CLASSIC *f*M
GOOD MUSIC GUIDE

CLASSIC *f*M
Good Music Guide

Jeremy Nicholas

Hodder & Stoughton

Copyright © 1999 Jeremy Nicholas

First published in Great Britain in 1999 by Hodder and Stoughton
A division of Hodder Headline

The right of Jeremy Nicholas to be identified as the Author of the Work has been asserted by
him in accordance with the Copyright, Designs and Patents Act 1988.

10 9 8 7 6 5 4 3 2 1

A CIP catalogue record for this title is available from the British Library

ISBN 0 340 75042 1

Designed by Ned Hoste

Printed and bound in Great Britain by
Clays Ltd, St Ives plc, Bungay, Suffolk

Hodder & Stoughton
A division of Hodder Headline PLC
338 Euston Road
London NW1 3BH

ACKNOWLEDGEMENTS

My thanks first and foremost to Rupert Lancaster of
Hodder & Stoughton who first ran the flag up this
particular pole to see if anyone saluted, and whose
enthusiasm and support throughout the book's long
gestation has been constant; I owe a huge debt of
gratitude to Anna Gregory, Classic FM's Head of Music,
for her generous help, guidance and suggestions; and to
Helen Garnons-Williams (Hodder & Stoughton), Ned
Hoste (who has designed the whole book so brilliantly),
all at Classic FM, (especially Robert O'Dowd and Kate
Sampson), Peter Robinson (my agent at Curtis Brown),
and Alison Waggitt (the best indexer in the business) for
their invaluable contributions. Finally, the biggest thanks
of all to Jill, for being there - all the way through.

CONTENTS

Foreword 9

How to Use this Book 11

Glossary 13

Music for Particular Occasions 17

1,000 Pieces of Classical Music 35

Index 361

DEDICATION

To Jill – whose date with Placido got me interested
To Rosie – who I hope will grow to love this music
and to Jeremy and Robin – who did.

FOREWORD

I started listening to classical music when I was three. My mother tells me I used to sit on the floor for hours on end with my ear pressed up to the speaker of our Murphy radiogram listening to Beethoven's Fifth Symphony. I can't remember doing this but it was obviously something that made me innately happy.

Classical music has been a passion, a hobby and an enthusiasm ever since: a passion because it is something I would find hard to live without; a hobby because it involves collecting discs, music, information and anecdotes; and an enthusiasm because it is such a stimulating subject to discuss, debate and discover.

One of the main reasons for wanting to write this book was due to some research material that came my way. Among other things, it revealed that some people are too frightened to enter the classical section of a record shop. Why? Because they have no idea where to start looking or what to look for, and are frightened of making fools of themselves by asking the wrong questions. The report also showed that there are a large number of people who consider listening to classical music to be 'elitist' and/or intellectual. Most surprising of all, the research disclosed that there are some people who listen to classical music in secret because they don't want their family and friends to find out.

I found this terribly sad.

Let's underline it, shout it out, and clear it up once and for all: there is no mystery to classical music!

This book assumes no previous knowledge of classical music. It takes nothing for granted except a spirit of curiosity. So to those who are new to the whole business, come with me to the bazaar. Hold my hand and we'll stroll along together. You can pick your own route through the crowded market place, stop as often as you want for as long as you want at whatever stall you like, sampling as much or as little as suits your personal taste. Some of you will already know your way around but there will, hopefully, be many things on offer you haven't encountered before and which will take your fancy.

It was fun deciding what should make up the 1,000 works for this book. The great, undisputed masterpieces of Western classical music are here of course, many of which are, in any case, voted annually by listeners into the Classic FM Hall of Fame. Nearly all the titles from the last few years' lists are included. The official Classic FM playlist and a number of personal favourites helped in compiling the remaining titles but I could easily have chosen a further 1,000 works of interest and/or significance. Even then we would only be scratching the surface - especially when you realise that the bible of recorded classical music, the R.F.D. catalogue, lists well over half a million titles.

Inevitably, there are dozens of works which have 'got away'. If you have any pieces you would like to see included in future editions of the book - 'how could you possibly leave out so-and-so?' - please let me know. Write to me via the publishers at Hodder & Stoughton, 338 Euston Road, London NW1 3BH or Email at JeremyNicholas@excite.com.

So this guide to Good Music is not making any claims to being 'definitive' or 'complete', but I like to think it will provide a paddling pool for anyone who has ever wondered about dipping their toes into the vast ocean of classical music. For others who know a thing or two already, I trust it will amuse, intrigue and provoke. In a magazine article in 1964, the great Russian composer Igor Stravinsky wrote: 'The trouble with music appreciation in general is that people are taught to have too much respect for music: they should be taught to love it instead'. Above all, I hope this book will inspire that.

Jeremy Nicholas
Barley Fen
1999

HOW TO USE THIS BOOK

The book has three sections:

1. MUSIC FOR PARTICULAR OCCASIONS

Classic FM are regularly asked to recommend pieces of music for particular occasions. Anna Gregory, Head of Music at Classic FM, has chosen sixteen occasions or events, some practical, others just fun, and has matched music from this book to fit them.

2. 1,000 PIECES OF CLASSICAL MUSIC

The music is listed by alphabetical title under its (alphabetical) composer. Sometimes this strict rule has been broken if a section (say an aria) from a work was separated from its source because of the A–Z order. The dates of each composer and their nationalities are shown at the start of the appropriate entry. Below that is the title of the work, the date of its composition and symbols identifying what sort of music it is (opera, orchestral, vocal, etc.) and what sort of mood it evokes.

CHOICE OF MUSIC

The works chosen are based - but not exclusively so - on the Classic FM playlist. The selection broadly reflects the listening policy of the station. Nothing specific should be read into the omission of certain composers (there had to be a cut-off point somewhere); however, few contemporary works written in the past 20 years or so have established themselves in the regular concert repertoire and/or in the public affection and that was one contributing factor to the final choice. Musical trifles, attractive obscurities, forgotten masterpieces and light music have been given the same consideration as well-known operas, symphonies and other works of the core classical repertoire.

TITLES OF MUSIC

In listing the titles of the music, I have partly followed tradition by including the key in which a work is written (this applies mainly to symphonies, concertos, chamber and instrumental pieces) and partly abandoned it: only when a work's identity required extra clarification (for example, where a composer has written two pieces in the same form and in the same key), have I included the Opus or catalogue number ascribed to it . The titles I have used are those by which a work is most commonly known (e.g. 'The Flying Dutchman', not 'Der Fliegende Holländer').

RECORDINGS

Occasionally I have mentioned a particular recording but only if it presents an unmissable account of a work. To find out about the best or currently available recordings of a work, you can ring the Classic FM Musicshop for advice: Tel. No. 08702 414242. Otherwise, recommended recordings can be found easily in a number of books where the merits of each performance and recording are discussed in more detail than would have been practicable here. The best of them are Rob Cowan's *Classical 1000* (Guinness), *The Penguin Guide to Compact Discs* and *The Gramophone Good CD Guide*.

SYMBOLS AND CATEGORIES

A quick look at the heading for each entry will tell you what kind of music you are reading about:

Chamber
Choral
Concerto
Instrumental
Opera
Orchestral
Vocal

Where a piece of music is well known, in more than one form (e.g. as an orchestral work) that is shown by two symbols, thus O/I.

One feature is new to this book. Every piece of music you read about has been given a symbol to convey - in a nutshell - its overall character. Music conveys an infinite variety of emotions and 'moods' so the categories that have been devised are intended only as the most approximate of indications to the general 'feel' of a piece. In a multi-movement work with many contrasting moods, more than one symbol is used. If you don't know a work, it seems to me a useful device to be shown at a glance if it's the sort of music you are likely respond to. The categories devised are:

Joyful / Celebratory
Merry / Sparkling
Romantic / Nostalgic
Spiritual / Inspirational
Smooth / Relaxing
Weepy

3. GLOSSARY AND INDEX

I have tried to describe the pieces of music, their character and how they sound, and to avoid writing about them using technical terms. However, at times the most precise way to explain a particular point has been to use musical jargon - andante, concerto, rondo, etc.. If a term is not defined within a particular entry, it can be found in the Glossary.

GLOSSARY

Only musical terms which appear and are not explained in the course of the main text are included.

adagietto - not quite as slow as adagio

adagio - 'leisurely', 'at ease', slower than andante; a slow movement; sometimes an independent work with that title

allegretto - not quite as fast as allegro

allegro - lively, fast (not as fast as presto)

andante - at moderate speed (between allegretto and adagio)

anthem - a short choral work, either patriotic or using words from the Bible or some other religious text

aria - a solo song, usually from an opera

baritone - male singing voice between tenor (high) and bass (low)

Baroque - period of European music written between (roughly) 1600–1750, after the Renaissance period and before the Classical

bass - the lowest male voice

bel canto - literally 'beautiful singing', describing the kind of smooth, agile singing required in operas by Donizetti, Bellini and Rossini

bourré - a lively French dance-movement found in many eighteenth century suites

BWV - *Bach-Werke-Verzeichnis*: the catalogue of J.S. Bach's works

cantata - a work with a sacred or secular text for chorus, with or without solo voices, usually with orchestra, divided into several sections

capriccio/caprice - a lively, light, usually instrumental piece

chaconne - originally a slow dance in 3/4 time, now a piece in which a theme is repeated over and over again in the bass with variations developed above it

chamber work - originally music suitable for performance in a room rather than a church or concert hall; now it describes music of an intimate character written for a small number of players

chorale - a hymn of the German Protestant church

choral(e) prelude - an organ piece based on a chorale tune

Classical - all the works described in the book are pieces of classical music but, 'Classical' is also the name given to the period of European music written between (approximately) 1750–1800 (i.e. Haydn, Mozart and early Beethoven)

coloratura - the art of great vocal agility and embellishment, usually applied to the soprano voice

concert - a performance of music in public, usually involving an orchestra, with a number of compositions on the programme. If there is a single performer (with or without accompaniment), it's called a recital

concerto - a work for orchestra and one (or more) instrumental soloist(s), usually with three or four movements

concerto grosso - a work in which a small group of instrumental soloists (the concertino) contrasts and alternates with a larger group (the ripieno); a very popular form in Baroque music

concert piece - a work (usually taken to mean an independent orchestral composition) suitable for performance in a concert

continuo - short for *basso continuo* (i.e. continuous bass) where the bass line of a work indicates the harmonies to be played by a keyboard instrument (often harpsichord)

contralto - the lowest of the three female singing voices, below a mezzo-soprano

13

conzertstück/konzertstück – *stück* is German for 'piece' or 'composition', applied usually to an instrumental concert piece (sometimes taking the form of a short concerto)

counterpoint/contrapuntal – the important art, when composing, of combining two or more melodies simultaneously to make musical sense

divertimento – a light, cheerful work in several movements, generally for a small instrumental group

elegy – an instrumental (originally vocal) lament; a piece in similar mood

étude – a 'study', usually a short solo instrumental piece designed to address a particular technical problem

fantaisie/fantasy/fantasia/fantasie – a piece in which the composer's fantasy or imagination runs 'free' (as opposed to a work with some formal structure such as a sonata or symphony); also a piece made out of tunes contained in a particular work

finale – the last (final) movement of a work

folk-music/tune/song – a work which has been handed down aurally from one generation to the next, often in several different versions, and which has no known composer

fugue – an elaborate contrapuntal (see above) composition in which different treatments of the same short theme(s) combine(s) together in separate voices of equal importance

G numbers – the numbering for Boccherini's works, named after Gérard, who catalogued them

gamelan – Indonesian instrumental ensemble using string, wind and percussion

harmony/harmonically – from the Latin and Greek *harmonia* meaning 'notes in combination', i.e. the sound that results when more than one note is played or sung at the same time. The study of harmony, a basic element in the art of composition, is the examination of how chords are built and move from one to another. A composer's unique style can be defined from the way he builds and uses chords

improvisation – to invent on the spot (as opposed to playing from music)

incidental music – composed for the accompaniment of a stage play

instrumental music – for, or produced by, a musical instrument; non-vocal music; often used to describe music for a solo instrument

intermezzo – a short piece of orchestral music inserted between the acts of an opera; also a short concert or instrumental piece

K or KV numbers – short for *Köchel-Verzeichnis* or 'Köchel catalogue', the chronological listing of Mozart's works by musicologist Ludwig von Köchel, published in 1864

key – the key in which a piece of music is written is determined by the set of notes chosen as the main material for its composition

Kk numbers – see entry on Domenico Scarlatti

L numbers – see entry on Domenico Scarlatti

larghetto – slow, but not as slow as largo

largo – slowly and with dignity

lento – slow

libretto – the verbal text of an opera or large-scale vocal work

lyric tenor – tenor voice (see below) suited to lighter, unhistrionic roles

madrigal – see entry on Gibbons

major – if a work is described as (for example) being 'in C major', it means that that particular work is predominantly in that key, i.e. using the notes in the scale of C major

mass – the most important regular ritual of the Roman Catholic Church consisting of a number of fixed prayers which, as far as musical settings of the mass are concerned, are *Kyrie, Gloria, Credo, Sanctus* with *Benedictus, Agnus Dei*

mezzo-soprano - the middle range female singing voice, between soprano (high) and contralto (low)

minor - same principle as major, using the notes in the scale of a minor key

molto - much or very, as in *allegro molto*

motet - a short sacred contrapuntal choral composition without accompaniment

motif - a short theme or musical passage from which a longer theme is often developed

movement - the self-contained section of a large composition, such as a symphony or concerto, each one having a different speed indication

Op. - short for Opus, the Latin for 'work', used, with a number, to help identify a composer's work; sometimes an opus contains more than one piece in which case it is subdivided (e.g. Op. 30 No. 4)

opera - a dramatic work in which all (or most) of the words are sung to orchestral accompaniment, the music being a principal element

operetta - an opera with a frivolous or comic theme, with tuneful music and spoken dialogue, virtually the same as 'light opera' (e.g. Offenbach's *Orpheus in the Underworld*)

Opus - see Op.

oratorio - a sacred work on the same scale as an opera but without scenery, action or costume (e.g. Handel's *Messiah*)

overture - the instrumental introduction to an opera or stage play; in Baroque music, the overture is often the first movement of a suite; it can also be an independent orchestral work (e.g. Mendelssohn's *Hebrides Overture*)

partita - a suite (mainly from the Baroque period) usually of dance movements

pas de deux - *pas* is 'step' in French, thus a dance for two persons (ballet)

passacaglia - piece of music (originally a dance) in 3/4 time with a repeated bass line, though, unlike the chaconne (q.v.) with which it has much in common, not necessarily always in the bass

pavane - a stately slow dance dating from the Sixteenth Century or earlier

pizzicato - direction to pluck a stringed instrument with the fingers

polonaise - a courtly Polish dance in 3/4 time

prelude - a piece preceding something (a fugue, for instance); the first movement of a suite, or the introduction to an opera; a short self-contained piece (see Debussy, Chopin and Rachmaninov)

quartet - a piece for four performers (instrumentalists or singers); most commonly used to describe a work in several movements played by two violins, viola and cello

quintet - a piece for five performers: a string quintet adds an extra viola or cello to a quartet; a piano quintet usually adds a piano to a string quartet

ragtime - early type of jazz composition featuring syncopated ('ragged') rhythm, especially associated with a style of piano playing (see Scott Joplin)

requiem - funeral mass, the service celebrated in the Roman Catholic Church for the repose of the soul of someone who has died; generally, a requiem omits the *Gloria* and *Credo* movements of the Mass but adds the *Dies Irae*

rhapsody - title especially popular from mid-Nineteenth Century to describe a work in one continuous movement without any formal structure and, like a 'fantasy', suggesting a romantic inspiration (see Liszt, Rachmaninov and Gershwin)

Romantic - the period in musical history following the Baroque and Classical periods, beginning and ending (approximately) with the Nineteenth Century

romanza/romance - often used to describe a slow movement with a mood of tenderness and intimacy; also an independent work with that title

rondo/rondeau - type of composition in which the same theme ('A') keeps recurring (ABACA, etc.) a popular device in the last movements of concertos and sonatas in (especially) the Classical period; rondeau is an alternative spelling, though was originally a type of French medieval song

RV numbers - identify Vivaldi's works (named after P. Ryom's *Verzeichnis der Werke Antonio Vivaldi*)

S numbers - identify Liszt's works (after Humphrey Searle's catalogue)

saraband(e) - a slow and stately dance originating from Spain, much used in Baroque suites

scherzo - literally 'joke', the scherzo movement of a symphony, sonata or quartet is always lively, is in 3/4 time and has a middle section called the *trio*; sometimes an independent work of its own (see Chopin)

score - the written copy of all the 'parts' (voices, instruments, etc.) of a composition placed systematically one above the other on separate lines of music manuscript; 'scored for ...' means the music has been written/arranged for a particular combination of voices and/or instruments

sextet - a piece for six instrumentalists or singers

sonata - 'to be sounded' (as opposed to cantata 'to be sung'); the sonata is the most important form of classical instrumental music, generally for piano (or solo instrument and piano) in three or four movements contrasted in character and tempo (see Scarlatti, Beethoven and Liszt for different examples)

song cycle - a collection of songs by one composer usually with a common subject and often performed consecutively

soprano - the highest type of the three categories of female singing voices

string quartet - see quartet

suite - an instrumental or orchestral work in several movements (in the Baroque period these were generally dance forms); also describes a set of movements assembled from a full ballet, theatre or film score

symphony - since the time of Haydn, this has described a substantial, serious work for orchestra in several (three, four or more) contrasted movements

tarantella - fast Italian dance in 6/8 time

tenor - the highest category of (normal) male singing voice (the alto or counter-tenor sings higher but uses falsetto)

theme - an air, subject or tune

toccata - literally 'touched' - a rapid solo instrumental piece that shows off the performer's agility (see Bach, Schumann and Widor)

tone poem - a one-movement piece for orchestra which tells a story (or programme) in music (see Richard Strauss, Debussy and Sibelius).

transcription - a) an arrangement of a piece of music for a different instrument or in a different form from the original; b) a brilliant paraphrase or showpiece based on some standard theme or composition

trio - a piece for three instrumentalists or singers; the central section of a scherzo, minuet or march

trouser role - the term used to describe operatic roles such as Cherubino (*The Marriage of Figaro*) or Octavian (*Der Rosenkavalier*) which, although sung by women, are male characters. Also called *travesti* role or breeches part

variations - a set of varied versions of a particular tune; 'Variations on such-and-such a theme' means a composition made up entirely of music inspired by different versions of the same tune (see Handel, Rachmaninov and Dohnányi)

viols - bowed string instruments of various sizes popular till about 1700 when the instruments of the violin family replaced them

virtuoso/virtuosic - an instrumental performer of exceptional technical brilliance/music requiring great technical accomplishment to play

Wq numbers - the numbering for C.P.E. Bach's works, after Wotquenne, who catalogued them

Music for Weddings

BACH, J.S.
'Jesu, joy of man's desiring' (page 47)

BOËLLMANN
Prière à Notre Dame from *Suite Gothique* (page 76)

BRAHMS
Es ist ein Ros' entsprungen (page 79)

BREWER
Marche Hèroïque (page 84)

CHARPENTIER
Trumpet Tune from *Te Deum* (page 92)

CLARKE
Prince of Denmark's March ('Trumpet Voluntary') (page 98)

GUILMANT
Grand Choeur in D (page 146)

HANDEL
Arrival of the Queen of Sheba from *Solomon* (page 148)

HANDEL
'Let the bright seraphim' from *Samson* (page 149)

KARG-ELERT
Nun danket alle Gott (page 169)

MENDELSSOHN
Wedding March from *A Midsummer Night's Dream* (page 194)

MOZART

Exultate, Jubilate (page 205)

PACHELBEL

Canon in D (page 220)

PURCELL

Rondo from *Abdelazar* (page 240)

PURCELL

Trumpet Tune and Air in D (page 241)

STANLEY

Trumpet Voluntary in D (page 296)

VERDI

Grand March from *Aida* (page 328)

VIERNE

Finale from *Organ Symphony No. 1* (page 334)

WAGNER

Bridal Chorus from *Lohengrin* (page 340)

WIDOR

Toccata from *Organ Symphony No. 5* (page 357)

Music for Funerals

BACH, J.S.
'In tears of grief' from *St. Matthew Passion* (page 49)

BARBER
Adagio for strings (page 52)

BEETHOVEN
Symphony No. 3 ('Eroica'), second movement (page 61)

BEETHOVEN
Symphony No. 7, second movement (page 62)

CHOPIN
Piano Sonata No. 2 ('Funeral March'), third movement (page 97)

CHOPIN
Prelude No. 4 in E minor (page 96)

WALFORD DAVIES
Solemn Melody (page 103)

ELGAR
Nimrod from *Enigma Variations* (page 119)

FAURÉ
Élégie (page 122)

FAURÉ
Pie Jesu from *Requiem* (page 123)

HANDEL
Largo from *Xerxes* (page 150)

LLOYD WEBBER, A.

Pie Jesu from *Requiem* (page 185)

MOZART

Ave verum corpus (page 202)

MOZART

Laudate Dominum (page 206)

MYERS

Cavatina (page 216)

PARRY

My soul, there is a country from *Six Songs of Farewell* (page 225)

PURCELL

'When I am laid in earth' (page 239)

SATIE

Gymnopédie No. 1 (page 269)

TAVENER

Song for Athene (page 313)

VERDI

Ingemisco from *Requiem* (page 329)

Music for Babies

BEETHOVEN
Für Elise (Bagatelle No. 25 in A minor) (page 55)

DEBUSSY
La Fille aux cheveux de lin from *Préludes* (page 105)

DELIBES
Pizzicato from *Sylvia* (page 106)

HANDEL
Water Music (page 151)

HUMPERDINCK
'Evening Prayer' ('Abenslied') from *Hansel and Gretel* (page 162)

MOZART
Clarinet Quintet in A (page 203)

PUCCINI
'Humming Chorus' from *Madame Butterfly* (page 236)

SAINT-SAËNS
Aquarium from *Carnival of the Animals* (page 261)

SCHUMANN
Daydreams from *Kinderszenen* (page 281)

STRAUSS, J.
The Blue Danube (page 297)

Music to DIY to

BEETHOVEN
'Prisoners' Chorus' from *Fidelio* (page 60)

COPLAND
Hoe-Down from *Rodeo* (page 101)

HANDEL
The Harmonious Blacksmith (page 148)

OFFENBACH
Cancan from *Orpheus in the Underworld* (page 219)

PONCHIELLI
Dance of the Hours from *La Gioconda* (page 228)

PROKOFIEV
Montagues and Capulets from *Romeo and Juliet* (page 231)

SCHUBERT
Marche Militaire No. 1 in D (page 273)

SIBELIUS
Alla Marcia from *Karelia Suite* (page 289)

TCHAIKOVSKY
Polonaise from *Eugene Onegin* (page 315)

VERDI
'Anvil Chorus' from *Il Trovatore* (page 331)

Music for Pure Self-Indulgence

ALBINONI *(arr. Giazotto)*
Adagio for organ and strings in G minor (page 38)

CACCINI
Ave Maria (page 90)

CANTELOUBE
'Baïlèro' from *Songs of the Auvergne* (page 90)

CHARPENTIER
'Depuis le jour' from *Louise* (page 91)

CHAUSSON
Poème (page 92)

GÓRECKI
Symphony No. 3 ('Symphony of Sorrowful Songs'),
second movement (page 139)

RACHMANINOV
'Vocalise' (page 245)

VERDI
Prelude to Act 1 of *La Traviata* (page 330)

VILLA-LOBOS
Aria from *Bachianas Brasileiras No. 5* (page 335)

WAGNER
Siegfried Idyll (page 342)

Music to Dine to

BACH, J.S.
Brandenburg Concertos Nos. 1-6 (page 45)

BACH, J.S.
Cello Suites (page 45)

BOCCHERINI
Guitar Quintets in D and E minor (page 75)

MENDELSSOHN
Octet for strings in E flat (page 194)

MOZART
Eine Kleine Nachtmusik (Serenade No. 13 in G) (page 212)

MOZART
Symphonies Nos. 38-40 (pages 213-14)

RESPIGHI
The Birds (page 250)

SCHUBERT
String Quintet in C (page 277)

TCHAIKOVSKY
Serenade for strings in C (page 318)

VIVALDI
Mandolin Concertos (page 338)

Music to Study to

BACH, J.S.
Concerto in D minor for two violins (page 46)

BACH, J.S.
The Well-Tempered Clavier (page 50)

BEETHOVEN
Piano Sonata No. 8 in C minor('Pathétique) (page 58)

CHOPIN
Prelude No. 7 in A (page 96)

MOZART
Horn Concerto No. 4 in E flat (page 206)

MOZART
Piano Sonata No. 11 in A (page 211)

SATIE
Trois Gymnopédies (page 269)

SCHUBERT
Octet in F (page 273)

TCHAIKOVSKY
Symphony No. 6 in B minor ('Pathétique') (page 320)

VAUGHAN WILLIAMS
Fantasia on a Theme of Thomas Tallis (page 325)

Music to Go to Sleep to

BACH, J.S.
Goldberg Variations (page 47)

BACH, J.S.
Orchestral Suite No. 3 in D, second movement
('Air on the G String') (page 48)

BEETHOVEN
Piano Sonata No. 14 in C sharp minor ('Moonlight')
(1st Movement) (page 58)

BRAHMS
Wiegenlied, Op. 49 No. 4 (page 84)

CHOPIN
Nocturnes (page 95)

ELGAR
Chanson de Nuit (page 114)

HUMPERDINCK
'Evening Prayer' ('Abenslied') from *Hansel and Gretel* (page 162)

LISZT
Liebestraüme No. 3 in A flat (page 181)

MASSENET
Méditation from *Thaïs* (page 191)

MENDELSSOHN
Nocturne from *A Midsummer Night's Dream* (page 193)

Music for Christmas

ADAM
'Cantique de Noël' (page 35)

BERLIOZ
The Childhood of Christ (page 67)

BRITTEN
A Ceremony of Carols (page 84)

CORELLI
Christmas Concerto (page 102)

MONTEVERDI
Vespers (page 200)

MOZART
Laudate Dominum (page 206)

PALESTRINA
Missa Papae Marcelli (page 224)

PROKOFIEV
Troika from *Lieutenant Kijé* (page 231)

TCHAIKOVSKY
The Nutcracker (page 316)

WALDTEUFEL
The Skaters' Waltz (page 346)

Music to Sing Along to

ARNE
'Rule, Britannia!' (page 41)

BEETHOVEN
'Ode to Joy' from Symphony No. 9 in D minor (page 63)

ELGAR
Pomp and Circumstance March No. 1 in D
('Land of Hope and Glory') (page 116)

HANDEL
'Hallelujah Chorus' from *Messiah* (page 149)

HANDEL
Zadok the Priest (page 152)

MOZART
'I am the jolly birdcatcher' from *The Magic Flute* (page 206)

ORFF
O Fortuna from *Carmina Burana* (page 220)

PUCCINI
'Nessun Dorma' from *Turandot* (page 238)

ROSSINI
'Largo al Factotum' from *The Barber of Seville* (page 255)

VERDI
'Sempre Libera' from *La Traviata* (page 331)

Music to Romance to

BARBER
Violin Concerto, second movement (page 53)

BRUCH
Violin Concerto No. 1 in G minor (page 87)

ELGAR
Salut d'Amour (page 117)

ELGAR
Serenade for strings (page 117)

MASCAGNI
Intermezzo from *Cavalleria Rusticana* (page 190)

MOZART
Clarinet Concerto in A (page 203)

RACHMANINOV
Piano Concerto No. 2 in C minor (page 242)

RACHMANINOV
Symphony No. 2 in E minor (page 244)

RODRIGO
Concierto de Aranjuez (page 254)

TCHAIKOVSKY
Andante Cantabile from String Quartet No. 1 in D (page 314)

Music to Drive to

BEETHOVEN
Romance No. 2 in F minor for violin and orchestra (page 60)

BIZET
Carmen (page 73)

CIMAROSA
Oboe Concerto in C minor (page 98)

HANDEL
Water Music (page 151)

KHACHATURIAN
Adagio from *Spartacus* (page 170)

MOZART
Don Giovanni (page 204)

ORFF
Carmina Burana (page 220)

ROSSINI
Overture to *The Barber of Seville* (page 255)

TCHAIKOVSKY
Violin Concerto in D (page 321)

VAUGHAN WILLLIAMS
Fantasia on 'Greensleeves' (page 326)

Music to Karaoke Conduct to

BEETHOVEN
Symphony No. 5 in C minor (page 61)

BERNSTEIN
Overture to *Candide* (page 71)

BERNSTEIN
Symphonic Dances from *West Side Story* (page 71)

COPLAND
Fanfare for the Common Man (page 101)

DELIBES
Pizzicato from *Sylvia* (page 106)

HOLST
Mars from *The Planets* (page 159)

RACHMANINOV
Piano Concerto No. 3, first movement (page 242)

TCHAIKOVSKY
1812 Overture (page 314)

VERDI
Dies irae from *Requiem* (page 329)

VERDI
Grand March from *Aida* (page 328)

Music to Cook to

BACH, J.S.
Concerto in D minor for two violins (page 46)

BOCCHERINI
Minuet from String Quintet in E (page 76)

GLUCK
Dance of the Blessed Spirits ('Mélodie') from *Orfeus and Euridice*
(page 137)

HANDEL
Arrival of the Queen of Sheba from *Solomon* (page 148)

HAYDN
Symphony No. 94 in G ('Surprise') (page 155)

SCHUBERT
Piano Quintet in A ('Trout') (page 274)

VAUGHAN WILLIAMS
Fantasia on 'Greensleeves' (page 326)

VIVALDI
Nulla in Mundo Pax Sincera (page 338)

WEBER
Grand Duo Concertant (page 351)

ZIPOLI
Elevazione (page 360)

Music to Bathe to

BARBER
Adagio for strings (page 52)

BERLIOZ
Summer Nights No. 4 (page 70)

DEBUSSY
Clair de lune from *Suite Bergamasque* (page 104)

FAURÉ
Cantique de Jean Racine (page 121)

MOZART
Concerto for flute and harp in C (page 204)

OFFENBACH
Barcarolle from *The Tales of Hoffmann* (page 218)

PACHELBEL
Canon in D (page 220)

RACHMANINOV
Rhapsody on a Theme of Paganini, Variation 18 (page 244)

SHOSTAKOVICH
Piano Concerto No. 2 in F, second movement (page 286)

VAUGHAN WILLIAMS
The Lark Ascending (page 326)

Music for Children

BRITTEN
The Young Person's Guide to the Orchestra (page 86)

DEBUSSY
Children's Corner (page 103)

DUKAS
The Sorcerer's Apprentice (page 110)

HUMPERDINK
Hansel and Gretel (page 162)

MENDELSSOHN
A Midsummer Night's Dream (page 196)

MOZART, L.
Toy Symphony (page 202)

PROKOFIEV
Peter and the Wolf (page 232)

SAINT-SAËNS
Carnival of the Animals (page 261)

TCHAIKOVSKY
The Nutcracker (page 316)

TCHAIKOVSKY
The Sleeping Beauty (page 318)

A

Adam said of himself, 'My only aim is to write music which is transparent, easy to understand and amusing to the public.' 'Oh, Holy Night!' is the English title of one of the most popular of Christmas songs, first performed at Midnight Mass in Paris in 1847. It featured in the 1990 film *Home Alone*.

ADOLPHE ADAM
1803–56
FRENCH
'CANTIQUE DE NOËL'

V

I've never been quite sure what *Giselle* is all about, despite it being one of the most celebrated of all ballets. So tuneful is the score that it's easy to overlook the story which, on closer inspection, concerns elves in white dresses (known as the *Wilis*) who died before their wedding day and emerge from their graves to dance till dawn. All the great ballerinas from Grisi to Pavlova, Fonteyn and Shearer have appeared as Giselle. If you prefer to listen to just a selection from the tuneful score, Constant Lambert, the twentieth century English composer, took four of the best bits – *Giselle's Dance*, *Mad Scene*, the Act 2 pas de deux and closing scene - and turned them into an orchestral suite.

ADAM
GISELLE
Ballet
(1841)

O
♥

Long-forgotten, *Le Toréador* was the *Joseph and the Amazing Technicolor® Dreamcoat* of its day. After its first performance in 1849, it received regular revivals for the next 20 years and was revived to acclaim in 1881 before falling victim to changing taste and fashion. That doesn't lessen the charm of this infectiously enjoyable two-act romp, a mix of opera and operetta, with its catchy overture that sounds a bit like one of Rossini's. Why do we never hear it in the concert hall? Adam wrote 53 operas in his brief 52 years, all now forgotten. This overture makes you wonder what his others are like.

ADAM
Overture to
LE TORÉADOR

O

ADAM
Variations on
'AH! VOUS DIRAI-JE,
MAMAN'
from Le Toréador

OP

The tune we know as 'Twinkle, twinkle, little star' and the Americans know as the 'Alphabet Song' ('A–B–C–D–E–F–G'), was first known as 'Ah! Vous dirai-je, Maman' and appeared (without words) in 1761. Our nursery rhyme version was first published in 1806 (with words by one Jane Taylor, a 'poetess' who died in Ongar, Essex in 1824 in case you'd like to know). Adam's variations on the theme are sung by the heroine Coraline (the wife of Don Belflor, the retired bullfighter of the title), and form a show-stopping aria for coloratura soprano. Mozart wrote 12 variations for piano on the same melody .

JOHN ADAMS
B. 1947
AMERICAN
SHORT RIDE IN A
FAST MACHINE
(1986)

O

The short (four minute) ride is underlined throughout by the relentless, steady beat of the woodblock ('almost sadistic', says the composer) while the high-spirited orchestra plays exuberantly in a completely different rhythm. 'You know how it is,' explains Adams, 'when someone asks you to ride in a terrific sports car, and then you wish you hadn't?' A fun piece of modern music.

STEPHEN ADAMS
1844–1913
ENGLISH
'THE HOLY CITY'
(1905)
and other songs

V

Stephen Adams was the pen-name of baritone Michael Maybrick who wrote some phenomenally successful songs around the turn of the century – 'The Holy City' ('Jerusalem, Jerusalem, lift up your gates and sing!') sold 50,000 sheet-music copies a year at the height of its popularity. The words were by the prolific barrister/poet Fred. E. Weatherly who, among his 1500 lyrics, also provided words to Adams' other hits, 'The Star of Bethlehem' (1890) and 'Nirvana' (1900). They're the sort of sentimental drawing-room ballads our great-grandparents sang around the piano but which are still undeniably stirring and effective.

This concert lollipop was an integral part of the 1941 film *Dangerous Moonlight* in which Polish concert pianist/fighter pilot Anton Walbrook escapes the Nazis and loses his memory after flying in the Battle of Britain. Though the main theme was originally a rumba Addinsell had composed in the twenties, most of the *Warsaw Concerto* was actually written and arranged by orchestrator Roy Douglas. Another good Addinsell work is his theme for *A Tale of Two Cities*, though you're likely to know another piece of his better – *Old Tyme Dancing* ('Stately as a Galleon') which he wrote with Joyce Grenfell.

RICHARD ADDINSELL
1904-77
ENGLISH
WARSAW
CONCERTO
(1941)

C

♥

Albéniz was an accomplished and original pianist (as a child he played the piano as a vaudeville stunt - standing with the keyboard behind him, he would play with the backs of his fingers!) and, amazingly, there are a few ancient, crackly cylinders of his playing. *Iberia* is Albéniz's masterpiece, a collection of 12 musical portraits of his homeland, impressionistic and immensely difficult to play. Many are equally well known in versions for orchestra. *Navarra*, left unfinished at Albéniz's death, forms a brilliant afterthought to *Iberia*, exultantly capturing the special character of the singing style found in that region.

ISAAC ALBÉNIZ
1860-1909
SPANISH
IBERIA *and*
NAVARRA
(1906-09)

I

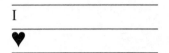

♥

Albéniz wrote over 250 pieces for piano besides *Iberia* and *Navarra*, many of which are rather weak. Among the better ones, though, are the first and third movements (*Preludo* and *Malagueña*) of the six-movement suite called *España*. But it is the second piece in the collection that is Albéniz's best known work by far, the prototype of all tangos, one of those seductive little tunes you recognise but can never put a name to. It is even more effective in an exotic piano transcription by Leopold Godowsky (q.v.).

ALBÉNIZ
TANGO IN D
from España, Op. 165
(1890)

I

♥

TOMASO ALBINONI
1671–1751
ITALIAN
OBOE CONCERTOS
(1710)

C

Albinoni was the first composer to have an oboe concerto published. Though others had certainly written for the instrument before (the oboe was introduced in about 1657), Albinoni's four concertos Op. 7 appeared in Amsterdam in 1710. No. 3 in B flat Op. 7 is popular, No. 6 in D is frequently (and effectively) played on the trumpet, but Op. 9 No. 2 (1722) is the jewel - it has one of Baroque music's most touching slow movements.

ALBINONI
(arr. Giazotto)
ADAGIO FOR ORGAN
AND STRINGS IN G
MINOR
(1958)

I

Albinoni was a celebrated opera composer (he wrote over 50) but is best known today for this work. Trouble is, he didn't compose it. It was pieced together, completed, and dressed up in a romantic arrangement by a distinguished Milanese scholar, Professor Remo Giazotto in 1958 using fragments of Albinoni's manuscript and his own intuition. It seemed to have a 'church' feel about it, hence the organ. John Cameron has made an effective choral arrangement of the Adagio taking as his text *The Beatitudes* (Christ's *Sermon on the Mount* from *St. Matthew's Gospel*).

JOHANN
ALBRECHTSBERGER
1736–1809
AUSTRIAN
HARP CONCERTO
IN C
(1773)

C

It's interesting to hear exactly what kind of music was written by the man who taught Beethoven and Hummel. I came across his charming harp concerto - it has a particularly catchy final movement (rondo) - in a recording by the great Spanish harpist Nicanor Zabaleta (1907-93). Listen out, too, for Albrechtsberger's lively Organ Concerto in B flat.

Sometimes called the 'British Sousa', Alford (whose real name was Frederick Ricketts) trained as a military bandsman. He composed *Colonel Bogey* in Inverness after hearing an impatient golfer trying to attract the attention of someone standing on the fairway by repeatedly whistling the notes C and A. Alford never allowed his own band to play the march on parade after that famous writer 'Anon.' added some ribald lyrics to the tune concerning the genitalia of leading figures in the Nazi Party. Colonel Bogey was revitalised in the 1957 film *The Bridge on the River Kwai* for which Malcolm Arnold (page 42) wrote the music.

KENNETH J. ALFORD
1881-1945
ENGLISH
COLONEL BOGEY
March
(1913)

O

A brief, heartfelt adagio movement from the music Alfvén had written for a play called *We* by Ludvig Nordström. It was composed for the tercentenary celebrations of the death of the Swedish King Gustav Adolf II in the Thirty Years' War. The Elegy is heard during the scene when, the day before the battle of Lützen in which he was killed, the King reminisces about a former love.

HUGO ALFVÉN
1872-1960
SWEDISH
ELEGY
from Gustav Adolf II Suite
(1932)

O

Using national Swedish dance rhythms and folk songs, the music describes the revels held in small Swedish towns during the St. John's Eve festival celebrating the longest day and the brightest night of the year. It was originally produced as a ballet, *La Nuit de Saint-Jean*, in Paris. In a shortened version, it was a much-requested record by Mantovani and His Orchestra on BBC Radio's *Children's Favourites* with Uncle Mac in the 1950s.

ALFVÉN
SWEDISH
RHAPSODY NO. 1
'MIDSUMMER VIGIL'
(1903)

O

**CHARLES-VALENTIN
ALKAN
1813–88**
FRENCH
12 ÉTUDES IN ALL
THE MINOR KEYS
(1857)

I

Those turned on by virtuoso piano music will revel in this monumental set of studies in which Alkan offers a thrill-a-minute roller-coaster ride of pieces so difficult that they are playable by only a handful of top-flight pianists. Unlike the famous ground-breaking set of études by Chopin (page 93), few of which last longer than five minutes, Alkan's are monsters - No. 8 alone lasts nearly half an hour! - physically-taxing assaults demanding the highest technical finish and musicianship. Studies 8, 9 and 10 are played together and known by the separate title of Concerto for Solo Piano. No. 12, the final study of this set, is Alkan's best-known work, the extraordinary *Le Festin d'Esope* (*The Feast of Aesop*) - 25 variations on a simple theme in which the pages of music are black with notes, the frantic piano imitating dogs barking and hunting calls. To hear the genius of Alkan at its best, listen to the recordings by the French-Canadian pianist Marc-André Hamelin.

**GREGORIO ALLEGRI
C. 1582–1652**
ITALIAN
MISERERE
(date unknown)

CHO

There are many fine recordings of this ethereal masterpiece, but none has replaced that of boy soprano Roy Goodman (now a successful conductor) and the Choir of King's College, Cambridge, directed by Sir David Willcocks. To hear it sung in this most beautiful of settings provided one of the most unforgettable musical experiences of my life. Allegri wrote this setting of *Psalm 50* ('Have mercy upon me, O God') for the Sistine Chapel choir in the early Seventeenth Century. Legend has it that the young Mozart scribbled down the score from memory after hearing it sung in St Peter's during Holy Week, though it is now established that he almost certainly knew the work beforehand.

Anderson was, arguably, the best known - and certainly the most successful - American composer of light orchestral classics. His *Blue Tango* was the first strictly instrumental composition ever to reach Number One in the Hit Parade, but his semi-classical 'novelty' items have also achieved enduring popularity – *Fiddle-Faddle* (inspired by Paganini's *Perpetuum Mobile*), *Plink, Plank, Plunk* (an effective pizzicato number), *Sleigh Ride, Bugler's Holiday, The Typewriter* and *Sandpaper Ballet* are recognisably 'Anderson country'. His *Irish Suite* is an under-rated six-movement adaptation of melodies by Thomas Moore.

LEROY ANDERSON
1908–75
AMERICAN
BLUE TANGO
and others

O

One of the most appealing chamber works in the repertoire, Arensky's trio was composed in memory of the great Russian cellist and composer Carl Davidov (1838-89), whose own cello concertos and brilliant *At the Spring* are worth investigating. The third of the trio's three movements is a deeply romantic elegy, while the second (scherzo) and finale bubble with vitality and memorable themes.

ANTON ARENSKY
1861–1906
RUSSIAN
PIANO TRIO IN D MINOR
(1894)

CH

♥

Wagner (page 339) said that the first eight notes of 'Rule, Britannia!' sum up the whole British character. The 'Celebrated Ode, in Honour of Great-Britain' received its first performance on 1 August 1740 at Clivedon, the Prince of Wales' residence in Buckinghamshire. It formed part of the masque *Alfred*, written to commemorate the succession of the House of Hanover to the throne. The original version of the words has 'Rule Britannia!/Britannia rule the waves' (not 'rules the waves' as we usually sing today, giving it a different meaning). Whichever, no one is sure who wrote them - either a David Mallett or a James Thomson.

THOMAS ARNE
1710–78
ENGLISH
'RULE, BRITANNIA!'
(1740)

CHO

MALCOLM ARNOLD
B. 1921
ENGLISH
CONCERTO FOR
TWO PIANOS
(1969)

C

♪ 𝅘𝅥

Commissioned for the BBC Proms in 1969, the *Concerto for Three Hands* (as it's invariably called) was written specifically for the husband and wife team of Cyril Smith and Phyllis Sellick. Smith had lost the use of his left hand after a stroke in 1956 but continued to enjoy a successful career alongside his wife until his death in 1974. After the dark, disruptive opening of the Concerto, the last movement is a riotous, irresistible rumba.

ARNOLD
EIGHT ENGLISH
DANCES
(1950-51)

O

𝅘𝅥

Arnold's publisher suggested these as companion pieces for Dvořák's *Slavonic Dances*. No. 5 is widely known as the signature tune of television's long-running *What the Papers Say*. Try also *Four Scottish Dances* (1957) and *Four Cornish Dances* (1966).

ARNOLD
A GRAND, GRAND
OVERTURE
(1956)

O

𝅘𝅥

A gallumphing *jeu d'esprit* composed for a concert of musical japes and jollity put on at the Royal Festival Hall by the cartoonist and musical humorist Gerard Hoffnung (1925-59). The Overture is written for full orchestra, but in addition demands virtuoso performances on three vacuum cleaners, one floor polisher and four rifles. Silly, perhaps, but how many composers today could come up with such a glorious tub-thumping main theme?

ARNOLD
PETERLOO
Overture
(1968)

O

🎺

The Peterloo Massacre occurred in August 1819 in St Peter's Fields, Manchester, when an orderly political meeting of 80,000 people was broken up by the cavalry, killing 11 people and injuring 400. Arnold was commissioned by the Trades Union Congress to celebrate the centenary of its first meeting in Manchester in June 1868 and chose to portray the incident with a hymn-like tune violently interrupted by an onslaught of percussion. The Bridgewater Hall in Manchester was built on the very site of the massacre and the Overture was played at its opening in September 1996.

A spirited orchestral showpiece first performed at the BBC Promenade Concerts of 1955, in which Arnold portrays the wild night ride of Tam, the hero of Robert Burns' 1790 ballad *Tam O'Shanter*, to the accompaniment of the bag-pipes and other tartan sounds. Like an earlier overture by Arnold, called *Beckus the Dandipratt* (1943), the central character has much in common with the rascally Till Eulenspiegel portrayed in Richard Strauss' famous piece of that name.

ARNOLD
TAM O'SHANTER
*Overture
(1955)*

O

Only the overtures to Auber's once vastly-successful operas have survived today - and even they are in danger of disappearing. If you like the curtain-raisers of Rossini and Suppé you'll love these for, while he doesn't quite equal the teaming invention of the other two, Auber provides lively alternatives which deserve to be heard more often. Rossini himself was a fan: 'Though Auber's music is light, his art is profound,' he wrote. The ones to go for are *Fra Diavolo* (1830), *Le Cheval de bronze* (1835), *Le Domino noir* (1837), *Les Diamants de la couronne* (1841) and, especially, *Masaniello* or *La Muette de Portici* (1828).

**DANIEL AUBER
1782-1871**
FRENCH
OVERTURES

O

B

One of C.P.E.'s last works. It shows that he still had an adventurous turn of mind, though, for this is an unusual combination of solo instruments in which the old world of his youth (represented by the harpsichord) meets the new world of his last years with the fortepiano. But by this time, all but two of Mozart's keyboard concertos had appeared and piano writing had entered another realm.

**CARL PHILIPP
EMMANUEL BACH
1714-88**
GERMAN
DOUBLE CONCERTO
FOR HARPSICHORD
AND FORTEPIANO
IN E FLAT
(1788)

C

C.P.E. BACH
FLUTE CONCERTOS
(1750-55)

C

C.P.E. was hired by the flute-playing Crown Prince of Prussia in 1738 as accompanist. He remained, reluctantly, at the court in Berlin for the next 28 years. Even better than Mozart's later efforts, C.P.E.'s flute concertos are full of surprises with sudden bursts of energy, abrupt contrasts and changes in rhythm. They demand great virtuosity (try the bustling last movement of the D Minor Concerto, one of my favourites) but have unusually eloquent slow movements. Those to go for are the flute concertos in G (Wq169), A minor (Wq166), D minor (Wq22), A major (Wq168) and B flat (Wq167), all composed in the 1750s.

C.P.E. BACH
HARPSICHORD
CONCERTO IN D
MINOR
(1748)

C

Nearly 20 years before C.P.E. escaped from the court of Frederick the Great, he composed (in Potsdam) this heroic, passionate concerto. It anticipates the kind of music he didn't get around to writing until he moved to Hamburg. As in most of C.P.E.'s music, it bowls merrily along down new roads taking unexpected twists and turns en route.

C.P.E. BACH
MAGNIFICAT IN D
(1749)

CHO

If you like the dramatic openings to Vivaldi's *Gloria* and Handel's *Zadok the Priest*, then this will knock you sideways (the whole work sounds more like Handel than C.P.E.'s father Johann Sebastian). It's the only sacred work C.P.E. composed in Berlin and is also his best - ironically, nothing he wrote while music director of Hamburg's five main churches equals it.

C.P.E. BACH
SIX HAMBURG
SYMPHONIES
(1773)

O

Dr Burney, the celebrated English music historian who met C.P.E. in 1772, described him as having 'a very animated countenance, and a cheerful and lively disposition'. These six symphonies reflect Bach's personality - vital, original and impetuous. Having extricated himself from the conservative Berlin court, Bach moved to Hamburg where he was given a free hand to write as he pleased. The most adventurous of his symphonies are these six three-movement works (agitated-sorrowful-joyful). They were commissioned by Baron van Swieten who was later one of Mozart's patrons.

Bach composed these masterpieces for the Margrave of Brandenburg and made a flowery dedication to him which (to quote musicologist Nicolas Slonimsky) 'is an extraordinary example of the verbal genuflection of a great composer before a member of petty royalty who vouchsafed him an emolument'. It is doubtful whether the Margrave actually liked Bach's *Brandenburgs* - he didn't even bother to include them in the catalogue of his music collection. All six concertos have something different to offer - No. 1 in F is the most richly scored, No. 2 in F is the one with the brilliant high trumpet part, No. 3 in G, has only two movements, No. 4 in G is the most light-hearted of the set, No. 5 in D is almost a harpsichord concerto, while No. 6 in B flat is the most solemn.

JOHANN SEBASTIAN BACH
1685–1750
GERMAN
BRANDENBURG CONCERTOS NOS. 1-6
(1720)

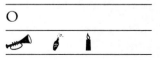

No one is quite sure why or for whom Bach wrote these suites for solo cello but whoever first tackled them must have been quite a player (the same holds true today). In each suite a different mood dominates; each one opens with a prelude and each is followed by a series of French dance movements with titles like Allemande, Courante and Sarabande. Amazingly, before the great Spanish cellist Pablo Casals (1876-1973) did so in 1900, no one had ever performed all six suites in public (his recording of them, made in the 1930s, is still revered). Now these works are among the touchstones of the cello's repertoire.

J.S. BACH
CELLO SUITES
(1717-23)

J.S. Bach
CHACONNE
(fifth movement of Violin
Partita No. 2 in D minor)
(1720)

I

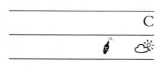

The violin equivalents of the unaccompanied cello suites are Bach's three sonatas and three partitas for solo violin. Of these, the fifth and final movement of the Partita No. 2 is a chaconne, by far the longest (nearly 15 minutes) and the most famous. It's de rigeur for all violinists to be able to master this, but the Chaconne is also well known through a splendid transcription for piano by Busoni. There's another piano version by Brahms, arranged to be played with the left hand alone. It featured in the 1948 horror film *The Beast With Five Fingers* in which a dismembered hand played the Chaconne. Look out, too, for the popular Prelude, Gavotte and Gigue from the Violin Partita No. 3 in E, also well-known in piano transcriptions by Rachmaninov.

J.S. Bach
CONCERTO IN D
MINOR FOR TWO
VIOLINS
(c. 1718-23)

C

The most celebrated concerto for two violins ever written and among the finest violin works of the entire Baroque period. The energetic first and third movements contrast with the concerto's central section (Largo). A distinguished writer on music, Ralph Hill, suggested that this wondrous passage of music might be thought of as a translation into musical terms of Sir Philip Sidney's poem, 'My true love hath my heart, and I have his/By just exchange the one to the other given...'. It is certainly one of the most serene and deeply spiritual eight minutes ever composed.

J.S. Bach
FANTASIA AND
FUGUE IN G MINOR,
BWV 542
'THE GREAT'
(c.1712)

I

The organ was Bach's favourite instrument and, while he was employed by Duke Wilhelm Ernst as court organist and chamber musician, he produced a number of masterpieces that are considered today to be cornerstones of the organ's repertoire. The magnificent Fantasia with its sprightly Fugue were composed as separate pieces in about 1712 (no one's quite sure when they became linked). The eminent music theorist Ebenezer Prout (1835-1909) took it into his head to provide 'lyrics' to be sung to many of Bach's keyboard works as an aide mémoire. He wrote some for the G Minor Fugue, which two of his students parodied: 'Oh Ebenezer Prout, you horrid little man/You just make Bach sound as silly as you can'. They were, apparently, sent down from university for their trouble.

One of the greatest creations for keyboard was written as a mild sedative. Count Kayserling, the Russian Ambassador at the court of Dresden, suffered from insomnia and commissioned Bach to write some music that would be 'soft and yet a little gay' to help him sleep. Johann Gottlieb Goldberg was his chamber musician who had the job of playing this series of 30 variations on the haunting tune of the opening aria, one which Bach had written for his second wife, Anna Magdalena. The 25th variation was dubbed by harpsichordist Wanda Landowska 'the supreme pearl of the necklace, the black pearl'.

J.S. BACH
GOLDBERG
VARIATIONS
(1741)

I

Concertos are traditionally written for a solo instrument playing with an orchestra, but Bach's *Italian Concerto* is for unaccompanied solo clavier (i.e. harpsichord or piano - it can be played on either). It's entitled *Italian* because Bach composed it in imitation of the earlier Italian style of concerto, emulating the works of Italian masters like Corelli. The two outer movements bubble away with tremendous rhythmic drive while the slow movement is a soaring aria.

J.S. BACH
ITALIAN CONCERTO
(1735)

I

The cantata *Herz und Mund und Tat und Leben* for solo voices, chorus and orchestra was written in Weimar for performance on the fourth Sunday of Advent. Its tenth section has a beautiful hymn-like melody called 'Jesu bleibt meine Freunde'. We know it as 'Jesu, joy of man's desiring', one of Bach's best-loved works. It's a perennial favourite at weddings and is almost as well known in its original choral version as in the famous piano transcription by Dame Myra Hess (1890-1965).

J.S. BACH
'JESU, JOY OF MAN'S DESIRING'
from Cantata No. 147, BWV 147
(1723)

CHO/I

**J.S. BACH
MASS IN B MINOR
*(1733-38)***

CHO

This, one of the greatest of all choral works, was never heard in Bach's lifetime. In fact, it was nearly a century after his death that it received its première (in Berlin in February 1834). It's a tribute to Bach's profound spirituality that he, a Protestant, should have felt inspired to write a mass belonging to a Catholic ritual. Amongst its 24 mainly choral sections, perhaps the most awe-inspiring are the *Gloria, Crucifixus, Sanctus* and *Credo*.

**J.S. BACH:
ORCHESTRAL
SUITES
*(c.1717-23)***

O

Bach composed four orchestral suites. No. 2 in B minor is scored for flute and strings, and the last of its six movements is the lively *Badinerie* (an old, vivacious dance form). If you want to hear the original version of what has come to be known as the *Air on the G String*, then listen to the second movement of Bach's Orchestral Suite No. 3 in D (five movements scored for oboes, trumpets, drums and strings this time). Can we edit out all the jokes about striptease artists? And can we stop calling it the *Air on the G String*? It only attracted this nickname in 1871 when the German violinist August Wilhelmj (1845-1908) made a violin and piano arrangement (or 'derangement' to some) of the second movement of this orchestral suite, changed the key into C major and directed that it should be played on the violin's G string alone. Jacques Loussier's arrangement for jazz trio was used for the long-running TV commercials for Hamlet cigars.

**J.S. BACH
PRELUDE AND
FUGUE IN D
*BWV532
(c. 1707-09)***

I

No one's quite sure when Bach composed this brilliant showpiece, a mixture of the solid, rather stodgy North German school of organ composition (in the Prelude) and the light-hearted gaiety of the Italian school (in the Fugue). The latter features what is known in the business as 'advanced pedal work'; in other words, as far as the organist's feet are concerned, it's a real pig to play.

'An act of worship which ... has the animation of a play' is how the American pianist and writer on music, Arthur Loesser, described *The Passion According to St. Matthew* (to give it its proper title). It is 'a marriage of the theatre and the church' and contains some of Bach's most exalted music. There are many moving arias ('Buss' und 'Reu'', for example, and 'Aus Liebe will mein Heiland sterben') as well as chorales, of which 'O Sacred Head, sore wounded' is the best known. The *St. Matthew Passion* lapsed into obscurity after Bach's death and was not heard again until the famous occasion in Berlin on 11 March 1829 when Mendelssohn conducted a revelatory revival, the first step in the restoration of Bach's music.

J.S. BACH
ST. MATTHEW
PASSION
(1727)

CHO

'Schafe koennen sicher weiden', in the German, is the familiar section of this secular cantata entitled *Was mir behagt*. I can still see the record player on the stage at my infant's school, as we all trooped in for morning assembly to the strains of 'Sheep may safely graze' - played on an old 78 rpm disc by the husband-and-wife two piano team of Ethel Bartlett and Ray Robertson. The Australian Percy Grainger used the same tune as the basis for an orchestral piece he called *Blithe Bells - a Free Ramble on Sheep May Safely Graze* which mixes Bach with Delius and Duke Ellington. (See also Walton.)

J.S. BACH
'SHEEP MAY SAFELY
GRAZE'
*from Cantata No. 208,
BWV 208
(1713)*

CHO

Bach wrote over 225 church cantatas (as opposed to about 25 lengthier secular ones). This one, written to be performed on the 27th Sunday after Trinity, has a text that concerns the parable of the wise and foolish virgins in chapter 25 of St. Matthew's Gospel. The most famous section of *Sleepers awake* (*Wachet auf, ruft uns die Stimme - Wake, awake, a voice is calling* is its proper title) is Part Four, the stately chorus 'Zion hört die Waechter singen' ('Zion hears the watchmen singing'). Bach borrowed the tune for this from an earlier hymn, also called 'Wachet auf', by Philipp Nicolai (1556-1608). Later, Bach adapted it as a choral prelude for organ, *Wachet auf*; later still, Ferruccio Busoni made a celebrated piano transcription of Bach's organ version.

J.S. BACH
SLEEPERS AWAKE
*(Cantata No. 140,
BWV 140)
(1731)*

CHO

**J.S. BACH
TOCCATA AND
FUGUE IN D
MINOR,
BWV 565
(c. 1708)**

I/O

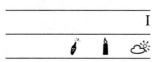

With Widor's Toccata, this is the most famous piece of organ music ever written. The opening toccata section is a series of bold, dramatic flourishes with crunching chords followed by the cumulative excitement of one of Bach's finest fugues. In fact, the piece probably wasn't written by Bach, was almost certainly not conceived for the organ and was probably originally for the violin. The conductors Leopold Stokowski and Sir Henry Wood both made effective orchestral arrangements of the work - Stokowski being largely responsible for the popularity of the work after it was featured, conducted by him, in Walt Disney's *Fantasia*.

**J.S. BACH
VIOLIN
CONCERTOS
IN A MINOR
& E MAJOR
(1717-23)**

C

These are the two earliest concertos for solo violin and orchestra to survive in the present-day repertoire. Many others pre-date them but none approaches them in style, substance or sheer musical craftsmanship. You have to wait until Mozart for the next great examples of the form. One of Bach's earliest biographers observed, 'The beauty of the A minor concerto is severe, that of the E major full of unconquerable joy of life that sings its songs of triumph in the first and last movements.' Listen, and you'll see just how right he was!

**J. S. BACH
THE WELL-
TEMPERED CLAVIER
(1722-44)**

I

This is the name by which Bach's mighty collection of 48 paired preludes and fugues for the clavier are known in English, usually referred to as *The 48*. They are in two sets, each with 24 preludes and fugues in all the major and minor keys, arranged in chromatic order (C major, C minor, C sharp major, C sharp minor, and so on up the black and white notes of the keyboard). Well-tempered? *Temperament* is the word used to describe the tuning of an instrument. Bach introduced a revolutionary way of tuning his clavier (i.e. harpsichord or piano), thus the *48 Preludes and Fugues* were written to be played on a keyboard that was 'well-tuned' or 'well-tempered'. The Prelude No. 1 in C (from Book 1) is the most famous (everybody who has ever touched a piano has had a crack at it) and Gounod used it as the basis for his version of 'Ave Maria'. For all *48*, the recordings made in the 1930s by Edwin Fischer remain indispensable for illuminating these miniature masterpieces.

Sir William Walton arranged movements from Bach cantatas (and a chorale prelude), selected by Constant Lambert, to create a war-time ballet for Sadler's Wells. Choreographed by Sir Frederick Ashton with one of the principal roles danced by Margot Fonteyn, it tells (rather loosely) the parable of the Wise and Foolish Virgins in *St. Matthew's Gospel* (Chapter 25). Walton selected six extracts from the complete ballet to make an orchestral suite, and the fifth section is his tender arrangement of 'Sheep may safely graze' (page 49).

J.S. BACH
(arr. Walton)
THE WISE VIRGINS
Ballet
(1940)

O

'Oriental fantasy for piano' is the subtitle of this barnstorming virtuoso work, still among the most difficult ever written for the instrument (it *looks* as difficult to play as it sounds!), 'accessible to only the most intrepid pianists', as one commentator put it. Try the recordings by Boris Berezovsky or Julius Katchen to hear it at its best. The *islamey* (a word derived from Islam) is a popular folk dance of the Caucasian tribe of the Kabardinians.

MILY BALAKIREV
1837–1910
RUSSIAN
ISLAMEY
(1869, rev. 1902)

I

Glinka's *A Life for the Tsar* (1836) was the first opera written by a Russian which quoted Russian folk songs, Russian church music, had a Russian subject and was concerned with peasants instead of the nobility. The 18-year-old Mily Balakirev's first piano composition was *Reminiscences on Glinka's A Life for the Tsar*, using tunes from the opera. It's a dizzyingly-difficult virtuoso piece (which fascinated Glinka himself, incidentally) and a virtual compendium of keyboard effects and devices. Listen to the recording by Earl Wild.

BALAKIREV
REMINISCENCES
ON 'A LIFE FOR
THE TSAR'
(GLINKA)
(1899, second version)

I

MICHAEL BALFE
1808-70
IRISH
'I DREAMT I DWELT
IN MARBLE HALLS'
from The Bohemian Girl
(1843)

OP

One of opera's most improbable stories didn't prevent Balfe's big hit from remaining popular right up until the 1930s. In fact, *The Bohemian Girl, Maritana* (by Wallace) and *The Lily of Killarney* (by Benedict) were known for years as *The English Ring* (though the implication that they rival Wagner's *Ring Cycle* shouldn't be considered too seriously). 'I dreamt I dwelt...' is Balfe's single most famous melody, in which Arline, the daughter of Count Arnheim but brought up by gypsies, recalls her childhood. This once universally-sung ballad returned recently as a pop single sung by Enya. Balfe's other chief claim to fame, incidentally, is as the composer of that quintessential Victorian ballad 'Come into the garden, Maud'.

SAMUEL BARBER
1910-81
AMERICAN
ADAGIO FOR
STRINGS
(1936)

O

Originally the slow movement (molto adagio) of Barber's String Quartet, Op. 11, this has become one of the most frequently performed short pieces by an American composer. It was at the suggestion of the great conductor Arturo Toscanini that Barber made an arrangement of the adagio movement for string orchestra (Toscanini premièred it in November 1938) and it was Barber who later recast it in 1967 as a choral work, *Agnus Dei*. Its sustained mood of solemn serenity rises to an intense pitch of grief, and for that reason the Adagio is often heard at funerals, most famously those of Franklin D. Roosevelt and Princess Grace of Monaco. Oliver Stone also made moving use of it in his Vietnam War movie *Platoon*.

BARBER
PIANO CONCERTO
(1962)

C

The publisher Schirmer commissioned Barber to celebrate its centenary and the result was this vivid and dramatic concerto, premièred in September 1962 at the opening of the new Philharmonic Hall at the Lincoln Centre, New York City. By turns tuneful, sensual and aggressive, it is an exciting and accessible work with a bombastic finale (a toccata) that's a riot. The original soloist was John Browning and his recording with George Szell and the Cleveland Orchestra remains as good as any.

Commissioned by a wealthy Philadelphia businessman to compose a violin concerto for a protégé of his, Barber composed the first two ravishing, lyrical movements before being told by the (unknown) protégé that it was 'too easy'. Barber then added a fiendishly taxing finale only to be told that it was 'too difficult'. The businessman demanded his money back. Albert Spalding gave the first performance with the Philadelphia Orchestra and Eugene Ormandy in 1941 - but only half the fee was returned by Barber. He'd already spent most of it on a holiday!

BARBER
VIOLIN CONCERTO
(1941)

C

Not a name to crop up in many music books, but Bargiel earns his entry here for this exquisite little jewel recently unearthed, polished and recorded by cellist Steven Isserlis. It's a yearning, wistful elegy that is really most moving. Bargiel, who was highly thought of in his day, was the half-brother of Clara Schumann, a protégé of her husband Robert, and later a champion of Brahms (you can hear something of the influence of Brahms - but more so of Hummel and Mendelssohn - in Bargiel's charming piano trios).

WOLDEMAR BARGIEL
1828-97
GERMAN
ADAGIO FOR CELLO
AND ORCHESTRA

I

Born in Barnstaple, Bath composed grand opera (*Trilby*), light opera (*Bubbles*), tone poems, cantatas and various orchestral works - all forgotten, except this atmospheric piece for piano and orchestra. It's the theme music for a mediocre 1944 British film called *Love Story* (no relation to the 1970 weepie with Ryan O'Neal and Ali McGraw). Known in the US as *The Lady Surrenders*, this one starred Stewart Granger and Margaret Lockwood as a concert pianist. Passionate themes, wild seas, seagulls calling – *Cornish Rhapsody* is a gem of its kind.

HUBERT BATH
1883-1945
ENGLISH
CORNISH
RHAPSODY
(1944)

C

London-born Bax was sympathetically drawn to the works of the great Irish poets and Celtic folklore. This evocative tone poem for orchestra is, wrote Bax, 'meant to capture the castle-crowned cliff of Tintagel, and more particularly the wide distances of the Atlantic as seen from the cliffs of Cornwall on a sunny but not windless summer day'. Towards the climax of the middle section, Bax introduces a sly quotation from Wagner's *Tristan and Isolde*. See if you can spot it!

ARNOLD BAX
1883-1953
ENGLISH
TINTAGEL
(1917)

O

ANTONIO BAZZINI
1818-97
ITALIAN
THE DANCE OF THE
GOBLINS
(1852)

I

A one-hit composer, the virtuoso Italian violinist Bazzini's single lasting gift to posterity is this ear-tickling encore *La Ronde des lutins, scherzo fantastique,* Op. 25. The other reason for its inclusion here is because it can be heard on one of the most astonishing violin recordings ever made - by the 16-year-old Jascha Heifetz on 19 December 1917. Listen and be amazed!

LUDWIG VAN
BEETHOVEN
1770-1827
GERMAN
CHORAL FANTASY
IN C
for piano, chorus
and orchestra
(1807)

C/CHO

An unusual work - part piano solo, part piano concerto, part choral symphony - which defies classification. It can be seen as a kind of trial run for the finale of the Ninth Symphony (the choral theme has a vague similarity to the *Ode to Joy*). The work is in one continuous movement lasting about 20 minutes, but it is only in the last four minutes that the chorus enters with a setting of a poem by Beethoven's friend Christopher Kuffner (1750-1846) in praise of music.

BEETHOVEN
CORIOLAN
Overture
(1807)

O

One of Beethoven's most powerful overtures, written not for a production of Shakespeare's tragedy but for one on the same subject, first produced in Vienna in 1802, by a certain Heinrich Joseph von Collin, a Viennese lawyer and playwright with whom Beethoven was negotiating over the collaboration of an opera. Collin's storyline deviates from Shakespeare's in that Coriolanus commits suicide - not that Beethoven had any intention of following either: the music selects dramatic highlights from the story.

You need to concentrate for this bit: *Fidelio*, Beethoven's only opera, was based on a French play by Bouilly called *Lénore, ou l'Amour conjugal* and first performed in 1805. It was a disaster. The overture he wrote for the première is now called *Leonore Overture No. 2*. After some drastic rewriting it was given again in 1806. For this, he rewrote the overture. This one is called *Leonore Overture No. 3*. Then there was a planned revival of Fidelio in Prague which never took place and Beethoven rewrote the overture again. This is known as (don't ask me why) *Leonore No. 1*. At last, after further rewrites, *Fidelio* was offered again in 1814 and this time it was a success. The overture heard was the fourth that Beethoven composed for *Fidelio* and, thank heavens, it's known as the *Fidelio Overture*. [See also 'Prisoners' Chorus'.]

BEETHOVEN
FIDELIO
Overture
(1814)

O

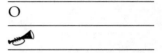

Für Elise is one of Beethoven's 27 little bagatelles or trifles. Second only to the first movement of the *Moonlight Sonata*, it's his most popular piano piece – who hasn't had a go at it in early lessons? But (and I'm sorry to disabuse you) it wasn't written for Elise at all. Beethoven's autograph manuscript reads: 'Für Therese am 27 zur Erinnerung and L. v. Bthvn' ('For Therese on the 27th April in remembrance of L. v. Bthvn'), the Therese being Therese Malfatti with whom Beethoven was then in love. But for an inept copyist, we would know the piece today as *Für Therese*.

BEETHOVEN
FÜR ELISE
(Bagatelle No. 25 in A minor)
(1810)

I

♥

I think we've done this one (see *Fidelio*). Just to say that in modern productions of *Fidelio*, the general practice is to play the *Fidelio Overture* at the beginning of the opera and to insert *Leonore No. 3* (which, I must say, I prefer) between the first and second scenes of Act 2.

BEETHOVEN
LEONORE
OVERTURE NO. 3
(1806)

O

BEETHOVEN
MISSA SOLEMNIS
IN D
(1823)

CHO

A mammoth work which, with Bach's Mass in B minor and Mozart's C Minor Mass ('The Great'), represents the pinnacle of religious music since the Sixteenth Century. Not that Beethoven saw his mass as a religious piece but as his personal testament, a hymn to the spirit of man, Nature and the creative process. He originally planned the work in 1819 to celebrate the installation of the Archduke Rudolph as Archbishop of Olmuetz the following year, but the work kept growing (music by Haydn and Hummel was used for the occasion instead). It took him a further three years to complete. Of the opening *Kyrie*, Beethoven wrote on the score, 'It comes from the heart - may it go to the heart'. You could say that of all its six sections – *Kyrie, Gloria, Credo, Sanctus, Benedictus* and *Agnus Dei* (which ends with a radiant setting of *Dona nobis pacem*).

BEETHOVEN
Overture to
THE CREATURES OF
PROMETHEUS
Ballet
(1800)

O

Based on the legend of the Greek god Prometheus, a potent symbol of independent thinking and the cause of freedom, this ballet was Beethoven's first dramatic work. It was commissioned by the celebrated dancer and choreographer Salvatore Vigno in honour of the Empress Maria Theresa. The only part of the whole score that is still played today is this overture and the Contredanse (a forerunner of the waltz) No. 7 in E flat, a tune which Beethoven also used in the finale of his *Eroica Symphony* and *Eroica Piano Variations*.

BEETHOVEN
Overture to
EGMONT
(1809)

O

The Overture is all that is heard today of the incidental music Beethoven wrote for a revival of Goethe's play which concerns Lamoral, Count of Egmont (1522-68), the Flemish statesman who liberated the Netherlands from Spanish domination. The theme of liberty and its denunciation of tyranny was close to Beethoven's heart (his veneration of Goethe was almost as fervent) and he responds with some of his most sublime and exultant music.

This is Beethoven writing incidental music for the theatre (if they'd had film in those days, Beethoven would have written for that too). One of the short plays to be performed at the opening of the new German theatre in Pest was *Die Ruinen von Athen* in which Minerva wakes from 2,000 years of sleep, finds Athens in ruins but is delighted to find that the new home of art is - heavens, what a coincidence! - Pest, as a result of the generous patronage of Emperor Franz. [See also *Turkish March.*]

BEETHOVEN
Overture to
THE RUINS OF
ATHENS
(1811)

O

Beethoven's first two piano concertos were written when he was in his twenties, when he was already noted as one of the most striking and original pianists around. (Concerto No. 2 in B flat was actually composed three years before No. 1 but not published until 1801, a short time after the C Major Concerto appeared.) Hard to imagine two centuries later, but this amiable masterpiece with its perky final movement (rondo) was rated as daring and novel when it was first heard in Prague with the composer as soloist.

BEETHOVEN
PIANO CONCERTO
NO. 1 IN C
(1798)

C

The key and the opening theme of the Concerto recall Mozart's Piano Concerto No. 24 which Beethoven held in great affection. But within a few bars it is clear that we have left Mozart's world behind and are veering off into new territory: the music is more dramatic, the orchestral writing is more sonorous and the piano part is more expressive (listen to the beautiful slow movement in the unexpected key of E major).

BEETHOVEN
PIANO CONCERTO
NO. 3 IN C MINOR
(1800)

C

This is the one which starts with the piano (five quiet introductory bars), a device unheard of until then. Then there's the second (slow) movement in which the piano has an almost tangible spoken dialogue with the orchestra (Liszt described it as 'Orpheus taming the wild beasts'). No. 4 is the most lyrical of Beethoven's five piano concertos and more - it's among the most sublime works ever written for piano and orchestra.

BEETHOVEN
PIANO CONCERTO
NO. 4 IN G
(1806)

C

BEETHOVEN
PIANO CONCERTO
NO. 5 IN E FLAT
'EMPEROR'
(1809)

C

'Music of sweeping and imperious grandeur unknown to any concerto written up to 1812, and beside which the dignity of emperors or archdukes loses all consequence', wrote the American critic John Burk. The striking opening movement and the exultant finale (a rondo in which Beethoven throws in a popular folk tune of the time) are glorious but, for me, it's the serene, hymn-like second movement that I can't live without. The work's nickname, by the way, was not Beethoven's idea. In 1809, Napoleon's troops were in Vienna and the story goes that a French officer in the audience at the first performance (when Beethoven's pupil Czerny was the soloist) proclaimed it 'an emperor of a concerto'.

BEETHOVEN
PIANO SONATA
NO. 8 IN C MINOR
'PATHÉTIQUE'
(1797-98)

I

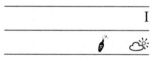

Pathétique (as in 'affecting' or 'moving' rather than 'God, how pathetic') was Beethoven's own subtitle for this, one of the best known of his 32 sonatas for piano. Its anguished opening page, frenetic first movement and playful, yet reflective finale, frame a second movement of almost religious tranquillity. I'm sorry to say that songwriters Norman Newell and Ernest Ponticelli turned it into a hideously-maudlin pop song called 'More Than Love', a hit (would you believe it?) for Ken Dodd in 1966.

BEETHOVEN
PIANO SONATA
NO. 14 IN C SHARP
MINOR
'MOONLIGHT'
(1801)

I

The nickname came from a Berlin critic named Ludwig Rellstab who interpreted the famous first movement as an aural picture of moonlight over Lake Lucerne (though it was more probably inspired by Beethoven's love for the Countess Giulietta Guicciardi to whom the work is dedicated). Rellstab's nickname overlooks the character of the rest of the sonata, which is far from moonlit. Beethoven himself subtitled the work 'Sonata quasi una fantasia' ('Sonata in the style of a fantasia'), but it is the fact that the slow movement opens the work that made it so original. Up until then, when writing a sonata every composer had followed the same established format of 1. fast - 2. slow - 3. fast.

Known by the name of its dedicatee, Count Ferdinand Gabriel von Waldstein, among the first to appreciate Beethoven's genius, this great sonata has always been a *pièce de resistance* for concert pianists. In effect, it has just two movements, for another piece (now called the *Andante Favori in F)* was originally its slow movement. Beethoven discarded this in favour of a brief but heartfelt *Introduzione* leading to the last movement, a rondo of 'radiant jubilance'.

BEETHOVEN
PIANO SONATA
NO. 21 IN C
'WALDSTEIN'
(1803-4)

I

Beethoven thought this the best of his sonatas and many critics agree ('holds the palm amongst all sonatas written for the piano', opined one). The two outer movements are deeply passionate and volatile, framing a languid slow movement *(andante con moto)* which consists of a short set of variations on what is surely one of the composer's most beautiful themes. The nickname is apt but, once again, it wasn't L.v.B.'s but his publisher's. Well, I suppose it might have helped sales.

BEETHOVEN
PIANO SONATA
NO. 23 IN F MINOR
'APPASSIONATA'
(1804-5)

I

Archduke Rudolf, Beethoven's patron and friend, beat a hasty retreat from Vienna in 1809 as French troops advanced on the city. Over the first three notes of the opening theme Beethoven scrawled 'Le-be-wohl' ('Farewell') - the following two movements are labelled 'Absence' and 'Return', a rare example of Beethoven composing a specific programme for a piece of music which, in his dedication to the Archduke, he said was 'written from the heart'.

BEETHOVEN
PIANO SONATA
NO. 26 IN E FLAT
'LES ADIEUX'
(1809-10)

I

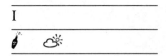

**BEETHOVEN
'PRISONERS'
CHORUS'**
*from Fidelio
(1804-14)*

OP

Beethoven was less happy writing for the voice and the stage than in any other forms. The theme of the opera appealed to him greatly – the unjustly imprisoned Florestan (a symbol of all the repressed peoples of the world) freed by the devoted love of Leonore (representing liberty and justice) – but its composition caused him agonies. He rewrote one aria no less than 18 times and, as we've seen (above), composed four different overtures. Ultimately, what emerged from this creative struggle and a series of unsuccessful early versions, is one of man's noblest utterances, more a symphony-drama than an opera. One of the highlights is 'O welche Lust' ('What happiness'), known as the 'Prisoners' Chorus'. It comes in Act 1 when Leonore persuades the jailer, Rocco, to let Florestan's fellow prisoners spend a few moments in the sunlight.

**BEETHOVEN
ROMANCES FOR
VIOLIN &
ORCHESTRA
NOS. 1 IN G & 2 IN F**
(1802-3)

I

♥

Here, for once, is Beethoven in non-revolutionary mode. These brief, lyrical, romantic pieces were written during the first period of mental anguish he suffered over his advancing deafness, a year, nevertheless, of great inspiration which included the *Moonlight Sonata*, the *Kreutzer Sonata* (for violin and piano) and the Second Symphony.

**BEETHOVEN
SYMPHONY
NO. 1 IN C**
(1800)

O

'A caricature of Haydn pushed to absurdity' was how one of Beethoven's critics described his First Symphony. To our ears it is an easy, agreeable listen but to contemporary audiences, who had heard Haydn's final symphony only five years earlier, Beethoven's effort was challenging and dissonant. The opening chords of the First Symphony represented a new world and his subsequent efforts in the genre reveal just what a revolutionary force Beethoven was and how far musical language developed under his leadership.

The first symphony to be inspired by non-musical ideas (as opposed to subjecting musical material to formal symphonic treatment), the *Eroica* was Beethoven's expression of his democratic ideals. One critic described the *Eroica* as 'the greatest single step made by an individual composer in the history of the symphony and the history of music in general'. It's really an epic four-movement musical essay on the subject of heroism and was the composer's own favourite among all his symphonies (its famous Funeral March is the second movement). Beethoven planned the work as a homage to Napoleon whom he perceived as a champion of liberty and freedom. Legend has it that when he heard that Napoleon had crowned himself Emperor, Beethoven's disenchantment with such self-aggrandisement and lust for power led him to scratch out the name 'Bonaparte' from the front page of the manuscript and replace it with the one word 'Eroica'. However, the published score still bore the words 'composed to celebrate the memory of a great man'. More important than any legends attached to this great work, though, is the powerful message that Beethoven wanted to convey to the world.

BEETHOVEN
SYMPHONY
NO. 3 IN E FLAT
'EROICA'
(1804)

O

'Da-da-da-daaah. Da-da-da-daaah'. Perhaps the most familiar opening to any piece of symphonic music – the three short notes, one long, then repeated – have had all kinds of interpretations attached to them. Beethoven's friend Schindler was the first to suggest they represented Fate knocking at the door. It's more probable that they were inspired by the song of the goldfinch. Latterly, it was the fact that three short dots and one long signified the letter V in Morse Code that 'V for Victory' became the effective call-sign for the Allied Forces during World War II. Beethoven wrote this great and profound work when he was 38 years old. Schumann wrote of it, 'So often heard, it still exercises its power over all ages... [it] will go on centuries hence, as long as the world and the world's music endure.' So far, he has been proved right.

BEETHOVEN
SYMPHONY NO. 5 IN
C MINOR
(1808)

O

**BEETHOVEN
SYMPHONY
NO. 6 IN F
'PASTORAL'**
(1808)

O

'Nature', according to Beethoven's companion Charles Neate, 'was almost meat and drink to [him]; he seemed positively to to exist upon it.' This, regularly voted the most loved of all Beethoven's compositions, is a hymn to Nature which originally bore the title *Characteristic Symphony: The recollections of life in the country*. The descriptive titles by which we know its five movements – *The Awakening of Joyful Feelings Upon Arrival in the Country, The Brook, Village Festival, The Storm* and *The Shepherd's Thanksgiving* - were added later. There are many people for whom this work has vivid associations - in my case, the last movement was my father's favourite piece of music and I can remember, as a very small boy, listening to it again and again on one of the first long-playing records that ever appeared. (That dates me!)

**BEETHOVEN
SYMPHONY
NO. 7 IN A**
(1812)

O

This life-enhancing work was famously described by Wagner as 'the apotheosis of the dance' because of the emphasis on rhythmic power that pervades all four movements. After hearing the end of the festive first movement, Weber (page 350) is said to have remarked that Beethoven was now 'quite ripe for the madhouse'. The second movement (allegretto) is particularly poignant and was an important influence on the Romantic composers, the third is a lively scherzo (sometimes heard separately), while the final movement is an irresistible Bacchanalian frenzy. The first performance was a benefit concert for Austrian soldiers and arranged by the musician and mechanic Johann Nepomuk Mälzel, the inventor of the metronome (he also invented an automatic chess player and a mechanical trumpeter). In the orchestra, under Beethoven's direction, were Spohr, Moscheles and Meyerbeer, while Hummel and Salieri were backstage priming the cannons for a performance of Beethoven's *Battle Symphony*.

'The Glorious Ninth of Ludwig Van' (as it was referred to in Stanley Kubrick's cult movie of Anthony Burgess' *A Clockwork Orange*) was many years in the making, but its most distinguishing feature, the choral finale, came at a late stage of the creative process. Beethoven had been attracted to Schiller's 'Ode to Joy' as early as 1792; his *Choral Fantasy* of 1807 (see above) has the germ of the idea; he was making sketches for the symphony from 1815 onwards, but only when he returned to its composition in earnest in 1822 did he finally decide that the finale was the right place for a setting of Schiller's 'Ode' (actually, he used only about a third of the original poem and re-ordered the verses to suit his own purposes). Despite some ungrateful vocal writing in the last movement, the work is a monumental achievement, for the emotional power of the whole score is one of the mightiest celebrations of the human spirit. How ironic, then, that its creator never heard it: at its first performance, after the close of the second movement, the totally deaf Beethoven was turned around on the conductor's stand to see the audience's gestures of approval - he had been unaware of the roars of applause behind him.

BEETHOVEN
SYMPHONY
NO. 9 IN D MINOR
'CHORAL'
(1824)

O/CHO

A strange and not wholly satisfying work redeemed by its vivacious finale (a rondo in the style of a polonaise). The three solo instruments (piano, violin and cello) are used in the same sort of way as in the old concerti grossi of the Italian masters of a century earlier, pitting a small group of instrumentalists (called the *concertino*) against a larger group (the *ripieno*). Though written after the two early piano concertos, this is nothing like as adventurous - an example of Beethoven, for once, looking backwards.

BEETHOVEN
TRIPLE CONCERTO
IN C
(1805)

C

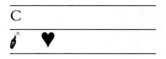

BEETHOVEN
TURKISH MARCH
from The Ruins of Athens
(1811)

O/I

Apart from the Overture (page 57), Beethoven wrote some choruses and marches to accompany this play. The only ones to have remained popular are the 'Chorus of Dervishes' and the *Turkish March*. The latter is written in the pseudo-Turkish style popular in Vienna around the turn of the Nineteenth Century. Beethoven made a version for piano with six variations - his Op. 76, but today it's heard more often than not in a famous piano transcription by the great Russian pianist and composer Anton Rubinstein (page 260) which imitates a marching band passing by and fading into the distance. You can hear both the chorus and the march (and much more) in Liszt's grand *Fantasy on Beethoven's 'Ruins of Athens'* for piano and orchestra, dedicated, incidentally, to Nicolas Rubinstein (Anton's brother) and premièred, appropriately, in Pest in 1853.

BEETHOVEN
VIOLIN CONCERTO
IN D
(1806)

C

It's a paradox that the three greatest violin concertos of the Nineteenth Century were written by composers who were pianists - Beethoven, Mendelssohn and Brahms. The latter two turned to professional violinists for advice (respectively David and Joachim); Beethoven, I need hardly tell you, turned to no one. A further paradox is that this most spiritual and profound of violin concertos was written for a violinist named Clement, a combination of musician and circus clown. He must have been quite a player for it is said that, at the first performance (23 December 1806), Clement had to sight-read the score of this exacting work without benefit of rehearsal. Then, supposing the audience to be in need of comic relief after the first movement, he played them a sonata of his own on one string and with the violin turned upside down. After the interval, he continued with the second and third movements of Beethoven's new concerto. Apparently the work was well received, though it took nearly 40 years to establish itself in the violin repertoire, thanks largely to Joachim (see above), who played it as a 13-year-old prodigy in London in May 1844, conducted by Mendelssohn.

Beethoven wrote ten sonatas for violin and piano, not all of them as good as the *Spring* and the *Kreutzer* (see below). Many were published as works 'for piano with the accompaniment of the violin', carrying on an eighteenth century tradition where the violin had a secondary role in duos. Here, the fiddle-player has anything but a secondary role and its general good-humour and ebullient high-spirits evoke the Sonata's nickname.

BEETHOVEN
VIOLIN SONATA
NO. 5 IN F
'SPRING'
(1801)

I

This, the finest of Beethoven's violin sonatas, was composed for a prodigiously-gifted violinist whom the composer met in 1802, a mulatto named George Augustus Polgreen Bridgetower, born in Poland of German parents and referred to in contemporary journals as an 'Abyssinian prince'. Bridgetower, sight-reading some of the solo part, and Beethoven gave the first performance in May 1803. Subsequently, though, the two quarrelled (presumably over a girl) and the composer dedicated the Sonata to the distinguished violinist Rudolph Kreutzer. Kreutzer, however, found the work 'outrageously unintelligible' and refused to play it. And thus he is remembered by posterity - oh, and for the fact that Tolstoy was so taken with the work that he was inspired to write his tale of passion and jealousy entitled *The Kreutzer Sonata*.

BEETHOVEN
VIOLIN SONATA
NO. 9 IN A
'KREUTZER'
(1803)

I

Norma is Bellini's *magnum opus*, set in Gaul during the Roman occupation of about 50BC. 'A great score that speaks to the heart,' wrote Wagner, a notoriously ungenerous critic, 'a work of genius.' It tells the story of Norma, High Priestess of the Druids, and her love for the Roman Pro-Consul Pollione. The title role is one of the most arduous in opera, a challenge to all the great sopranos who have relished its dramatic and vocal opportunities, not least Maria Callas who left two unmissable recordings of the part. 'Casta Diva' ('Chaste goddess') from Act 1 is one of opera's best loved arias. Personally, I've always preferred the last 20 minutes and the orgasmic ensemble which ends the opera, 'Deh! non volerli vittime', and which also features in a glittering piano transcription of some of the opera's themes by Liszt.

VINCENZO BELLINI
(1801–35)
ITALIAN
'CASTA DIVA'
from Norma
(1831)

OP

BELLINI
I PURITANI
(1835)

OP

Bellini was not yet 34 when he died in Paris, eight months after the première of this, his last opera – *I Puritani di Scozia* (*The Puritans of Scotland*) to give it its full title. Here is some of Bellini's most dazzling and demanding vocal writing with highlights such as Elvira's radiant 'Son vergin vezzosa' (a sparkling polonaise) and her moving mad scene aria 'Qui la voce soave'. The stirring bass/baritone duet 'Suoni la tromba' was used by Liszt as the theme for his *Hexameron Variations* written by himself, Chopin and four other fashionable pianists for a charity fund raiser in Paris in 1837.

BELLINI
LA SONNAMBULA
(1831)

OP

The Sleepwalker or *The Sleepwalking Girl* was Bellini's seventh opera - he wrote only ten in his short life - and one which you don't go and see for the plausibility of its plot. But Bellini's melodic outpouring is irresistible in arias like 'Ah, non credea mirarti' in the final sleepwalking scene (Act 3), and 'Ah, non giunge' (one of opera's most brilliant coloratura arias) when Amina, the heroine, awakens.

RALPH BENATZKY
1884-1957
CZECH
THE WHITE HORSE INN
(1930)

OP

Im Weissen Rössel (its original German title) was arguably the most successful operetta produced between the two world wars and one of the last of its kind in the tradition of *Die Fledermaus*, *The Merry Widow* and *The Chocolate Soldier*. 'Goodbye' ('Goodbye, goodbye/I wish you all a last goodbye') is its best-known number. Benatzky, whose other big success was his 1928 Johann Strauss II revue-cum-operetta *Casanova* (from which comes the famous 'Nun's Chorus'), was amazingly prolific and is credited with over 90 theatre shows, 250 film scores and 5000 songs.

ARTHUR BENJAMIN
1893-1960
AUSTRALIAN
JAMAICAN RUMBA
(1938)

O/I

The rumba is a Cuban dance - 'not suggestive, as has been alleged, since it leaves nothing to suggest' - and this is the composer's single (and singularly unsuggestive) hit, usually heard in its two-piano arrangement. His *Romantic Fantasy* for violin and viola (which Jascha Heifetz and William Primrose recorded) is worth a listen, as is his bustling *Overture to an Italian Comedy*, an overlooked curtain-raiser. Though born in

Australia, Benjamin spent most of his career in London, including a period teaching at the Royal College of Music. By some circuitous route, my late father-in-law bought his Armstrong Siddley Sapphire car from him.

The vivacious opening to Berlioz's last work was first heard in August 1862. The opera, based on Shakespeare's *Much Ado About Nothing*, was a triumph, though poor Berlioz was too ill to enjoy its success. America did not hear the opera until a concert version nearly a century later in New York's Carnegie Hall in 1960.

HECTOR BERLIOZ
1803–69
FRENCH
BEATRICE AND
BENEDICT
Overture (1862)

O

This is the original overture for Berlioz's first full-length opera (see *Roman Carnival*) which was such a fiasco at its first performance at the Paris Opera in 1838 - it was nicknamed 'Malvenuto Cellini', the audience almost started a riot and, after three performances, it was not given another outing until 1913. After the first night, Berlioz recorded, 'The overture received exaggerated applause, but the rest was hissed with admirable energy and unanimity.'

BERLIOZ
BENVENUTO
CELLINI
Overture
(1837)

O

The Childhood of Christ is an oratorio in three sections: *Herod's Dream*, *The Flight into Egypt* (this part has the lovely 'Shepherd's Farewell' chorus) and *The Arrival at Saïs*. For a self-confessed agnostic it's a deeply spiritual work - hear this and it's hard to believe that the *Grande Messe des morts* is by the same composer. Its first performance in Paris was a huge success; in Bordeaux the audience was so ecstatic they rushed to crown the composer with a laurel wreath; in Strasbourg an audience of 8,000 continually interrupted the music with their outbursts of enthusiasm.

BERLIOZ
THE CHILDHOOD
OF CHRIST
(1845)

CHO

BERLIOZ
THE CORSAIRE
Overture
(1844)

O

Some writers think that the inspiration for this dramatic orchestral showpiece was Byron's poem 'The Corsair' (1814) about a pirate chief; others are convinced that James Fennimore Cooper's novel *The Red Rover* was its basis (Berlioz changed the overture's title to *Le Corsaire rouge*). There again, it was called *La Tour de Nice* at its first performance in 1845 because the original version, completed in 1831, was composed in a tower overlooking the sea at Nice. Whatever, it is 'as salty a sea piece as has ever been written' according to Sir Donald Tovey, the eminent English musicologist.

BERLIOZ
DANCE OF THE
SYLPHS & MINUET
WILL-O'-THE-WISPS
from The Damnation
of Faust
(1846)

O

♥

Two short excerpts from Berlioz's 'dramatic legend' *The Damnation of Faust* are now designated 'orchestral lollipops' of the sort championed (and much-recorded) by Sir Thomas Beecham. The *Dance of the Sylphs* is a short waltz which conjures up for Faust the image of his beloved Marguerite while he is sleeping. The Minuet is a serenade given at the command of Mephistopheles by the spirits and Will-o'-the-wisps under Marguerite's window at night. Will-o'-the-wisps? They're defined as '*Ignis-fatuus* - the light of combustion from marsh-gas, apt to lead travellers into danger; any deceptive or elusive person'.

BERLIOZ
LES FRANCS-JUGES
Overture
(c. 1826)

O

Berlioz's original intention was to write an opera about the *Vehmgerircht*, a secret tribunal that flourished in Westphalia in the late medieval period. After completing the Overture, Berlioz abandoned the project. You may know the second theme of this vivacious orchestral favourite as the signature tune for BBC TV's series of *Face to Face* interviews with John Freeman in the early 1960s.

BERLIOZ
HAROLD IN ITALY
(Symphony in G for viola
and orchestra)
(1834)

C

The great violin virtuoso Paganini (page 221) commissioned Berlioz to write a viola concerto for him after hearing a performance of the *Symphonie fantastique* (see below). After seeing the sketches for the first movement, though, he was so disappointed with what Berlioz had written that he lost all interest. Berlioz then proceeded to weave a series of scenes very loosely based on Byron's *Childe Harolde* and his own 'impressions recollected from wandering in the Abruzzi mountains'. The two most celebrated parts of the work's four movements are the second movement *March of the Pilgrims Singing Their Evening Prayers* and the last movement, the *Orgy of the Brigands*. Paganini, to do him credit, after first hearing the work in 1838, realised he'd made an error of judgement and presented Berlioz with a gift of 20,000 francs.

No one quite knows who wrote the original march but it certainly wasn't Berlioz - who receives the credit for it today. The tune was popularised by the army of Prince Ferencz Rakoczy, the leader of the Hungarian revolt against Austria in 1703-11. It was his favourite march and was named after him. But it did not become more widely known until Berlioz inserted it into his *Damnation of Faust*. Liszt also used the same theme in his *Hungarian Rhapsody No.15* for piano.

BERLIOZ
HUNGARIAN
MARCH
'RAKOCZY MARCH'
(1846)

O

'If I were threatened with the burning of all my works except one,' Berlioz once confessed, 'it is for the *Requiem* that I would ask for mercy.' Originally intended as a work honouring the dead of the 1830 revolution, it was first heard at the Invalides in Paris in December 1837 at the funeral service of General Damremont, hero of the Algerian campaign. Berlioz asks for huge forces - 400 voices in the chorus, 100 in the orchestra plus, in the *Tuba Mirum* movement, four brass bands placed at the four points of the compass to conjure up the Day of Judgement. The work contains some of the most awesome and grandiose music ever written which Berlioz himself described as 'overwhelming and horrifying grandeur'.

BERLIOZ
REQUIEM
'GRANDE MESSE
DES MORTS'
(1837)

CHO

'It exploded like a mass of fireworks,' wrote the composer after conducting a performance in Vienna. The themes come from Berlioz's opera *Benvenuto Cellini*, composed between 1834-37 but which, when it was premièred at the Paris Opera in September 1838, was a dismal failure. So, six years later, Berlioz salvaged some choice bits and whipped them into this high-powered and exuberant concert favourite.

BERLIOZ
THE ROMAN
CARNIVAL
Overture
(1844)

O

BERLIOZ
SYMPHONIE
FANTASTIQUE
(1830)

O

One of the great revolutionary works of classical music which broke rules and new ground in every page. The innovations and imaginative forces at work in this masterpiece represented a new sound world. (Rossini said of it, 'What a good thing it isn't music!') Subtitled *An Episode in the Life of an Artist*, the composition of the *Fantastic Symphony* was closely bound up with Berlioz's stormy affair with the English actress Harriet Smithson, but based on De Quincy's *Confessions of an Opium Eater* in which a young, sensitive musician with a vivid imagination poisons himself in a fit of love-sick despair. Its five sections trace the hero as he falls in love: *Dreams, Passions; The Ball* (its famous waltz movement); *Scene in the Country; The March to the Scaffold; Dreams of the Witches' Sabbath.*

BERLIOZ
SUMMER NIGHTS
'LES NUITS D'ÉTÉ'
(1841)

V

♥

Generally sung by a soprano (in the original piano version and in Berlioz's later orchestral arrangement) these six settings of poems by Théophile Gautier are languid, serene songs which constitute the first important song cycle in French up to that time, complementing those of Beethoven, Schubert and Schumann. No. 1 ('Villanelle') and No. 4 ('Absence') are particularly popular.

BERLIOZ
TROJAN MARCH
from The Trojans
(1856-58)

O

Les Troyens is an oversized masterpiece inspired by Virgil's *Aeneid* - with intermissions it takes about four-and-a-half hours to perform. You won't get a chance to see it very often: it's simply too expensive to mount. It's in five acts but divided into two separate operas (*The Fall of Troy* and *The Trojans at Carthage*) and was not heard in its entirety until 1969. Critic Ernest Newman decribed it as 'a truly stupendous work, and until a man has seen and heard it he can hardly claim to much more than a rudimentary knowledge of the composer'. Two orchestral excerpts are often heard in concert: the *Royal Hunt and Storm*, and this, the *Trojan March*, which appears in both parts of the opera.

Perhaps the most popular choice for an opening number at orchestral concerts today, this breathless four minutes of tongue-in-cheek orchestral fireworks certainly gets things off with a bang. It uses the duet 'Oh Happy We' from the operetta as a lyrical contrast to the middle section before a sparkling conclusion featuring part of the witty coloratura aria 'Glitter and be Gay'.

LEONARD BERNSTEIN
1918–90
AMERICAN
Overture to
CANDIDE
(1956)

O

🎵

In 1948, the bandleader Woody Herman commissioned Bernstein to write him a work for solo clarinet and jazz ensemble. When it was finished, Herman was unable to pay Bernstein and, though one of the *riffs* found its way into Bernstein's 1952 musical *Wonderful Life*, it wasn't until October 1955 that Bernstein's friend and neighbour Benny Goodman brushed the dust off this catchy score and performed it for the first time. The work is dedicated to him.

BERNSTEIN
PRELUDE, FUGUE
AND RIFFS
(1949)

I

🎵

Like Handel and many others before him, Bernstein was not against plagiarising himself and giving extra mileage to some of his most inspired music. This one-movement suite lasting 20-odd minutes is an orchestral fusion of some of *West Side Story*'s most effective passages, including *Somewhere, Cool* and *The Rumble*.

BERNSTEIN
SYMPHONIC
DANCES
from West Side Story
(1957)

O

🎵

As an introduction to Bernstein's serious side (as opposed to his West Side) you could do a lot worse than start with this, reflections on the poem of the same title by W.H. Auden. Admittedly, it's a difficult listen first time through, but is ultimately rewarding. That being said, the fifth of its six sections (*The Masque*), featuring virtuosic jazz piano and percussion, is immediately appealing and winningly on-Broadway.

BERNSTEIN
SYMPHONY NO. 2
'THE AGE OF
ANXIETY'
(1949)

O

BERNSTEIN
THREE DANCE
EPISODES
from On the Town
(1944)

O

On The Town took Broadway by storm in December 1944. It is a spirited musical with book and lyrics by Betty Comden and Adolph Green about three sailors on 24-hour shore leave in New York City. Bernstein took three sequences - the *Dance of the Great Lover* (which accompanies the Coney Island dream sequence of Gabey, one of the sailors), *Lonely Town* and *Times Square* (from Act 1) - and presented them as orchestral dance movements.

FRANZ BERWALD
1796-1868
SWEDISH
GRAND SEPTET
IN B FLAT
(1828)

CH

I rather like Berwald with his echoes of Weber and Mendelssohn: his music has the same sunshine feel to it. His Septet is a deliciously airy work with charming tunes and ideas (it's scored for clarinet, bassoon, horn, violin, viola, cello and double bass). Its jokey finale shows that Berwald, though described by contemporaries as arrogant and intransigent, had an excellent sense of humour.

BERWALD
SYMPHONY
NO. 3 IN C
'SINGULIÉRE'
(1845)

O

Unable to find an audience in the provincial atmosphere of his native Sweden, Berwald went off to central Europe to make a career. Liszt was among the few impressed with his talents but, to make a living, Berwald at various times ran an orthopaedic establishment in Berlin, became manager of a glassworks, then part-owner of a sawmill. Much of his music was not heard until this century. Listening to this richly-melodic, original work makes you wonder why. It's as light as Haydn and as individual (or should that be 'singular'?) as Berlioz. Symphonies Nos. 2 and 4 are also well worth a listen.

Bizet's most widely-known orchestral work was fashioned from the 27 numbers he composed as incidental music to a drama by Daudet, set in the Provençal city of Arles (hence the work's English translation *The Woman of Arles*). Suite No. 1's opening Prelude is popular (a march tune based on an old French Christmas song) as are the following Minuet (Rachmaninov transcribed it for piano) and the gentle Adagietto. Suite No. 2, arranged by Ernest Guiraud after Bizet's death, is not heard as often, though the music of the Intermezzo movement was put to yet another use - given words and turned by Guiraud into an effective setting of the *Agnus Dei* (from the Mass).

GEORGES BIZET
1838-75
FRENCH
L'ARLÉSIENNE
SUITES NOS. 1 *(1872)*
& 2 *(1876 arr. Guiraud)*

O

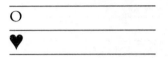

Les Pêcheurs de perles is set on the island of Ceylon (Sri Lanka) in ancient times and tells of the love two fishermen (Nadir and Zurga) have for the same girl, Leïla, the beautiful High Priestess of the Brahmin temple. It all ends in disaster, of course, but in Act 1 the two men believe themselves cured of their infatuation with Leïla and swear eternal friendship. That's what 'In the Depths of the Temple', by far the most popular duet in all opera, is all about. The historic recording of it made in 1950 by Jussi Björling and Robert Merrill has yet to be bettered.

BIZET
'AU FOND DU TEMPLE SAINT'
from The Pearl Fishers (1863)

OP

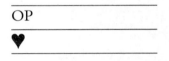

With its succession of classical 'pops', compelling story and exotic settings, it's no wonder that *Carmen* is the most frequently performed of all operas. It's that rare thing, a truly great work with universal appeal. There are four or five tunes that everyone can sing in the bath: 'L'amour est un oiseau rebelle' ('Love is a rebellious bird') - the famous 'Habanera', so-called because it's written in the rhythm of the Cuban dance, though in fact the tune is not by Bizet (he thought it was a folk song and inserted it into the opera only to discover that it was a recently-composed ditty called 'El Arreglito' by Sebastián de Yradier, 1809-65); 'Les Tringles des sistres tintaient' ('To the sound of tambourines') known as the 'Chanson Bohème' - Carmen's wild gypsy dance at the inn of Lilas Pastia; then there's Escamillo's 'Toreador's Song', Don José's

BIZET
CARMEN
(1875)

OP

'Flower Song' and a string of others. Many composers have written fantasies and variations on the themes from *Carmen*. Among those to look out for are by Sarasate and Waxman (both for violin), and Busoni and Horowitz (both for piano). There are also two *Carmen* suites, effective orchestral arrangements of the music.

BIZET
JEUX D'ENFANTS
(1871)

I/O

12 short pieces make up this enchanting suite about childhood subjects. They were also written for children to play (four-hands, one piano), though any child would have to be pretty good to tackle some of them. Bizet later made orchestral versions of five of them: *Trumpeter and Drummer, The Doll, The Top, Little Husband, Little Wife* and *The Ball*, a lively gallop with which to end the *Children's Games.*

BIZET
SYMPHONY IN C
(1855)

O

A delightful work that's guaranteed to put a spring in your step. Bizet began writing it while still a student on 29 October 1855. He finished it within a month and then forgot all about it. It was discovered in a bundle of his manuscripts which the composer Renaldo Hahn (page 147) presented to the Paris Conservatoire in September 1935. He didn't find the Symphony particularly interesting. A Mr D.C. Parker, Bizet's English biographer, thought otherwise and handed the score to the great conductor Felix Weingartner who gave the world première of Bizet's youthful Symphony in Basle on 26 February 1935, 80 years after its composition. You can hear hints of Mozart, Rossini, Mendelssohn and Gounod (no one's music would be the worse for that!), but Bizet produced a real charmer all his own.

ARTHUR BLISS
1891–1975
ENGLISH
CHECKMATE
Ballet
(1937)

O

A game of chess played by Love and Death and danced out on a huge chess board in which the old King is eventually struck down - checkmate! The first of Bliss's four ballets, this one was written for the Royal Ballet's first visit to Paris in 1937. The cast included Margot Fonteyn, Michael Somes and Robert Helpmann and the choreography was by Ninette de Valois. The finale is particularly arresting. Other works of Bliss to try are: *A Colour Symphony,* Introduction and Allegro, the Clarinet Quintet and his muscular Piano Concerto.

Knighted in 1950, succeeding Sir Arnold Bax as Master of the Queen's Musick in 1953, Bliss was hailed as one of the foremost British composers of his generation (in fact, he was half American). H.G. Wells approached him to write the music for the film of *Things To Come* which prophesied war in 1940 followed by plague, rebellion, a new glass-based society and the first rocket-ship to the moon. It's still one of the great film scores, subsequently turned into a concert suite with its terrifying march especially outstanding.

BLISS
March from
THINGS TO COME
(1935)

O

Boccherini was a virtuoso cellist and wrote 11 concertos for the instrument. The one in G major (G480, composed in 1770) is worth investigating, though the only one that still receives regular performance in concert is this one. Until very recently, though, Boccherini's original was never played. It was almost always heard in the version by the renowned German cellist Friedrich Grützmacher (1832-1903), who published in 1895 a romantic conflation of the B Flat Concerto and an earlier one in G minor. Pablo Casals made a famous recording of this arrangement in 1936 and many other great virtuosi have since followed his example.

LUIGI BOCCHERINI
1743-1805
ITALIAN
CELLO CONCERTO
IN B FLAT, G482
(1780)

C

Lured away from his native Italy to become Royal Composer in Residence at the court of the Infante Don Luis in Aranjuez, it was only natural that Boccherini would be attracted to the national instrument of Spain. A guitar quintet combines a string quartet with a guitar and Boccherini's are the first important examples of their kind. He wrote 12 of them, though four are lost. These two are highly popular with Classic FM listeners.

BOCCHERINI
GUITAR
QUINTETS IN D,
G449 *(1779)*
& E MINOR,
G451 *(1796)*

CH

BOCCHERINI
Minuet from
STRING QUINTET
NO 5 IN E
G275
(1771)

CH

Known as *Boccherini's Minuet* - which is pretty meaningless as he composed hundreds of other minuets - this particular one (in A major) has become so hackneyed that it's hard to succumb any longer to its dainty, innocent charm after over-enthusiastic use in television commercials in which lazy directors use it to instantly convey eighteenth century elegance and refinement to a modern audience. Mind you, its use in the 1955 Ealing comedy *The Ladykillers* was a stroke of genius.

LEON BOËLLMANN
1862-97
FRENCH
SUITE GOTHIQUE
(1895)

I

This short-lived French composer and organist left behind one masterpiece for the organ. Its four movements include *Prière à Notre Dame* (often played during the signing of the register at weddings) and a final Toccata. This is one of the most delirious and exhilarating of its kind - against the right hand's whirlwind of notes and the left hand's stabbing chords, a threatening theme, played on the pedals, grows ever louder as the movement progresses, finishing in a triumphant blaze of full organ. I shall never forget the first time I heard it, sitting alone at the back of the school chapel with tears streaming down my face as I eavesdropped on my organ teacher.

ALEXANDER
BORODIN
1833-87
RUSSIAN
IN THE STEPPES OF
CENTRAL ASIA
(1880)

O

A 'musical picture' - literally, for this, one of Borodin's most popular works, was conceived to accompany a *tableau vivant* intended to glorify the Central Asian campaigns of Alexander II. (Borodin was one of 12 Russian composers commissioned to write similar works to mark the 25th anniversary of the Tsar's reign.) The music, with Borodin's typical juxtaposition of folk-based Oriental and Russian themes, depicts a caravan crossing the steppes 'under the surveillance of the terrible armed forces of the [Russian] victors', as Borodin's original programme note put it (a note that was swiftly 'demilitarized' by the authorities, by the way).

Borodin's masterpiece, the opera *Prince Igor*, was left incomplete at his death. Among its missing parts was the Overture. This was added in 1887 by Glazunov who, apparently, created it by writing down from memory the overture he remembered from Borodin's own improvisations. Essentially, it's a potpourri of melodies from the opera. So, for 'Borodin's Overture to Prince Igor' read 'Glazunov's version of how he thought Borodin intended his Overture to Prince Igor to go'.

BORODIN
Overture to
PRINCE IGOR
(1887)

O

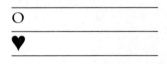

While Borodin's fragmentary manuscript of Prince Igor was completed by Glazunov and Rimsky-Korsakov, the *Polovtsian Dances* were one of eight numbers completed by Borodin himself (with his public duties as an eminent scientist and research chemist, it's no wonder that so much of his music was left abandoned or incomplete at his death). The dances were premièred separately in 1879 and have remained a favourite on concert programmes ever since, though the opera itself, concerning the capture of Prince Igor in the Twelfth Century, is rarely performed.

BORODIN
POLOVTSIAN
DANCES
from Prince Igor
(1869-79)

O

♥

You may think you've never heard anything from this quartet, but you have! The third of its four movements, a nocturne, was used in the 1953 Wright/Forrest musical *Kismet* which was entirely based on themes culled from Borodin's works. Now it's impossible to hear this tender melody without singing the lyrics attached to it - 'And this is my beloved'. Not inappropriate as it turns out, for Borodin dedicated his Second String Quartet to his wife to mark the twentieth anniversary of their first meeting. From the same quartet, the second movement (Scherzo) provided most of the music for another hit from *Kismet* - 'Baubles, Bangles and Beads'.

BORODIN
STRING QUARTET
NO. 2 IN D
(1881)

CH

SERGEI BORTKIEWICZ
1877-1952
RUSSIAN
PIANO CONCERTO
NO. 1 IN B FLAT
(1912)

C

♥

No one would claim that Bortkiewicz was a great or even important composer, but this concerto is a memorable flash in the pan. Its lush orchestration, surging melodies and virtuosic solo part make this one of the most seductive of romantic concertos. Hollywood never had it this good! Over-the-top, heart-on-sleeve and verging on the vulgar at times, nevertheless it makes a welcome alternative to other over-played works of this ilk. What a shame it never gets played in concert. The only current recording is by the excellent Stephen Coombs.

WILLIAM BOYCE
1711-79
ENGLISH
GAVOTTE
from Symphony
No. 4 in F
(1751)

O

Boyce's eight symphonies, none with the exception of No. 8 lasting over ten minutes, are busy, boisterous (or should that be 'Boyceterous'?) affairs, originally designed as overtures or 'between acts' theatre music. Anyone who loves the orchestral music of Handel will find much to enjoy in all eight symphonies, but this gavotte is the best known movement from its use as the signature tune for the long-running BBC Radio 4 programme *These You Have Loved*.

JOHANNES BRAHMS
1833-97
GERMAN
ACADEMIC FESTIVAL
OVERTURE
(1880)

O

Brahms' generally melancholic muse is blown away in this 'very jolly potpourri on students' (as he described it). The University of Breslau had made him an honorary Doctor of Philosophy in recognition of his contribution to 'music of the more severe order', so you can imagine the reaction of the University dignitaries to this selection of popular student tunes - most of them associated with beer drinking - used as a concert overture. The work climaxes with a triumphant setting of the most famous student song of all, 'Gaudeamus igitur'.

BRAHMS
ALTO RHAPSODY
(1869)

CHO

Brahms had just emerged from an unhappy love affair and the general mood is (you've guessed) one of gloom, despite the optimism of the radiant ending. The official title of the work is *Rhapsody for Alto Voice, Men's Chorus and Orchestra* and it is a setting of three of the 11 verses of Goethe's 'Harzreise im Winter'.

Brahms' little-known organ works include 11 choral preludes, his final works. They were written during his last summer, which he spent at Ischl in Upper Austria and when he was in a sombre frame of mind, ill, tired, and bereaved at the loss of several close friends. Among them is this beautiful and tranquil meditation, justly popular at weddings.

BRAHMS
ES IST EIN ROS'
ENTSPRUNGEN
(A ROSE HAS
BLOOMED)
from 11 Choral Preludes
(1896)

I

'German' because the agnostic Brahms chose sections of the Lutheran Bible to set to music, rather than the traditional text of the Catholic liturgy. It differs again from other requiems in that it is not a solemn mass for the dead, but rather a work of solace for those left behind. It took Brahms 11 years to complete the work, first inspired by the death of his friend Robert Schumann and then, in 1865, by the death of his mother. The *Requiem*, lasting over an hour and a quarter, is in seven sections, scored for soprano and baritone soloists, chorus and orchestra, and is one of the loftiest of all choral works.

BRAHMS
A GERMAN
REQUIEM
(1868)

CHO

Brahms' lifelong fascination with Hungarian gypsy music was first kindled when he toured Germany as a 19-year-old with the Hungarian violinist Edouard Remenyi. Many gypsy elements can be found in Brahms' works - the finales of the Piano Quartets Nos. 1 and 2, Piano Concerto No. 1, Violin Concerto and *Double* Concerto are rousing Magyar dances. The melodies of the Dances (with the exceptions of Nos. 11, 14 and 16) were not composed by Brahms, but arranged by him - 'Genuine gypsy children which I did not beget but merely brought up with bread and milk,' he wrote. They were an immediate success and made a small fortune for the publisher. Brahms, unwisely, sold them for a fixed price. The most popular are Nos. 1, 5, 6 and 7.

BRAHMS
21 HUNGARIAN
DANCES
(1869-80)

O/I

BRAHMS
PIANO CONCERTO
NO. 1 IN D MINOR
(1854-58)

C

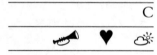

Now one of the cornerstones of the concerto repertoire, it was hissed at its première and did not become popular until the 1950s. This was Brahms' first large-scale work (it pre-dates the First Symphony by a full 17 years). Much of the music in the two outer movements is stormy and turbulent, though the wistful second theme of the first movement is immensely touching (it was used in the 1962 British film *The L-Shaped Room*). Its yearning slow movement comes as a contrast and, with its inscription 'Benedictus qui venit in nomine Domine' on the score, is understood to have been written in memory of his friend Schumann.

BRAHMS
PIANO CONCERTO
NO. 2 IN B FLAT
(1878-81)

C

More serene than the D Minor, Brahms' B Flat Concerto is among the longest (about 45 minutes) and physically taxing of all piano concertos. It is conceived on an epic scale with four movements, yet it somehow also manages to be intimate, 'as of a great man talking to us but not haranguing us', as one critic put it. Brahms himself described the work facetiously to a friend as 'a tiny, tiny piano concerto with a tiny, tiny wisp of a scherzo'. The restful third movement (andante) opens with a beautiful melody for the cello, one of the composer's finest passages.

BRAHMS
PIANO SONATA
NO. 3 IN F MINOR
(1853)

I

The piano was Brahms' own instrument. He admitted that he wrote for it in an entirely different way from instruments that he knew only from hearing them. This sonata is an important work in the composer's development, now free of the earlier influence of Beethoven, Schumann and Mendelssohn, extending the four-movement sonata to five movements, letting the finale refer back to themes in the third movement (scherzo), and also linking the second and fourth movements thematically.

While on a visit to the Court of Meiningen, Brahms heard the great German clarinettist Richard Mühlfeld (1856-1902) play. It inspired four works: the Trio, Op. 114, the two Clarinet Sonatas, Op. 120 and this most cherishable of chamber works. It was composed in Brahms' mountain retreat of Ischl and looks back on his youth and forward, with patient resignation, to death.

BRAHMS
QUINTET FOR CLARINET AND STRINGS IN B MINOR
(1891)

CH

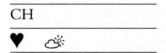

'A symphony is no joke,' wrote Brahms. He was 43 before he was satisfied with his first attempt at the form. He had written and destroyed many earlier experiments having been inhibited by what he felt to be the overwhelming greatness of Beethoven. Indeed, Hans von Bülow described Brahms' First Symphony enthusiastically as 'Beethoven's Tenth Symphony', praise underlined by the similarity between the second theme of the finale and the *Ode to Joy* from Beethoven's Ninth Symphony ('Any fool can see that,' snapped Brahms when someone pointed it out). Also in the last movement, listen out for the tune played by the horns with its resemblance to the clock chimes known as the *Cambridge Quarters*.

BRAHMS
SYMPHONY NO. 1 IN C MINOR
(1855-76)

O

The Second Symphony is a sunny and (by and large) cheerful work after the gloom and solemnity of the First. Taking the comparison with Beethoven further, some critics dubbed Brahms' D Major 'The Pastoral'. For some reason, the whimsical composer led his friends to believe that his Second Symphony was going to be even more serious and portentous than the first. 'It is in F minor,' he informed them. 'It is forceful and stern.' Nothing could be further from the truth - it is the happiest in mood of the four.

BRAHMS
SYMPHONY NO. 2 IN D
(1877)

O

BRAHMS
SYMPHONY
NO. 3 IN F
(1883)

O

This is the shortest of Brahms' four symphonies and also the least performed. While the First is tragic and the Second full of pastoral joy, the Third is vibrant and heroic, lyrical and vigorous. Brahms uses a particular theme throughout the Symphony to unify it - three notes (F, A flat, F) which symbolize Brahms' optimistic saying 'Frei aber Froh' ('Free but happy'). Some say his Third Symphony is the greatest of the four; its third movement is surely one of the loveliest.

BRAHMS
SYMPHONY
NO. 4 IN E MINOR
(1885)

O

Brahms' lack of confidence in his Fourth Symphony is shown by the fact that he first presented the work in a two-piano arrangement to friends to see what they thought of it. The critic Eduard Hanslick remarked after the first movement, 'Really, you know it sounds like two tremendously witty people cudgelling each other.' Brahms, typically tongue-in-cheek when describing his own music, called it his 'Waltz and Polka Affair' (the last movement being the 'waltz', the 'polka' the third), but it was his own favourite orchestral work - perhaps because it is the most self-revelatory. The last movement, far from being a waltz, is a passacaglia (a form that had last been fashionable in Bach's day) involving 31 variations on a theme derived from Bach's Cantata No. 150, in exultant, breathtaking counterpoint. The Fourth Symphony was played at the last concert Brahms ever attended, an occasion of valedictory emotion for audience and dying man alike.

BRAHMS
TRAGIC OVERTURE
(1880)

O

♥

At the same time as producing his spirited *Academic Overture* (see above), Brahms 'could not refuse my melancholic nature the satisfaction of composing an overture for a tragedy'. He had no particular tragic story in mind when he wrote it, no fictional subject such as Hamlet or Faust which he wanted to depict in music. No, Brahms just liked writing tragic music. He himself described his two contrasting overtures simply, 'One of them weeps, the other laughs.'

Originally written for two pianos, these orchestral variations have proved to be among Brahms' most frequently heard works. There are eight variations played without a break, followed by a finale which is itself an unbroken chain of 18 variations. The chorale theme is not actually by Haydn but was used by him in the second movement of an unpublished Divertimento composed in about 1781. It's an old hymn tune (composer unknown) called the *Chorale St. Antoni*.

BRAHMS
VARIATIONS ON A THEME BY HAYDN 'ST. ANTHONY CHORALE'
(1873)

O/I

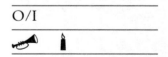

The theme is the same Paganini Caprice No. 24 in A minor for solo violin that is the basis for variations by Rachmaninov, Lutoslawski, Andrew Lloyd Webber and others. Brahms described the 28 variations (published in two sets) as 'études' and they do indeed cover the entire gamut of pianistic difficulties, as thrilling to hear as they are to play. In performance, many virtuosos omit some of the weaker variations and combine the best numbers from both sets.

BRAHMS
VARIATIONS ON A THEME OF PAGANINI
(1863)

I

Like Beethoven, Brahms was not a violinist, composed just one violin concerto and, in so doing, produced one of the great masterpieces for the instrument. This, as one writer put it, is 'a song for violin on a symphonic scale'. Brahms' friend, the great violinist Joseph Joachim, was on hand to advise, inspire and give the Concerto its first performance, but it was seen to be so fraught with difficulties that it was dubbed as a concerto not *for* but *against* the violin. Many years later, the celebrated virtuoso Bronislav Hubermann disputed this: 'No,' he corrected, 'it's a concerto *for* violin *against* orchestra – and the violin wins!' Every famous fiddler has this wonderful work in their repertoire, the finest recorded version being by Jascha Heifetz and conductor Fritz Reiner.

BRAHMS
VIOLIN CONCERTO IN D
(1878)

C

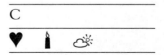

BRAHMS
WALTZES
(1865)

I

Brahms much admired the waltzes of Johann Strauss. Famously, on one occasion he autographed the fan of Frau Strauss by quoting the opening bars of *The Blue Danube* and adding, 'Unfortunately - not by me.' Brahms' 16 waltzes for piano (many were arranged for piano duet) owe more to Schubert than to Strauss, though some also have a gypsy flavour. By far the most popular is No. 15 in A flat.

BRAHMS
WIEGENLIED,
OP. 49 NO. 4
(1868)

V

The most famous lullaby of all is the fourth of a set of *Five Songs* composed in July 1868. The first child who had it sung to her was its dedicatee, one Bertha Faber. Brahms later suggested there should be a special edition in a minor key for naughty children!

HERBERT BREWER
1865-1928
ENGLISH
MARCHE
HÉROÏQUE
(1915)

I

A magnificent organ solo that's a first cousin to Elgar's *Pomp and Circumstance Marches* (Brewer was a friend of Elgar's, organist of Gloucester Cathedral from 1896 to 1928 and knighted in 1926). It begins with a brisk march, followed by a noble, slower theme; the march returns, with the second theme then repeated with all the stops pulled out - a real spine-tingler. The Countess of Wessex (or Miss Sophie Rhys-Jones as she still was) walked up the aisle to this in St. George's Chapel, Windsor in June 1999. The march was also played in Westminster Abbey for the funeral of Earl Mountbatten in 1979.

BENJAMIN BRITTEN
1913-76
ENGLISH
A CEREMONY OF
CAROLS
(1942)

CHO

A book of carols purchased in Halifax, Nova Scotia on his return from America in 1942 was the inspiration behind this, Britten's first work to utilise boys' voices. The texts for the carols are mainly from the Fourteenth and Fifteenth Centuries and Britten recaptures in this perennially popular work the joyousness, simplicity, mystery and even the physical rigours of Christmas in the Middle Ages. There are 11 sections, the longest of which is the Interlude for solo harp.

The première of Britten's opera on 7 June 1945 at Sadler's Wells is often cited as the turning point for English opera. Set in an East Anglian fishing village, the opera tells the story of Peter Grimes, a hard, solitary fisherman treated with distrust after the death of an apprentice at sea. The *Four Sea Interludes - Dawn, Sunday Morning, Moonlight* and *Storm* - are often played as independent concert works and are powerful evocations of the sea, while also cleverly reflecting Grimes' own inner turmoil.

BRITTEN
FOUR SEA INTERLUDES
from Peter Grimes
Opera
(1945)

O

The titles of the four movements convey the character of the music: *Boisterous Bourré, Playful Pizzicato* (the best known section), *Sentimental Saraband* and *Frolicsome Finale*. It's scored for string orchestra and uses material from pieces composed by Britten between the ages of 9 and 12.

BRITTEN
SIMPLE SYMPHONY
(1934)

O

Between 1935 and 1938 Britten composed the music for nearly 30 short films, the most famous of which is *Night Mail*, an illustration of the travelling Post Office between London and Glasgow, with words by W.H. Auden. In 1936 Britten wrote the score for an animated film called *The Tocher* (a Scots word for dowry) in which he used some then little-known tunes by Rossini. He later re-scored three movements and added a further two to complete the collection - March, Canzonetta, Tirloese, Bolero and Tarantella. There's also a second suite, *Matinées musicales*, composed five years later.

BRITTEN
SOIRÉES MUSICALES
adapted from Rossini
(1936)

O

**BRITTEN
THE YOUNG
PERSON'S GUIDE TO
THE ORCHESTRA**
(1946)

O

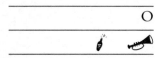

Variations and Fugue on a Theme of Henry Purcell, to give the work its formal title, was originally conceived as a score for a documentary film, *Instruments of the Orchestra*, made by the Crown Film Unit and first shown at the Empire Theatre, Leicester Square on 29 November 1946 (Sir Malcolm Sargent had conducted the first concert performance, in Liverpool, a month earlier). The theme is the Rondeau from the incidental music Purcell wrote for a play called *Abdelazar or The Moor's Revenge* and Britten takes us on a brisk tour of all sections of the orchestra before ending with a riotous fugue and a grand restatement of Purcell's theme. A terrific work best heard without the dull spoken commentary by Eric Crozier that formed part of the film.

**MAX BRUCH
1838–1920**
GERMAN
KOL NIDREI
(1880)

I

On the eve of their Day of Atonement (Yom Kippur), Jews sing a prayer called the *Kol Nidrei*. Its melody is one of the most celebrated in all Hebrew liturgy and it's this that Bruch used as the basis for this moving work for cello and orchestra – and which led most people to assume that Bruch himself was Jewish (in fact, he came from a clerical Protestant family). It was written for the Jewish community in Liverpool, where Bruch was conductor of the Liverpool Philharmonic Orchestra.

**BRUCH
SCOTTISH FANTASY**
(1880)

C

♥

Fantasia on Scottish Folk Tunes for Violin, Orchestra and Harp is the official title of the work in which Bruch, inspired by his love of the novels of Sir Walter Scott, took a series of simple Scottish folk melodies and wove them into the form of a violin concerto. The first movement uses 'Auld Rob Morris', the second 'The Dusty Miller'; the slow movement (especially touching in the unmissable recording by Jascha Heifetz) uses 'I'm a doun for lack o' Johnny', while 'Scots wha hae' features in the lively finale.

Dedicated to the great violinist Joseph Joachim, to whom Brahms was to dedicate his violin concerto, the *Bruch G minor* is one of the finest works of the Romantic period and has regularly topped the popularity polls with Classic FM listeners. Why? Because it is unapologetically and frankly sentimental in a quite endearing way, because it speaks directly and unaffectedly, because it is expertly crafted and because it is flooded with the most beguiling melodic charm from beginning to end. Each of its three movements are, in their different ways, equally appealing. Listen out for the theme from the *Perry Mason* TV series in the first movement!

Though nowhere near as popular as No. 1, Bruch's other two violin concertos are well worth a listen. No. 2 was championed (and first recorded) by Jascha Heifetz in 1954, while Salvatore Accardo has made a persuasive recording of No. 3. If Bruch's music appeals to you, you might like to get to know a couple of other even less well-known Bruch concertos that have the same richly-romantic, lyrical appeal - the Concerto for Two Pianos, and the Concerto for Viola and Clarinet (written in 1911 but in the same style as the G Minor Concerto of 43 years earlier).

Bruckner's symphonies, someone said, are the symphonies that Wagner never wrote. They are on the same grand scale as Wagner's operas and have been described as 'Gothic cathedrals of sound'. No. 4 (the most frequently performed of Bruckner's 11 symphonies) is the best one with which to begin exploring Bruckner's world and, except for its slow movement - a funeral march - is a lively, buoyant affair throughout its hour-long duration. There are five different versions of the work, the second 'Vienna' version of 1878-80 is the one you usually hear.

BRUCH
VIOLIN CONCERTO
NO. 1 IN G MINOR
(1868)

C

♥

BRUCH
VIOLIN
CONCERTOS NOS. 2
IN D MINOR
(1878)
& 3 IN D MINOR
(1891)

C

♥

ANTON BRUCKNER
1824-96
AUSTRIAN
SYMPHONY
NO. 4 IN E FLAT
'ROMANTIC'
(1874)
(rev. 1878-80 & 86)

O

♥

BRUCKNER
SYMPHONY
NO. 7 IN E
(1883)

O

♥ ◗

This was the work that brought Bruckner most success during his lifetime and its second movement adagio, lasting over 20 minutes, is reckoned to be his finest - 'one of the most eloquent dirges in symphonic music' - said to be a lament for the death of his hero, Wagner (actually, Bruckner began sketching the movement a year before Wagner died; it was completed nine weeks after Wagner's death). Throughout the work there are indications of how much the organ influenced and inspired Bruckner.

BRUCKNER
SYMPHONY
NO. 8 IN C MINOR
(1885)

O

♥

Having spent the first 60 years of his life searching for success, by the time his Eighth Symphony was premièred, Bruckner was acknowledged even by his enemies (and they were many) as a master symphonist. The first performance (Vienna, December 1892) elicited a congratulatory wreath from the Emperor and a telegram from Johann Strauss II. 'Boisterous rejoicings, wavings of handkerchiefs from those standing, innumerable recalls, laurel wreaths' greeted the ending. Can you think of a composer today whose work would generate such a reaction?

BRUCKNER
TE DEUM
(1881, rev. 1883-84)

CHO

The critic Neville Cardus described Bruckner in this work and his setting of Psalm 150 as 'God intoxicated... no fumes, no incense... his Catholicism is Austrian and as likeable and humane as Haydn's'. It's a grand but brief (20 minutes) affair which Bruckner regarded as his finest: 'When God calls me to Him and asks me, "What have you done with the talent I gave you?" then I shall hold out the rolled up manuscript of my *Te Deum* and I know He shall be a compassionate judge.'

Busoni's opera (not produced until 1917) used the same fairy-tale by Carlo Gozzi that Puccini was later to use for his more familiar version. The six-movement orchestral suite gives a fair idea of Busoni's sumptuous orchestral style; in the fourth (*Das Frauengemach*, the intermezzo from Act 2), you'll be surprised to hear the familiar strains of 'Greensleeves'. Busoni apparently thought the tune was of Oriental origin. Besides being a significant Italian composer, Busoni was one also of the great pianists of the day. You should try his *Chamber-fantasy on Carmen*, his many keyboard transcriptions of the music of J.S. Bach and, if you want to hear a mammoth piano concerto with a choral finale, then look no further than Busoni's.

FERRUCCIO BUSONI
1866–1924
ITALIAN
TURANDOT
Suite
(1904)

O

A defining piece of English pastoral music. Butterworth (Eton and Oxford educated) immersed himself in English folk music while an undergraduate under the influence of Vaughan Williams (he was befriended by V.W. and helped him in the preparation of his *London Symphony*). Butterworth was all set for a brilliant career when he was killed during the Battle of the Somme, winning a posthumous Military Cross. Listen also to his unsurpassed settings of Housman's 'A Shropshire Lad'; his rhapsody *A Shropshire Lad* uses some of the same musical themes in orchestral guise.

GEORGE
BUTTERWORTH
1885–1916
ENGLISH
THE BANKS OF
GREEN WILLOW
(1914)

O
♥

Byrd's masterpieces are considered to be his *Anglican Great Service* and his three settings of the Latin Mass. But, arguably, his greatest single choral work is this motet which comes from a collection of settings for the church's year. This appeared in 1605 under the title *Gradualia*. Here is Byrd at his most intimate and concentrated.

WILLIAM BYRD
1543–1623
ENGLISH
AVE VERUM CORPUS
(1605)

CHO

C

GIULIO CACCINI
c. 1545–1618
ITALIAN
AVE MARIA

V

Caccini was the first composer to have an operatic work published (Jacobo Peri was the first composer to have an opera produced, beating Caccini to it by just three days). His song 'Amarilli, mia bella' has been recorded by Beniamino Gigli, Janet Baker, Cecilia Bartoli and others, but it was the Lithuanian soprano Inessa Galante who recently introduced listeners to Caccini's radiant setting of *Ave Maria* (albeit in a lush orchestral arrangement). Just these two pieces make you curious to hear more of his music.

JOSEPH CANTELOUBE
1879–1957
FRENCH
SONGS OF THE AUVERGNE
(1923-55)

V

♥

The dramatic and mountainous area of the Auvergne, dominated by its chain of extinct volcanoes, is rich in folk-song. Canteloube scoured the whole of France in search of such material not merely because the songs were fresh and charming, but because he believed they could help revive French music. From the four sets of songs he collected and orchestrated, by far the most popular (from Set 1) is 'Baïlèro', used for years in a Dubonnet TV commercial. The best of the others are 'Passo pel prat', 'Brezairola' (from Set 3) and 'Chut, chut' (Set 4).

EMMANUEL CHABRIER
1841–94
FRENCH
ESPAÑA
(1883)

O

A favourite orchestral showpiece, *España* was composed after a Spanish holiday. Chabrier uses two traditional Spanish folk melodies and one of his own invention to exhilarating effect. Waldteufel (page 346), the 'French waltz king', turned the work into a waltz; in 1956, two songwriters, Al Hoffman and Dick Manning, added lyrics to Chabrier's opening theme and called it 'Hot Diggity' - a pop hit for Perry Como and Michael Holliday.

Said to be a depiction of a group of drunken musicians staggering home after an evening on the town, the work was originally a piano composition which Chabrier wrote as a sight-reading test for students at the Bordeaux Conservatory. It proved to be too difficult and so he turned it into a boisterous orchestral burlesque.

CHABRIER
MARCHE JOYEUSE
(1888)

O

♪

When it was first published, *Autumn* sold over 6000 copies a year. It could be found in every piano stool in the land, the archetypal drawing-room piece, just within the playing capabilities of a good amateur player (though the 'storm' section in the middle has its tricky moments). Despite its graceful writing and tunes, I have never heard any concert pianist include it in a recital - too sentimental, I suppose. *Autumn* is actually the second of Chaminade's *Six Études de Concert*, Op. 35, all composed very much in the Chopin-Liszt mould. There are a number of other short, charming piano pieces by her on disc which you might enjoy, among them *Sérenade espagnole*, *Scarf Dance*, *La Lisonjera (The Flatterer)* and, especially, *Autrefois (In Days of Yore)*.

CÉCILE CHAMINADE
1857-1944
FRENCH
AUTOMNE
(c. 1890)

I

♥

None of Chaminade's large-scale works has survived in the repertory (she composed a symphony, two orchestral suites and ballets). This short (less than eight minutes) concerto in a single movement is further evidence of her skill and melodic invention. It wasn't just the piano she knew how to write for, as flautist James Galway's recording proves.

CHAMINADE
CONCERTINO FOR FLUTE
(1902)

C

♥

Charpentier's fame rests securely on the success of this one opera, a triumph when it was first seen in Paris in February 1900. A sequel, called *Julien* (1913), was a failure. After that, Charpentier wrote almost nothing more despite living to the age of 95. But then you could live to a hundred and still never write anything quite as beautiful as this aria from Act 3 in which Louise looks out over the rooftops of Paris at twilight and tells her lover, Julien, that she has never been so happy 'Since the day I gave myself to you'.

GUSTAVE
CHARPENTIER
1860-1956
FRENCH
'DEPUIS LE JOUR'
from Louise
(1889-96)

OP

♦

MARC-ANTOINE CHARPENTIER
1643-1704
FRENCH
PRELUDE
(Trumpet Tune)
from Te Deum
(c. 1690)

I

A popular choice for weddings - a good one to go down the aisle - the magnificent opening Prelude is the only piece of Charpentier's that most people know (it was written for the Jesuit church of St Paul in Paris where Charpentier was head of music). But there are other lovely moments in the work (the soprano solo, *Te ergo quaesumus*, for instance). Charpentier's sombrely-beautiful *Missa Assumpta est Maria* is also well worth tracking down.

ERNEST CHAUSSON
1855-99
FRENCH
POÈME
(1896)

I

♥

One of the great lyrical masterpieces for violin, *Poème*, as its composer explained, has 'no description, no story, nothing but sensation'. The highly-critical, fastidious Debussy said of it, 'Nothing touches us more with dreamy sweetness than the end of this *Poème*, where the music, leaving aside all description and anecdote, becomes the very feeling that inspired its emotion.' The work is dedicated to the great Eugène Ysaÿe who gave its first performance in London, exactly a week after the premature death of Chausson in a cycling accident. A must for every lover of romantic music - try the recordings by David Oistrakh (who captures its wistful character to perfection) or Jascha Heifetz who goes for intensity and passion.

CHEN KANG
B. 1935
HO ZHAN HAO
B.1933
CHINESE
BUTTERFLY LOVERS VIOLIN CONCERTO
(1958)

C

♥

To have a concerto written by two composers is not unique but it is unusual (an earlier Chinese concoction, the *Yellow River Piano Concerto* was written by a committee). It doesn't always make for the best results musically. Almost as unusual is the fact that the Concerto has a programme (story) which unfolds over its three movements - two young, star-crossed lovers from Chinese folklore rebel against an arranged marriage, the young man loses his beloved and dies of a broken heart, he is followed by the girl who jumps into his tomb to join him. In the mystical, nostalgic third movement it's clear that the two lovers have returned as butterflies 'united in an eternally happy dance among the flowers'. The work, which has become very popular in the West, incorporates Chinese melodies, harmonies, rhythms and sounds, adapted into the format of a late-nineteenth century European romantic concerto.

The polonaise had long been out of fashion as a dance form when Chopin revived it. He wrote 18, all for piano solo except two: his *Introduction and Polonaise brillante* (for cello and piano) and this one. It's a good example of what Chopin was writing at the age of 20, yet this was to be the last of his six compositions using an orchestra. Both parts of the work are heard as often as not as a piano solo these days. The Polonaise (and you'll hear within a few bars why it's called *grand* and *brilliant*) is preceded by the nocturne-like Andante ('It makes one think of a lake on a calm bright summer day,' wrote one commentator). *Spianato*? *Spiana* is Italian for a carpenter's plane and so it becomes an apt description for 'planed, level, smooth' music.

**FRÉDÉRIC CHOPIN
1810–49**
POLISH
ANDANTE
SPIANATO AND
GRANDE
POLONAISE
BRILLANTE
IN E FLAT
(1830)

C

♥

'Arias without words', 'poetic stories' - these are the best ways to describe the four masterpieces for solo piano that Chopin called Ballades. Almost every pianist has (or has had) them in their repertoire: No. 1 in G minor (Chopin's own favourite) and No. 3 in A flat (which Sir Winston Churchill called 'the rocking-horse piece' - he was particularly fond of it) are the most heard. No. 2 in F has been interpreted as 'the struggle between a wild flower and the wind', while the pianist John Ogdon thought No. 4 in F minor was the most powerful of all Chopin's compositions. Its technical difficulties apparently infuriated Chopin's contemporaries!

**CHOPIN
4 BALLADES
*(1836-42)***

I

♥

**CHOPIN
ÉTUDES
(1829-34)**

I

There are numerous books of piano études (studies), each study devoted to one aspect of technique (the execution of scales, octaves, arpeggios, etc.). Most of them are boring beyond belief. All that changed with Chopin's two sets of 12 studies (Op. 10 and Op. 25 as they're known in the trade) which lifted the ordinary étude into the realm of poetry. Perhaps the most loved is Op. 10 No. 3 in E (*Tristesse*), a study to develop expression, turned into a song in 1939 ('So Deep is the Night'). The best known is a study for the left hand - Op. 10 No. 12 in C minor (the *Revolutionary*, composed in 1831 under the impression that Warsaw had been captured by the Russians) which a generation of young music lovers first heard played by Sparky (or was it his magic piano?). But if you dip in anywhere you will come up with a treasure - Op. 25 No. 1 in A flat (known as the *Aeolian Harp*), Op. 25 No. 11 (*Winter Wind*), for instance, or the two studies in G flat, Op. 10 No. 5 (*Black Keys*) and Op. 25 No. 9 (*Butterfly*). Leopold Godowsky (q.v.) went a step further and composed *53 Studies on Chopin Études*, works of incredible complexity. One of them, which he jokingly called *Badinage*, is a study made up of the two G flat studies played simultaneously!

**CHOPIN
FANTAISIE IN F
MINOR
(1841)**

I

♥

This work, as much as any other, displays every facet of Chopin's genius. Written at the height of his creative powers, it is said to depict (and have been inspired by) a quarrel and reconciliation between Chopin and his paramour George Sand. But everyone will read what they want into this marvellous work for solo piano, by turns heroic, melancholic and tender.

**CHOPIN
'FANTAISIE-
IMPROMPTU'
(Impromptu No. 4 in C
sharp minor)
(1835)**

I

This is among the most popular of all piano works, yet Chopin himself thought so little of it that he kept it in his bottom drawer and did not permit its publication (it appeared only after his death). It's the earliest of three other *impromptus* which *were* published. The middle section (trio) provided two American songwriters with a hit tune in 1919 – 'I'm always chasing rainbows'.

Here is another musical form invented or developed by Chopin. The term *nocturne* was first coined (in musical terms) by the Irish composer and pianist John Field in 1814, but Chopin 'invested it with an elegance and depth of meaning which had never been given to it before', as the critic James Huneker wrote. The most popular (probably the most popular of all Chopin's compositions) is No. 2 in E flat, Op. 9 No. 2. But, like the Études, whichever one you alight on will be an exquisite gem - and quite unlike the previous one. Personally, I wouldn't be without No. 5 in F sharp, Op. 15 No. 2, No. 8 in D flat, Op. 27 No. 2 (the most serene of piano compositions) and No. 13 in C minor, Op. 48 No. 1.

CHOPIN
NOCTURNES
(1827-46)

I

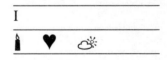

Chopin composed two piano concertos. Both date from early in his career (1829 and 1830). This one in E minor was the second to be written but the first to be published and so designated No. 1. In a letter to his friend Titus Wojciechowski, Chopin described the slow movement (*Romanza*) as, 'intended to convey the impression one receives when gazing on a beautiful landscape that evokes in the soul beautiful memories - for example, on a fine moonlit spring night.' The first performance took place in Chopin's home city of Warsaw on 11 October 1830. It was a huge success ('I was not in the least nervous,' wrote Chopin, 'but played as I do when I am by myself.'). It was the last time he played in Poland. Three weeks later, Chopin left never to return. He was then just 20.

CHOPIN
PIANO CONCERTO
NO. 1 IN E MINOR
(1830)

C

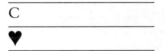

Introduced by Chopin in Warsaw on 17 March 1830, the Second Concerto's slow movement (larghetto) is 'possibly one of the greatest pages ever written by Chopin' according to one critic. It was inspired by Constantia Gladowska, a young voice pupil with whom Chopin was madly in love. The Concerto itself is dedicated to the Countess Delphine Potocka, among the very few people to whom Chopin dedicated more than one piece (her name also appears on the 'Minute' Waltz) and it was she who sang to Chopin on his death-bed.

CHOPIN
PIANO CONCERTO
NO. 2 IN F MINOR
(1829-30)

C

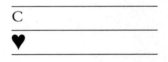

**CHOPIN
POLONAISES
*(1817-46)***

I

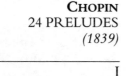

The first two of Chopin's polonaises (officially No. 13 in G minor and No. 14 in B flat) were written in 1817 when Chopin was only seven. The character and rhythm of this old Polish dance form attracted Chopin throughout his life and the later polonaises reflect the hapless condition of his native land, full of defiance and pride. No. 3 in A major (*Military*) is one of Chopin's best known works, closely followed by No. 6 in A flat (*Heroic*) with a 'cavalry charge' in the middle. You should also try the *Polonaise-Fantaisie in A flat*, a more extended piece in which Chopin strives to develop the form. Many consider this to be among his most profound and personal creations.

**CHOPIN
24 PRELUDES
*(1839)***

I

The prelude was originally an introductory piece of music (the opening movement of a suite, say). Chopin liked to create new forms from old titles and these preludes preface nothing - they are their own self-contained thoughts. There is one written in each major and minor key. Many were composed at Valdemossa in Majorca where Chopin and George Sand spent a few unhappy months. Look out for No. 7 in A, No. 15 in D flat (*The Raindrop*) and No. 20 in C minor (Rachmaninov and Busoni each wrote sets of variations on this, and Barry Manilow used it as the basis for his hit song 'Could it be magic?'). Nos. 4 in E minor and 6 in B minor were played on the organ at Chopin's funeral.

**CHOPIN
4 SCHERZI
*(1832-42)***

I

It was Haydn who developed the stately 3/4 minuet into the scherzo (which means, literally, 'joke' in Italian); Beethoven's scherzos are more bustling, humorous affairs; to Mendelssohn, the scherzo was synonymous with a light-hearted caprice. Chopin saw the scherzo as 'breathings of stifled rage and of suppressed anger' (Liszt). The opening pages of No. 1 in B minor demonstrate just that, though its middle section could hardly offer a greater contrast. No. 2 in B flat minor is the best known (at one time nicknamed *The Governess' Scherzo*, even if the music must have been way above the capabilities of most governesses). No. 3 in C sharp minor has a central section that might remind you of a hymn played on the organ. No. 4 in E is glittering, intense and passionate.

One of the priceless gems of music, this is known as the *Funeral March Sonata* because of its celebrated and sombre third movement, played at every state funeral (usually by a military band). It's followed by a brief final movement in which the whirling right hand plays in unison with the left to create the impression (according to Anton Rubinstein) of 'night winds sweeping over churchyard graves'. There is something doom-laden and threatening about the opening two movements as well (just listen to the opening bars of the Sonata and the anxiety behind the first theme). Strangely, though, the last thing you ever feel after listening to the work is depressed. Just the opposite, in fact.

CHOPIN
SONATA
NO. 2 IN B FLAT
MINOR
(1839)

I

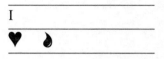

A flawed masterpiece compared to No. 2 (the earlier Sonata No. 1 in C minor is far inferior to both and rarely played). The first movement is overflowing with ideas, though the scherzo (which follows) is succinct and graceful; the nocturne-like slow movement is (for me) one of Chopin's weakest but has the effect of building anticipation for the gloriously jubilant finale (a fast rondo) that brings the work to a thrilling conclusion. This is one of the most difficult of all Chopin movements to play and is certainly one of the most effective.

CHOPIN
SONATA
NO. 3 IN B MINOR
(1844)

I

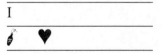

Johann Strauss I was at the peak of his popularity when Chopin arrived in Vienna in 1829. Though Chopin thought those composed by the Strauss family quite vulgar ('I have acquired nothing particularly Viennese,' he wrote, 'and I still cannot play waltzes'), he was nevertheless inspired by the form. His efforts are Parisian more than Viennese, 'never meant to be danced by ordinary mundane creatures of flesh and blood', as one commentator put it. Listen out for the *Grande Valse brilliante in E flat*, Op. 18, the one in A minor, Op. 34 No. 2 (said to be Chopin's favourite), the A flat Waltz Op. 42 (arguably the best and certainly the most difficult to play) and of course...

CHOPIN
WALTZES

I

CHOPIN
WALTZ NO. 6 IN D
FLAT, OP. 64 NO. 1
'MINUTE WALTZ'
(1847)

I

Impossible to play in 60 seconds, even if you rush the more lyrical middle section (which would be criminal). On average it takes about 90 seconds - the shortest (hence the French description 'minute') and most popular of Chopin's waltzes. Barbra Streisand, lyricist Richard Stilgoe and the great coloratura soprano Amelita Galli-Curci are just three people who have recorded 'song' versions of the waltz; pianists Alexander Michailowski and Moriz Rosenthal both made clever arrangements playing the two tunes of the waltz simultaneously!

**DOMENICO
CIMAROSA
1749-1801**
ITALIAN
(arr. Benjamin)
OBOE CONCERTO
IN C MINOR

I

It was his numerous operas for which Cimarosa was most famous in his day, but it's this oboe concerto (which he didn't compose) that is most frequently heard today. It was arranged in 1942 by Arthur Benjamin, of *Jamaican Rumba* fame, specially for Evelyn Rothwell (Lady Barbirolli), using music from four of Cimarosa's 32 short, single-movement keyboard sonatas. Listening closely, you'll hear some very non-eighteenth century harmonies in the orchestration! Incidentally, Cimarosa is a strong entry for 'composers who died unusual deaths' quizzes: he was rumoured to have been poisoned by order of the Queen of Naples as a dangerous revolutionary, but on examination was found to have expired from a gangrenous abdominal tumour.

**JEREMIAH CLARKE
C. 1673-1707**
ENGLISH
PRINCE OF
DENMARK'S
MARCH
(Trumpet Voluntary)

C

This is the *Trumpet Voluntary*, which for years was mistakenly attributed to Henry Purcell (Clarke, poor chap, shot himself for the love of a lady, not because a fellow composer had been given the credit for one of his works). It comes from the Suite in D for trumpet and strings written to celebrate the arrival in England of Prince George of Denmark, consort of Queen Anne, but was popularised in the last (twentieth) century in a grand orchestral arrangement by Sir Henry Wood. A popular choice for weddings.

Second to *The Archers* (see entry on Arthur Wood), this is the most famous signature tune on radio, introducing (with seagulls added to the recording later) thousands of castaways on *Desert Island Discs*. The dreamy waltz was intended to conjure up pictures of warm blue seas, sandy beaches and palm trees but was actually inspired by a view of Bognor Regis seen from Selsey in the fading light. The tune was given lyrics and twice topped the charts in America. Another set of (anonymous) lyrics goes like this: 'It wasn't the breeze/ that tickled her knees/It was her suspenders'.

ERIC COATES
1886–1957
ENGLISH
BY THE SLEEPY
LAGOON
(1930)

O

♥

'My best inspiration,' wrote Coates, 'is to walk down a London street and a tune soon comes to me. When I can think of nothing I walk down Harley Street and there is a lamppost. Every time I catch sight of it a tune comes to my mind. That lamppost has been my inspiration for years.' The three movements of the *London Suite* (*Covent Garden - Tarantella*, *Westminster - Meditation* and *Knightsbridge - March*) are among the most popular pieces of British light music ever written. When the BBC first used the *Knightsbridge March* as a signature tune (it introduced the variety show *In Town Tonight* for 23 years), over 20,000 people wrote in to find out what it was called. There's a second *London* suite, *London Again*, which portrays Oxford Street (where Classic FM is situated), Langham Place, and Mayfair.

COATES
LONDON SUITE
(1932)

O

𝄞

Calling All Workers was the march that introduced BBC Radio's long-running *Music While You Work*. Then there are the scintillating *London Bridge March* and *London Calling*, the latter commissioned by the BBC for its overseas children's programmes. Most popular of all is *The Dam Busters March,* written for the 1954 film about the raids in 1943 to destroy the Ruhr dams using Dr Barnes Wallis' bouncing bombs. And somehow, after all these years, no one has quite yet matched the *brio* and dash of the composer's own recordings of these and his other works.

COATES
MARCHES
and other works

O

𝄞

COATES
SUMMER DAYS
SUITE
(1919)
and others

O

♥

Coates' longer works include *The Three Bears* (an orchestral fantasy on Goldilocks' adventure), *Cinderella Fantasy* and the *Saxo-Rhapsody* (a concertino for saxophone), further impressive examples of a fecund melodic gift and expert orchestration. He also wrote a large number of suites in three or four movements: *Summer Days Suite* has one of his loveliest slow movements (*On the Edge of the Lake*), but you should also look up *The Three Men Suite*, *Four Ways Suite*, *Four Centuries Suite*, *From Meadow to May Fair Suite* and...

COATES
THE THREE
ELIZABETHS SUITE
(1944)

O

♥

A clergyman, Rev. Arthur Hall, vicar of Barnes in London, suggested to Coates the idea of a suite reflecting the world of past, present and future monarchs. The first movement, *Halcyon Days*, representing Elizabeth I, was used as the opening music for the BBC's classic TV adaptation of Galsworthy's *The Forsyte Saga*. The second movement, *Springtime in Angus*, hints at the (now) Queen Mother's Scottish roots, while the concluding *Youth of Britain* march celebrates the young Princess Elizabeth.

NORMAN COCKER
1889–1953
ENGLISH
TUBA TUNE

I

Yorkshire-born Cocker became assistant organist of Manchester Cathedral in 1920, taking over as organist in 1943. He was simultaneously the organist at the Gaumont Theatre in Manchester and an amateur conjurer of some note. This maddeningly-catchy organ solo was written to show off the *solo tuba*, usually the most powerful stop on a pipe organ.

SAMUEL COLERIDGE-
TAYLOR
1875-1912
ENGLISH
HIAWATHA'S
WEDDING FEAST
(1898)

CHO

♥

Coleridge-Taylor was only 23 when he composed this setting of Longfellow's poem, the first of a trilogy (*The Death of Minnehaha*, 1899, and *Hiawatha's Departure*, 1900, are not as inspired). Until the mid-1950s, *Hiawatha* and Mendelssohn's *Elijah* vied for second place to *Messiah* as the most popular choral work in the repertoire. Today it is relatively unfamiliar, though occasionally you might hear its sole tenor aria, the striking 'Onaway! Awake, beloved'. A pity - it's a fine and endearing work.

A quintessential piece of British light music - you know it when you hear it! - lasting just a few minutes and included here as a masterly example of this underrated genre. Collins, like his near-contemporary Eric Coates, started out as a violist but eventually became better known as a conductor than composer - his early LP recordings of Sibelius' symphonies are still landmarks. Hastings-born, Collins died in Los Angeles to where he'd moved in 1939 to write and conduct film music.

ANTHONY COLLINS
1893–1963
ENGLISH
VANITY FAIR

O

Copland's shortest work is also his best known, a brief but arresting curtain-raiser. It was one of ten patriotic fanfares commissioned from different composers by the Cincinnati Symphony Orchestra for their 1942/43 season, specifically designed to introduce their concert programmes. Each composer was asked to write a conventional fanfare but to give it a contemporary feel. Copland wrote his with typical economy, using just brass and percussion.

AARON COPLAND
1900–90
AMERICAN
FANFARE FOR THE COMMON MAN
(1942)

O

The ballet tells the story of a cowgirl who is infatuated with both the Head Wrangler and the Champion Roper, and tries to gain their attention by displaying her own prowess as a rider. The *Four Dance Episodes* (the orchestral suite that Copland adapted from the full score) end with the exuberant *Hoe-Down*.

COPLAND
HOE-DOWN
from Rodeo
Ballet
(1942)

O

Composed in California and Mexico, this ballet score, written for the renowned dancer and choreographer Martha Graham, is a tonal portrait of Pennsylvania farmland. The penultimate section of the orchestral suite (No. 7, entitled *Scenes of Daily Activity for the Bride and her Farmer-Husband*) is a series of variations on the traditional Shaker tune *Simple Gifts*. The words to the hymn we sing using the same tune ('Dance, then, wherever you may be/I am the Lord of the Dance, said he') were written in 1963 by Sydney Carter.

COPLAND
VARIATIONS ON A SHAKER HYMN
from Appalachian Spring
Ballet
(1944-45)

O

ARCANGELO CORELLI
1653-1713
ITALIAN
12 CONCERTI GROSSI, OP. 6
(pub. 1714)

O

The *concerto grosso* was the most favoured instrumental form of the Baroque era and those by Corelli are, in historical terms at least, the most important, for they established the form, one which led to the idea of the solo concerto. Corelli's 12 concertos had been circulating in manuscript for a quarter of a century before they finally appeared in print the year after Corelli's death (he had personally prepared them for publication in December 1712, just months before he died) and were enthusiastically taken up – '[they] are to ye musicians like ye bread of life,' wrote one Roger North at the time. Each concerto, scored for string orchestra and continuo (harpsichord) with 'soloists' on two violins and cello, has between three and five short contrasted movements. No. 8 is the most frequently played, known as the *Christmas Concerto* (though the spiritual finale is the only part with any bearing on the Nativity), while No. 2 is the work on which Tippett (page 324) based his *Fantasia Concertante on a Theme of Corelli*.

BERNHARD CRUSELL
1775-1838
FINNISH
CLARINET CONCERTO NO. 2 IN F MINOR
(1808)

C

Crusell was the greatest clarinet player of his day (he is said to have given the first performance of Mozart's Clarinet Concerto after its publication). Few people would have heard his name before the enterprising Emma Johnson won the 1984 *BBC Young Musician of the Year* competition playing this remarkable forgotten masterpiece for the instrument. The mellow, slightly melancholy nature of the first two movements superbly illustrates one side of the clarinet's character; the perky, jaunty finale (a catchy rondo) matches the other. Johnson has recorded it – and the other two clarinet concertos by Crusell, also well worth getting to know.

D

A child prodigy who played for Louis XIV at the age of six, Daquin became one of the greatest keyboard players of the age. *The Cuckoo* comes from a collection called *Pièces de clavecin* and wittily imitates the calling of the bird. For other musical cuckoos, see Delius (*On Hearing the First Cuckoo in Spring*), Handel (Organ Concerto) and Saint-Saëns (*Carnival of the Animals*).

LOUIS-CLAUDE DAQUIN 1694-1772
FRENCH
LE COUCOU
(1735)

Walford Davies succeeded Elgar as Master of the King's Musick in 1934 (he'd been knighted in 1922). His moving elegy, originally for organ and string orchestra, never fails to stir the emotions when it is heard at the annual Service of Remembrance held at the Cenotaph in Whitehall. Clearly modelled on Elgar's *Nimrod* - and none the worse for that - it is an indispensable part of the nation's music for mourning. Walford Davies was the Royal Air Force's Director of Music in the latter part of the First World War and composed the *RAF March Past March* in 1919. And, while organist and choirmaster at the Temple Church in London (a post he held for 25 years), wrote that magical sung prayer 'God be in my head'.

(HENRY) WALFORD DAVIES 1869-1941
ENGLISH
SOLEMN MELODY
(1908)
and others

Debussy and his second wife, Emma Bardac, had a daughter ('Chouchou') to whom he dedicated this charming piano suite in six movements. Among them are *Doctor Gradus ad Parnassum* (conjuring up memories of piano practice), *Serenade for the Doll* and *Jimbo's Lullaby* (Chouchou rocking her toy elephant to sleep); the final movement is the popular *Golliwog's Cakewalk*: this is Debussy's version of the cakewalk, a popular Negro dance of the time (though it includes a tune Debussy heard played by the Band of the Grenadier Guards in London and, in the middle section, a sly quote from Wagner's *Tristan and Isolde*). Sadly, Chouchou died at the age of only 14 in July 1919.

CLAUDE DEBUSSY 1862-1918
FRENCH
CHILDREN'S CORNER SUITE
(1908)

**DEBUSSY
CLAIR DE LUNE**
*from Suite bergamasque
(1890, rev. 1905)*

I

Among Debussy's early works, by far the most popular is the third movement from this piano suite. Never has there been a more effective keyboard evocation of a moonlit night. Debussy took the title (it means, of course, 'Light of the Moon' not, as the great humorist Victor Borge would have us believe, 'Clear the Saloon') from a poem by Paul Verlaine and he sold the rights to a publisher for a few pounds.

**DEBUSSY
IMAGES**
*for orchestra (1905-12)
and*
IMAGES
*Sets 1 & 2 for piano
(1905 and 1907)*

O/I

Though they share the same title, the orchestral and piano suites are unconnected musically, though all are concerned with tonal impressions. *Iberia*, for example, the second section of the orchestral suite, is a colourful three-movement evocation of Spain, while the first piano suite has such masterly miniatures as *Reflets dans l'eau* (*Reflections in the Water*) and *Poissons d'or* (*Fishes of Gold*), the latter inspired by a piece of Oriental lacquer work.

**DEBUSSY
LA MER**
(1905)

O

For all his many musical 'water impressions', Debussy was none too fond of sea travel (though he managed to cross the Channel, for the last movement of these three ambitious symphonic sea 'sketches' was completed in Eastbourne). Some critics have condemned the work as formless (which rather suggests that Debussy succeeded in his task of evoking the ocean); after hearing the first movement, *From Dawn to Noon on the Sea*, the composer Erik Satie said, 'I liked the bit that comes at about a quarter to eleven', while one American musicologist attempted to explain the last movement (*Dialogue of the Wind and the Sea*) by saying it depicted a sea traveller who gets seasick and finally throws up.

**DEBUSSY
LA PLUS QUE LENTE**
(1910)

I

This has become one of Debussy's best-known piano works (orchestrated in 1912), a gentle send-up of the fashionable salon waltzes of the day, hence the humorous (to Debussy, anyway) title *Slower than Slow*. It's said that the composer gave the manuscript to a gypsy violinist at the New Carlton Hotel in Paris.

Mallarmé's poem of the same title, which inspired Debussy's most famous orchestral work, tells the story of a faun experiencing the delicious state between waking and dreaming. It imagines it has seen a nymph, awakens, its feelings intense and turbulent, and then returns once more to sleep. This piece, perhaps more eloquently than any other of Debussy's, links his musical inspiration with the Impressionist painters and Symbolist poets of the time.

DEBUSSY
PRÉLUDE À L'APRÈS-MIDI D'UN FAUNE
(1892-94)

O

♥

The two sets of piano preludes are a distillation of Debussy's art and also represent the first change of character and technique in piano writing since Chopin. Each is a miniature tone poem conjuring up pictures as diverse as *La Fille aux cheveux de lin* (*The Girl with the Flaxen Hair*), *Minstrels* (music-hall and black-faced minstrels), *Feux d'artifice* (*Fireworks*), *General Lavine - eccentric* (a famous wooden puppet at the Folies Bergère) and *La Cathédrale engloutie* (*The Sunken Cathedral*), which depicts the cathedral of Ys rising to view from the depths of the translucent sea.

DEBUSSY
PRÉLUDES
(1910 and 1913)

I

The big solo vocal hit from *Lakmé* is known as the 'Bell Song' (more properly 'Où va la jeune Hindoue?' or 'Where is the young Hindu maiden?'). It's one of the most testing of all coloratura soprano arias, which sends the leading lady's voice up into the stratosphere as bell-like effects mingle with a seductive oriental melody. There is a famous recording of this by the glamorous French-born opera star Lily Pons (1898-1976) who, incidentally, remains the only opera singer ever to have a town named after her (Lilypons in Maryland, USA).

LÉO DELIBES
1836-91
FRENCH
'BELL SONG'
from Lakmé
(1883)

OP

DELIBES
'FLOWER DUET'
(*'Dôme épais le jasmin'*)
from Lakmé
(1883)

OP
♥

'O thick canopy of jasmine,' sing Lakmé and her slave Mallika as they prepare to bathe in the gardens of the sacred temple. It's a sensuous, languorous barcarolle now indelibly associated with an international airline's television commercials. Set in nineteenth century India, *Lakmé* is Delibes' single opera that survives in the repertoire today and concerns the love of Lakmé, daughter of a fanatical Brahmin priest, for Gérald, a young English officer.

DELIBES
MAZURKA and
CZARDAS
from Coppélia,
Ballet
(1870)

O
♪

Coppélia or *The Girl with the Enamel Eyes* is a ballet based on a story called *Der Sandmann* by E.T.A. Hoffmann, the same story that Offenbach used a year later for his opera *The Tales of Hoffmann*. It was the first ballet about a doll come to life, the first to use European folk dances like the czardas and mazurka (*Coppélia*'s two most popular sections together with the elegant *Waltz of the Doll*) and one of the first ballet scores arranged as a suite and heard in the concert hall in its own right - without dancers.

DELIBES
SYLVIA
Ballet
(1876)

O
♪

Following the immense success of *Coppélia*, *Sylvia* or *The Nymph of Diana* established Delibes as the foremost composer of ballet music in France. This, too, has a popular orchestral suite adapted from the full score, its most celebrated single number being the *Pizzicato* danced by Sylvia disguised as a slave. It has inspired numberless send-ups, usually involving huge, ungainly men tripping about in tutus.

FREDERICK DELIUS
1862-1934
ENGLISH
LA CALINDA
(1904)

O
♥

This little piece comes from Delius' second opera *Koanga* but didn't really catch on until Eric Newby made an arrangement of it for concert orchestra in 1938. In fact the music made its first appearance even earlier - in 1887 as part of Delius' very first orchestral composition, the *Florida Suite*.

Delius' summer holidays were invariably spent in Norway, in the hills of Jotenheim. This wonderfully-evocative masterpiece, a tone-poem for orchestra, not only paints a picture of the awakening of springtime in England but reflects Delius' nostalgic yearning for Norway (its second theme, 'In Ola Valley', is a Norwegian folk-song). It was introduced together with its companion piece, *Summer Night on the River* (1911), in Leipzig in 1913.

DELIUS
ON HEARING THE FIRST CUCKOO IN SPRING
(1912)

O

♥

No one who has seen Ken Russell's film biography of the same title can forget the powerful effect of this richly-scored work as Eric Fenby (Christopher Gable) and the blind and paralysed Delius (Max Adrian) make for the sun-bathed summit of a mountain. The score, dictated by Delius and notated by his amanuensis Fenby, was adapted from an earlier unpublished work entitled *A Poem of Life and Love*.

DELIUS
A SONG OF SUMMER
(1930)

O

♥

An orchestral interlude, often heard on its own, this piece comes between the fifth and sixth scenes of Delius's opera *A Village Romeo and Juliet*. It tells the story of the love between the children of two quarrelling farmers. From the fair in the Paradise Garden they wander to the river and die together in a barge that sinks as it floats downstream. Not a lot of laughs, but the music is ravishing.

DELIUS
THE WALK TO THE PARADISE GARDEN
(1907)

O

♥

Dinicu, a gypsy violinist who studied at the Bucharest Conservatoire, is remembered for this one short, dazzling display piece which he is said to have introduced at his graduation in 1906. Jascha Heifetz heard it and made his own arrangement of it in 1930, since when it has been a firm favourite as a fiddle encore. The *hora* is an exciting Rumanian folk dance, reflecting Dinicu's musical background.

GRIGORAS DINICU
1889-1949
RUMANIAN
HORA STACCATO
(1906)

I

ERNST VON
DOHNÁNYI
1877–1960
HUNGARIAN
RHAPSODY
IN C, OP. 11 NO. 3
(1903)
and other piano works

I

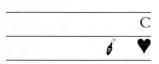

Pianist, conductor, composer and teacher (Georg Solti and the virtuoso pianist Cziffra were among his pupils), Dohnányi wrote music that has been described as 'the last flowering of European Romanticism' - that is, it's twentieth century but melodic. This rhapsody is a testament to his legendary prowess as a pianist and there are many other appealing short piano works that are sure to please - like his Capriccio in F minor, Op. 28 No. 6 and his stunning transcription of the *Pas de Fleurs* from Delibes' ballet *Naïla*.

DOHNÁNYI
SUITE IN F SHARP
MINOR
(1909)

O

Though Hungarian, Dohnányi's music sounds more German than anything. Brahms praised his early compositions - indeed, there's more than a touch of Brahms in this delightful four-movement suite, a favourite of the conductor Sir Malcolm Sargent but, for some reason, rarely encountered in the concert hall. The first movement is a set of variations, the second a breezy scherzo, while the gorgeous third (*Romanza*) has a serene oboe melody over plucked strings. The finale is an exuberant rondo.

DOHNÁNYI
VARIATIONS ON A
NURSERY SONG
(1913)

C

The nursery song in question is our 'Twinkle, twinkle, little star'. (First known as 'Ah, vous dirai-je, Maman', it appeared without words in 1761.) The introduction is amusingly over-the-top, followed by the tongue-in-cheek soloist playing the simple theme with two fingers. The 14 witty variations that follow are a compendium of virtually every nineteenth century musical trend. Dohnányi dedicated the score 'to the enjoyment of lovers of humour and the annoyance of others.'

Donizetti's comic masterpiece was written at the height of his creative powers, a non-stop riot of invention and sparkling wit (the finale to Act 2 is unmissable). There's no lack of lyricism either - try Ernesto's fervent serenade to Norina, 'Com'è gentil'. Shortly after the success of *Don Pasquale*, Donizetti began to suffer from bouts of intense depression, headaches and fevers and, after a paralytic stroke in 1845, lapsed into insanity.

GAETANO DONIZETTI
1797-1848
ITALIAN
DON PASQUALE
(1843)

OP

Written in just 14 days, *The Elixir of Love* is one of Donizetti's finest comic creations (it was his 41st opera) and contains this, one of the most frequently-heard of all tenor arias. A good example of *bel canto* singing, 'A Furtive Tear' is sung in Act 2 by Nemorino, a role that has attracted all the great lyric tenors from Caruso and Gigli to Di Stefano and Pavarotti.

DONIZETTI
'UNA FURTIVA LAGRIMA'
from L'elisir d'amore
(1832)

OP

♥

One of the most performed operas, *Lucia* also has one of opera's most ludicrous libretti offering an incredible sequence of madness, deception, treachery and suicide. The music is something else and the title role is one of the great soprano vehicles (the famous *Mad Scene* from Act 3 is a veritable lexicon of coloratura technique). There are many other thrilling passages (try the Act 1, Scene 3 duet 'Se tradirmi tu potrai', especially in the recording with Joan Sutherland and Sherrill Milnes) but these are crowned by the famous Sextet (Act 1, Scene 4), one of the great episodes in Italian opera and, as an ensemble number, rivalled only by the Quartet from *Rigoletto*.

DONIZETTI
Sextet from
LUCIA DI LAMMERMOOR
(1835)

OP

♥

RICCARDO DRIGO
1846–1930
ITALIAN
Pas de Deux from
LE CORSAIRE
Ballet
(1899)

O

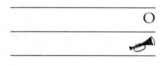

A minor figure, true, but one who deserves a mention just for this. It's the only part of the ballet seen in the West, thanks mainly to the unforgettable filmed performance of Rudolf Nureyev and Margot Fonteyn. The original score, dating from 1856 by Adam (p.35) and others, was revised for its 1899 production in St. Petersburg and Drigo was asked to provide two extra numbers (for no extra payment, he noted in his memoirs) of which this pas de deux is one. Why Drigo? Besides composing, from 1886 to 1917 he conducted every important ballet première in St. Petersburg, including the first performances of Tchaikovsky's *The Sleeping Beauty* and *Nutcracker*. You sometimes come across one other Drigo composition, the once-popular Serenade from his ballet *Harlequin's Millions*.

PAUL DUKAS
1865–1935
FRENCH
THE SORCERER'S
APPRENTICE
(1897)

O

No, this wasn't composed for Walt Disney's brilliant 1940 cartoon *Fantasia*, but this exhilarating orchestral scherzo is now indelibly associated with Mickey Mouse battling in vain against the rising water as it invades his master's enchanted castle. The music is a literal musical translation of Goethe's ballad 'Der Zauberlehrling' – 'L'Apprenti Sorcier' in French which, to be pedantic, should more correctly produce the English title of *The Apprentice Sorcerer*. Dukas didn't write much after 1910 (and, before his death, destroyed most of what he had written) and this piece proves to be quite unlike the rest of his music which tends to be gloomy and rather dour.

ANTONIN DVOŘÁK
1841–1904
BOHEMIAN (CZECH)
CARNIVAL
Overture
(1891)

O

Dvořák planned a cycle of three overtures to portray 'three great creative forces of the Universe - Nature, Life and Love', each to be linked by the same melody representing 'the unchangeable laws of Nature'. He abandoned this scheme and published separate overtures - *In Nature, Carnival* and *Othello*. The story of the music was described by Dvořák as 'a lonely, contemplative wanderer reaching the city at nightfall where a carnival of pleasure reigns supreme. On every side is heard the clangour of instruments, mingled with shouts of joy and the unrestrained hilarity of the people giving vent to their feelings in songs and dances'.

In 1893, Dvořák was offered the directorship of the National Conservatory of New York at a salary of $15,000 a year. While in New York he heard the composer Victor Herbert (better known today as the composer of *Naughty Marietta* and a string of other incredibly successful operettas) as soloist in his own Cello Concerto No. 2. This provided the inspiration for what is unquestionably one of the greatest works for the instrument. In the second movement you can hear a quotation from Dvořák's song 'Lass mich allein', a special favourite of Josefina Kaunitzová with whom he had fallen in love 30 years earlier (she later became his sister-in-law) and who died a few months after Dvořák completed the first draft of this masterpiece. He re-wrote the ending to incorporate the song again as a memorial to Josefina.

DVOŘÁK
CELLO CONCERTO
IN B MINOR
(1895)

C

♥

The great violinist Fritz Kreisler visited the ailing Dvořák in 1903 and was handed a pile of (mostly unknown) music. Among them was this, one of a set of eight *humoresques* for solo piano composed in 1894 (musical history has decided that the other seven should be completely ignored). Dvořák intended it as a quick, light, whimsical piece but Kreisler's arrangement/ recording for violin and piano, through which the work became universally popular, was played at a much slower tempo - and that's how it is always performed today. It's sometimes sung too: 'Gentlemen should please refrain/From using toilets while the train/Is standing in the station/I love you'.

DVOŘÁK
HUMORESQUE IN
G FLAT, OP. 101 NO. 7
(1894)

I

Rusalka is a water nymph who, in the first scene of the opera, confesses to her father that she has fallen in love with a prince and wants to become human (for obvious reasons). She then confides to the moon her longing, and the result is this celebrated aria, one of the most touching yet chaste of all operatic love songs.

DVOŘÁK
'O SILVER MOON'
from Rusalka
(1901)

OP

♥

DVOŘÁK
PIANO QUINTET
IN A
(1887)

CH

♥ ☼

There are three acknowledged masterpieces in this form - one by Schumann, one by Brahms, and this. A piano quintet is scored for piano and string quartet (two violins, viola and cello) and this one has four movements, each reflecting Dvořák's preoccupation with the Bohemian folk idiom (you should also try the Piano Quartet in E flat and the *Dumky Piano Trio* from the same period). So it's full of piquant melodies and dance rhythms - a thoroughly sunny, uplifting work. Chamber music needn't be an ordeal!

DVOŘÁK
SCHERZO
CAPRICCIOSO
(1883)

O

🎷

This is one of those fizzing, effective orchestral showpieces that audiences love but which conductors rarely offer in concert programmes. It lasts about 14 minutes (a bit long as a curtain-raiser or encore) which makes it awkward to programme. It's a piece that uses the Bohemian dance rhythms of which Dvořák was so fond and there's a particularly lovely theme for the cor anglais, almost as lovely as that in the slow movement of the *New World Symphony*.

DVOŘÁK
SERENADE FOR
STRINGS IN E
(1875)

O

🎷 ☼

Dvořák was 33 and not yet widely known in Europe (the *Slavonic Dances* were still three years away) when he wrote this lovely suite of five short movements. Composed very quickly in the space of just 12 days, the suite comprises a Waltz (second movement), Scherzo, Larghetto and a lively Finale that quotes melodies from the first and fourth movements. A companion work for the string serenades by Tchaikovsky (composed four years later) and Elgar (1892).

DVOŘÁK
SONGS MY MOTHER
TAUGHT ME
(1880)

V

♥

Round the turn of the last (twentieth) century, this ballad used to be a hugely popular drawing-room favourite but even this, the only one of Dvořák's 50 songs that achieved lasting fame, is rarely performed now. It comes from a collection of *Seven Gypsy Songs* for voice and piano, though you're more likely to hear it today in a transcription for violin or cello.

These are the pieces that made Dvořák's name internationally famous. They were composed at the request of his publisher who was hoping to cash in on the success of Brahms' *Hungarian Dances* - and cash in he did. Dvořák originally scored them for four-hands-one-piano but after their initial success made orchestral versions. Where Brahms used original gypsy tunes, Dvořák invented his own and borrowed the dance rhythms of his native Bohemia. Top favourites are Nos. 1 and 8 of Op. 46 and Nos. 1 and 2 of Op. 72.

DVOŘÁK
SLAVONIC DANCES
OP. 46 AND OP. 72
(1878 and 1886)

O/I

It's been called Dvořák's *English Symphony* and the *Pastoral Symphony*, but it's better labelled his *Bohemian Symphony* because it's the one that reflects, more than the eight others, Dvořák's national identity. It's such a cheerful piece, described by one critic as 'a lovable expression of a genius who can rejoice with the idyllic simplicity of his forebears'. The second movement is the most original of all Dvořák's slow movements - a miniature portrait of Czech village life with bird song and a rustic band.

DVOŘÁK
SYMPHONY
NO. 8 IN G
(1889)

O

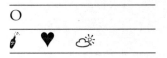

High in the popularity ratings with Classic FM listeners, the *New World Symphony* has never waned in its appeal since its very first performance in New York by the New York Philharmonic in 1893. 'I felt like a king in my box,' wrote Dvořák at the time. The themes are all Dvořák's own, though he had so thoroughly absorbed Negro folk melodies during his time in America that he convinces you that you're listening to genuine spirituals (listen to the first movement with its echoes of 'Swing low, sweet chariot', and the famous slow movement, adapted into a pseudo-spiritual as a song entitled 'Goin' Home'). American-inspired it may be but there's a strong hint of Bohemian homesickness in the jubilant third and final movements.

DVOŘÁK
SYMPHONY
NO. 9 IN E MINOR
'FROM THE NEW
WORLD'
(1893)

O

E

EDWARD ELGAR
1857–1934
ENGLISH
CELLO CONCERTO
IN E MINOR
(1919)

C

♥ ♪

Written at *Brinkwells*, a cottage near Fittleworth in the peaceful Sussex countryside, this poignant, elegiac masterpiece reflects Elgar's state of mind after the First World War, anxiety over his wife's failing health and other personal concerns. All of Elgar's opulent, ceremonial style is on display but transformed into an introspective essay of sadness and regret. The first performance in October 1919 was not a success due to lack of rehearsal but the second was, featuring a young John Barbirolli as soloist. It was Barbirolli who, 46 years later, conducted the much-loved recording of the work with Jacqueline du Pré as the eloquent soloist.

ELGAR
CHANSON DE
MATIN
and
CHANSON DE NUIT
(1897)

O/I

♥

Chanson is the French word for 'song' - so *Night Song* (Elgar's original title was *Evensong*) and *Morning Song*, two short pieces written for violin and piano which attained immense popularity as soon as they appeared and for which many people still have much affection. *Matin* is suitably fresh and bright while *Nuit* is more characteristically melancholy. They appeared just two years before the *Enigma Variations*, the work which finally established Elgar as a major figure.

ELGAR
COCKAIGNE
OVERTURE
'IN LONDON TOWN'
(1901)

O

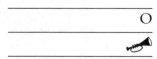

'Cockaigne,' Elgar told the conductor Hans Richter, 'is the old, humorous (classical) name for London and from it we get the term Cockney.' Thus 'Mr. Elgar's clever and humorous new overture' (as it was described in the Philharmonic's programme at its first performance) is a portrait of London seen through the eyes of a pair of lovers as they stroll through the city - the hubbub of the streets, the quiet parks, a brass band, a church, and the romantic ardour of the young couple.

The text for this magnificent choral work was by Cardinal Newman and depicts the death of Gerontius and the journey of his soul towards the judgement seat of God. Dvořák had been offered the text first (he turned it down) but Elgar transformed it into a powerful meditation on the soul's immortality (it is often described as an oratorio, but the composer disapproved of the description and it doesn't appear anywhere in the score). For many, it's an overwhelming work with its massive forces and three soloists in music that veers from the still and spiritual to the passionate and blazing. Not everyone liked it: the composer Delius thought it 'a nauseating work', while another, Sir Charles Stanford, found it 'stinking of incense'. The Irish writer George Moore described it as 'Holy water in a German beer barrel'.

ELGAR
THE DREAM OF GERONTIUS
(1900)

CHO

Elgar called this piece a 'symphonic study' (in other words, an orchestral portrait) of the Falstaff of Shakespeare's *Henry IV* plays (not so much the buffoon of *The Merry Wives of Windsor*) and his relationship with Prince Hal (afterwards Henry V). You can hear how the music portrays life at the Boar's Head Tavern in Eastcheap, the restful scenes in Justice Shallow's orchard in Gloucestershire, battle scenes, the coronation and Falstaff's death when he 'babbled of green fields'. A work full of humour and pathos.

ELGAR
FALSTAFF
(1913)

O

The earliest orchestral march from Elgar's pen was written to celebrate Queen Victoria's Diamond Jubilee. Its first performance was at the Crystal Palace in a concert of massed bands in April 1897, but when it was later played at a Royal Garden Party, it so touched the Queen that she commanded its inclusion in the official State Concert in July. The March is also well known in an arrangement for organ by Sir George Martin - not the Beatles man but the then celebrated organist (from 1888) of St. Paul's Cathedral.

ELGAR
IMPERIAL MARCH
(1897)

O/I

**ELGAR
INTRODUCTION
AND ALLEGRO**
(1905)

O

♥

Here is Elgar, bright and breezy, striding over the Malvern Hills (though the opening theme in fact came to him a few years earlier when on holiday in Wales), pausing occasionally to reminisce. It's a wonderfully accomplished work scored for a string quartet set against a full string orchestra, one that undoubtedly influenced the later compositions of Vaughan Williams and Tippett.

**ELGAR
POMP AND
CIRCUMSTANCE
MARCH NO. 1 IN D**
(1901)

O

The middle section (known as the Trio) of this grand ceremonial march is the tune to which we sing 'Land of Hope and Glory'. Elgar knew it was a winner the moment he wrote it ('I've got a tune that will knock 'em – knock 'em flat,' he said) and it's now a second national anthem, but it was not originally conceived to be sung. The words (by Elgar's friend Arthur C. Benson, Master of Magdelene College, Cambridge) were added a year after the March was premièred, when Elgar used the same melody to end his *Coronation Ode* (composed for the accession of Edward VII).

**ELGAR
POMP AND
CIRCUMSTANCE
MARCH NO. 4 IN G**
(1907)

O

Elgar wrote a further four marches with the same title. It comes from Shakespeare's *Othello* (Act 3): 'Farewell the neighing steed and the shrill trump,/The spirit-stirring drum, the ear-piercing fife,/The royal banner, and all quality,/Pride, pomp, and circumstance of glorious war'. Each march follows the same pattern – a vigorous first section followed by a stately trio, both then repeated – one which has been emulated by many composers including William Walton and Eric Coates. No. 4 (the second most popular) was also given words (by A.P. Herbert) and called 'Song of Liberty'. It's never quite caught on.

**ELGAR
QUINTET FOR
PIANO AND STRINGS
IN A MINOR**
(1919)

CH

♥ ◗

Composed in the same tranquil country home as the Cello Concerto (see above), the Quintet was begun before the First World War's end but seeks to capture the vanished world of a decade earlier. The Adagio (the second of its three movements) is sublime, one of Elgar's finest achievements, easily recognisable as being by the same creative genius of *Nimrod*.

Used by film-makers to evoke instantly the (mythical?) sunlit innocence of the late-Victorian era, this tiny piano solo went round the world, arranged for violin and piano, cello and piano, orchestra, piano and harmonium, and even two mandolines and guitar! Its title translates as *Love's Greeting* and it is dedicated 'à Carice', an Elgarian pun on his fiancée's Christian names Caroline Alice.

ELGAR
SALUT D'AMOUR
(1888)

O/I

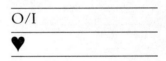

Elgar's settings of lyrics are not as assured as his settings of texts, but this cycle of five songs (for contralto and full orchestra) is his best effort in this field. The second poem ('In Haven') is by Elgar's wife, while the most popular (No. 4, 'Where Corals Lie') is by the forgotten critic and biographer Richard Garnett (1835-99), one-time keeper of books at the British Museum. *Sea Pictures* received its first performance at the Norwich Festival in October 1899 sung by its dedicatee Dame Clara Butt (who twice recorded 'Where Corals Lie' in 1912 and 1920). Elgar told a friend after the occasion that 'she dressed like a mermaid'.

ELGAR
SEA PICTURES
(1899)

V

This charming, early suite in three short movements owed much to the inspiration and encouragement of Elgar's wife who was still waiting for some signs of recognition of her husband's genius (he was 35 when the Serenade appeared). It was turned down by his publishers but eventually won through and was among the final works that Sir Edward himself recorded in 1933.

ELGAR
SERENADE IN E
MINOR FOR
STRINGS
(1892)

O

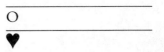

**ELGAR
SYMPHONY
NO. 1 IN A FLAT
*(1908)***

O

Unlike most great composers, Elgar had no formal academic musical training and, regarding the symphony as 'the highest development of art', left writing in this form until he was 50. The mighty Hans Richter, who conducted the première, declared to the orchestra, 'Gentlemen, let us now rehearse the greatest symphony of modern times, written by the greatest modern composer, and not only in this country.' The noble opening theme of the first movement tells you all about Elgar and where he's coming from.

**ELGAR
SYMPHONY
NO. 2 IN E FLAT
*(1911)***

O

King Edward VII had died in 1910 and this symphony, dedicated to his memory, has a funereal slow movement. But, by and large, it's a more optimistic and approachable work than No. 1 (try the rumbustious third movement rondo and the undisguised triumph of the end of the Symphony). It is a superb piece but one to which its first audience reacted with puzzlement. To Elgar's disappointment 'they sat there like a lot of stuffed pigs'. There's a famous out-take of Elgar rehearsing his recording of the Symphony, a fascinating glimpse of a great composer/conductor at work.

**ELGAR
TRIUMPHAL
MARCH
from Caractacus
*(1898)***

CHO

After *The Black Knight* (1893), *The Light of Life* (1896) and the Nordic saga *King Olaf* (1896) came this, the fourth major choral work Elgar composed within five years. It's half opera, half dramatic cantata with many splendid and rousing passages (listen to the thrilling final chorus), though the actual libretto is irredeemably dated. Ignore this and treat it as the period piece it is, telling the story of Caractacus, the British chieftain who is defeated by the Romans, captured, taken to Rome and pardoned. The *Triumphal March* opens the final scene in Rome when the captive Britons are led in to face the Emperor Claudius.

The *Enigma Variations*, one of the great original masterpieces of English music, is a series of musical portraits of Elgar's friends, his wife and (in the last section) himself. The Variations are based on a hidden (enigmatic) theme which Elgar teasingly always refused to reveal. The debate goes on as to whether hidden in the score is 'Auld Lang Syne', 'Rule, Brittania!', a theme from a Mozart symphony or Chopin's Nocturne No. 11 in G minor, all of which have been considered as candidates. The 14 variations include *Nimrod* (Variation No. 9), among the most requested pieces of music on Classic FM. *Nimrod*'s popularity was recently boosted by the success of John Cameron's choral arrangement, entitled *Lux Aeterna*. Why *Nimrod*? Elgar loved word-play and riddles. His publisher was his friend August Jaeger; the German for 'huntsman' is *jaeger* and in Genesis we read of 'Nimrod, the mighty hunter before the Lord'.

ELGAR
VARIATIONS ON AN ORIGINAL THEME 'ENIGMA'
(1899)

O

Elgar's own instrument was the violin - at one time his ambition was to become a soloist - a love that continued all his life. Though slow to be accepted (the solo part is technically very difficult) his concerto is now admired as one of the finest for the instrument. The score is inscribed somewhat mysteriously (Elgar loved to be enigmatic!) 'Acqui està encerrada el aima de...' ('Herein is enshrined the soul of...'). It was dedicated to the great violinist Fritz Kreisler who gave its first performance but who, to music's loss, never recorded it. The most celebrated recording of the work was made in 1932 with Elgar conducting the 15-year-old Yehudi Menuhin (it's a wonderful interpretation), but an earlier (1929) one by Albert Sammons and Sir Henry Wood is arguably more faithful to Elgar's original intentions.

ELGAR
VIOLIN CONCERTO IN B MINOR
(1910)

C

♥ ♦

GEORGES ENESCU
1881-1955
RUMANIAN
RUMANIAN
RHAPSODY
NO. 1 IN A
(1907)

O

Enescu was Rumania's most famous composer and one of the Twentieth Century's great all-round musicians (he was also a violinist and conductor). By far his most popular composition is the first of two *Rumanian Rhapsodies* for orchestra (the second is not nearly as attractive), and is really a medley of various folk melodies - some sad, some boisterous - dressed up in Enescu's scintillating orchestration.

F

MANUEL DE FALLA
1876-1946
SPANISH
NIGHTS IN THE
GARDENS OF SPAIN
(1907-16)

C

♥   ☁☀

Falla's music is imbued with the rhythms and character of Spanish music though he was strongly influenced by the French Impressionist works of Debussy, Ravel and Dukas. Here is Falla's musical impression of the fountains, cypresses, Moorish palaces, orange groves, palm trees and guitars of his native country in the form of a gentle, melancholic three-movement piano concerto.

FALLA
RITUAL FIRE DANCE
and
DANCE OF TERROR
from El amor brujo
Ballet
(1915)

O

♪

Love, the Magician is a ballet-pantomime (which the composer subtitled *Gypsy Life*) based on a play, itself derived from an old Andalusian folk-tale of a sensuous gypsy girl who falls in love after her husband's death only to be haunted by her husband's ghost; she finds a beautiful friend for the ghost, leaving her free to carry on with her lover. The orchestral suite has 12 numbers of which the *Ritual Fire Dance* is the best known (it's also Falla's most celebrated piece) often heard as an exciting piano solo.

The famous impresario Sergei Diaghilev commissioned Falla to compose a score which would 'synthesize all Spanish folk arts'. The first performance (it took place in London in 1919) of the resulting ballet, *El sombrero de tre picos*, was extraordinarily successful. Besides Falla's music, it had scenery by Pablo Picasso and choreography by Leonide Massine. The *Miller's Dance* from the first orchestral suite is often heard on its own.

FALLA
THE THREE-CORNERED HAT
Ballet
(1919)

O

♥

Fauré is one of the most significant French song writers (he wrote over 100). This exquisitely beautiful example was originally one of a set of three but is now much more familiar in transcriptions for cello, violin or orchestra.

GABRIEL-URBAIN FAURÉ
1845-1924
FRENCH
'APRÈS UN RÊVE'
(1878)

V/I/O

This delicate, refined work - a single movement for piano and orchestra lasting a mere 13 minutes - shows Fauré at his finest, restrained, lyrical and undeniably French. There are many other eloquent Fauré works for the piano which are equally unknown to most people - listen to his nocturnes (the early ones influenced by Chopin and Schumann, the later ones echoing Debussy), barcarolles and impromptus and you'll discover many delights.

FAURÉ
BALLADE IN F SHARP
(1881)

C

♥

Fauré's *Requiem* is among the most loved of all choral works. Well, here is its little (elder) sister. It was written when Fauré was still a student at the École Niedermeyer in Paris (it won the composition prize), an assured piece of writing for a 20-year-old, which features many of the elements of his later music, not least those ravishing melodies. It's a brief (five minute) choral work of moving serenity scored for organ and choir, a setting of a religious text in a translation by the seventeenth century French dramatist Jean Racine.

FAURÉ
CANTIQUE DE JEAN RACINE
(1865)

CHO

FAURÉ
DOLLY SUITE
(1897)

I/O

♥ ☼

If you're old enough to remember BBC Radio's *Listen With Mother* then the *Berceuse* (the first of the suite's six movements) will be instantly familiar as its signature tune, played in its original piano duet version. Fauré wrote the music for his young friend Hélène ('Dolly') Bardac, the daughter of the woman who later became Debussy's wife.

FAURÉ
ÉLÉGIE
for cello and orchestra
(1880)

I

◗

Fauré wrote quite a few pieces for the cello (including two sonatas), but this is the one favoured by every great soloist from Guilhermina Suggia and Pierre Fournier to Jacqueline du Pré and Steven Isserlis, a fine example of a composer being able to convey much by the simplest of means.

FAURÉ
PAVANE
(1887)

O

☼

A short work of stately beauty which survived being used (bizarrely) as the signature tune for the BBC's coverage of the 1998 Football World Cup. It is usually heard in its original orchestral setting - the BBC's arrangement with chorus was not an original idea: Fauré did it himself the year after the Pavane first appeared.

FAURÉ
PELLÉAS AND
MÉLISANDE
Suite
(1898-1909)

O

☼

The celebrated actress Mrs Patrick Campbell commissioned Fauré to write some incidental music for a series of performances in London of Maeterlinck's drama *Pelléas et Mélisande*. It was the first score to be inspired by this influential play - it would be followed with works by Debussy, Schoenberg and Sibelius among others. Fauré turned the music into a three-movement orchestral suite, later adding the graceful Sicilienne (its best-known section, adapted from an earlier piece for cello and piano) to complete the suite we know today.

Unlike most requiems, Fauré's much-loved setting of the words of the Mass for the Dead concentrates on the serenity and tranquillity of death, rather than its torment and pain. Fauré himself was 'not a believer but a sceptic' (as his son confirmed) and was inspired to write the *Requiem* in memory of his father who died in 1885. Its first performance was at the funeral of a well-known Paris architect, a Monsieur Lesoufaché. In this form it had only five sections. Fauré later added the *Offertory* and *Libera me* sections and altered some of the orchestration - this second version is the one generally heard today, though there is also a grander (over-elaborate?) third 'symphonic' version - the choice is yours. Of the seven magical sections, the most requested are *Sanctus*, *Pie Jesu* (for soprano or treble soloist), *Libera me* and *In Paradisum*, the latter two using words from the Office for the Dead.

FAURÉ
REQUIEM
(1888, rev. 1893 and 1900)

CHO

Though the nocturne is a musical form indelibly associated with Chopin, it was the Irish composer-pianist John Field who first used the word to describe a particular kind of piano composition. The word means 'night piece' and, typically, the right hand plays a gentle song-like melody accompanied by a flowing left hand. Field composed 19 of them, though included in this number are re-arrangements of movements from other works.

JOHN FIELD
1782-1837
IRISH
NOCTURNES
(1812-32)

I

The best of Field's seven piano concertos - and the only one never to have gone out of print - this charming work was part of the repertoire for over 100 years. Now you will only get to hear the A Flat Concerto on disc. Schumann described it as 'divinely beautiful', Chopin admired it (he was much influenced by Field's music) and many of the great pianists of the last century played it as a matter of course. The final rondo is really catchy - astonishing to realise it was written not in the 1830s, as one might think, but at roughly the same time as Beethoven's Fourth Concerto.

FIELD
PIANO CONCERTO NO. 2 IN A FLAT
(c. 1808)

C

FIELD
(arr. Harty)
A JOHN FIELD SUITE
(1939)

O

Sir Hamilton Harty (1879-1941) was not only a fine pianist and distinguished conductor, notably of the Hallé Orchestra, but also a composer and arranger. The 'Handel-Harty' suite from Handel's *Water Music* was preferred to the original for many years until the current enthusiasm for authentic instruments displaced it. Here Harty chose three solo piano pieces and a movement from a piano quintet by his fellow Irishman and transformed them into a delightful orchestral suite - Polka, Nocturne, Slow Waltz and another catchy rondo (known as *Le Midi*).

GERALD FINZI
1901-56
ENGLISH
CLARINET
CONCERTO IN C
MINOR
(1949)

C

Finzi's is the finest concerto for the clarinet written by an Englishman this century, first heard in Hereford Cathedral during the 1949 *Three Choirs Festival* played by its dedicatee, Frederick Thurston. It was an entirely appropriate setting, for Finzi lets the clarinet sing (and not battle) with the string orchestra throughout - carefree, soaring, lyrical - in music that is quintessential pastoral England.

FINZI
DIES NATALIS
(1939)

CHO

Most of Finzi's music is for voices - try *Intimations of Immortality* (his settings of Wordsworth poems) or 'Lo, the full, final sacrifice' - but start, perhaps, with *Dies Natalis*, a cantata for soprano or tenor and strings. After an orchestral introduction, the remaining four sections are settings of words by the seventeenth century mystic Thomas Traherne. One critic described the setting of *Centuries of Meditation* (Finzi's second section) as 'one of the most beautiful specimens of melodic speech in all music'.

One friend of mine, having heard a recording of this serene 10 minutes of hushed magic for the first time, was so moved that she sat there all evening playing it over and over again. It may have the same mesmerising effect on you. Finzi originally intended it as a movement of a concerto but in the end was content to let it stand on its own. It was first performed after his death at his memorial concert in January 1957 at the Victoria and Albert Museum.

FINZI
ECLOGUE
for Piano and String Orchestra
(late 1920s, rev. 1940s)

O

♥ ◐

There is one famous aria from *Martha* that is not by Flotow at all (though, for simplicity's sake, he is credited with it in this setting). It's an old Irish tune which the celebrated poet and composer Thomas Moore (1779-1852) used for a setting of his lyric 'The Groves of Blarney'; Moore in turn had pinched it from an earlier song called 'Castle Hyde'. Beethoven made an arrangement of the tune, Mendelssohn wrote a piano fantasia on it – and Flotow knew a winner when he heard it. He uses it several times during the course of the opera in different guises, a technique which the Hollywood musicals of the 1930s adopted with great success.

FRIEDRICH VON FLOTOW
1812-83
GERMAN
'THE LAST ROSE OF SUMMER'
from Martha
(1847)

OP

♥

Flotow, descended from an ancient Prussian aristocratic family, was not by any stretch of the imagination one of the great composers, but he was a pretty good tunesmith, as proved by the only one of his 30 operas to be remembered today – *Martha, or The Market at Richmond*. The role of Lionel, among the favourites of the great Italian tenor Enrico Caruso, includes this memorable Act 3 aria (translated as 'Like a Dream') that expresses Lionel's longing for Lady Harriet, the opera's heroine.

FLOTOW
'M'APPARI'
from Martha
(1847)

OP

♥

CÉSAR FRANCK
1822-90
BELGIAN
LE CHASSEUR MAUDIT
(1882)

O

'The Accursed Huntsman' is a tone poem for orchestra. Franck wrote five of them. This one is based on the legend of the wild Count of the Rhine who went hunting on a Sunday morning and, refusing to stop, was cursed as a 'desecrator' to be forever pursued by the Evil One. His fate is to be terrorised (as we can hear!) by a pack of demons, fleeing from them eternally by day and night, tortured by leaping flames.

FRANCK
LES DJINNS
(1884)

C

Here's another tone poem, but this one, unusually, incorporates a piano into the score, creating a kind of one-movement piano concerto. The piece translates into music a poem by Victor Hugo called 'Les Orientales'. It's all about the aerial flight of *Djinns* over a city in the dead of night. A *Djinn*? He is 'a good or evil genie, a child of fire able to assume any form he wishes', a character found in Arabian mythology.

FRANCK
'PANIS ANGELICUS'
(1872)

V

This is Franck's most recorded work by a long chalk, a sacred song that is as popular with tenors and choirs as it is with over-ambitious boy sopranos. It's a rather theatrical piece of church music which Franck himself thought so highly of that he added it to his earlier (1860) Mass for Three Voices.

FRANCK
PIÈCE HÉROÏQUE
(1878)

I

Franck, though Belgian by birth, spent the whole of his career in Paris - he was organist of Sainte-Clothilde from 1858 until his death. This impressive organ solo is the last of three pieces Franck wrote for the inauguration of the huge organ at the Trocadéro during the 1878 Paris Exhibition. Stand by for the final pages!

With a failed marriage behind him, the affection of his pupils was some recompense to Franck. He is said to have had an affair with one of them, the beautiful Franco-Irish composer and poetess Augusta Holmès and this tremendous work is a love letter to her, full of erotic intensity. Franck dedicated the work to Saint-Saëns who was the pianist at its first performance in 1880. For reasons of professional jealousy and because he himself was more than a little taken with Miss Holmès, Saint-Saëns stalked off the stage in a huff at the conclusion of the Quintet, refused to return to acknowledge the applause and discourteously left the music on the piano which Franck had publicly offered to him.

FRANCK
PIANO QUINTET IN F MINOR
(1878-79)

CH

♥

Don't be put off by the titles. These are bewitching works in which we find a blend of the Romantic, the mystic and – as you might have guessed from the names given to each movement – J.S. Bach. The earlier work has a distinctive religious flavour, the later one a more secular tone yet, though both are deeply felt and, at times, sombre, they are curiously uplifting and reassuring. Track down the recordings by Alfred Cortot or, if you prefer a modern version, by Stephen Hough.

FRANCK
PRELUDE, CHORALE AND FUGUE FOR PIANO
(1884)
PRELUDE, ARIA AND FINALE FOR PIANO
(1887)

I

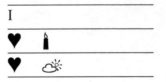

This stands alongside the violin sonatas of Beethoven, among the finest in the repertoire. It was written as a wedding present for the renowned Belgian violinist Eugène Ysaÿe and his wife Théophile. Its first performance was played in a room in Brussels in which were some valuable paintings and where no artificial light was permitted. It was a winter's afternoon and after the first movement it was so dark neither Ysaÿe or the pianist could see the music. They suggested abandoning the concert but the audience would have none of it and demanded to hear the whole sonata (Franck's music very often roused its hearers in this way). So, with a cry of 'Allons! Allons!', Ysaÿe and his pianist plunged into the other three movements playing in the dark from memory!

FRANCK
SONATA FOR VIOLIN AND PIANO IN A
(1886)

CH

♥

FRANCK
STRING QUARTET
IN D
(1889)

CH

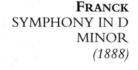

For most of his life, Franck's music was ignored and unappreciated though he always remained untouched by the lack of worldly recognition. His one and only quartet, though, was a resounding success and, when he mounted the stage to acknowledge the applause, it was the first time that he had experienced a public ovation. He was 69. 'There,' he is said to have remarked after the concert, 'the public is beginning to understand me at last.' One critic has described the work as 'perhaps one of the most beautiful of all in the whole realm of chamber music'.

FRANCK
SYMPHONIC
VARIATIONS FOR
PIANO AND
ORCHESTRA
(1885)

C

A good introduction to Franck's music, this is his most frequently-heard orchestral work, a piano concerto in miniature (it's in one continuous movement and lasts about 15 minutes). After its sombre opening, the music alternates between the dramatic and quietly poetic before the brilliant finale. Frederick Ashton used it as a ballet score in 1946, counted among his finest achievements.

FRANCK
SYMPHONY IN D
MINOR
(1888)

O

What a noble, compelling work this is, full of dramatic effects, colourful orchestration and soaring themes. It's hard to understand today why it was treated with open contempt on its first outing - the Paris Conservatory Orchestra for a while refused to play any of it and Gounod described it as 'the affirmation of incompetence pushed to dogmatic lengths'. The audience, too, was unenthusiastic. Yet, on emerging from the hall, one of his pupils described the composer as 'radiant'. Franck's only comment was, 'It sounded well, just as I thought it would.' No anger, no bitterness. Small wonder he was known as 'Pater Seraphicus' - 'Angel-like Father'.

Like Bach and Brahms, Franck's last musical utterances were choral preludes for the organ (indeed, these three masterpieces were at Franck's bedside when the priest came to administer the last rites). There's a feeling of serenity and simple acceptance in most of his music with, at times, a kind of mystical exaltation. The *Three Chorales* (in E major, B minor and A minor) combine all these idiomatic qualities.

FRANCK
THREE CHORALES
for organ
(1890)

I

Bring on the clowns, the acrobats, the Ringmaster! Here they come into the Big Top to the accompaniment of Fučik's 'triumphal march' which is, for some unknown reason, played whenever the circus comes to town (in fact it's rarely heard anywhere else). Fucik was a Bohemian composer and bandmaster, a composition pupil of Dvořák, who wrote an immense number of other marches of which *Florentiner* (his Op. 214) is an exuberant rival to *The Gladiators*.

JULIUS FUČIK
1872-1916
BOHEMIAN (CZECH)
THE ENTRY OF THE GLADIATORS
March
(1903)

O

G

An ardent collector of folk-songs, Gardiner's music reflects his love of England and its countryside. He was a great friend of Delius (and also the great-uncle of the conductor Sir John Eliot Gardiner) and was inspired to write this evergreen classic of light music by an episode in Thomas Hardy's *Wessex Tales*. Try also his jolly *Overture to a Comedy* (even though Gardiner himself loathed the piece!).

BALFOUR GARDINER
1877-1950
ENGLISH
SHEPHERD
FENNEL'S DANCE

O

FRANCESCO GEMINIANI
1687–1762
ITALIAN
CONCERTI GROSSI
(1732-46)

○

Listing the different concerti grossi that Geminiani wrote over the years doesn't make for riveting reading – he published four sets (Op. 2, 3, 4 and 7) totalling 30 concertos in all – but the music is something else. If you like Handel's concerti grossi you'll like these with their varied dance movements and Geminiani's strong gift for melody. The Concerto Grosso in G minor, Op. 3 No. 2 is a good one to begin with.

EDWARD GERMAN
1862–1936
ENGLISH
THREE DANCES
FROM HENRY VIII
(1892)

○

Listening to German's music you can understand why Elgar held it in such high regard – in fact Sir Edward admitted that he could never listen to the *Shepherd's Dance* (the second of these three) without a lump in his throat. The *Dances* were adapted from the incidental music German composed for Sir Henry Irving's production of Shakespeare's play at the Lyceum Theatre in London. They made his name.

GERMAN
THREE DANCES
FROM NELL GWYNN
(1900)

○

Anthony Hope, the best-selling author of *The Prisoner of Zenda* and *Rupert of Henzau*, wrote a play called *English Nell*, first staged in London in 1900 as a vehicle for the famous actress Marie Tempest. It was she who insisted that the incidental music should be written by German and the *Three Dances*, arranged as a concert suite from the score, have always been popular. There's also a lively overture which incorporates the song 'Early One Morning'.

GEORGE GERSHWIN
1898–1937
AMERICAN
AN AMERICAN
IN PARIS
(1928)

○

Inspired by a trip to Europe in 1926, Gershwin sketched this tone poem two years later in Paris, wrote the orchestral score in Vienna and had the work premièred in New York. It describes the experiences of an American tourist strolling along the boulevards of Paris, nostalgically thinking of home. Gershwin calls for four actual Parisian taxi horns in the score which was memorably choreographed and danced by Gene Kelly in the 1951 MGM film of the same title.

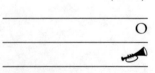

Originally called *Rhumba*, Gershwin's concert overture was written after a visit to Cuba where he had been fascinated by the dance and the Cuban bands he heard in Havana (you can hear the rhumba in the opening bars). Gershwin changed the title to *Cuban Overture* soon after its first performance when a group of 200 out-of-work musicians included it in a benefit concert at the New York Metropolitan Opera House in late 1932. Listen out for the Cuban percussion instruments (cuban stick, bongo, gourd and maracas) in the electrifying final pages.

GERSHWIN
CUBAN OVERTURE
(1932)

O

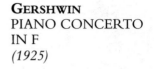

The day after the historic première of *Rhapsody in Blue* (12 February, 1924), Walter Damrosch, the eminent American conductor of the New York Symphony Orchestra, commissioned Gershwin to compose a full-length piano concerto. The première, with Gershwin as soloist and Damrosch conducting, took place in Carnegie Hall on 3 December 1925. It has remained one of the most popular twentieth century concertos with its opening Charleston theme, lyrical slow movement and exciting jazz finale.

GERSHWIN
PIANO CONCERTO
IN F
(1925)

C

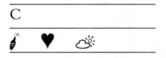

This was Gershwin's last major classical work and his greatest, the first American opera. It's based on the play *Porgy* (1927) by Dorothy and DuBose Heyward, itself adapted from DuBose Heyward's novel of the same name. It tells the story of the crippled beggar Porgy and his love for Bess. Gershwin immersed himself in the local colour and music of Charleston, South Carolina, where the opera is set. It took him two years to write the score which draws on indigenous folk songs and speech patterns, popular music idioms, jazz and spirituals. The hit arias (or songs, whatever you like to call them) include 'Summertime', 'Bess, you is my woman', 'I got plenty o' nuttin'' and 'It ain't necessarily so'.

GERSHWIN
PORGY AND BESS
(1935)

OP

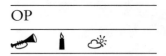

GERSHWIN
RHAPSODY IN BLUE
(1924)

C

The most frequently performed piece of American twentieth century music was written in the space of a few weeks. The dance-band leader Paul Whiteman, the self-styled 'King of Jazz', had asked Gershwin for a jazz piano concerto. Gershwin had declined due to pressure of work (he was busy writing Broadway musicals), when his brother Ira spotted a newspaper item announcing George's forthcoming participation in Whiteman's next concert. There's nothing that inspires like a deadline. This ground-breaking work 'for piano and jazz band', orchestrated by Whiteman's arranger Ferde Grofé (page 146), was premièred in front of the musical world's elite with triumphant success. It was one of the first pieces successfully to combine the jazz and classical worlds and it made Gershwin internationally famous overnight. The title of the work, incidentally, was the inspiration of George's brother Ira who, on the very day that George first played the work through, had been to an exhibition of Whistler's paintings, one of which was entitled *Nocturne in Blue and Green*. The original title of the music, *American Rhapsody*, was changed there and then, encapsulating as it does the European musical elements (rhapsody) and the American (blues).

GERSHWIN
THREE PRELUDES
FOR PIANO
(1926)

I

Gershwin composed six piano preludes in the mid-twenties and performed them all in public. He eventually decided to publish just three - the first and third are rhythmically exciting using elements of the tango and the Charleston, while the middle prelude (the best-known) is a 'blues lullaby'. Talking of lullabies, look out for the tender Lullaby from Gershwin's early string quartet in its arrangement for string orchestra.

A madrigal is a setting of a poem sung by unaccompanied voices in an elaborate contrapuntal style. Gibbons published one collection of these (Madrigals and Motets) all for five voices, all in sombre mood, their texts dealing with death, unrequited love and sadness. 'The Silver Swan' is exquisite, but 'What is our life' and 'How art thou thralled' are also moving and impressive.

ORLANDO GIBBONS 1583-1625
ENGLISH
'THE SILVER SWAN'
and other madrigals
(1612)

CHO

Gibbons raised the standard of English music to make it the envy of all Europe and became the first composer of sacred music to write exclusively for the Anglican church. One of his important innovations was the *verse anthem*, a work for solo voices and choir in which the solo passages have an independent accompaniment (played by viols and/or organ). *This is the record of John* is the best known of these.

**GIBBONS
THIS IS THE RECORD OF JOHN**
(c.1616)

CHO

One of the great love songs, its directness and simplicity proving the old dictum that less is more. Great singers from Amelita Galli-Curci to Cecilia Bartoli and Giuseppe De Luca to Luciano Pavarotti have recorded it. Little else of Giordani's music is known, few of his 30 operas have survived and, poor chap, some scholars question whether it was he who composed this.

GIUSEPPE GIORDANI 1743-98
ITALIAN
'CARO MIO BEN'

V

It says something for a composer writing in a late-Romantic style and in the last year of his life to embrace an instrument which, with few exceptions, was the property of the jazz world. Berlioz, Bizet, Richard Strauss and others had earlier made use of the saxophone in their scores, but Debussy's *Rapsodie* (1908), Ibert's *Concertino* (1936) and Glazunov's single movement concerto were the first to exploit the saxophone as a solo instrument in classical music.

ALEXANDER GLAZUNOV 1865-1936
RUSSIAN
CONCERTO IN E FLAT FOR ALTO SAXOPHONE
(1936)

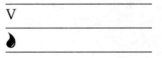

C

♥

GLAZUNOV
MÉDITATION
IN D
(1891)

I

Glazunov's most successful short piece, a lusciously romantic sister of Massenet's *Méditation* from *Thaïs*, has long been a favourite encore for fiddle players. It was written at the composer's summer home in Oserki and reflects the affection Glazunov had for the place.

GLAZUNOV
THE SEASONS
(1899)

O

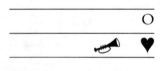

Glazunov inherited his skills as an orchestrator from his teacher Rimsky-Korsakov, the supreme master of the art. They're on show throughout this colourful score. Always heard in its form as an orchestral suite, the music comes from a forgotten ballet first performed in St Petersburg in 1900. It interprets the four seasons of the year, the lusty opening bacchanal of the final section (*Autumn*) being the most familiar part.

GLAZUNOV
STENKA RAZIN
(1885)

O

A tone poem portraying the ruthless seventeenth century Cossack Stenka Razin who led daring raids on the Czarist regime. He was captured and given amnesty in return for an oath of allegiance, but then raised an army to have another bash at the government. This time, when he was captured in 1671, he was executed. Glazunov turns him into something of a romantic hero and begins and ends the work with the 'Song of the Volga Boatman' (the one that goes 'Yo-ho, heave-ho').

GLAZUNOV
VIOLIN CONCERTO
IN A MINOR
(1904)

C

One of the staples of the violin repertoire, Glazunov's fiddle concerto is gloriously melodic in a richly romantic style - thoroughly old-fashioned for its day, especially when compared with Sibelius' rugged violin concerto completed the same year - but its three-movements-in-one don't contain a dull moment. It is dedicated to the great Russian violinist and teacher Leopold Auer who was as fond of the work as were his pupils Jascha Heiftez and Nathan Milstein (both of whom recorded it more than once).

Like Glazunov, Glière was a superb craftsman, a fecund melodist - and a Russian musical conservative (listening to this soul-stirring work, you'd never guess that it was written during the terrible years of 1942-3). Russian music boasted previous examples of singing without words (Rachmaninov's *Vocalise* is the most famous example) but Glière was the first to use the human voice as a virtuoso solo instrument in a concerto. There are two movements; the second is a brilliant concert waltz.

REINHOLD GLIÈRE
1875-1956
RUSSIAN
CONCERTO FOR COLORATURA SOPRANO
(1943)

C

♥

A work that has become a favourite with Classic FM listeners. The Russian harpist Ksenia Erdeli first met Glière when he was preparing the first production of *The Red Poppy* (see below). She noticed how significant a part the harp played in the score and pressed him to compose a concerto for her. Erdeli eventually got her wish and gave it its first performance. Why its three lyrical movements, full of glowing romantic melodies, are not better known must remain a mystery.

GLIÈRE
CONCERTO FOR HARP AND ORCHESTRA
(1938)

C

♥

The glamorous allure of China caught the attention of many composers in the twenties - Puccini was working on *Turandot* until his death and Lehar's *The Land of Smiles* came out just two years after Glière's ballet score. In it, the Chinese lover of a fine young Russian sailor meets her death at the hands of his evil capitalist rival. Her dying act is to present a red poppy as the symbol of freedom. Oh dear - for its rare revivals, the ballet had to be re-titled *The Red Flower*: it would never have done for the glorious symbol of Communism to be associated with the opium of the masses. The dance, by the way, comes last in the orchestral suite, an exuberant showpiece.

GLIÈRE
RUSSIAN SAILOR'S DANCE
from The Red Poppy Ballet
(1927)

O

MIKHAIL GLINKA
1804–57
RUSSIAN
GRAND SEXTET IN
E FLAT FOR PIANO
AND STRINGS
(1832)

CH

There's nothing very Russian about this sparkling chamber work from 'the father of Russian music'. Composed amidst the striking landscape of Lake Como before Glinka became immersed in Russian folklore and music, it is clearly inspired by the Italian surroundings and bubbles with Mendelssohnian high spirits. Scored for piano, string quartet and double bass, the Sextet sounds at times almost like a piano concerto.

GLINKA
JOTA ARAGONESA
(1845)

O

Also known as the *Spanish Overture No. 1*. The *jota* is a lively northern Spanish dance, usually performed with castanets, so this is Glinka's picture postcard of Spain (he was enchanted by the country when he first visited it in 1845), resulting in one of the first attempts by a European composer to capture Hispanic melodies and rhythms.

GLINKA
KAMARINSKAYA
(1848)

O

Glinka called this an 'orchestral fantasy'; it turned out to be an influential work in Russian musical history. Tchaikovsky wrote of it, 'From [Kamarinskaya] all Russian composers (including myself) draw contrapuntal and harmonic combinations whenever they have to deal with a Russian dance tune.' Glinka takes two Russian folk songs (a wedding song called 'Over the hills, the high hills' and a dance-song, 'Kamarinskaya') and transforms them with counter-melodies and brilliant scoring.

GLINKA
Overture to
RUSLAN AND
LUDMILLA
Opera
(1842)

O

A pioneering work in creating almost at a stroke a Russian nationalist school of music, the opera *Ruslan and Ludmilla* is a fantasy of fairy-tale charm based on a poem by Pushkin (the two lovers of the title, unusually in opera, end up happily married). Glinka makes much use of Russian folk song and dance – with a dash of Orientalism. This was the first time such a trait appeared in Russian music and it had a great effect on subsequent Russian composers. Though the opera is rarely mounted these days, the ebullient Overture is a perennially popular first item on concert programmes.

The famous flute solo, *Dance of the Blessed Spirits*, comes from the ballet sequence in Act 2 of Gluck's best known work. Orfeo has been allowed by the Furies to enter the Valley of the Blessed, a tranquil spot where the good spirits in Hades find rest, expressed in this ethereal slow dance. It is also well known under the title of *Mélodie* in a masterly transcription for piano by Giovanni Sgambati (1841-1914), a pupil of Liszt and friend of Wagner, who enjoyed a high reputation in Germany and Italy during his lifetime, but who is remembered for just this one piece today. It was a favourite encore of Rachmaninov (who recorded it) and many other great pianists.

CHRISTOPH GLUCK 1714-87
GERMAN
DANCE OF THE BLESSED SPIRITS 'MÉLODIE'
from Orpheus and Euridice
Opera
(1762)

O/I

Originally written for a *castrato*, this ravishingly lovely aria ('O thou belov'd') is sung by Paris as he arrives in Greece, happy in the knowledge that he will soon be with his Helen. There is a heart-melting recording of this by the great mezzo-soprano Teresa Berganza which brings out the chaste elegance of Gluck's music to moving effect and was used in the 1979 Italian art film *Forget Venice*.

GLUCK
'O DEL MIO DOLCE ARDOR'
from Paride ed Elena
(1770)

OP

'All forms of language have been exhausted to praise the stupor of grief, the passion, the despair expressed in this sublime number,' we read in the Larousse opera dictionary. It is sung in Act 3 by Orfeo (a contralto 'trouser' role) after he has ignored the warning of Amor, God of Love, and clasped his beloved Euridice in his arms. She immediately dies, but Amor is so affected by the aria Orfeo sings that Euridice is restored to life. 'Che farò senza Euridice?' is the original Italian but a whole generation was introduced to this number through a recording in English by the much-loved contralto Kathleen Ferrier (1912-53) who died from cancer at the height of her career. 'What is life to me without thee?' is the translation she sings (literally it should be 'What can I do without Eurydice?'), though in the last verse of Ferrier's evergreen disc she gets it the wrong way round and sings, 'What is life to thee without me?'

GLUCK
'WHAT IS LIFE'
from Orpheus and Euridice

OP

LEOPOLD GODOWSKY
1870-1938
POLISH-AMERICAN
ALT WIEN
(1919)

I

♥

Godowsky was one of the greatest pianists in history and wrote some of the most elaborate and difficult works for the instrument. Only now are pianists coming to terms with the extraordinary legacy he left them. This little piece, though, *Old Vienna*, achieved wide popularity and can be played by the average amateur (it comes from a collection of 30 short pieces in waltz time which Godowsky called *Triakontameron*). *Alt Wien* is a wistful look back at the glory days of the Waltz City before the First World War. It was played by the dance band in the 1932 film *Grand Hotel* starring Greta Garbo and both the Barrymores, John and Lionel. As for Godowsky's other works (all for solo piano), these will appeal mainly to the virtuoso/ transcription fancier - his concert paraphrases on themes by Johann Strauss and the 53 elaborate versions he made of Chopin's studies (see entry).

KARL GOLDMARK
1830-1915
AUSTRO-HUNGARIAN
RUSTIC WEDDING
SYMPHONY
(1876)

O

If the word 'symphony' means something forbidding and serious to you, then this is the symphony to change your mind. Hungarian-born, Goldmark spent most of his life in Vienna, a fact reflected in this loveable, high-spirited work. Its five movements (*Wedding March, Song of the Bride, Serenade, In the Garden* and *Dance*) are far removed from the worlds of Beethoven and Brahms and more akin to those of Schubert and Johann Strauss II. The rustic wedding is seen through the eyes of a Victorian romantic - an innocent village maiden, a faithful bucolic swain and the villagers turning out to celebrate the nuptials with music and dance.

GOLDMARK
VIOLIN CONCERTO
IN A MINOR
(1877)

C

This is one of the finest of Romantic violin concertos and one that for some reason or other has never achieved the popularity of the Brahms or Tchaikovsky concertos. Nathan Milstein, Itzhak Perlman and other leading players have recorded it but, to the shame of the rest of their profession, it is rarely heard in the concert hall. Its glorious themes (especially its central second movement, andante) are real crowd pleasers while the solo part is full of virtuoso opportunities. Try it! I guarantee you won't be disappointed.

Górecki's name and music were virtually unknown in the West until 1992 when a recording of his Third Symphony appeared with David Zinman conducting the London Sinfonietta and the young American soprano Dawn Upshaw. The hypnotic, haunting score caught the imagination of Classic FM listeners (though some thought it pretentious and sleep-inducing) and, uniquely, a contemporary work reached the top of the classical charts, staying there for months. To date it has sold well over a million copies. Perhaps its most moving section is the (second movement) setting of the prayer inscribed on a cell wall of the Gestapo headquarters in Zakopane, written by an 18-year-old girl in 1944.

HENRYK GÓRECKI
B. 1933
POLISH
SYMPHONY NO. 3
'SYMPHONY OF
SORROWFUL
SONGS'
(1976)

O

♪

The piano was phenomenally popular during Gottschalk's time and he composed dozens of (mainly) short works of all sorts: variations on national tunes and operatic themes, pieces using the dance rhythms of Latin America, ragtime (50 years before Scott Joplin) and Chopinesque mazurkas and waltzes. There are a number of recorded collections on the market (those by Philip Martin are wide-ranging and engaging). For an overview look out *The Union* (a paraphrase on American national airs), *Le Banjo*, *Souvenir de Porto Rico*, *Ojos Criollos* and *Manchega*.

LOUIS MOREAU
GOTTSCHALK
1829–69
AMERICAN
PIANO WORKS

I

♪

Gottschalk was the first American-born composer to achieve international fame. He was a virtuoso pianist, European-trained (praised and befriended by Berlioz and Chopin) and spent most of his short career touring all over America, especially South America and the West Indies. His First Symphony, completed during a stay at Guadeloupe, has two movements, the first exotic and slow (like Wagner with palm trees), followed by an infectiously-lively samba, the first time the dance rhythm had been used in a symphony.

GOTTSCHALK
SYMPHONY NO. 1
'A NIGHT IN THE
TROPICS'
(1859)

O

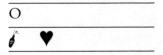

GOTTSCHALK
SYMPHONY NO. 2
'À MONTEVIDEO'
(1865-68)

O

More a rhapsody than a symphony, the work's single movement (composed in Uruguay) is in seven linked sections and features an arrangement of the Uruguayan national anthem, 'Hail Columbia', 'Yankee Doodle' and other patriotic airs cleverly and wittily interwoven. Great fun.

CHARLES GOUNOD
1818-93
FRENCH
AVE MARIA
(1859)

V

'Ave Maria' or 'Hail, Mary' are the first words of the prayer of the Roman Catholic Church (from the Angel Gabriel's address to Mary, in Luke i, 28). Many composers have set them to music, but Gounod's version came about after he had written, in 1853, a violin melody to be played to the accompaniment of the Prelude No. 1 in C from Bach's *Well-Tempered Clavier* (page 50). Listening to this piece, which Gounod called 'Méditation', you'd never guess the two tunes were written by composers who lived a century apart. Three years later, in 1856, words were added – but not those of the *Ave Maria* (it was still called 'Méditation'). It was another three years after that that someone had the bright idea of fitting 'Ave Maria' to Gounod's tune. (See also Schubert: Songs.)

GOUNOD
FUNERAL MARCH
OF A MARIONETTE
(1872)

O

Gounod's most popular concert work began life as a piano piece (he'd intended it to be the first movement of a *Suite Burlesque*) but success came when he turned it into a light orchestral number. It describes the funeral procession of a puppet that has been killed in a duel. Halfway to the cemetery the pallbearers stop off at an inn for a drink and then continue on their sombre way.

Gounod's opera is based on the Faust legend in the version by the great German poet and dramatist Johann Wolfgang von Goethe. Up until the 1930s it was by far the most frequently performed opera in the world - wonderful writing for the voice, rousing choruses, memorable melodies, exotic settings and costumes. Now it is rarely revived. The 'Jewel Song' ('Ah! Je ris de me voir' - 'I am laughing with joy') remains a favourite soprano showpiece sung in Act 3 by the heroine Marguerite as she examines the jewels Faust has given her.

GOUNOD
'JEWEL SONG'
from Faust
(1859)

OP

Beloved of Welsh male voice choirs, this was originally written for Gounod's unfinished opera *Ivan the Terrible*. Too good a tune to waste - so the 'Soldiers' Chorus' ('Gloire immortelle' - 'Immortal Glory') was transplanted to Act 4 of *Faust* as the soldiers return triumphantly from the war, watched by Faust and Mephistopheles. Among their number is Marguerite's brother, Valentine. He hears the Devil insult his sister's name, challenges Faust to a duel and is killed.

GOUNOD
'SOLDIERS' CHORUS'
from Faust

OP

After 1880, Gounod abandoned opera and devoted his time to sacred music, reflecting his deep-rooted religious convictions. Among this is an oratorio called *Mors et Vita* (*Life and Death*) dedicated to Pope Leo XIII and first heard at the 1885 Birmingham Festival. From it comes this short, serene orchestral interlude *The Judge*, reminiscent of Verdi (there's even a phrase from the *Ingemisco* section of the Italian's *Requiem*) and the Intermezzo from Mascagni's *Cavalleria Rusticana* composed six years later.

GOUNOD
JUDEX
from Mors et Vita
(1884)

O

GOUNOD
ST CECILIA MASS
(1855)

CHO

Messe Solonelle de Sainte Cécile (its French title) is just one of 16 masses that Gounod wrote but the only one that is heard today. Composed in the country near Avranches, it's among his most impressive works (try the splendid *Gloria!*) and dedicated to the patron saint of music. After its first performance in Paris, Saint-Saëns wrote, 'At first one was dazzled, then charmed, then conquered.' You may well agree.

GOUNOD
'WALTZ SONG'
from Roméo et Juliette
(1867)

OP

Though fairly faithful to Shakespeare's version of the story, Gounod's *Romeo and Juliet* is an inconsistent work. Nevertheless there are many passages of Gounod at his best (Romeo's aria in the garden scene, for example, or the lovers' parting duet) but most popular of all is 'Ah! Je veux vivre dans ce rêve' ('Ah! I want to live in this giddy dream'), known as the 'Waltz Song', which Juliet sings to her nurse in Act 1 just before her first meeting with Romeo.

PERCY GRAINGER
1882–1961
AUSTRALIAN
CHILDREN'S
MARCH
(1917)
and
IN A NUTSHELL
Suite
(1916)

O

Written during World War 1 for the United States Army Band, *Children's March: Over the Hills and Far Away* is one of those maddeningly catchy tunes you can't get out of your head, a jaunty open-air piece typical of Grainger. *In a Nutshell* has four movements, the first called *Arrival Platform Humlet* - simply a tune to hum or whistle while you're standing on a railway platform waiting for the train. The second movement (*Gay and Wistful*) reminds you of music hall, *Pastoral* is exactly that, while the final part is another march - *The Gum-suckers' March. Gum-suckers* are apparently the inhabitants of Victoria (Australia), so-called because of their habit of sucking the leaves of the Eucalyptus tree!

Grainger's best-known music tends to exuberant high-spirits but there are many poignant and extremely moving quieter pieces. Both *Harvest Hymn* and *Colonial Song* (which Sir Thomas Beecham once described as 'the worst orchestral piece of modern times') fall into this category, lushly-romantic and rather endearing. His tender *Bridal Lullaby* (a short piano piece) was used effectively in the film *Howard's End*, while for an unusual and intense choral setting, try his version of the folk-song 'Shallow Brown'.

GRAINGER
COLONIAL SONG
(1911)
HARVEST HYMN
(1905)
and others

O/CHO

♥   ☼

♥   ☼

Under the collective title of *British Folk-Music Settings* (the whole set 'lovingly and reverently dedicated to the memory of Edvard Grieg'), Grainger 'dished up for piano' (his description) a series of lively traditional dances. The bucolic *Country Gardens* and *Shepherds Hey* are morris-dances, *Molly on the Shore* is an Irish Reel. *Handel in the Strand*, another favourite Grainger work, is a 'clog dance' from a collection which he called *Music-Room Tit-Bits*. He also made successful orchestral versions of these and others: British light music at its best - composed by an Australian.

GRAINGER
COUNTRY
GARDENS
(1908-18)
and other folk-song
arrangements

I/O

♪

Inspired by the paintings of Goya, this remarkable series of seven ballades for piano is Granados' lasting monument. He captures not only the spirit of Goya's work but also reflects their eighteenth century world (Granados much admired the music of Domenico Scarlatti who spent much of his career in Spain). Spanish life, scent, dance and song pervade every page. Perhaps the finest is No. 4 – *Quejas, o la Maja y el Ruiseñor* which we know as *The Maiden and Nightingale* (there's also, not surprisingly, a beautiful vocal version).

ENRIQUE GRANADOS
1867-1916
SPANISH
GOYESCAS
(1911)

I

♥

GRANADOS
SPANISH DANCES
(1892-1900)

I

Falla, Albéniz and Granados were the Spanish composers responsible for the establishment of a modern Spanish school of music that reflected the country's indigenous dance, song and character. Granados' 12 *Spanish Dances* are good examples - No. 5, *Andaluza* (also known as *Playera*), is especially popular in its original form as a piano solo or on the guitar.

EDVARD GRIEG
1843–1907
NORWEGIAN
HOLBERG SUITE
(1884)

O/I

Norway's greatest composer established almost single-handedly a modern Norwegian school of music, though this work, *From Holberg's Time* (to give it its official title), written to celebrate the bi-centenary of the birth of Ludvig Holberg, is in a classical style to reflect the era in which Holberg lived (there's a prelude, sarabande, gavotte, air and rigaudon). Holberg (1684-1754), a poet, playwright and philosopher, is regarded as the founder of Danish literature, though he was Norwegian-born and shared Grieg's birthplace of Bergen.

GRIEG
HOMAGE MARCH
from Sigurd Jorsalfar
Suite
(1872)

O

A grandiose, triumphant march - trumpets blaring, full orchestra - ends the suite Grieg made from the incidental music he wrote for a historical drama of the same name produced in Oslo in 1872. The central character is the twelfth century Norwegian king Sigurd, who joins the Crusades to fight against the Saracens.

Grieg was essentially a miniaturist. In other words he was at his best in short works, as these 62 piano pieces prove. Every music lover should get to know *Papillons* (*Butterflies*), *To Spring* and *Wedding Day at Troldhaugen* (all of which Grieg himself recorded in 1903 in very primitive sound) as well as the five numbers that Grieg orchestrated for his *Lyric Suite*, Op. 54 (1904) – *Shepherd's Boy*, *Norwegian March*, *Nocturne* (my particular favourite), *March of the Trolls* and *Bell Ringing*. But dip in anywhere in this collection – there are many more delights than these.

GRIEG
LYRIC PIECES
(1867-1901)

I/O

The Norwegian poet and dramatist Henrik Ibsen (1828-1906) asked Grieg to write the incidental music for the first production (in Oslo, then called Christiania) of his verse play *Peer Gynt*. The title role was based on a character from Scandinavian legend, a lovable liar and rogue. Grieg was unhappy about the music he composed ('I had no opportunity to write as I wanted') but the result was an instantaneous success. From the two suites he fashioned from the original 23 numbers, *Morning*, *Ase's Death*, *Anitra's Dance* and *In the Hall of the Mountain King* (all from Suite No. 1) have always been firm favourites. The second suite (less popular) has the lovely 'Solveig's Song', a haunting Norwegian air portraying Solveig, the bride whom Gynt abducts then abandons but who remains faithful to him. It's typical of Grieg's other songs (he wrote 140 of them), the most famous of which is 'Ich liebe dich' ('I love thee') written for his wife Nina in 1865 with words by Hans Christian Anderson. The Broadway operetta, *Song of Norway* (1944), tells the story of the love affair between Nina and Grieg and uses this song and other Grieg pieces for its score.

GRIEG
PEER GYNT
Suites Nos. 1 and 2
(1876)

O/V

GRIEG
PIANO CONCERTO
IN A MINOR
(1868)

C

There are many good reasons why this is among the most frequently-played and best known of all concertos. From its arresting opening bars to its brilliant finale with all the colour of a Norwegian folk festival, it is a work of white-hot inspiration. The second movement is surely one of the most lyrical in the entire piano concerto repertoire. Grieg was 25 when he wrote this, the first time he had composed anything in which an orchestra was used.

FERDE GROFÉ
1892-1972
AMERICAN
GRAND CANYON
SUITE
(1931)

O

The American composer, pianist and arranger is best known as the man who orchestrated Gershwin's *Rhapsody in Blue*. At the time (1924) Grofé was band-leader Paul Whiteman's in-house arranger but Grofé was an interesting composer in his own right, using jazz rhythms and tuneful themes in light music vein. This suite is an orchestral description in five movements of one of America's natural wonders: *Sunrise*, *The Painted Desert*, *On the Trail*, *Sunset* and *Cloudburst*. Other Grofé works well-worth exploring are the *Mississippi Suite* (1925), *Aviation Suite* (1946) and *Hudson River Suite* (1955).

ALEXANDRE
GUILMANT
1837-1911
FRENCH
GRAND CHOEUR
IN D, OP. 18
(1866)

I

'Grand choeur' is simply the French for 'full chorus' or, in this context, 'full organ' - and in this thunderous and exciting organ solo all the stops are pulled out. Guilmant was one of the greatest French organists in history who wrote prolifically for the instrument. Another winner is the march he wrote based on 'Lift up your heads' from Handel's *Messiah*. Both are good choices for going down the aisle.

Guilmant wrote eight organ sonatas (for solo organ) but turned the first two into 'symphonies' by reworking the material with orchestral accompaniment, organ concertos in all but name. In either solo or orchestral version, the First Sonata/Symphony (especially) comes across as a thrilling work - if you want to give your loudspeakers a workout I suggest you start with the Finale, a tumultuous toccata with a wall-shaking last couple of pages. If you like Saint-Saëns' *Organ Symphony* you're sure to like this.

GUILMANT
ORGAN SYMPHONY
NO. 1 IN D MINOR
(1874)

C

H

Venezuelan-born Hahn came to Paris at the age of five and is considered as a thoroughly French composer, a pupil of Massenet and Saint-Saëns whose influences can be heard in this mellifluous and witty concerto. It's not widely played, or indeed widely known, but its one modern recording (with Stephen Coombs as soloist) is a real charmer. The only other time it has appeared on disc was in a 1937 (slightly abridged) performance with Hahn himself conducting the work's dedicatee, Magda Tagliafero.

REYNALDO HAHN
1874-1947
VENEZUELAN-FRENCH
PIANO CONCERTO
NO. 1 IN E
(1931)

C
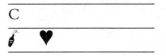

It is as a composer of songs that Hahn is mostly remembered today. He himself had a light tenor voice and was a favourite in fashionable Parisian drawing-rooms where he would sing, accompanying himself with a cigarette drooping gracefully from the corner of his mouth (he recorded a number of them in the thirties). His most famous song, 'Si mes vers avaient des ailes' ('If only my poem had wings') was written when he was only 16. 'Á Chloris' ('To Chloris'), 'L'Heure exquise' ('The Exquisite Moment'), 'Le Rossignol des lilas' ('The Nightingale in the Lilacs') and 'Tyndaris' are popular requests on Classic FM.

HAHN
SONGS
(1895-1918)

V
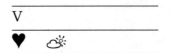

**GEORGE FRIDERIC
HANDEL
1685-1759**
GERMAN-ENGLISH
ARRIVAL OF THE
QUEEN OF SHEBA
from Solomon
(1748)

O

♪

The words for the seldom-performed oratorio from which this classical 'lollipop' comes are based on the books of *Kings* and *Chronicles*. They concern three aspects of Solomon's greatness: his piety, his conjugal bliss and his wisdom. Though designated an oratorio, 'in hardly another of [Handel's] great oratorios does the purely religious side play so modest a part', according to Sir Thomas Beecham. It was Beecham who made a particularly famous recording of this brief, jaunty orchestral piece that features two oboes in duet and which heralds the entrance of the Queen of Sheba in Act 3. It also often heralds the arrival of a bride - it's one of the top choices for a church wedding.

**HANDEL
12 CONCERTI
GROSSI, OP. 6
(1739)

O

♪

These peaks of Baroque instrumental music were, incredibly, composed in the space of a month: Handel completed the first concerto on 29 September, the last on 30 October. Even considering that he borrowed some themes from Scarlatti, Muffat, Telemann and (as was his habit) himself, it represents an amazing achievement - they fill three CDs! And this is no 'Baroque wallpaper music'. They represent the highest manifestation of Handel's compositional skills. Each concerto has five or six contrasted movements, all scored for a string orchestra pitted against two solo violins, a cello and harpsichord.

**HANDEL
THE HARMONIOUS
BLACKSMITH
(1720)

I

♪

From the Harpsichord Suite No. 5 in E comes one movement in which Handel takes a stately eight-bar theme and writes some jolly variations on it (the rest of the suite is seldom played). It has nothing whatsoever to do with a blacksmith, harmonious or otherwise. Legend had it that Handel invented the tune while sheltering in a smithy during a storm (untrue), but the work got its nickname about 1820 when a publisher in Bath issued the work saying he had heard a local blacksmith whistling Handel's theme.

One of the most dramatic of Handel's soprano arias, it's still remembered as the number in which Dame Kiri te Kanawa dazzled the congregation at the marriage of the Prince and Princess of Wales. The singer soars jubilantly into the stratosphere with a high trumpet. Handel added the number to his oratorio *Samson* a year after he'd completed the score, a score he had completed only a month after finishing *Messiah*!

HANDEL
'LET THE BRIGHT SERAPHIM'
from Samson
(1743)

V

'Unquestionably one of the greatest works of its kind ever conceived by the mind of man,' wrote one commentator, 'In its pages will be found music of both the simplest and most complex nature, but all of it is on the highest plane of inspirational beauty.' Incredibly, Handel wrote the entire work (which lasts two and a half hours complete) in the span of 24 days. There is no space to examine each section but this one masterpiece includes 'Every valley shall be exalted', 'For unto us a Child is born', 'I know that my Redeemer liveth' and 'The trumpet shall sound' - as well as the 'Hallelujah Chorus'. It was first performed on 13 April 1741 in Dublin. At the oratorio's London première in March 1742, King George II is said to have risen to his feet at the close of the great celebratory chorus. Of course, the rest of the audience followed suit and ever since, in England at any rate, it has been the custom to stand for the 'Hallelujah Chorus'.

HANDEL
MESSIAH
(1741)

CHO

You thought monster concerts in Hyde Park were a recent invention? King George II commissioned Handel to write a suite of celebratory music to be played alfresco as part of a huge entertainment in Green Park, London, on 27 April 1749. The rehearsals in Vauxhall Gardens attracted a crowd of 12,000 and the event itself even more. Alas, the gigantic firework display to accompany the music (or was it the other way round?) was not a success: the rockets went off alright but the Catherine-wheels wouldn't light - except for one which ignited the specially-built wooden Temple of Peace and caused total panic. The music was a triumph, however. The suite consists of an overture followed by five short movements.

HANDEL
MUSIC FOR THE ROYAL FIREWORKS
(1749)

O

HANDEL
'OMBRA MAI FU'
'HANDEL'S LARGO'
from Serse ('Xerxes')
Opera
(1738)

V

This is an aria from one of Handel's operas and describes the beauty of the cool shade of a palm tree. Universally known in its instrumental version as *Handel's Largo*, this has come to be a meditative, religious piece (often played at funerals). The Italian *largo* means 'wide, roomy, generous' or, in musical terms, 'slow and broad', though Handel's score is actually marked *larghetto* ('less slow than largo'), added to which he composed many other movements which *were* marked *largo*! Still, *Handel's Largo* it has come to be called, and a magical five minutes it is too, in whatever form you hear it.

HANDEL
ORGAN
CONCERTOS
(1735-51)

C

High among music's most life-enhancing creations are Handel's organ concertos. If ever you're feeling a bit down, put on one of these to pep you up - the fast movements simply bubble along, contrasted by serene or magisterial slower sections. There are 16 in all, most of them written as interludes for Handel's oratorios. Handel was a shrewd businessman-composer and one of London's most famous figures, as well as being the finest organist of his day. By appearing as organ soloist in the midst of one of his popular oratorios he added to his allure and purse. The public lapped it up. The most popular concerto, No. 13 in F (known as *The Cuckoo and Nightingale* because of its bird imitations in the second movement) was composed for the first performance of *Israel in Egypt*. But dip in anywhere - there's not a dud amongst them.

Frederic, Prince of Wales, asked Handel to write something to celebrate the return of his son, the Duke of Cumberland, from his victory at Culloden in Scotland. What he got was this oratorio based on the *First Book of Macabees* (in the *Apocrypha*), a work that not only won Handel further success but offered a rare (for England) favourable representation of a Jew. This is one of Handel's greatest choruses. From the same work comes one of his most heroic tenor arias 'Sound an alarm'.

HANDEL
'SEE THE CONQU'RING HERO COMES'
from Judas Maccabeus (1746)

CHO

Three years after George I had ascended the throne, he asked Handel to compose some music specially to accompany a royal pageant on the River Thames. While the royal family floated along in barges they listened to a suite of 20 pieces consisting of all kinds of dance music, airs and fanfares, a kind of early disco. The King liked it all so much that everything had to be repeated three times. The music wasn't printed until 1741 by which time Handel had added a few more movements. Until recently, the *Water Music* was heard most frequently in the modern orchestral arrangement (six movements only) made by Sir Hamilton Harty (page 152) in 1922. The second of these is the gentle *Air* (one of Handel's best-known tunes, popular at weddings), No. 6 of the original *Water Music Suite No. 1 in F*.

HANDEL
WATER MUSIC
(1717)

O

Neither an oratorio nor an opera, *Semele* is a mixture of the two, the unlikely tale of Semele (daughter of the King of Thebes) falling in love with Jupiter and upsetting everyone in the process. The story doesn't get in the way of one of Handel's finest scores and there are few more serene arias than this, one of his most graceful tunes. It is sung in Act 2 by Jupiter as he announces his intention of transporting Semele and her sister Ina to a peaceful Arcadian grove. It works just as well (better?) without knowing that.

HANDEL
'WHERE E'ER YOU WALK'
from Semele (1744)

V

HANDEL
ZADOK THE PRIEST
(1727)

CHO

Handel composed four anthems for the coronation of George II in Westminster Abbey. This one has been heard at every coronation since, sung during the anointing of the sovereign. Its magnificent opening never fails to send a tingle down the spine. The words come from the *First Book of Kings* ('Zadok the priest and Nathan the prophet... anointed Solomon king'). And Zadok? He was a decendant of Aaron and a priest in Jerusalem under King David and Solomon.

HANDEL
(arr. Beecham)
THE GODS GO A'
BEGGING
and others
(1928-45)

O

Now wildly unfashionable, the four ballet scores that Sir Thomas Beecham fashioned from a wide variety of Handel's works and scored for the modern orchestra retain a period charm of their own. The recordings he made of *The Gods go a'begging*, *Love in Bath* (or *The Great Elopement*), *The Origin of Design* and *The Faithful Shepherd* are full of Handelian *joie de vivre* and affectionate music-making.

HAMILTON HARTY
1879-1941
IRISH
WITH THE WILD
GEESE
(1910)

O

There's an old Irish legend that the spirits of the dead return to Ireland in the guise of a large flock of wild geese, unseen in the depths of night. Harty's tone poem tells the story of Irish exiles who fought with distinction with the French army at the Battle of Fontenoy in 1745. They recall their days in Ireland before the battle. Afterwards, we hear a lament for the fallen, rising to a triumphant conclusion as the 'wild geese' fly home. Harty himself left a superb recording of this from way back in 1926. Other works of Harty's worth looking out for are his Violin Concerto, Piano Concerto and the arrangements of music by Handel and Field (page 123).

With over 100 symphonies to his credit, Haydn wrote comparatively few concertos - so far, 24 have been authenticated of which only about half a dozen are heard regularly. The two cello concertos are among them. The one in D major, composed about the same time as Symphonies 79, 80 and 81, has always been played (the dance-like finale, especially, represents a real challenge) but the C major is a newcomer. Why? The manuscript was only discovered in 1961 in the Prague National Museum - Rostropovitch was the first cellist to record it in the West and the Concerto quickly established itself in the repertoire. The last movement is a real thriller reminiscent of C.P.E. Bach.

JOSEPH HAYDN
1732-1809
AUSTRIAN
CELLO CONCERTOS
NOS. 1 IN C
(1784)
and
2 IN D
(1783)

C

This magnificent, sprawling choral work has some of the most adventurous orchestral writing of the entire Eighteenth Century and throughout the following 100 years was Haydn's most popular work. The text is in English, a setting of words from the *Book of Genesis* and Milton's 'Paradise Lost', for the subject of the oratorio is chaos being resolved into order, darkness turning into light. One of the highlights is the mighty chorus 'The heavens are telling the glory of God'. Hearing this as a small boy was one of the things that turned me on to classical music.

HAYDN
THE CREATION
(1796-8)

CHO

Haydn composed 14 settings of the Mass, most of them rather jolly affairs. He himself acknowledged that 'at the thought of God his heart leaped for joy, and he could not help his music doing the same'. The *Nelson Mass* (also known as the *Imperial Mass, Missa in Augustiis* or *Mass in Time of Straightened Circumstances*) was begun when the Austrian army was under threat from Napoleon. Haydn finished the work on 31 August 1798. A month later, news reached Vienna of Nelson's victory at the Battle of the Nile when the French fleet was blown out of the water. Two years after that Nelson and Lady Hamilton paid a visit to Haydn when this mass was performed. The three got on famously (Nelson gave Haydn his watch, Haydn gave Nelson his pen) - and that's how the work got its nickname.

HAYDN
NELSON MASS
(1798)

CHO

HAYDN
PIANO CONCERTO
IN D,
Hob XVIII:11
(1784?)
and
PIANO CONCERTO
IN F,
Hob XVIII:3
(c. 1766)

C

'I was never a wizard on any one instrument, but I knew the power and effectiveness of all of them,' Haydn told his biographer. His 12 piano concertos have suffered, comparatively, from neglect, though the D major has always been around (even if no one is still quite sure if Haydn wrote it), played by many great pianists. It's in three short movements (fast-slow-fast) like most of Haydn's concertos, with a sparkling Hungarian-style rondo for the finale. The F Major Concerto, written around 1766, is definitely by Haydn, more difficult to play than the D major but with the same intimate chamber-music feel about the music. (Note: Haydn's works are known by their Hob[oken] numbers, after Anthony van Hoboken, the Dutchman who catalogued all Haydn's work in 1957-71; they are given here, and below, to distinguish these concertos and the Piano Trio from other works in the same forms and keys.)

HAYDN
PIANO TRIO IN G,
Hob XV:25
(1795)

CH

The amazingly prolific Haydn wrote over 40 piano trios (that's a work composed for keyboard, violin and cello). The only one that is heard frequently is No. 25 composed in 1795 and sometimes called the *Gypsy Trio*, a nickname it acquired because of its celebrated last movement, another of Haydn's Hungarian-style rondo tunes (the *Gypsy Rondo*). A famous recording of this was made in 1927 by the great pianist Alfred Cortot, violinist Jacques Thibaud and cellist Pablo Casals, one which in many people's opinions has never been bettered.

HAYDN
THE SEASONS
(1799-1801)

CHO

Haydn had been inspired to write his oratorio *The Creation* after hearing some of Handel's oratorios in London. If *The Creation* is Haydn's response to his deep religious beliefs, *The Seasons*, his second oratorio, reflects his profound love of nature. The words come from a poem of the same name by the English writer James Thomson and, of course, it's in four sections. *The Seasons* was Haydn's last major work, yet you wouldn't know it was the work of an elderly man, so full is it of impish humour and vivid musical pictures. But though he lived for another eight years after completing it, Haydn wrote little else of importance.

Between 1791 and 1795, Haydn wrote two sets of *London* symphonies, so-called because they were composed for his two visits there under the auspices of the London violinist and impresario J.P. Salomon. No. 94 (the second symphony of the first set) acquired its nickname because of the second movement which opens with a sweet, simple tune played very softly by the orchestra which is then repeated. At the end of the repeat, the full orchestra comes in unexpectedly with a crashing chord (in Austria it's called the *Paukenschlag Symphony* - literally 'drumstroke'). It was said that Haydn put it in to wake up his audiences who fell asleep during his slow movements! Alas, it's a myth - though Haydn's sense of humour is there for all to hear.

HAYDN
SYMPHONY
NO. 94 IN G
'SURPRISE'
(1791)

Like the *Surprise*, the *Miracle* has four contrasted movements and acquired its nickname through a myth. When the work was first played (at the Hanover Rooms in London on 11 March 1791), the audience was so curious to see this most famous of all musicians conduct that they left their seats to get a better view. No sooner had they done this when a huge chandelier fell from the ceiling into the area where the audience had been sitting. Naturally, cries of 'A miracle, a miracle!' went up. In fact (sorry to spoil a good story), the chandelier came down during a performance of Haydn's Symphony No. 102 in the first half of the programme: the *Miracle* was played in the second half *after* the miracle!

HAYDN
SYMPHONY
NO. 96 IN D
'MIRACLE'
(1791)

There's nothing very much that's military about the music - no portrait of a soldier's life or battle scenes. No, it's just that towards the end of the second movement Haydn introduces an Austrian bugle call on the trumpet and includes a bass drum, triangle and cymbals in the score, instruments that, in the Eighteenth Century, were particularly associated with military music (often called 'Turkish' music). This same second movement opens with a tune Haydn borrowed from a French song called 'La Gentille et jeune Lisette', one he had already used in a lute concerto and his Symphony No. 85, known as *La Reine*.

HAYDN
SYMPHONY
NO. 100 IN G
'MILITARY'
(1794)

HAYDN
SYMPHONY
NO. 103 IN E FLAT
'DRUM ROLL'
(1795)

O

Here is another nicknamed symphony from the *London* set, all of which show Haydn at the peak of his creative powers. Haydn himself has been nicknamed the 'Father of the Symphony' and, though this is not strictly accurate, he certainly developed the symphony to a higher degree than anyone else at the time and showed the way forward. The *Drum Roll* gets its name from the kettledrum roll (unusual in those days) heard over the slow introduction to the first movement.

HAYDN
SYMPHONY
NO. 104 IN D
'LONDON'
(1795)

O

Confusingly, this, the final symphony of the two sets of *London* symphonies is itself known as the *London Symphony*, perhaps because it was this one that was given at Haydn's last benefit concert. Haydn wrote in his diary, 'The hall was filled with a picked audience. The whole company was delighted and so was I. I took in this evening 4000 guilden. One can make as much as this only in England.' When he left the country for the last time in August 1795, he was given many parting gifts by friends, including a talking parrot, which brought 1400 florins at Haydn's death. He was thought of so highly in England that nine years after his departure he was sent six pairs of cotton stockings by a firm in Leicester into which were woven themes from his music.

HAYDN
TRUMPET
CONCERTO IN
E FLAT
(1796)

C

The most popular of all trumpet concertos was composed in 1796 for the Viennese virtuoso Anton Weidlinger. He must have been quite a player for the bustling finale (a rondo) is a real workout for the soloist, even for today's artists who have the advantages of a modern valve trumpet. Haydn wrote this for an instrument called the keyed trumpet, invented by Weidlinger and which worked by having keys covering holes in the side of the tube, rather on the same principle as the modern saxophone. It made it easier for the trumpeter to play all the notes of the scale, but never caught on and, in any case, was soon superseded in the early years of the Nineteenth Century by the instrument we know today. Hear the Concerto at its best in the recordings of Maurice André or Wynton Marsalis.

You won't find Henselt (let alone his Piano Concerto) in every music book but this particular work of his is really special. If you like the big Romantic piano concertos of, say, Schumann or Chopin you'll love this - it was once as popular as Tchaikovsky's First Piano Concerto is today. Many great pianists included it in their repertoire; many others gave a sigh of relief when other concertos (Grieg's, for instance) became fashionable, because the Henselt is so enormously difficult to play (the composer himself never played it in public for that reason). Clara Schumann (Robert's wife) gave the first performance. There is a superb CD of it played by Marc-André Hamelin.

ADOLF VON HENSELT
1814-89
GERMAN
PIANO CONCERTO
IN F MINOR
(1844)

C

The English title for this evergreen ballet is *Vain Precautions* or, sometimes, *The Unchaperoned Daughter*. Its musical origins are a bit of a mish-mash - the original 1789 production consisted of folk-songs and popular tunes which were then re-arranged in 1828 by Hérold who was then the chorus master at the Paris Opéra (he added numbers by himself and pinched bits from Rossini's operas). In 1864 another arrangement was made by an obscure German composer called Peter Hertel. Paradoxically, it was he who wrote what is now the most popular number from the ballet, the famous *Clog Dance*. Finally, the score we hear today was assembled in 1959 by John Lanchbery for a revival by Sir Frederick Ashton. But it's Hérold who gets all the credit for this colourful score while poor old Hertel is totally forgotten.

FERDINAND HÉROLD
1791-1833
FRENCH
LA FILLE MAL
GARDÉ
Ballet
(1789, 1828, 1864, 1959)

O

The only other work of Hérold still heard today is his rousing overture *Zampa*, the curtain-raiser to his opera about Zampa, a sixteenth century pirate who is dragged under the sea and drowned by a marble statue of his former bride (I know, I know, but this is opera). Beloved of brass bands, the piece is a real firecracker, in the same vein as Rossini's and Suppé's overtures.

HÉROLD
Overture to
ZAMPA
Opera
(1831)

O

BERNARD HERRMANN
1911-75
AMERICAN
ARIA
FROM SALAMMBÔ
(Citizen Kane, 1940)

V

♥

The first of Herrmann's 61 film scores, *Citizen Kane* (1940) is regarded as a classic of its kind. In the course of the film, Kane's second wife, Susan Alexander, is due to make her (disastrous) debut in opera and for that sequence Herrmann composed a clever and extremely effective pastiche of the type of showy aria you'd hear in a nineteenth century opera - too demanding for a second-rate voice to sing and one which brilliantly underlined Susan's inadequacy in the film. But when you hear the whole thing sung by Kiri te Kanawa... wow!

JONNY HEYKENS
1884-1945
SERENADE
(1920)

O

One of those quintessential pieces of light music you know so well but can never put a name to. Known simply as *Heykens' Serenade*, it was enormously popular between the two Wars, having been penned in 1920 by this Dutch violinist and composer. It was his one big hit, played by all the light orchestras and even recorded as a song ('Starlight Serenade') in 1940 by the great tenor Richard Tauber.

GUSTAV HOLST
1874-1934
ENGLISH
FUGAL CONCERTO
FOR FLUTE, OBOE
AND STRINGS
(1923)

C

Don't let the rather portentous title put you off. This is a delightful little work for an unusual combination. Holst himself described it as 'the world's shortest concerto'. He sketched the piece in April 1923 while crossing the Atlantic on board the *Aquitania*, finished it in the States and had it performed by members of the Chicago Symphony Orchestra during the same visit. There's a fugue in each of the three movements, the last one includes a version of the country dance tune *If all the world were paper*.

One of English music's twentieth century masterpieces, this seven-movement orchestral suite was suggested (in Holst's words) 'by the astrological significance of the planets'. In other words they are not intended to portray the deities after whom they are named. The subtitles of each section confirms what Holst was on about: 1. *Mars, the Bringer of War.* 2. *Venus, the Bringer of Peace.* 3. *Mercury, the Winged Messenger.* 4. *Jupiter, the Bringer of Jollity.* 5. *Saturn, the Bringer of Old Age.* 6. *Uranus, the Magician.* 7. *Neptune, the Mystic.* (Pluto had not been discovered when Holst composed the work between 1914 and 1916 and which was first performed complete in 1920.) The best-known section is *Jupiter* which contains a tune also known as *Thaxted* (an Essex town where Holst played the organ) to which the hymn 'I vow to thee, my country' is sung.

HOLST
THE PLANETS
(1914-16)

O

Holst was an inspirational teacher, perhaps most notably at St. Paul's Girls' School, Hammersmith (London) where he was director of music from 1905 till his death in 1934. The Suite, written for the St. Paul's orchestra, is typical of his ingenuity in writing fine music for amateur players that was within their capabilities yet would also stretch them. A mood of innocence and English folk-song pervades the score (the last movement is a clever combination of the the old dance tune *Dargason* with 'Greensleeves'), while the Intermezzo includes a melody Holst picked up in Algeria.

HOLST
ST. PAUL'S SUITE
(1913)

O

Mouvement symphonique No. 1 (to give it its French sub-title) is a musical picture of a steam locomotive, the best-known and most realistic example in music. *Pacific 231* was an American class of train designated 2-3-1 by the number of its axles (in Britain, where we count the wheels instead, it would be a 4-6-2). The Franco-Swiss Honegger had a passionate love of steam locomotives all his life and set down this vivid impression of 300 tons of metal getting up steam, moving off on its journey and finally snorting, grinding and squealing to a halt. *Mouvement symphonique No. 2* is called *Rugby* - a musical depiction of the game. There's also a third *Mouvement* which has no other title.

ARTHUR HONEGGER
1892-1955
FRENCH-SWISS
PACIFIC 231
(1923)

O

JOHANN NEPOMUK HUMMEL
1778-1837
GERMAN
BASSOON CONCERTO IN F
(c. 1805)

C

The three greatest bassoon concertos (Mozart's, Hummel's and Weber's) were all written within 50 years of each other, 1774-1822. Strange that the instrument's lyrical and comedic potential have not attracted more composers. Hummel's is a refined work combining virtuosity with drama and flowing melodies, the last of its three movements an irresistible, perky rondo. It was composed in about 1805 but remained almost completely forgotten until a modern edition of the music appeared in 1957.

HUMMEL
PIANO CONCERTO IN A MINOR
(1821)

C

Hummel, like Mozart, was a child prodigy pianist and toured Europe as a youngster with his father. He was adjudged to be among the finest of living pianists, the equal even of Beethoven (they were pupils together under Albrechtsberger). His piano concertos stand somewhere between Mozart and Chopin - in other words, there is Mozart's delicacy and melodic invention, some of Beethoven's gravitas and a surprising amount of music that anticipates Chopin (the A Minor Concerto was written eight years before Chopin's First Concerto).

HUMMEL
PIANO CONCERTO IN B MINOR
(1819)

C

The A Minor and B Minor Concertos had rarely been heard this century before they appeared on an award-winning recording by the young English pianist Stephen Hough in 1986. It was a good example of a recording persuasively reclaiming unjustly neglected music and allowing us to re-evaluate and hear with fresh ears music that had been condemned as slight and superficial. Both are technically highly demanding works but no one could deny their originality, quality, high good spirits and memorable themes.

Some idiot in the first edition (1889) of Grove, the famous music dictionary, opined that Hummel was 'quite incapable of humour or passion, but fully equipped with every musical virtue that can be acquired by steady plodding, he appears expressly to be cut out for the hero of respectable mediocrity'. The writer had clearly never heard this outstanding chamber work scored for piano and string quartet - the finale, especially, will send you on your way rejoicing.

HUMMEL
PIANO QUINTET
IN E FLAT
(1802)

CH

For this septet, Hummel replaces the oboe and viola with the clarinet and (making its first appearance in chamber music) trumpet - listen to Saint-Saëns' later Septet and you'll see where he got the idea from. Again, there are fizzing outer movements (the piano writing in the finale looks forward to Mendelssohn) with an elegiac slow movement and humorous minuet/scherzo. Look out too for Hummel's piano trios, seven more neglected gems of chamber music.

HUMMEL
PIANO SEPTET IN C
'MILITARY'
(1829)

CH

Hummel is fairly placed to win the 'most underrated composer of the first half of the Nineteenth Century' award. This was the work that established Hummel's reputation in his own lifetime. It was composed in 1806, scored for piano, flute, oboe, French horn, viola, cello and double bass, and for the next 100 years was one of the most popular of all chamber works. Why it is so rarely heard these days is a mystery with its exuberant first movement (dominated by the piano), minuet (really a scherzo), andante (a set of variations) and vigorous rondo finale.

HUMMEL
PIANO SEPTET IN D
MINOR
(1806)

CH

**HUMMEL
TRUMPET
CONCERTO IN E
FLAT**
(1803)

C

Hummel, pupil of Mozart and Albrechtsberger, also studied for a time with Haydn. His trumpet concerto was written in 1803 for the same virtuoso, Anton Weidlinger, for whom Haydn had written his famous E Flat Concerto seven years earlier. On the eve that Hummel took over from Haydn as Kapellmeister to the Eisenstadt court (New Year's Day, 1804), he and Weidlinger gave the first performance of this brilliant concerto. You could dance the polka to the final movement, a breathtaking display, deservedly popular on Classic FM.

**ENGELBERT
HUMPERDINCK
(1854-1921)**
GERMAN
DANCE DUET
*from Hansel and Gretel
(1893)*

OP

No, not the hirsute purveyor of 'Please release me' who changed his name from Arnold Dorsey, but the German-born composer whose one big international success this opera was. It was based on the tale by the Brothers Grimm, and Humperdinck provided a suitably fairy-tale-folk-tune inspired score which has enchanted generations since it was first performed. Try as he wanted, Humperdinck was never able to repeat the triumph. The Dance Duet, in which the two children sing 'Brother come and dance with me', was made familiar to thousands of non-opera-goers by the famous recording made in 1929 by the Manchester Schoolchildren's Choir. It has rarely been out of the catalogue since.

**HUMPERDINCK
EVENING PRAYER**
*from Hansel and Gretel
(1893)*

OP

♥

In Act 2, the two children have spent the day looking for strawberries in the forest. Suddenly they become aware of the gathering darkness, realise they are lost and start to panic. At the height of their terror, the Sandman appears through the rising mist and, having gained their confidence, drops into the children's eyes magic grains that bring deep sleep. Gradually, Hansel and Gretel grow calmer. They kneel and sing the famous 'Evening Prayer' ('Abenslied') about the 14 angels who gather in pairs around their bed to guard them while they sleep. 'Abends, will ich schlafen gehn' ('When at night I go to sleep') is an enchanting duet, a hymn of innocence at the end of which the orchestra echoes the prayer's theme as darkness falls and Hansel and Gretel fall asleep on the moss clasped in each other's arms.

I

Like many French composers of his generation, Ibert preferred the musical chuckle to the furrowed brow, and in this suite drawn from the incidental music he wrote for a production of the play *Le Chapeau de paille d'Italie* (*The Italian Straw Hat*), he indulges his taste for comedy. First heard in Paris in 1930, its six movements include send-ups of Mendelssohn's *Wedding March* (raspberries from the trombones), Johann Strauss's *Blue Danube Waltz* and Offenbach's Cancan. It's a riot!

**JACQUES IBERT
(1890–1962)**
FRENCH
DIVERTISSEMENT
(1930)

O

♪

The title translates as *Ports of Call.* During his tour of duty in the French Navy during World War I, Ibert visited many Mediterranean ports and in 1922 was inspired to write a suite of orchestral pieces reflecting the different atmosphere and character of three of them – Palermo, Tunis-Nefta and Valencia: colourful picture postcards which were heard for the first time in Paris in 1924. Ibert himself made a recording of them in 1954.

IBERT
ESCALES
(1924)

O

♪

The French title for this beguiling three-movement work for piano and orchestra is *Symphonie sur un chant montagnard 'Cévenole'.* It's the one work of d'Indy that is heard regularly today. As a teenager he visited the Cévennes area of France (the French Alps) for the first time and was so impressed that he went back at least once a year for the rest of his life. He built up a collection of Cévenole songs and one particular one, a shepherd's song, appears in different guises throughout this wonderfully-evocative work. If you like *Songs of the Auvergne* (Canteloube) you'll go for this too.

**VINCENT D'INDY
1851–1931**
FRENCH
SYMPHONY ON A
FRENCH
MOUNTAIN SONG
(1886)

C

♥

**MIKHAIL
IPPOLITOV-IVANOV
1859-1935**
RUSSIAN
CAUCASIAN
SKETCHES
(1894)

O

♥

A pupil of Rimsky-Korsakov, Ippolitov-Ivanov rose to great eminence in Russian musical circles and was even able to maintain his prestige under the Soviet regime, ending up as Director of the Moscow Conservatoire. While conductor of the symphony concerts in Tiflis he made a penetrating study of the folk music of the Caucasus, wrote exhaustively on the subject and composed this suite, once the staple diet of orchestras everywhere. Its four parts depict *In the Mountain Pass*, *In the Village*, *In the Mosque* and (most popular) *March of the Sirdar* (an Oriental commander-in-chief) with tunes derived from war songs and marches of western Armenia.

**JOHN IRELAND
1879-1962**
ENGLISH
GREATER LOVE
HATH NO MAN
(1912)
and other works

CHO

Ireland's music is varied and unpredictable - his best known piece is his setting of John Masefield's poem 'Sea Fever', while there's also a rousing *London Overture* and an attractive piano concerto. Among his many hymns and choral works, this brief but powerful motet for soprano, baritone and chorus stands out. Written for the choristers of St. Paul's Cathedral, it takes its text from a selection of verses from the New Testament but opens with words from *The Song of Solomon*.

**CHARLES IVES
1874-1954**
AMERICAN
VARIATIONS ON
'AMERICA'
(1891)

I

Ives' most frequently performed piece of music was written for the organ when he was just 17 (though listening to the treatment of the theme it's hard to believe it wasn't written yesterday) and gives a strong hint of the wildly unconventional orchestral and instrumental music that was to follow. Here is our national anthem (which the Americans pinched for their own ends in the 1830s and added different words) subjected to a series of extravagant variations. At turns imposing, whimsical, humorous and silly, it's great fun... for the first couple of hearings.

J

Janáček was not a religious man (he described churches as 'concentrated death') and showed little interest in writing sacred music. However, as a fervent Czech nationalist he loved the language of the *Old Church Slavonic Mass*, a text rendered into Slav by the ninth century missionaries Cyril and Methodius. The result was this celebratory choral masterpiece - lashings of brass fanfares and bursting with energy - which he composed towards the end of his life. *Glagolitic*, by the way, simply means 'pertaining to Glagol', the ancient Slavonic alphabet.

**LEŎS JANÁČEK
1854–1928**
CZECH
GLAGOLITIC MASS
(1926)

CHO

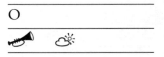

Dedicated to 'the free Czech men and women of today', the bright, optimistic Sinfonietta was inspired initially by a fanfare Janáček had written for a gymnastic festival in Prague in 1926. The fanfare became the musical material for the first movement and the end of its final (fifth) movement. Moravian folk tunes and dance rhythms reflect Janáček's deeply-felt pride in his country's new-found independence - the Czech Republic had been founded in 1918.

**JANÁČEK
SINFONIETTA**
(1926)

O

Janáček composed this three-movement symphonic rhapsody intending it not only as an act of homage to the Russian troops whom he hoped would free his country from Habsburg rule, but also to encourage his compatriots' struggle for independence. Murder, revenge, torture and execution are the order of the day, for the subject of the music (based on a novel by Gogol) is the seventeenth century Cossack leader Taras Bulba, who died a hero's death fighting the Poles in 1628. A doom-laden work but one which ends radiantly as Taras Bulba joins the angels.

**JANÁČEK
TARAS BULBA**
(1915-18)

O

ARMAS JÄRNEFELT
1869-1958
FINNISH
PRAELUDIUM
(1900)

O

☁

Järnefelt (a minor composer who was Sibelius's brother-in-law) is one of those whose name is remembered because of a single work - and this one lasts all of two and a half minutes. His *Praeludium*, written for a small orchestra, begins in jogging tempo with plucked strings underneath a catchy oboe tune. It was played all over the world and, in the oh-so-charming words of one reference book, 'made [Järnefelt's] name known even amongst simple-minded music-lovers'.

KARL JENKINS
B. 1944
ADIEMUS
from Songs of Sanctuary
(1995)

CHO

🕯 ☁

Of Welsh and Swedish parentage (he hails from the Gower Peninsula), Jenkins has embraced the classical, jazz and rock worlds during his performing career - principal oboe in the National Youth Orchestra, jazz saxophonist and member of the progressive seventies band Soft Machine. *Songs of Sanctuary*, an extended song cycle for voice, percussion and string orchestra, uses the musical language of the European classical tradition combined with ethnic/world music ideas. It topped the classical and pop charts in Europe and Japan. The *Adiemus* section achieved even greater popularity from its use in an airline commercial and boosted it high into the Classic FM Hall of Fame.

JENKINS
ADIEMUS II
'CANTATA MUNDI'
(1996)

CHO

🕯 ☁

Cantata means a piece that is sung (as opposed to a sonata, which is played), usually by a chorus and containing several movements; *mundi* means 'of the world'. Using the same devices as in *Songs of Sanctuary* (European classical music with an invented language for the text using Eastern European, Arabic, Celtic and African sounds), Jenkins adds woodwind, brass and an augmented percussion section to the strings. Not so much a development as a re-visit to the same country.

JENKINS
IMAGINED OCEANS
(1998)

CHO

🕯 ☁

Contemporary pastiche of Vivaldi, Bach, Fauré and others, combined with the instrumental and vocal techniques used in *Adiemus* (though here Jenkins uses fragments of Latin for his words). This is 'a musical interpretation of 13 of the Latin titles given to what was believed to be areas of water on the Moon' - an attractive idea resulting in some pretty music. Whether or not Jenkins' music will retain its current appeal only Time will tell.

More pastiche - three-movements for string orchestra in the style of a Baroque Italian concerto, a work inspired, according to the composer, by the renowned Italian architect Andrea Palladio (1508-80), though there is nothing of the Sixteenth Century reflected in the music. Jenkins' score is attractive enough and uses the musical language of the Eighteenth Century, reminiscent of Vivaldi and Albinoni, for inspiration.

JENKINS
PALLADIO
(1995)

O

Jessel, a theatre conductor and composer of operettas, wrote this little march originally as a piano piece entitled *Parade der Zinnsoldaten* (his Op. 123). Its orchestral version (1911) became familiar to thousands after the Second World War as the signature tune of BBC Radio's *Toytown* series on *Children's Hour* (remember? - the one with Larry the Lamb and Mr Mayor).

LÉON JESSEL
1871-1942
GERMAN
PARADE OF THE TIN SOLDIERS
(1905)

O

One of that rare breed of 'famous Belgians', Jongen's finest piece of music is this powerful work for organ and orchestra. The first three movements have elements of Vierne and Fauré, as well as looking forward to Duruflé, Messiaen and the Organ Concerto of Francis Poulenc. The final movement is a rip-roaring, non-stop-whirlwind toccata with all the stops pulled out and the orchestra in full cry. It comes as a surprise that a director of the Brussels Conservatoire could have so much fun. The recording to get is by Virgil Fox who did much to popularise the work in America.

JOSEPH JONGEN
1873-1953
BELGIAN
SYMPHONIE CONCERTANTE
(1926)

C

SCOTT JOPLIN
1868-1917
AMERICAN
PIANO RAGS
(1899-1914)

I

♪ ♥

As one noted music historian put it, Joplin's piano rags are 'the precise American equivalent in terms of native dance music of minuets by Mozart, mazurkas by Chopin or waltzes by Brahms'. Joplin's first success was with *Maple Leaf Rag* (1899, and still the most popular of all piano rags) and he went on to attempt what Gershwin was later to do – marry European classical and American popular music (his ragtime opera *Treemonisha* is an ingenuous example). Like Gershwin, he died before fulfilling his potential. All but forgotten before the 1974 film *The Sting* revived his 1905 ragtime two-step *The Entertainer*, Joplin became a cult figure and his music widely played once more. Some of the best of the others are: *Elite Syncopations*, *Gladiolus Rag*, *Solace*, *Paragon Rag*, *The Ragtime Dance* and *The Easy Winners*.

K

DMITRI KABALEVSKY
1904-87
RUSSIAN
Galop from
THE COMEDIANS
(1940)

O

♪

Kabalevsky wrote some wonderful music for children to play – as well as for children's plays. This suite is taken from the incidental music for one of them, *The Inventor and the Comedians*. Ten brief contrasting movements reveal Kabalevsky's gift for humour, melody, gentle lyricism and joy. The frenetic Galop is almost as popular as Khachaturian's *Sabre Dance*.

KABALEVSKY
Overture to
COLAS BREUGNON
Opera
(1937)

O

♪

One of the first composers educated under the Soviet system, Kabalevsky was a musical conservative whose musical language was that of the previous century (Tchaikovsky was his greatest influence), and who was therefore the ideal 'Soviet composer'. He wrote an opera called *Colas Breugnon* based on a short novel by the French writer Romain Rolland (an approved Soviet writer). The Overture serves as an exuberant portrait of the opera's hero, a crafty Burgundian rogue of the Sixteenth Century who loved the good things of life.

One of a *Youth Trilogy* comprising the Violin Concerto (1948) and Cello Concerto (1949), Kabalevsky's Third Piano Concerto (1952) was written for students to play but, like all good works of its kind, transcends the purpose for which it was conceived. From its opening bars, the Concerto sparkles with life, energy, memorable themes and ideas, notably the incisive use of percussion. Far from profound, but uninhibited fun.

KABALEVSKY
PIANO CONCERTO NO. 3 IN D 'YOUTH'
(1952)

C

Heavyweight organist and composer Karg-Elert (his original name was Karg, which means 'avaricious' - so he changed it) wrote a series of 66 *Choral Improvisations* between 1908 and 1910. In other words, rather like Bach before him, he'd take a hymn tune and weave his own music round it. This one, No. 51, is based on the tune we know as *Now thank we all our God*, though it's cleverly hidden in Karg-Elert's version. If you like a grand, exultant processional march on the organ, and if you want to be different, it's a good choice for going down the aisle.

SIGFRID KARG-ELERT 1877-1933
GERMAN
MARCHE TRIOMPHALE - NUN DANKET ALLE GOTT
(1910)

I

Despite his French-looking surname, Ketèlbey was actually born in Birmingham. It's a name that always raises a mocking smile among the stuffier critics because of the series of short, tuneful and sentimental pieces of light music he wrote with exotic titles, among them *In a Persian Market*, *Bells Across the Meadows*, *In a Monastery Garden* and this one. They are completely unfashionable now but in their day (the 1920s and 1930s) were immensely popular and deserve a little corner to themselves today. *Sanctuary of the Heart* (subtitled *Méditation religieuse*), sometimes performed with vocal chorus, is unashamed kitsch but a cracking good tune.

ALBERT KETÈLBEY 1885-1959
ENGLISH
SANCTUARY OF THE HEART
(1924)
and other works

O

**ARAM
KHACHATURIAN
1903–78**
RUSSIAN-ARMENIAN
Adagio from
SPARTACUS
*Ballet
(1956)*

O

♥

Most of us hearing this will recognise it as the theme from *The Onedin Line*, BBC Television's long-running family shipping saga of the 1970s. The Adagio is in fact a love duet danced by Spartacus and his wife Phrygia from the ballet Khachaturian first composed in 1956 for the Leningrad Kirov Ballet (he revised it for the Bolshoi Ballet's visit to London in 1969). It tells the story of the slave revolt in 73BC against the Romans by the Thracian Spartacus.

KHACHATURIAN
DANCE OF THE
YOUNG MAIDENS
and
SABRE DANCE
*from Gayaneh
(1942)*

O

The *Sabre Dance* from this ballet made Khachaturian's name world-famous - it's been arranged and transcribed for every possible instrument and instrumental combination (my favourite is an outlandish virtuoso piano solo version by George Cziffra). It is the celebratory dance in the last act of the ballet which tells the story of Gayaneh (the worker-heroine of the title) who works on a collective farm in Armenia and wins the love of a young frontier-guard commander in the Red Army. The folk-style *Dance of the Young Maidens* sets the scene before the festive finale.

KHACHATURIAN
PIANO CONCERTO
IN D FLAT
(1936)

C

This is the work by which Khachaturian's name became known in the West when the pianist Moura Lympany introduced the work in 1940. It had been completed four years earlier by this Soviet-approved composer, and is an exotic, fiery, rhythmically-exuberant work in which Liszt meets Borodin and Prokofiev. There are no actual folk tunes quoted in the work but there are many themes that echo the spirit of Armenian music, and the whole work has an Oriental flavour. The slow movement features the unusual and ghostly sound of the *flexatone*, a kind of sophisticated musical saw.

Here is Khachaturian as light music composer, for *Masquerade* is a suite fashioned from the incidental music he wrote for a production of *Masquerade*, a play by Mikhail Lermontov (1814-41) about the upper classes of Russia in 1830. The opening Waltz, very much in the style of Tchaikovsky, is the most popular of the five sections with the final Galop coming a close second.

KHACHATURIAN
Waltz and Galop from
MASQUERADE
(1940)

O

Háry János, a boastful, pompous liar, is a familiar figure in Hungarian folklore and in this, his most famous work, Kodály turned the story into a comic opera (first seen in Budapest in 1926). The music is better known through the *Háry János Suite* which opens with an orchestral 'sneeze', for Hungarian legend has it that if someone sneezes while a tale is being told, the story must be true. The six movements include *Viennese Clock* (Háry visits Vienna and stands entranced by the musical clock and its mechanical figures) and the Intermezzo, an electrifying Hungarian dance in the best tradition.

ZOLTÁN KODÁLY
1882-1967
HUNGARIAN
VIENNESE CLOCK
and
INTERMEZZO
*from Háry János
Opera
(1926)*

O

Robin Hood was Warner Brothers' most ambitious and expensive production to date. It starred Errol Flynn, Olivia de Havilland and Basil Rathbone at his villainous best as Sir Guy of Gisbourne. From its frequent television showings, this is Korngold's most celebrated film score and he won his second Academy Award for it. It was with music like this that Korngold set the standards for film music with his innate ability to give impetus to the action and at the same time colour character and situation.

**ERICH WOLFGANG
KORNGOLD
1897-1957**
AUSTRO–HUNGARIAN–
AMERICAN
THE ADVENTURES
OF ROBIN HOOD
*Film
(1938)*

O

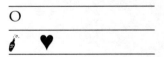

KORNGOLD
'GLÜCK DAS MIR
VERBLIEB'
*from Die tote Stadt
(1920)*

OP

♥

Korngold was hardly out of his teens when he began work on his opera *The Dead City*, the jolly tale of Paul who, in a nutshell, strangles a dancer (Marietta) whom he thinks is his late wife after she (Marietta) has been unfaithful to him. But it's all a dream. Thank heavens. It's a lush, romantic score that puts you in mind of Richard Strauss and Puccini (both of whom greatly admired it) and the vocal highpoint is this exquisitely-beautiful duet in Act 1, sung by the two protagonists. It was one of the sequence of opera arias filmed in Don Boyd's intriguing 1987 movie *Aria*.

KORNGOLD
KING'S ROW
*Film
(1942)*

O

♪ ♥

The tenth of Korngold's 16 full length film scores was for one of Warner Brothers' greatest films and contains his best known title theme. Released in 1942 and starring Ann Sheridan, Robert Cummings and the young Ronald Reagan, the film takes place in a small mid-Western town which Korngold reflects in just the right note of bitter-sweet nostalgia, able to conjure up an American setting as masterfully as he produced an English 'feel' in other films.

KORNGOLD
MUCH ADO ABOUT
NOTHING
*Suite
(1920)*

O

♪

Before he went to Hollywood in 1934, Korngold was revered as one of the most important contemporary composers in Europe. Operas, symphonic works and instrumental works of all kinds flowed from the pen of this amazing child prodigy. In 1919 he wrote the music for a production in Vienna of Shakespeare's play *Much Ado About Nothing*. The five short movements of the concert suite he produced are a delight (*Overture, Bridal Morning, Dogberry and Verges, Intermezzo* and *Masquerade*), full of wit and gaiety. A good one with which to begin investigating Korngold's non-Hollywood music.

This is the one with Bette Davis as Queen Elizabeth I and Errol Flynn as the Earl of Essex (Olivia de Havilland and Vincent Price were also in the cast). The tragic romance between Elizabeth and Essex appealed to Korngold and this 1939 score with its poignant melodies and dramatic power won him a third Academy Award. He also composed specially for the film's première an overture using the film's main themes. The conductor Charles Gerhardt, the man who did more than anyone to champion Korngold's film music, made a fine recording of this – and much else of this great composer's movie music.

KORNGOLD
THE PRIVATE LIVES OF ELIZABETH AND ESSEX
Film
(1939)

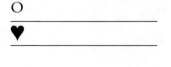

Korngold's film music was richly orchestrated in the Wagner-Richard Strauss-Mahler-Puccini tradition and never to better effect than in this score for what was to be Korngold's last historical swashbuckling movie (it was the sixth of this type, all starring Erroll Flynn). For this one, he needed to capture the grand sweep of sixteenth century England, the Spanish Armada and the escapades of Sir Francis Drake (Flynn) in the service of Queen Elizabeth (Flora Robson on this occasion). Even when the privateers are set free and sing (in harmony) a rollicking operatic chorus as they catch sight of Dover, Korngold convinces you that they might have done just that.

KORNGOLD
THE SEA HAWK
Film
(1940)

Korngold turned 50 in 1947 and had announced his retirement from Hollywood when he suffered a major heart attack. The *Symphonic Serenade* was composed while he was recuperating. It's in four movements and is as long as a symphony, opening with an innocent Viennese theme (that soon becomes transformed into an aggressive one). The Intermezzo that follows is a furiously fast pizzicato movement, after which the magical, moving slow movement unfolds with unbearable intensity. The final section's *perpetuum mobile* is interrupted by a rapturous theme that reminds us of Korngold's gift as one of the most inspired of all twentieth century melodists. Surprisingly, this masterly score, premièred in 1950 by Furtwängler and the Vienna Philharmonic, is rarely heard in the concert hall.

KORNGOLD
SYMPHONIC SERENADE IN B FLAT
(1950)

**KORNGOLD
SYMPHONY IN F
SHARP
*(1950)***

O

♥ ☀

Apart from its unusual key of F sharp major, the Symphony is written in the same tradition as the great symphonists of the past (in four movements) with Korngold's own special brand of Romanticism and glorious themes. At its heart is the sublime slow movement, with a tune that could have come straight out of one of his Hollywood film scores. Conductor Dmitri Mitropoulos wrote, 'All my life I have searched for the perfect modern work. In his symphony I have found it.' Korngold dedicated it to the memory of Franklin D. Roosevelt.

**KORNGOLD
VIOLIN CONCERTO
IN D
*(1945)***

C

♥ ☀

Some critics still look down their noses at this wonderful work - 'more corn than gold' is their little joke about it. Why? Because of its unabashed heart-on-sleeve emotion and because its themes are film themes. Korngold wrote the Concerto for the celebrated violinist Bronislav Hubermann who, alas, died before playing it. It was then taken up by Jascha Heifetz (whose recording of it remains peerless - try the yearning slow movement) and subsequently many other violinists. So when you hear Korngold's Concerto and also happen to catch on television *Another Dawn, Juarez, Anthony Adverse* and *The Prince and the Pauper* (all Korngold scores), you'll know where its themes come from.

**FRITZ KREISLER
1875-1962
AUSTRIAN-AMERICAN
VIOLIN PIECES
*(c. 1905)***

I

♥ ☀

Kreisler was one of the most acclaimed and certainly the most beloved of all violinists during the first half of the Twentieth Century, an artist whose humanity and generosity of spirit is tangible even in his recordings. He composed many charming short pieces for his instrument, among them *Liebesleid, Liebesfreud* and *Schön Rosmarin* which appeared in 1905. Kreisler announced that they were 'folk melodies' by the Viennese composer Joseph Lanner, the man who, with Johann Strauss I, is credited with the popularisation of the Viennese waltz. Rachmaninov made celebrated piano transcriptions of *Liebesleid* and *Liebesfreud*. Similarly, another short work, *Praeludium and Allegro* was one of many pieces 'in the olden style' purportedly by minor classical masters of the past, which Kreisler 'discovered and edited'. This one was allegedly by

Pugnani (others were by Francoeur, Martini, Couperin, Boccherini and Dittersdorf). Kreisler was eventually revealed as the sole source of these pieces, a hoax he perpetuated until 1935 when he 'owned up'. He also issued compositions under his own name. *Caprice viennois* and *Tambourin chinois* are two of them, perhaps his most popular. A *caprice* is a light whimsical piece - so *Viennese Caprice* (Kreisler himself recorded it six times); *Tambourin chinois* translates as *Chinese Drum*, much requested on Classic FM.

L

Lalo was over 50 before he had any great success as a composer and it was with this work that he finally made it. It's called a 'symphony' but is really a five-movement violin concerto (though the third movement, Intermezzo, is generally omitted today, considered of inferior quality to the rest of the music). Lalo had written a formally-entitled violin concerto earlier in the same year (1873) and dedicated it to the great Spanish violinist Sarasate. Bearing in mind Sarasate's nationality, Lalo wrote this *symphonie* for him too - hence the pronounced Spanish flavour of the themes and rhythms.

EDOUARD LALO
1823–92
FRENCH
SYMPHONIE
ESPAGNOLE
(1873)

C

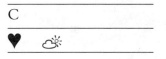

Lambert, a pupil of Vaughan Williams, spent much of his career composing and conducting ballets, but he wrote a number of other works unconnected with dance of which Rio Grande is not only the most successful but a minor masterpiece. It's a setting of Sacheverell Sitwell's poem, for mezzo-soprano, chorus, piano and orchestra (using a vast array of percussion), in a single movement and which Lambert wrote in 1927 when he was only 22. If you like works of jazzy exuberance, the rhythms of South America and music with an immediately likeable lyrical warmth then Rio Grande is irresistible.

CONSTANT LAMBERT
1905–51
ENGLISH
RIO GRANDE
(1927)

CHO

**LOUIS LEFÉBURE-
WÉLY
1817-69**
FRENCH
SORTIE IN B FLAT
(c. 1860)

I

♪

Sortie is the French for a voluntary (organ solo) at the end of a service and this one is guaranteed to send you out with a smile on your face. Though written in the mid-Nineteenth Century, it sounds like an American fairground organ playing ragtime, quite a contrast to the respectable solemnity of César Franck and Lefébure-Wély's other contemporaries. The composer was reckoned to be one of the finest organists of the day and it was he who played the organ at Chopin's funeral. Today, his tombstone in Paris's Père-Lachaise cemetery is worn and neglected.

**FRANZ LEHÁR
1870-1948**
AUSTRO-HUNGARIAN
GOLD AND SILVER
WALTZ
(1902)

O

♥

Before the theatre dominated Lehár's attention, he wrote many concert works and songs. One of these is a waltz which closely rivals the *Merry Widow Waltz* in popularity and helped make him famous. It was composed not as part of an operetta but as a straightforward concert work for an elaborate ball given by Princess Metternich in January 1902. Lehár was an authoritative conductor and made many fine recordings of his music including, in 1947, one of the *Gold and Silver Waltz*.

LEHÁR
THE MERRY WIDOW
*Operetta
(1905)*

OP

♥

The musical heir to Johann Strauss II and the last of the great Viennese operetta composers, Lehár brought a blend of nostalgia and sophisticated humour to the frivolous world of operetta, which suited perfectly the spirit of privileged gaiety in Vienna at the turn of the last century. *Die Lustige Witwe* (its German title) was an instant hit when it was first performed in 1905 - and within 12 months had been performed more than 5,000 times in the United States alone. In Buenos Aires, five different productions were playing simultaneously in five different languages. Eat your heart out, Andrew Lloyd Webber. It made Lehár an international name and a dollar millionaire by the time he was 35. Its two most popular vocal numbers are: 'Vilja Song' (Hanna's solo from Act 1 - 'Vilia, oh Vilia, you witch of the woods' - when she reminds her guests of her native land); 'Lippen schweigen' ('Love Unspoken'), the lovely duet near the end of the opera, perhaps only second to the *Blue Danube* as the most beloved of waltz tunes.

Frequently heard separately to the operetta, the Overture is a potpourri of the main melodies with the famous waltz at its centre. Lehár wrote two versions, one for the original 1905 production, then a second in 1940 with more ambitious orchestration which Lehár dedicated to the Führer. It was Hitler's favourite operetta but whether the dedication was an act of homage or an effort to save his Jewish wife from the Gestapo is questionable.

LEHÁR
Overture to
THE MERRY WIDOW
(1905 and 1940)

O

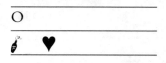 ♥

Many of Lehár's later operettas were specifically tailored to the magnetic personality and lyric tenor voice of Richard Tauber (1891-1948). The Tauber numbers (*Tauberlied*) were always the highspots - the Serenade from *Frasquita*, 'Girls were made to love and kiss' from *Paganini* and 'O maiden, my maiden' from *Friederike* are some of the best known. The all-time favourite, though, is 'You are my heart's delight' which Tauber is said to have sung over 3,000 times - and no one has ever done it better (for proof, you can hear Tauber conducted by Lehár on a disc made back in 1929).

LEHÁR
'YOU ARE MY HEART'S DELIGHT'
from The Land of Smiles Operetta
(1929)

OP

♥

Lemare (born on the Isle of Wight, died in Los Angeles) was regarded as the greatest organist of his day. He must have been remarkable judging from his ingenious and very difficult transcriptions of standard orchestral works arranged for the organ. His own compositions vary from the striking and distinguished to the second-rate and banal. Lemare's *Rondo Capriccio* and *Bell Scherzo* are fine works, but none came anywhere near achieving the popularity of his Andantino - everyone played it, either on the organ, the piano, or the violin. To Lemare's chagrin it was given a new lease of life in 1925 when two American songwriters added lyrics and called it 'Moonlight and Roses'. Lemare made a dim-sounding recording of the Andantino - and wrote an immensely dull autobiography wondrously entitled *Organs I Have Met*.

EDWIN LEMARE
1865-1935
ENGLISH
ANDANTINO IN D FLAT
(1892)

I

♥

RUGGIERO LEONCAVALLO 1858–1919
ITALIAN
'MATTINATA'
(1904)

V

Is there a tenor dead or alive who hasn't sung this ever-popular number, the quintessential Neapolitan folk-song? Leoncavallo provided his own words when he wrote it, more than a decade after the triumph of *Pagliacci*, and also made a record of it the same year with a young tenor named Enrico Caruso, bashing out the accompaniment on the piano with more enthusiasm than subtlety.

LEONCAVALLO
'VESTI LA GIUBBA'
from Pagliacci
(1892)

OP

♥

The first performance of *Pagliacci* (*Clowns*) was conducted by Toscanini in Milan in 1892. Ever since, it has been, with Mascagni's *Cavalleria Rusticana*, the most popular of all one-act operas. 'Vesti la giubba' is one of the greatest tenor arias in opera. It's sung by Canio in Act 1 after he has been told his wife has a lover. 'On with the motley' is how it is usually (but confusingly) sung in English - *motley* is a long-obsolete word describing the kind of multi-coloured costume a clown would wear. When Caruso made a record of the aria in 1902 he became the earliest recorded artist to sell more than a million copies of one disc.

ANATOLI LIADOV 1855–1914
RUSSIAN
THE ENCHANTED LAKE
(1909)

O

♥

My favourite of Liadov's fairy-tale pieces for orchestra is this, in which the shimmering waters of the enchanted lake are magically captured by Liadov, achieving an effect of mysterious tranquillity. This and the other two tone poems (below) were worked together as a ballet by Diaghilev in 1917 entitled *Contes russes* together with Liadov's suite for orchestra entitled *Eight Russian Folk-songs*.

LIADOV
THE MUSIC-BOX
(1893)

I

♥

The son and grandson of eminent Russian conductors, Liadov was a pupil of Rimsky-Korsakov at the St. Petersburg Conservatory (although he was expelled for not attending classes) and later taught Prokofiev. He was at his best as a *miniaturist*, in other words as a composer of short pieces. *The Music-Box* as it's known (but more properly *A Musical Snuff-box*) is an elegant little trifle imitating on the piano the tinkling tune of a music-box.

Liadov was fascinated by Russian folklore. Kikimora is a witch who was nursed in her cradle by a wise cat. For its troubles, the cat is pursued by the evil Kikimora and decapitated. Just the subject for a vivid orchestral showpiece that recalls Dukas' *The Sorcerer's Apprentice*. Liadov wrote another (shorter) 'witch piece' depicting Baba-Yaga, the same character familiar from Mussorgsky's *Pictures at an Exhibition* who lives in a hut supported on fowl's legs.

LIADOV
KIKIMORA
(1909)
and
BABA-YAGA
(1904)

O

♥

♥

Like Liadov, Liapunov was strongly influenced by Russian folk music (and also the works of Liszt, Glinka and Balakirev). The Ukraine was a rich source of material for Russian composers and this one-movement work for piano and orchestra uses folk themes from the area. It's a highly effective mix of contrasted dance rhythms - immediately appealing and culminating in a brilliant whirlwind finale in which the soloist has his work cut out. Fans of virtuoso piano playing should also seek out Liapunov's Piano Concerto No. 2 in E and (especially) his *12 Transcendental Studies*, modelled on Liszt's (see below).

SERGEI LIAPUNOV
1859-1924
RUSSIAN
RHAPSODY ON UKRAINIAN THEMES
(1907)

C

Liszt was not quite 20 when he first heard the fabled Italian violinist Paganini play his first concert in Paris. It made him realise for the first time that flawless virtuosity coupled with dramatic effects and a powerful personality could overwhelm an audience and he set about emulating on the piano what he had heard on the violin. Among the results were five piano versions of Paganini's Caprices for solo violin and a sixth, *La Campanella*, using the theme from the last movement of Paganini's Violin Concerto No. 2 in B minor. Ask any pianist, it's a fearsomely difficult piece to play! *Campanella* is Italian for 'little bell' - and when you listen to the concerto you'll hear one ringing in the orchestra each time the theme is played.

FRANZ LISZT
1811-86
HUNGARIAN
**LA CAMPANELLA
(PAGANINI)**
(1838)

I

**LISZT
CONSOLATION
NO. 3 IN D FLAT
*(1850)***

I

The six short pieces Liszt composed under the title *Consolations* were inspired by the poetry of Charles Sainte-Beuve (1804-69). All of them have an unpretentious, nocturne-like quality and were conceived to be played as a unity. Today, only No. 3 is ever heard regularly, a single work in its own right and among Liszt's most popular.

**LISZT
FAUST WALTZ
(GOUNOD)
*(1861)***

I

Liszt was a great champion of other people's music and made myriad piano transcriptions of orchestral, operatic and instrumental works by fellow composers. Sometimes these are straightforward arrangements without elaboration; at other times he transforms the piece into something grander. One of the finest examples of the latter is his version of the Waltz from Act 2 of Gounod's opera *Faust*. Liszt not only reinvents it as a virtuoso piano solo but captures the dark, demonic side of the opera as well.

**LISZT
FEUX FOLLETS
*from 12 Transcendental
Studies
(1851)***

I

Feux follets is the French equivalent of *Ignis-fatuus* or *Will-o'-the-wisp*, the flickering light from marsh gas (see also Berlioz's *Minuet Will-o'-the-wisp*). So, this is Liszt's attempt to portray the phenomenon on the piano. The result is one of the most taxing and difficult short works in the whole of piano literature. It is No. 5 of a set called *12 Transcendental Studies* in which Liszt threw down a challenge to all other pianists as if to say, 'This is what is now possible on the piano – if you're good enough!'

**LISZT
HUNGARIAN
FANTASY
*(1852)***

C

The correct title for Liszt's most popular piano-and-orchestra work is *Fantasia on Hungarian Folk Themes*. It's actually a version of his *Hungarian Rhapsody No. 14* for piano solo (this same piece became No. 1 in the series of six of the rhapsodies that he chose to orchestrate). The Fantasy begins with an imposing introduction leading to a scintillating czardas and was first performed in 1853 by the pianist Hans von Bülow, the same man who married Liszt's daughter Cosima (1857) and who later, despite being cuckolded by Wagner, was only too happy to continue promoting the music of his rival-in-love.

The rhapsody became a popular musical form because of Liszt and the 20 *Hungarian Rhapsodies* he composed for solo piano. Usually a rhapsody is a free-wheeling, brilliant work with the feeling of improvisation that treats the music in, well, a rhapsodic manner. Liszt made extensive researches into Hungarian folk music. Using Gypsy and Magyar melodies and dance rhythms, he created some of his best-loved compositions. Most begin with the slow, sensual *lassan* section and build up to a pulsating *frissan*, with many abrupt contrasts and changes of tempo and mood along the way. No. 2 in C sharp minor is by far the most famous (some would say hackneyed) but Nos. 9, 12, 14 and 15 are also much played. To hear them at their best, track down the electrifying recordings of them by Georges Cziffra.

LISZT
HUNGARIAN
RHAPSODIES
(1846-85)

Liszt's many études (studies) for the piano opened up new ways of playing the instrument, musical ideas that allowed a wider range of expression. His collection of *3 Études de concert* (S144) are subtitled *Il Lamento, La Leggierezza* and *Un Sospiro*, and just from their titles you can tell what kind of mood Liszt was attempting to paint in keyboard terms: *Lament* (this one is rarely played), *Light, Swift, Delicate* and *A Sigh*.

LISZT
LA LEGGIEREZZA
and
UN SOSPIRO
(1848)

Arguably Liszt's most familiar work and unquestionably among the most popular (and over-played?) of all piano compositions, this is in fact the third and final number of three pieces all bearing the title *Liebestraüme* (*Dreams of Love*). But when we talk of *Liszt's Liebestraüme* it is always No. 3 that is being referred to: the other two are rarely played. All began life as songs (which are never sung nowadays) that Liszt turned into works for solo piano. This *Liebestraüme* is similar in style to a nocturne but with an impassioned middle section.

LISZT
LIEBESTRAÜME
NO. 3 IN A FLAT
(c. 1850)

LISZT
MEPHISTO WALTZ
NO. 1
(1860)

I

This is not like one of Chopin's elegant Parisian waltzes or Johann Strauss's exuberant Viennese soufflés. This is the dance of the Devil (and it's a devil of a job to play, too). Subtitled *The Dance at the Village Inn*, this miniature tone-poem for piano was inspired by Nikolaus Lenau's dramatic poem 'Faust' and, after the daring opening when we hear Mephistopheles tuning up his violin, the amorous Faust dances in mad abandonment with a village beauty, whirling away into the woods.

LISZT
PIANO CONCERTO
NO. 1 IN E FLAT
(1849, rev. 1853 and
1856)

C

You could call the *Liszt Number One* (as it's known in the business) the *brilliant-spectacular Concerto*, while No. 2 (see below) is the *poetic-spiritual* one. No. 1 is the concerto in which, famously, the triangle plays a small but prominent role (in the Scherzo). What was more unusual about the work at the time it was written (1849) is that instead of having three or four separate movements unconnected musically (as in the traditional concerto), Liszt linked them all together by returning to themes he'd used earlier in the Concerto as a kind of unifying element. The work is dedicated to the pianist-composer Henry Litolff (page 185) of *Litolff's Scherzo* fame. The first performance was given in 1851 by Liszt himself with Berlioz conducting and it's still one of the most played of all piano concertos. Apparently Liszt, whenever he played the Concerto, used to sing along with the opening theme, 'Das verseht ihr alle nicht!' ('None of you knows how to do this!')

LISZT
PIANO CONCERTO
NO. 2 IN A
(1839, rev. 1849-61)

C

Liszt developed the one-movement idea with his Second Concerto, but instead of linking three or four movements into one, he wrote in a series of highly-contrasted sections using fewer themes but harking back to them in various guises throughout the work. One critic described it as 'the life and adventures of a melody'. It's in a more pensive, less showy vein than No. 1, though it's not without its flashy moments. Liszt dedicated the work to one of his pupils, Hans von Bronsart (1830-1913), who gave the first performance with Liszt conducting.

This is not just one of Liszt's greatest works but one of the greatest masterpieces for the piano. It lasts about half an hour in one continuous movement (though it's easy to spot the different sections of the traditional sonata: fast-slow-fast) and uses five different themes (or motifs) throughout to weld the Sonata together. You don't need to worry about all that when you hear it though, for the music seems to create its own momentum, carrying you along on an epic journey which Wagner thought 'beyond all conception, beautiful, great, lovely, deep and noble'.

LISZT
PIANO SONATA
IN B MINOR
(1853)

I

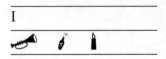

You want a dazzling, pyrotechnical show-stopper? Look no further. The *Spanish Rhapsody* was written during Liszt's tour of Spain (though the music wasn't published until 1887, after his death). It uses two famous Spanish dance tunes - *La Folia* and *Jota Aragonesa*, both of which have inspired many other composers. Superficial and noisy it may be, but there's no doubting the effect when played by a great no-holds-barred pianist like Georges Cziffra or, from a previous generation, Simon Barere. There's also a version for piano and orchestra by Busoni.

LISZT
RAPSODIE
ESPAGNOLE
(1845)

I

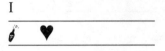

Réminiscences is Liszt's word for *fantasy* and here he does not merely borrow and arrange themes from Mozart's opera *Don Giovanni*, but weaves them into an elaborate tapestry that seems to condense the entire opera. It's an extremely demanding but effective solo (all the great pianists have risen to its challenge) lasting over a quarter of an hour. The effect of hearing Liszt himself play *Don Juan* and other pieces was recorded in 1842 by a young music student in Russia: 'We scarcely exchanged a word [after the concert], but hurried home, each to write down his impressions, dreams and raptures. But we both vowed to keep this anniversary sacred for ever, and never, whilst life lasted to forget a single instant of it.'

LISZT
RÉMINISCENCES
DE DON JUAN
(MOZART)
(1841)

I

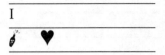

**LISZT
RIGOLETTO
PARAPHRASE
(VERDI)
(1859)**

I

One of Liszt's best known opera transcriptions, there was a time when every pianist had this in his or her repertoire. It's an ingenious piano transformation of the famous (vocal) Quartet from Act 3 of Verdi's *Rigoletto*, ingenious because the piano is a percussive instrument, yet Liszt manages to persuade you that you are listening to four voices accompanied by an orchestra. At the same time, you don't have to know the opera to revel in the acrobatic piano writing.

**LISZT
TOTENTANZ
(1849, rev. 1853 and
1859)**

C

Totentanz means *Dance of Death* and was inspired by a fresco, *The Triumph of Death*, in the Campo Santo in Pisa. It is a single-movement fantasy for piano and orchestra using, as one of its themes, the *Dies Irae* (Latin for *Day of Wrath*), a plainsong tune from the Requiem Mass (Berlioz uses it in his *Symphonie fantastique*, Saint-Saëns in his *Danse Macabre* and Rachmaninov in his *Rhapsody on a Theme of Paganini*). Turn up the stereo full volume - there are spectacular flights of virtuosity from the piano and the whole work exudes terror and diabolism.

**LISZT
WALDESRAUSCHEN
and
GNOMENREIGEN,
S.145
(1862)**

I

Forest Murmurs and *Dance of the Gnomes* are two further *Études de concert* (*Concert Studies*) for piano solo, deservedly popular with pianists and audiences alike. Don't let that forbidding description 'study' put you off - it's true that the studies of lesser composers are strictly finger exercises with no musical content. These are different, almost miniature tone-poems which dazzle the ear (just listen to a great pianist like Sviatoslav Richter play *Gnomenreigen* and you'll hear what I mean).

There is little of Litolff's music available on disc and it's never heard in the concert hall, the sole exception being the occasional outing for this one movement. A pity, because what there is shows a skilful and appealing composer. This scherzo comes from his Fourth Piano Concerto (he called it a *concerto symphonique* to emphasise the equal importance of orchestra and piano). It's unusual in that Litolff includes a triangle and piccolo in the score and introduces a mock-solemn chorale in the middle, offset with some chirpy piano writing.

After his youthful success as a composer before the Second World War, Lloyd suffered a complete lack of interest in his music (it was shamefully blacklisted by the BBC for years because of its conservative nature - i.e. it has tunes). This was offset to some degree by the huge revival of his fortunes in the decade or so before his death. This glorious work, commissioned for the 1993 Brighton Festival, is already well on its way to becoming one of the favourite choral works of the past 50 years, thanks in no large measure to Classic FM, the first radio station to broadcast it. The same melody links the work, with a powerful setting of the words of the *Sanctus* in the middle and ending with a touching *Dona nobis pacem*.

Long before his immersion in the West End and Broadway, Lloyd Webber was thoroughly at home with the Anglican choral tradition - regular services in Westminster Abbey and the influence of his composer father William saw to that. The *Requiem*, written in memory of his father, features boy treble, high soprano and tenor soloists, chorus, organ and orchestra and is a dark, subdued and sombre piece, except for the athletic *Hosanna*. The treble/soprano setting of *Pie Jesu* is, justifiably, the 'hit' of the score, a beautifully-judged and imaginative passage likely to have a longer shelf life than the rest of the work.

HENRY LITOLFF
1818–91
ANGLO–FRENCH
Scherzo from
CONCERTO SYMPHONIQUE NO. 4
(1852)

C

GEORGE LLOYD
1913–98
ENGLISH
A SYMPHONIC MASS
(1993)

CHO

ANDREW LLOYD WEBBER
B. 1948
ENGLISH
PIE JESU
from Requiem
(1984)

CHO

**WILLIAM LLOYD
WEBBER
1914–82**
ENGLISH
AURORA
(1951)

O

♥

Over the past few years, due mainly to the advocacy of his cellist son Julian Lloyd Webber, the neglected and unpublished works of William Lloyd Webber have been brought to public attention for the first time. Not that a work like *Aurora* needs any special pleading to establish itself in the standard repertoire. This is a short, expertly-crafted orchestral tone poem that portrays the Roman goddess of the dawn and 'the inherent sensuality of her nature'. Fans of Delius and the heart-on-sleeve emotionalism of Rachmaninov will fall for this which shows that Andrew Lloyd Webber's father could match his son's gift for melody and surpass his skills of orchestration.

**WILLIAM LLOYD
WEBBER**
INVOCATION
(1957)

O

♥

A modest and introspective man, William Lloyd Webber stopped composing in the 1950s and 1960s, realising that the style and language of the music he wanted to write was out of joint with the times. There was little chance of any performance given the hostility of the musical establishment to anything tonal or melodic. Now the tide is turning away from ugliness and incomprehensibility, and pieces like this slight but evocative piece for strings, harp and timpani can be heard and enjoyed as they deserve. What a pity no one thought to ask Lloyd Webber Snr. to write for films!

**ALEXANDRE LUIGINI
1850–1906**
FRENCH
BALLET ÉGYPTIEN
*Ballet
(1875)*

O

♪ ♥

The son of an Italian-conductor father who worked in Paris, Luigini enjoyed a successful career as a ballet composer - and his *Ballet égyptien* composed in 1875 was very successful indeed, so successful that Verdi gave permission for it to be inserted into performances of *Aida* when it was presented in Lyons in 1886. The score was a long-time favourite with light orchestras everywhere (the first two movements especially), striking for its Oriental-type melodies.

The theme on which Lutoslawski based his variations (written for four hands, two pianos) was the same Paganini caprice for solo violin that attracted Rachmaninov, Brahms, Andrew Lloyd Webber and many more - No. 24 in A minor (composed in about 1805). But Lutoslawski went further, using Paganini's own variations on the theme as the model for his own set - and with pungent, exuberantly-twentieth century harmonies.

WITOLD LUTOSLAWSKI
1913-94
POLISH
VARIATIONS ON A
THEME OF PAGANINI
(1941)

I

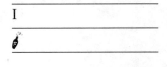

M

It's rare enough to come across a Scottish composer but rarer still to come across such an accomplished piece by a teenager. MacCunn wrote it when only 18 just after he'd resigned his scholarship to the Royal College of Music in London in a fit of pique (at 15 he'd been the College's youngest student). Mendelssohn and Bruch may be close at hand in this invigorating, open-air overture but MacCunn was clearly his own man in this unmistakably tartan tone poem. The title comes from Sir Walter Scott's poem 'The Lay of the Last Minstrel'.

HAMISH MACCUNN
1868-1916
SCOTTISH
LAND OF THE
MOUNTAIN AND
THE FLOOD
Overture (1887)

O

Though one of America's most significant composers of the Nineteenth Century, MacDowell was deeply rooted in the tradition of Schumann, Liszt, Grieg and other European composers. This concerto is not only his best work but also one of the finest of Romantic piano concertos with grand gestures, sweeping themes and a showy virtuoso solo part. The sparkling Scherzo is sometimes heard separately but if you like Saint-Saëns' Second and Grieg's Piano Concerto you're sure to enjoy the whole of this.

EDWARD
MACDOWELL
1860-1908
AMERICAN
PIANO CONCERTO
NO. 2 IN D MINOR
(1886)

C

♥

Despite the European tradition of his music, MacDowell was among the first to use the melodic and rhythmic material of the American Indian (try his *Indian Suite* of 1892) and to interpret the beauty of the American landscape in music. His *Woodland Sketches* for piano include his most familiar piece, a delicate gem entitled *To a Wild Rose*.

MACDOWELL
TO A WILD ROSE
(1896)
and other miniatures

I

☁️☀️

GUSTAV MAHLER
1860-1911
AUSTRIAN
SYMPHONY
NO. 1 IN D
(1896)

Mahler's symphonies are all conceived on a massive scale using a large orchestra and addressing lofty concepts such as Life and Death, and the human condition. His First Symphony was finished in 1888 when he was 28 (he revised it twice afterwards) and called *Titan* after the novel *Titan* by the German poet Jean Paul which he greatly admired at the time (he dropped the subtitle later). Although it has four movements, the Symphony breaks into two parts - the first celebratory and joyful, the second gloomy and troubled. The second movement (often heard separately) is like one of the jolly Moravian peasant dances to which Mahler often listened in his childhood

MAHLER
SYMPHONY
NO. 2 IN C MINOR
'RESURRECTION'
(1896)

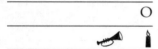

If 'Mahler One' calls for a large orchestra, 'Mahler Two' needs a gargantuan one augmented with an organ, church bells, off-stage horns, trumpets and percussion, soprano and contralto soloists, and chorus. Its five movements, which Mahler saw as a sequel to the *Titan* (see above), probe the reasons for human existence and suffering, an allegory on the life of Man, culminating in Judgement Day - among the most shattering and thrilling climaxes of any symphony.

MAHLER
SYMPHONY
NO. 4 IN G
(1892, rev. 1899-1910)

Not many laughs in Mahler, but this is the nearest you get. 'Mahler Four' is in complete contrast to the soul-searching of the *Resurrection Symphony*: look at the headings of its four movements - *Gay and Unhurried, Leisurely, Peacefully, Very Easily*. It's all sunshine and warmth, the most joyous and good-humoured of all Mahler's symphonies and also the shortest. He himself described it as 'a child's conception of heaven and the colour of blue sky'. The last movement has a soprano soloist singing the verses of an old Bavarian folk song.

MAHLER
SYMPHONY
NO. 5 IN C SHARP
MINOR
(1902)

Lasting over an hour and a quarter, 'Mahler Five' has five movements beginning, unusually, with a funeral march. Mahler insisted that 'not a single note points to the influence of extra-musical thoughts or emotions upon the composition of the Fifth', yet it seems to tell a story of passionate intensity. The Adagietto, the Symphony's fourth movement, is even more popular than Barber's Adagio for Strings as an outpouring of grief and yearning, and was made famous by its effective use in Visconti's film of Thomas Mann's novel *Death in Venice* (a rouged Dirk Bogarde sitting in a deckchair pining for a blonde Adonis).

Another epic score written on a vast scale, 'Mahler Eight' was the first completely choral symphony ever written. The first part is a setting of the Latin words of the Whitsuntide hymn 'Veni, creator spiritus', the second a setting of the closing scene of Goethe's *Faust* in which Faust's redeemed body is drawn up to heaven. Mahler's purpose was to link the power of Christian belief in the Holy Spirit with the idea of mankind's redemption through love. On another level, the work is a hymn of love to his wife Alma, the Symphony's dedicatee.

MAHLER
SYMPHONY
NO. 8 IN E FLAT
'SYMPHONY OF A
THOUSAND'
(1907)

CHO

For many years this, one of the loveliest of all Baroque oboe works, was attributed to Vivaldi, then to J.S. Bach and then to Benedetto Marcello (1686-1739), Alessandro's brother. At the moment Alessandro seems to have the honour - and of having written it in the key of D minor (my copy of the score says it's by Benedetto and is in C minor). Ah well, it's the quality of the music that's important and he would be hard of heart who failed to respond to the slow movement. Heartbreaking or what? Bach, incidentally, turned the work into a solo for harpsichord (very effective) and there's a magical old recording of the great pianist Edwin Fischer playing the slow movement on the piano.

ALESSANDRO
MARCELLO
1669-1747
ITALIAN
OBOE CONCERTO
IN D MINOR
(c. 1717)

C

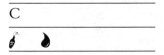

Not to be confused with Padre Martini (1706-84), the Italian composer and teacher of Mozart, our Martini was a German whose real name was Johann Paul Schwarzendorf, made his career in France, became Master of the King's Music and survived the Revolution despite his staunch support for the royalist cause. He is remembered now for this one song, everpopular and recorded by artists as diverse as John McCormack and Joan Baez. Strange the number of couples who choose it to be sung at their wedding. Despite its title 'Love's Pleasure' and its sentimental tune, it's all about the inconstancy of lovers and the fleeting delight of love itself.

JEAN PAUL MARTINI
1741-1816
GERMAN
'PLAISIR D'AMOUR'
(date unknown)

V

PIETRO MASCAGNI
1863-1945
ITALIAN
EASTER HYMN
from Cavalleria Rusticana
(1890)

OP

Cav and Pag, as they're known for short, are the most performed one-act operas, usually presented together - Leoncavallo's *Pagliacci* (*Clowns*) and this one, *Rustic Chivalry*. It's a passionate love story that ends in tragedy and is set in a Sicilian village on Easter Day. As the villagers make their way to church, they sing a magnificent Resurrection chorus led by the heroine, Santuzza - 'Inneggiamo, il Signor nonè morto' ('Let us sing of the Lord now victorious'). We know it as the 'Easter Hymn'.

MASCAGNI
Intermezzo from
CAVALLERIA
RUSTICANA

O

Much-used by the makers of television commercials, this is a purely orchestral number played between the two scenes of the opera while the stage is empty, to denote the passage of time. The Italian word *intermezzo* literally means 'insertion' and it was a popular device of opera composers - other famous examples are in Puccini's *Manon Lescaut*, Leoncavallo's *Pagliacci* and Massenet's *Thaïs* - but Mascagni's is the best known, one of the most celebrated melodies of all opera and one which never fails to stir the emotions. High in the Classic FM Hall of Fame.

JULES MASSENET
1842-1912
FRENCH
'ADIEU, NOTRE PETIT TABLE'
from Manon
(1884)

OP

Based on the 1731 novel *L'Histoire du Chevalier des Grieux et de Manon Lescaut* by Abbé Provost, Massenet's opera tells the tragic story of the beautiful but misguided Manon who gives in to her weakness for the good things of life at the expense of her true feelings of love (Puccini wrote his own version entitled *Manon Lescaut*). Manon falls for the young, impecunious Chevalier des Grieux and elopes with him but is later persuaded by the wealthy nobleman de Brétigny to leave and live with him instead. From Act 2 comes Manon's lovely aria 'Farewell, our little table' as she looks sadly at the table at which des Grieux and she had sat.

Massenet's *Elégie* is one of those classical pops you know but can never put a name to. It was originally a piano piece called *Mélodie* (No. 5 from a collection entitled *Dix Pièces de genre*, written in 1866). Then Massenet used the same melody in his orchestral music for a play by Leconte de Lisle where it was called *Invocation* (it was this score that gave Massenet his first big success). Not one to waste a good tune, he then turned it into a piece for cello and piano in the same year (1873) and repackaged it as *Elégie* - it sold like hot cakes.

MASSENET
ELÉGIE
(1866)

I

♥   ⛅

Thaïs was first produced at the Opéra Comique, Paris, in March 1894. It's a tale set in fourth century Egypt and tells how the monk Athanaël converts the courtesan Thaïs to become a nun. He, though, falls in love with her and, in the best tradition of opera, confesses as much to her at the moment she dies. The *Méditation*, now more usually heard as a violin solo, is a symphonic interlude (or intermezzo) played between the change of scenes in Act 2 and is repeated in an extended and modified form at the death of Thaïs.

MASSENET
MÉDITATION
from Thaïs
Opera
(1894)

O/I

♥   ⛅

Another tragic story of unrequited love (this one based on a novel by Goethe) provided Massenet with a huge success. Werther is a young poet in love with Charlotte who, despite returning his affection, goes off and marries Albert. Result? Werther gets hold of Albert's pistols and shoots himself. Before this, though, the lovelorn Werther is seen reading some verses by the third century Gaelic poet Ossian and realises that they reflect his own feelings. 'Why awaken me' from Act 3 is a soaring tenor aria, typical of Massenet's romantic, melodic score, but (coincidence or not) opens with a minor-key version of 'Ta-ra-ra-boom-di-ay'.

MASSENET
'POURQUOI ME RÉVEILLER'
from Werther
(1892)

OP

♥

PAUL MCCARTNEY
B. 1942
ENGLISH
STANDING STONE
(1997)

CHO

EMI commissioned McCartney to write a work to celebrate the record company's centenary and mark the former Beatle's long association with EMI. The result was this four-movement work for chorus and orchestra. It reflects McCartney's interest in the mysteries of the ancient world, folk legends and his own Celtic roots. The tunes are immediately appealing, as you'd expect from McCartney, and the orchestration colourful and expert, as you'd expect from professionals like David Matthews, Sir Richard Rodney Bennett and the rest of the team who helped McCartney knock the 75-minute score into shape.

FELIX MENDELSSOHN
1809-47
GERMAN
ANDANTE AND
RONDO
CAPRICCIOSO
(1830 and 1828)

I

One of Mendelssohn's earliest works for solo piano is also one of his finest. The Rondo, written in 1828, is straight out of the same world as *A Midsummer Night's Dream*, a brilliant, playful showpiece in E minor that ends in a storm of octaves. The reflective Andante, in E major, was added a couple of years later as a songful introduction.

MENDELSSOHN
ELIJAH
(1846)

CHO

Mendelssohn had the idea of writing a choral work about the prophet Elijah in 1836, soon after he had completed the writing of his first oratorio, *St. Paul*. But it was not until 1845 when the Birmingham Music Festival invited him to compose a work for the 1846 Festival that he set to work on the project. The first performance with the composer conducting was an overwhelming success and, for over a century, *Elijah* was second only to Handel's *Messiah* in popularity when it came to great oratorios. Among the stirring solos, duets and choruses are 'O rest in the Lord', 'If with all your hearts', 'Hear Ye Israel' and 'Baal we cry to thee'.

In the spring of 1829, Mendelssohn made his first visit to Britain and, accompanied by his friend Klingemann, journeyed up to Scotland. They made a trip to Staffa, off the Isle of Mull, and saw the celebrated Fingal's Cave. The very same day, Mendelssohn wrote to his sister Fanny, 'That you may understand how extraordinarily the Hebrides affected me, the following came into my mind' - and he sent her 21 bars of music that were to form the opening of the Overture. Cynical musicians of my acquaintance remember this famous theme by singing, 'Thank God when it's over/Thank God when it's over' (repeated ad nauseam). But it's a terrific 'sea piece' - you can just see the waves rolling into the cliffs round Staffa - which gets its double title from the fact that Mendelssohn scribbled 'Fingal's Cave' on the front of the original score, while the orchestral parts were marked 'The Hebrides'.

MENDELSSOHN
FINGAL'S CAVE
'THE HEBRIDES'
Overture
(1830)

O

One of the miracles of music, the Overture was written when Mendelssohn was only 17. It is not only a masterly essay on Shakespeare's play but reveals Mendelssohn's own distinct, individual musical style fully formed, a world inhabited by fairies and elves, and an imagination matched only by deft, delicate orchestration. After its mysterious opening, the whole orchestra bursts into a joyous dance, and a little later you'll hear the bray of the brass depicting Bottom in his ass's head.

MENDELSSOHN
Overture to
A MIDSUMMER
NIGHT'S DREAM
(1826)

O

The second most popular number from this score is the delicate, fairylike Scherzo (used as a prelude to Act 2 when it's played in the theatre). 'Chattering elves and their mischievous gambols' is how one writer characterised it. The orchestral original is also well known in an ingenious (and prodigiously difficult) transcription for solo piano by Rachmaninov. He himself, a master pianist, recorded it (it's said that he took 49 takes to perfect it) while his friend Benno Moiseiwitsch recorded it at the end of a session in 1939 as a fill-up and achieved the impossible in a single take.

MENDELSSOHN
Scherzo from
A MIDSUMMER
NIGHT'S DREAM
(1842)

O/I

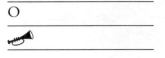

MENDELSSOHN
WEDDING MARCH
*from A Midsummer Night's
Dream
(1842)*

O/I

You'd never guess that the rest of the incidental music Mendelssohn wrote for *A Midsummer Night's Dream* was composed 16 years later. He had lost nothing of the wonder and delight of his youth in the meantime, and the 13 pieces, added at the command of King William IV of Prussia, have the same sense of magic and fantasy. The *Wedding March* has accompanied countless couples down the aisle, a tradition that was established after the wedding of Queen Victoria's daughter, the Princess Royal in 1858. It's a tune that has been quoted and sent-up by many composers since (try Ibert's *Divertissement* for a start!).

MENDELSSOHN
OCTET FOR
STRINGS
IN E FLAT
(1825)

CH

The Mendelssohn family lived in a large house on the outskirts of Berlin and, on Sunday mornings, held concerts - an excellent training ground for the young composer. Here Mendelssohn played and absorbed the chamber works of the great composers and was able to hear his own music played and criticised by fine musicians. By the age of 12 he was an experienced writer for stringed instruments. Even so, the Octet of 1825 is an amazing achievement. Not even Mozart or Schubert produced anything of this maturity at a comparable age, added to which it was the first truly integrated work for eight string players. In four movements (a richly-textured Allegro, elegiac Andante, gossamer-light Scherzo and high-spirited Presto), the Octet is one of the marvels of all chamber music.

MENDELSSOHN
'O FOR THE WINGS
OF A DOVE'
*from Hear My Prayer
(1844)*

CHO

In 1844 Mendelssohn was working in Berlin with responsibility for, among other things, a newly-formed cathedral choir. The anthem (or motet as it's more correctly labelled) *Hear My Prayer* is a setting of a paraphrase of the opening verses of Psalm 55 and scored for soprano soloist, choir and organ. The second of its two sections, 'O for the wings of a dove', is dominated by the soprano. It has always been a classic of the choral repertoire but became more widely-known through an inspired recording made in 1927 by the Temple Church Choir, London, and its remarkable boy soprano soloist Ernest Lough. The disc went on to sell a million and is still in the catalogue.

Mendelssohn composed nearly 100 songs but easily the most popular is 'Auf Flügeln des Gesanges' (words by Heine), translated as 'On Wings of Song', the second of six verse settings in a collection that appeared in 1836. Sopranos from Isobel Baillie to Barbara Bonney have recorded it but it's also well-known in an effective transcription for violin and piano by Joseph Achron, a version much-favoured by the great violinist Jascha Heifetz.

MENDELSSOHN
'ON WINGS OF SONG'
. *(1836)*

V

♥

'When he sat at the piano, music poured out of him with the richness of an inborn genius', wrote Mendelssohn's close friend and fellow composer Ferdinand Hiller. In this concerto and his other works for piano and orchestra, the music does indeed seem to pour forth, spontaneous, untroubled and teeming with ideas. The G Minor Concerto used to drive audiences wild and was a favourite war-horse of pianists. It's a vivacious and brilliant work with a dramatic first movement, a song-like slow movement and a breathless galop for the finale. Today, in some quarters, it's viewed as superficial and even banal. Take no notice if you like colourful, entertaining, musical fireworks.

MENDELSSOHN
PIANO CONCERTO NO. 1 IN G MINOR *(1832)*

C

The D Minor Concerto is slightly darker in mood, perhaps reflecting the deep depression Mendelssohn had suffered after the death of his father. But *joie de vivre* and sunshine are never far away in Mendelssohn's music, emphasised here by the fact that the Concerto was written just after the composer had returned from his honeymoon (it was composed for the Birmingham Festival of 1837). The slow movement is one of Mendelssohn's most heartfelt inspirations.

MENDELSSOHN
PIANO CONCERTO NO. 2 IN D MINOR *(1837)*

C

MENDELSSOHN
PIANO TRIO
NO. 1 IN D MINOR
(1839)

CH

Robert Schumann, a discerning critic as well as a great composer, judged this trio to be 'the master trio of the age, as were the B flat and D major trios of Beethoven and the E flat trio of Schubert in their times'. Opinions have not changed since, with others writing of its 'inspired melodies, incredible mastery of form, rich and idiomatic part writing, and warm emotional character'. Here and there we catch a glimpse of Liszt or Chopin and a snatch of Schumann (all three knew each other and there are many tributes and cross-references to each other in their music) but this is Mendelssohn at the height of his powers - and a life-enhancing work it is too.

MENDELSSOHN
SONGS WITHOUT
WORDS
(1825-45)

I

Over the years, Mendelssohn composed 48 short, graceful, charming piano works to which he gave the collective name of *Lieder ohne Worte* (*Songs Without Words*). An apt description, for here the piano is the wordless singer in what are generally sentimental, atmospheric and tuneful musical pictures. Each one has a title but, with four exceptions (the three *Venetian Boat Songs* and *Duetto*), these were concocted by Mendelssohn's publishers. *Spring Song* (Op. 62 No. 6) is among the most famous of all piano pieces - it was a constant stand-by in the era of silent films to denote soppy infatuation (often for comic effect).

MENDELSSOHN
SYMPHONY
NO. 3 IN A MINOR
'SCOTTISH'
(1842)

O

The inspiration for the Symphony came during the same visit to Scotland that resulted in the *Fingal's Cave Overture*, but it wasn't until 12 years later that Mendelssohn finally completed the work. It opens with a slow, brooding theme, one which occurred to him as he visited the old chapel at the Palace of Holyrood (it recurs throughout the Symphony); the second movement, rather than the third, is the scherzo - perhaps the best of the four - followed by a gloomy slow movement and a breezy finish. No bagpipes, no claymores, no folk-songs, just Mendelssohn's impression of Scotland.

Here is Mendelssohn's impression of Italy. He visited the country after his 1829 trip to Britain and, still only 22, wrote this ebullient, carefree response. Listen to the opening of the first movement – you can taste the excitement Mendelssohn must have felt at the prospect before him. The slow movement has been referred to as a 'pilgrim's march' but, though he witnessed the coronation of Pope Gregory XVI while in Rome, there's no evidence to confirm that this was what Mendelssohn intended. This is followed by a lively Scherzo and then the finale, the only genuine Italian thing about the Symphony: it's a *saltarello*, a vigorous Italian peasant dance.

MENDELSSOHN
SYMPHONY
NO. 4 IN A
'ITALIAN'
(1833)

O

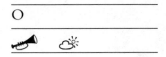

The *Mendelssohn Violin Concerto* as it's universally referred to (though he did compose one other violin concerto) came about as the result of his long friendship with the composer and celebrated violinist Ferdinand David (1810-73). It was written over a period of five years with many consultations between violinist and composer, and it was not until 13 March 1845 in Leipzig that it received its first performance – David the soloist, Niels Gade, the Danish composer, on the podium (Mendelssohn was having an enforced rest in Frankfurt). Its popularity with violinists and audiences has not diminished one jot since that day. Some have detected a similarity between the theme of the slow second movement with the Andrew Lloyd Webber/Tim Rice song 'I don't know how to love him' (from *Jesus Christ Superstar*), but appearances can be deceptive.

MENDELSSOHN
VIOLIN CONCERTO
IN E MINOR
(1844)

C

♥ ☁☀

SAVERIO MERCADANTE 1795-1870
ITALIAN
CONCERTO FOR FLUTE AND STRINGS
(c. 1819)

C

Mercadante was one of those myriad composers whose star shone oh-so-brightly during his lifetime but mysteriously flickered and vanished after his death. His main reputation was as an opera composer (he produced over 60, none of which is ever heard today) who was favourably compared with Donizetti and Rossini (a recent recording of his songs shows exactly why). But he earns a place here for his delightful Flute Concerto in E minor, graceful and appealing with a *Russian Rondo* finale (James Galway among others has recorded it). You should also look out his appealing Concerto for Clarinet (Op. 101) and Concertino for French Horn.

OLIVIER MESSIAEN 1908-92
FRENCH
JOY OF THE BLOOD OF THE STARS
from Turangalîla-symphonie
(1948)

O

Messiaen's music can be forbiddingly austere and sometimes downright bizarre, but the mystic and celebratory nature of much of his music can be exhilarating as well as rewarding. The massive *Turangalîla Symphony* (*Turangalîla* is a word derived from Sanskrit meaning 'time' and 'love') is a work of complex structure and rhythms that requires many hearings to absorb. To get to grips with it, a good starting place is this, the fifth of its ten movements entitled *Joie du sang des étoiles*, a rapturous, extravagant proclamation of love, which is 'a transformation on a cosmic scale,' Messiaen explained.

MESSIAEN
TRANSPORTS DE JOIE
from L'Ascension
(1934)

I

An early work, *The Ascension* was originally a four movement suite for orchestra, each movement illustrating a specific text from the Catholic liturgy. This was in 1933. The following year, Messiaen, a devout Roman Catholic, arranged the music for organ - far more effective - re-writing and re-titling the third movement. On a big organ, the cascades of sound with all the stops pulled out make this an awe-inspiring expression of 'ecstasy experienced in the contemplation of the risen and ascended Christ'. Hence Messiaen's full title: *Outburst of Joy from a Soul Before the Glory of Christ Which is its Own Glory*.

The high priest of French grand opera specialised in spectacular, star-studded extravaganzas of which *Le Prophète* was the grandest. It tells the cumbersome (true) story of the uprising of the Anabaptists in Holland and the coronation in 1535 of Jan Beuckelszoon, the Dutch Anapbaptist 'prophet' who was crowned in Münster, Westphalia. The swaggering *Coronation March* accompanies the stately procession to the cathedral. Listen to its second theme and you might wonder if this is where Verdi got the idea for the *Grand March* from *Aida*.

GIACOMO MEYERBEER 1791-1864
GERMAN
CORONATION MARCH
from Le Prophète Opera (1849)

O

The African Maid, Meyerbeer's final opera, is based on the exploits of the famed fifteenth century Portuguese explorer Vasco da Gama. He's shipwrecked off the African coast and falls in love with one of his captives, Selika, the African queen of the title. When he returns to his former love, Selika kills herself by breathing the poisonous scent of the manchineel tree. 'Twas ever thus. In Act 4, Vasco sings 'Oh paradise', one of the most enduring of tenor arias - a favourite on record with everyone from Caruso to Pavarotti - as he surveys the wonderful tropical scene before him.

MEYERBEER
'O PARADIS'
from L'Africaine (1865)

OP

It's difficult to pin down Milhaud's musical style, he adopted so many of them - symphonic jazz, early electronic music, densely-textured string quartets - but it is his lighter fair influenced by South American music that has stayed the course. *The Ox on the Roof* takes its title from a popular Brazilian song and is a colourful orchestral score awash with the Latin-American rhythms of the tango and samba. It's subtitled *Cinéma-Symphonie* because, in Milhaud's words, 'I thought that the character of this music might make it suitable for an accompaniment to one of Charlie Chaplin's films.'

DARIUS MILHAUD 1892-1974
FRENCH
LE BOEUF SUR LE TOIT
(1919)

O

MILHAUD
SCARAMOUCHE
(1937)

I

The prolific Milhaud produced over 500 works of every type but by far the best known (to his own great surprise) was this three-movement suite for two pianos. The themes he used were taken from the incidental music he had written for several plays, including one by Molière. The first movement could easily come from a French farce, while the second is tender and amorous, and the finale a rollicking samba. Scaramouche is the rascally character from traditional Italian comedy.

CLAUDIO MONTEVERDI
1567–1643
ITALIAN
'PUR TI MIRO'
from L'incoronazione di Poppea
(1642)

OP

Credited with writing the first opera with any truly dramatic character, Monteverdi must be considered as one of the great original minds of music. Forever experimenting and innovating, he was 75 years old when he composed his last opera *The Coronation of Poppea*, the first to make use of an historical event as its subject rather than mythology. 'Pur ti miro', the final number, sung by Nero to Poppea, remains one of the most touching love duets in opera: 'I gaze on you, I rejoice in you, I embrace you, I chain you to me…'

MONTEVERDI
VESPERS
(1610)

CHO

Shortly before the composition of *Vespero della Beata Vergine* (*Vespers of the Blessed Virgin*), to give this exalted work its formal title, Monteverdi had suffered the loss of both his wife (1607) and his only child (1608), a promising young singer. This is Monteverdi's outstanding achievement in religious music, a richly-scored setting of the service of *Vespers*. The variety of ways in which he uses the instrumental and vocal forces sets it apart from those of his contemporaries. It is dedicated to Pope Paul V.

Moszkowski was not one of those Olympian composers who develop the language of music and create new sound worlds like Wagner or Debussy. His talents lay elsewhere in the composition of tuneful, elegant miniatures for the piano, sneeringly referred to by the sniffier critics as 'salon music'. Paderewski considered that 'after Chopin, Moszkowski understands best how to write for the piano' and, certainly, if you like Chopin, Mendelssohn and Liszt you'll fall for Moszkowski. For tasters, try his Study in A flat, Op. 72 No. 11 and *Etincelles* (*Sparks*, Op. 36 No. 1) in breathtaking recordings by Vladimir Horowitz, the virtuosic *Caprice espagnol*, *La Jongleuse* (*The Lady Juggler*) and the affectingly simple *Serenata*, Op. 15 No. 1.

**MORITZ
MOSZKOWSKI
1854-1925**
GERMAN (SILESIAN)
CAPRICE ESPAGNOL
(c. 1885)
and others

I

♪

For the first decade of the Twentieth Century, Moszkowski's Piano Concerto was an international favourite, championed by most of the major pianists of the day. It was dedicated to Josef Hofmann, a remarkable tribute to a 22-year-old musician who would later be acknowledged as one of the greatest piano virtuosi in history (Rachmaninov later dedicated his Third Piano Concerto to him). Though Moszkowski's Concerto has been recorded several times, it is hardly ever heard in concert for reasons that must remain a mystery. It's a real crowd-pleaser written in four movements and in the unusual key of E major - a brilliant showpiece, dramatic, theatrical and romantic, with one memorable theme following the next. Moszkowski's Violin Concerto is another winning work waiting to find a champion (it's only been recorded once). It will surely find an audience given the chance.

MOSZKOWSKI
PIANO CONCERTO
IN E
(1898)

C

♥

MOSZKOWSKI
SPANISH DANCES
(c. 1875)
and
FROM FOREIGN
LANDS
(1884)

O/I

A century ago, Moszkowski's *Spanish Dances*, Op. 12 for piano duet were in virtually every piano stool in Europe, among the best-selling pieces of music of all time. They made their composer rich and famous (he made a spirited orchestral version of all five and produced a less-successful follow-up in the 1890s, his Op. 65) but, with changing musical taste, Moszkowski's brand of expertly-crafted, tuneful miniatures went out of fashion. From the same picture postcard shop come six short impressions of 'foreign lands' - Russia, Germany, Spain, Poland, Italy and Hungary - at one time rivalling the *Spanish Dances* in popularity. The attractive orchestral versions of these piano duets put you in mind of the ballet music of Tchaikovsky and Glazunov.

LEOPOLD MOZART
1719-87
GERMAN
TOY SYMPHONY
(date unknown)

O

The craze for writing symphonies using toy instruments came in the Eighteenth Century from the existence of a toy industry in the mountains near Salzburg. Many 'serious' composers from C.P.E. Bach and Michael Haydn to Reinecke and Méhul were attracted to rattles and whistles (Mendelssohn wrote two but they are lost). The most famous is attributed to Leopold Mozart, the father of Wolfgang Amadeus, though it's now thought that he merely arranged it from a work by 'Anon.'. Whoever was responsible had a lively sense of humour, for the *Kindersymphonie* is scored for two violins, double-bass, keyboard, toy trumpet, drum, rattle, triangle, 'quail', 'cuckoo' and 'nightingale' (i.e. bird warbler).

WOLFGANG AMADEUS
MOZART
1756-91
AUSTRIAN
AVE VERUM CORPUS
(1791)

CHO

One of the most profound and celebrated sacred works ever written lasts barely three minutes. In stark contrast to much of Mozart's church music which is celebratory and brilliant, this setting of the anonymous Latin hymn composed six months before his death, is understated, concise and direct, scored for chorus, strings and organ. The text, which has attracted composers from Josquin des Prés to Gounod and Elgar, means, literally, 'Hail, true body' but is usually translated as 'Word of God incarnate'.

One of Mozart's earliest concertos and the first he wrote for a wind instrument is this bassoon concerto (he composed at least three others for the instrument but they have disappeared). The two outer movements display the soloist's agility. Bearing in mind that the instrument Mozart knew was primitive compared with today's bassoon, the original player must have been quite an acrobat as he is sent scurrying up and down the full compass with many humorous touches. The slow movement is another matter, written *con amore*, exploiting the bassoon's capacity for wistfulness and tenderness.

MOZART
BASSOON
CONCERTO
IN B FLAT
(1774)

C

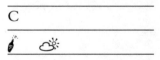

The Clarinet Concerto was written in the last few months of Mozart's life. It is said that he started work on it on 28 September 1791 and completed it on 7 October – the same week that he was conducting the first performances of *The Magic Flute*! Like the Clarinet Quintet (see below), the Concerto was written for Mozart's friend the celebrated virtuoso Anton Stadler (1753-1812). Mozart wrote for the very limit of the contemporary instrument's potential – it had only six keys whereas the modern clarinet has nearly 20. The two outer movements are lively allegros but the heart of the work is the central Adagio, surely one of the most beautiful slow movements in music. It has always been in the top ten of the Classic FM Hall of Fame.

MOZART
CLARINET
CONCERTO
IN A
(1791)

C

The gifted principal clarinet of the Imperial Court Orchestra of Vienna, Stadler was, by all accounts, a bit of a rogue, sponging off his friend Mozart, never repaying money he'd been lent and even stealing and selling Mozart's pawn tickets. Mozart's enduring affection for him and his instrument, though, inspired him to write this masterpiece which he finished on 29 September 1789. In four sections, the second (larghetto) is another slow movement so lovely it makes you hold your breath, followed by an expressive minuet and, for the finale, a set of variations on a folk-like theme.

MOZART
CLARINET
QUINTET IN A
(1789)

CH

MOZART
CONCERTO FOR
FLUTE AND HARP
IN C
(1778)

C

Arriving in Paris in March 1778, Mozart found himself well received by the Parisian socialites but not well paid. Soon his finances were running low and he acquired a few pupils to make ends meet. Among these was the daughter of the Duc de Guines who, Mozart wrote to his father, 'plays the flute extremely well and plays the harp magnifique.' The result was this concerto, a soft-spoken, delicate creation, relaxed in tone with a deft balance between the two instruments. The last of its three movements (a rondo) teems with melodies, as one writer put it, 'like an eighteenth century jam session with [each soloist] challenging the other to outdo its latest melodic inspiration.'

MOZART
COSÌ FAN TUTTE
(1790)

OP

The title translates literally as *Thus Do All [women]* but is usually given as *That's What All Women Do* or something similar. The opera's subtitle tells you what it's all about - *La Scuola degli Amanti* (*The School for Lovers*). On one hand it can be seen as a romantic comedy, on the other as a cynical and rather dark look at love and relationships. *Così* did not achieve the popularity of Mozart's other three great operas (*The Marriage of Figaro*, *Don Giovanni* and *The Magic Flute*) until this century and its American première had to wait until 1922! The most famous passage is the trio from Act 1, 'Soave sia il vento' ('May the gentle breeze'), one of opera's most sublime creations, sung by Don Alfonso and the two girls, Fiordiligi and Dorabella, as they bid farewell to their lovers. Listen out also for the Overture and Fiordiligi's aria 'Come soglio' ('Like a rock') with its spectacular vocal leaps, a test for any soprano.

MOZART
DON GIOVANNI
(1787)

OP

Although at least 30 other operas have been written around the legend of Don Giovanni (or Don Juan), the seducer and blasphemer who mocks the conventions of Man and God, Mozart's is the only one of any consequence. It's a mixture of the comic and serious with a fast-moving plot, a masterpiece that was a triumph at its first performance in Prague in 1787 and has never lost its popularity. It's said that Mozart had forgotten to write the Overture until the eve of the première when friends reminded him of the fact. He began composing at midnight and finished it three hours later, a work that comments on the whole opera itself. The many celebrated arias in *Don Giovanni* include the 'Catalogue Aria' (Act 1) in which the Don's servant Leporello lists his master's female conquests, 'Là ci darem la mano' ('Give me your hand', the Don's amorous duet with the peasant girl Zerlina), 'Dalla sua ace' ('Mine be her burden') in which Ottavio sings of his love for Donna Anna, and Ottavio's 'Il mio tesoro' ('My treasure'), a classic tenor solo.

MOZART
EXULTATE, JUBILATE
(1773)

V

The variety of music that Mozart composed while still a teenager is astonishing - concertos, divertimentos, symphonies, chamber works, church music and all kinds of vocal pieces. He was 16 when, while visiting Milan, he wrote this motet for Venanzio Rauzzini, a castrato who had appeared the previous month in his opera *Lucio Silla*. Today, of course, it's always sung by a soprano. Using a Latin text, the music is in three parts – the vigorous opening title section, followed by a solemn and deeply spiritual Andante (*Tu virinum corona*) and the concluding Allegro (very popular and often heard separately) which is spun brilliantly round the single word 'Alleluia'.

MOZART
HORN CONCERTO NO. 3 IN E FLAT, K447
(c. 1784-87)

C

Generally, the concertos that Mozart wrote for wind instruments are display pieces conceived for specific performers or occasions. His more profound concertos are those for the piano and violin. That said, there are many pages of deep feeling and nobility in the wind concertos, as in the last two of his four concertos for the French horn. All these were written between 1782 and 1787 for the same friend, a Viennese player called Ignaz Leutgeb who had retired from the Salzburg orchestra to become a cheesemonger. The Third Concerto is the best of the bunch and in the last movement (a rondo), Mozart litters the score with teasing insults and jokes directed at Leutgeb.

MOZART
HORN CONCERTO NO. 4 IN E FLAT
K495
(1786)

C

Ignaz Leutgeb (see above), who was already 50 when Mozart produced these concertos, must have been a very able player to negotiate the many demanding passages Mozart wrote for the French horn of his time. Modern day instruments make the solo part easier to play but, like all Mozart, it is never easy to play well. Though many fine versions have appeared subsequently, the classic recordings of all four were made in 1953 by the English virtuoso Dennis Brain. No. 4 has one of the composer's best-known movements (the final Rondo) turned into a comic song by Michael Flanders and Donald Swann called 'Ill Wind'.

MOZART
LAUDATE DOMINUM
from Solemn Vespers
(1780)

CHO

Among Mozart's most important works of church music (not as well known as the *Requiem* or *Great Mass*, see below) is the *Vesperae Solennes de Confessore* (*Solemn Vespers*), scored for soloists, chorus and orchestra. It's a setting in Latin of six psalms and the fifth of these, *Laudate Dominum* (Psalm 117), is one of the most moving and eloquent works of spiritual music, sung by the soprano: 'O praise the Lord, all ye nations: praise him all ye people'. From the late 1930's to the early 1950's a recording of this made in 1928 by the German soprano Ursula van Diemen was voted in an American poll as 'most popular classical request of all time'.

MOZART
THE MAGIC FLUTE
(1791)

OP

Beethoven considered this opera to be Mozart's greatest work and the distinguished critic Neville Cardus wrote, 'The opera... is the only one in existence that might conceivably have been composed by God.' *The Magic Flute* works on many levels - as a fairy tale, an allegory, a pantomime or a glorification of freemasonry (Mozart and his librettist Schikaneder were members of the brotherhood). After its première in Vienna in 1791, its popularity was such that it was performed more than 100 times in the first year alone - not that Mozart knew, for a little over two months after the opening night he was dead. The Overture begins with three heavy chords, said to represent knocking on the door of the masonic lodge. The vocal highlights include Papageno's introduction 'Der

Vogelfänger bin ich ja' ('I am the jolly birdcatcher'), Tamino's beautiful tenor aria 'Dies Bildnis ist bezaubernd schön' ('O loveliness beyond compare'), the two taxing arias for the Queen of the Night, 'O zittre nicht' ('Be not afraid') in Act 1 and 'Der Hölle Rache' ('I'll have revenge') in Act 2 which take the soprano up into the stratosphere, and 'Pa-pa-pa', the jolly final duet sung by Papageno and Papagena.

Mozart wrote nearly 20 settings of the Mass, most of them triumphal, bustling with energy and distinctly unsolemn. This one, known as the *Great*, was inspired by the illness of his then sweetheart, Constanza. He vowed that should she recover he would write a mass in gratitude. She did recover, she became his wife in August 1782, and he kept his promise. Or nearly. For some reason or other, perhaps because during the course of composition he became disenchanted with the marriage, Mozart never completed the work. Nevertheless, what we have represents one of the masterpieces of religious music. The first performance of what he did write - the *Kyrie*, *Gloria*, *Sanctus* and *Benedictus* - was given in Salzburg in 1783 fleshed out by earlier pieces of church music.

MOZART
MASS
NO. 18 IN C MINOR
'GREAT',
K427
(1882-3)

CHO

Figaro, as everyone calls it, is Mozart's comic masterpiece, one of the most popular and frequently performed of all operas. The opening night (1 May 1786 in Vienna) ran twice as long as planned because everything was encored. The complicated plot is based on the second of three plays by Beaumarchais (Rossini's opera *The Barber of Seville* is based on the first) featuring the rascally Figaro, the amorous exploits of Count and Countess Almaviva, and Cherubino and Susanna, their page and maid. The Overture is the most beloved of all opera, a sparkling mood-setter, while the many vocal highlights include Cherubino's 'Non so più' ('I know not what I am') and 'Voi che sapete' ('You who understand'), Figaro's 'Non più andrai' ('No more games') and the Countess's two exquisite arias 'Porgi amor' ('Grant, o love') and 'Dove sono' ('I remember days long departed').

MOZART
THE MARRIAGE OF
FIGARO
(1786)

OP

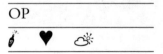

**MOZART
PIANO CONCERTO
NO. 9 IN E FLAT
'JEUNEHOMME',
K271
*(1777)***

C

More of Mozart's personality is revealed in his 27 piano concertos than any of his other works. The keyboard was how he expressed himself most openly and the whole collection can be seen as a kind of autobiography. Collectively, they are among the high points of Western culture. Among the earliest is this, written in January 1777 when a French virtuoso called Mademoiselle Jeunehomme visited Mozart in Salzburg (hence the work's nickname). Nobody seems to know anything about Mlle. Jeunehomme but she must have been quite a player for it is one of the most heroic and difficult concertos written up to that time.

**MOZART
PIANO CONCERTO
NO. 10 IN E FLAT
FOR TWO PIANOS
*(1779)***

C

After his return to Salzburg from Paris in 1779, Mozart composed two concertos, both of which require two soloists - the *Sinfonia Concertante*, K364 for violin and viola and this, its joyful, bubbling companion. It was written for himself and his sister Nannerl for ' home use' and, though it is outwardly a light-hearted romp, there are many tricky moments to overcome in performance, the sort that the audience would be unaware of and which Mozart must have put in with a nod and a wink. There's a wonderful description of two pianists preparing the concerto in Frank Conroy's novel *Body and Soul*, just about the best fictional account of what it takes to be a great concert pianist.

**MOZART
PIANO CONCERTO
NO. 20 IN D MINOR
*(1785)***

C

For the most part, Mozart's piano concertos are sunny and optimistic. This one, right from the opening bars, is turbulent and angry in mood. 'It seizes the listener forcibly' as one commentator observed, 'a rare thing for a Mozart concerto to do.' It was the first he wrote in a minor key and its drama and passion, a clear break from all his earlier essays in the form, was a musical signpost to the future. It was in 1785, round about the time this concerto was written, that Joseph Haydn wrote to Mozart's father, Leopold, 'Before God, and as an honest man, I tell you that your son is the greatest composer known to me either in person or by name.'

Mozart composed three piano concertos in C major (this is the middle one) and it's a measure of his genius that K467 was finished within weeks of the D Minor Concerto (see above). In fact, it seems likely that he was writing both masterpieces simultaneously - he liked to produce contrasting works in pairs and these two works could not be more different in mood. The two ebullient outer movements are full of the joys of spring but it's the slow movement that is hugely and rightly popular, a ravishing, dreamlike andante of heartfelt beauty and simplicity. Less is more. It was used in the 1967 Swedish film *Elvira Madigan* (about a tight-rope walker who falls in love with an army officer), making the Concerto a rare (unique?) example of a classical work acquiring its nickname nearly two centuries after its publication.

MOZART:
PIANO CONCERTO
NO. 21 IN C
'ELVIRA MADIGAN',
K467
(1785)

C

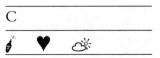

Here is another pair of piano concertos written simultaneously (March 1786) in contrasting moods. One writer characterised the opening of K488 as having 'the smiling maturity of a late Shakespearean drama'. It's a suave, welcoming theme which introduces the most lyrical of all Mozart's 27 piano concertos. The central Adagio is profoundly moving, a sombre song of yearning in F sharp minor, the only time Mozart ever wrote in that key. Typically, it's followed by a scintillating rondo guaranteed to put a spring in your step.

MOZART
PIANO CONCERTO
NO. 23 IN A
(1786)

C

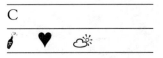

Many musicologists and music-lovers agree that this is one of the greatest piano concertos ever written, completed in March 1786 a matter of weeks after K488. How did he do it, while working on *The Marriage of Figaro* at the same time? Beethoven is reputed to have said to his pupil Ries when discussing K491, 'Oh, my dear fellow, we shall never get any idea like this.' The character of this concerto is light years away (though, in reality, less than a decade) from the dapper entertainments of the earlier ones. This is a turbulent, epic journey with no happy ending (unlike the D Minor Concerto), though the lovely slow second movement has a lyrical, hymn-like serenity.

MOZART
PIANO CONCERTO
NO. 24 IN C MINOR
(1786)

C

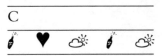

MOZART
PIANO CONCERTO
NO. 27 IN B FLAT
K595
(1791)

C

Mozart's final piano concerto, composed in January 1791 at the beginning of the last year of his life, has a valedictory, autumnal air about it. Is it a coincidence that the music has such a restless, foreboding quality, that even in the final rondo, where Mozart generally signs off on a cheerful note, there's a feeling of enforced jollity? There are too many associations with what we know of Mozart's life at the time to separate them from the innocent gaiety and quiet resignation of the music.

MOZART
PIANO SONATA NO. 8
IN A MINOR
K310 *(1778)*
and
FANTASIA
AND SONATA
IN C MINOR,
K457 *and* K475 *(1785)*

I

The 18 sonatas for solo piano are less consistently exalted as a group compared with the piano concertos, but almost all have something unique and original to say. A few are undisputed masterpieces, including the only two Mozart piano sonatas written in minor keys. The A Minor has a heroic opening theme - indeed, the whole work is an impassioned drama, caught to perfection in an historic recording by Dinu Lipatti. The Fantasia and Sonata, written in separate years (1784 and 1785) but intended to be played together, is regarded as Mozart's finest solo keyboard work, one of dramatic and ever-changing moods. The second movement Adagio of the Sonata must surely have been an inspiration for Beethoven's early sonatas.

MOZART
PIANO SONATA
NO. 10 IN C,
K330
(1781-3)

I

Is there a budding pianist in the world who hasn't had a crack at the first movement? It's one of the most played pieces ever written, though its cause was not helped when, in 1939, it was hijacked for a ghastly popular dance number entitled *In an Eighteenth Century Drawing-Room*. The Sonata is known as the *Sonate Facile* or *Little Sonata for Beginners* but it's difficult to play well. In the placid slow movement, crafty Mozart plants a quote from the slow movement of his own *Eine kleine Nachtmusik*.

The first movement is unusual for being a theme and set of (six) variations, the very essence of Mozartean elegance. This is followed by a minuet and rounded off with the celebrated *Turkish Rondo*, so famous that it's often played separately and as an encore. Among the many transcriptions made of it, the most spectacular is by the Russian pianist Arcadi Volodos. Why *Turkish?* Turkish or *Janissary* music was highly popular in Central Europe in the Seventeenth and Eighteenth Centuries and many composers incorporated their versions of the distinctive percussion instruments used. Mozart made further use of the Turkish flavour in his opera *The Abduction from the Seraglio* and the finale of his Violin Concerto No. 5 (see below).

Those who have seen the film or play *Amadeus* will know that this is the work that came about after a visit to Mozart by a tall, thin stranger who delivered an anonymous letter requesting a requiem to be written in the shortest possible time for an anonymous patron. Mozart, already suffering from the illnesses that were to prove fatal, became convinced that a messenger from another world had invited him to write his own *requiem*. Its composition did indeed prove to be a race with death. (The anonymous stranger proved to be the steward of Count Franz von Walsegg who wanted a requiem in memory of his late wife, but Mozart never learned this.) The composer managed to finish 12 of the *Requiem*'s 15 sections before he died. It is an extraordinary work ranging from despair and terror to exaltation and elegiac peace.

Mozart was already an experienced composer of 20 when he wrote this – no one's sure for whom or what occasion. What's unusual about it is that it is scored for two 'orchestras': one consists of two violins and double bass, the other of two violins, viola, cello and drums. Rather like the old Baroque concerto grosso of Bach and Handel, the two bands play question and answer with each other, but this one is heard at its best if the two groups play at opposite ends of a room. A musical novelty, yes, but with some of Mozart's most eloquent pages.

MOZART:
PIANO SONATA
NO. 11 IN A,
K331
(1781-3)

I

MOZART
REQUIEM
K626
(1791)

CHO

MOZART
SERENADE
NO. 6 IN D
'SERENATA
NOTTURNA'
(1776)

O

MOZART
SERENADE
NO. 13 IN G
'EINE KLEINE
NACHTMUSIK'
(1787)

O

Curiously, though *A Little Night Music* is arguably Mozart's most popular work, very little is known about its composition. All we know is that it was finished on 10 August 1787 while Mozart was still working on *Don Giovanni* - a further example (see piano concertos, above) of Mozart being able to write two pieces simultaneously of diametrically opposed moods. The four movements are Mozart in 'light music' mode but with his usual astonishing wealth of melodic invention, contrasting moods and witty asides.

MOZART
SERENADE NO. 10 IN
B FLAT FOR 13 WIND
INSTRUMENTS
(1781-84)

CH

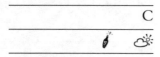

For all that the serenades, divertimenti and other chamber works were written for entertainment purposes, Mozart invested in the music his innermost feelings and all the gifts at his disposal. The extraordinary Serenade for 13 wind instruments is like a symphony in its structure except that it's longer than any of Mozart's symphonies (it lasts about 50 minutes) and is in seven movements. The score requests a pair each of oboes, clarinets, basset-horns and bassoons, plus four horns and a contra-bassoon. At its core is one of Mozart's most sublime slow movements in which passages from a solo oboe and clarinet waft above a murmuring, pulsating accompaniment. In Peter Shaffer's play *Amadeus*, the composer Salieri hears it through an open window and dashes home in despair: 'It seemed to me I had heard a voice of God.' Quite so.

MOZART
SINFONIA
CONCERTANTE
IN E FLAT
for violin and viola
(1779)

C

The finest of Mozart's concertos featuring a string soloist, the *Sinfonia Concertante* was composed in Salzburg the same year in which he wrote another concerto for two soloists, the Piano Concerto No. 10 (see above) and in the same key (E flat). His unhappiness in the service of the Archbishop of Salzburg and disappointment at the unsatisfactory trip he had recently made to Mannheim and Paris are disguised in this masterpiece - the work overflows with a cavalcade of tunes and unstoppable energy - but it is probable that the moving slow movement is a reflection on the death of his mother.

With such a deep treasure chest to dig into, which of Mozart's more than 200 chamber works do you choose from? There are 23 string quartets alone, a medium which, inspired by those of Joseph Haydn, he took to new heights. The best of them are the six *Haydn Quartets*, Nos. 14–20, dedicated in tribute to his friend. The first movement of No. 15 in D minor, K421 is said to have been inspired by the labour pains of Mozart's wife Constanza, while No. 19, K465 is known as the *Dissonance*, because in the opening of the quartet it is hard to pin down exactly what key Mozart is writing in: the effect is to produce dissonant sounds far in advance of Mozart's day. The String Quartet in B flat, K458 is known as *The Hunt* because of the first movement's imitation of a hunting call - and the chase!

MOZART
STRING QUARTETS
(1782-85)

CH

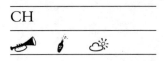

Prague was the scene of some of Mozart's greatest triumphs in the last years of his life. The public had gone wild over *The Marriage of Figaro* in the winter of 1786-87, just as they were to do a year later with the first performance of *Don Giovanni*. In fact there are several passages in this symphony which seem like sketches for *Don Giovanni* - the unusual slow introduction, for instance, resembles the music of the avenging stone statue in the opera. Another unusual feature is the absence of a minuet (the Germans know the *Prague* as *Mozart's Symphony Without a Minuet*, though there are others without minuet movements). The acclaim for the *Prague* was so enthusiastic at its first performance in January 1787 that Mozart was not allowed to leave until he had improvised at the piano for over half an hour.

MOZART
SYMPHONY
NO. 38 IN D
'PRAGUE'
(1786)

O

MOZART
SYMPHONY
NO. 39 IN E FLAT
(1788)

O

It is one of musical history's miracles that Mozart could have produced three of the greatest symphonies ever written, all very different in style and character, in the space of six weeks, to be exact between 26 June and 10 August 1788. Symphony No. 39 was composed at a time when Mozart was in debt, depressed about his inability to secure a court position and in despair about his future. Yet the music is consistently bright and optimistic or contentedly serene, 'a summer symphony of leisurely gait' as one writer aptly put it. One unusual musicological feature is the Andante movement written in the key of A flat, the only time Mozart used the key in a large-scale work; apart from Elgar's First Symphony, written over a century later, it's difficult to think of another symphony that uses it.

MOZART
SYMPHONY
NO. 40 IN G MINOR,
K550
(1788)

O

Without any formal introduction, Mozart launches into one of the most lyrical openings of any symphony, a work of which Schubert said, 'You can hear the angels singing in it.' Another writer described the opening theme as 'the consoling thoughts that spring out of human suffering'. A pity that such a divine and dignified idea should have been mangled in a hideous rhythm arrangement by Waldo de los Rios that became popular in 1971. The whole symphony, which is in four movements, has a quiet character that suggests the end of summer and the first shades of autumn.

MOZART
SYMPHONY
NO. 41 IN C
'JUPITER'
(1788)

O

No one seems sure how the *Jupiter* acquired its nickname. Some think it arose in England in the 1820s due to the German-born pianist, composer and publisher Johann Baptist Cramer who was impressed by the God-like perfection of the work. The work is not so much Olympian as jovial – Jupiter being 'the bringer of jollity' – and the last of its four movements is a compositional tour de force: even seasoned conductors and musicians enthuse about the way in which Mozart juggles five themes simultaneously without most listeners being aware of such incredible skill, so naturally does the music flow. This, his final symphony, is the crowning glory of any work in this form written in the Eighteenth Century.

The concerto was central to the way in which Mozart expressed himself – it's no accident that this book, like any other of its kind, will feature more concertos by Mozart than by any other composer. The trumpet, cello and double bass are the only regular members of the orchestra not to have a concerto written for them by him. Mozart completed five violin concertos in the same year, 1775, though only Nos. 3, 4 and 5 are heard regularly today. The G Major is the slightest of these three, written for himself to play as court Kapellmeister and leader of the orchestra in Salzburg.

MOZART
VIOLIN CONCERTO
NO. 3 IN G
(1775)

C

Mozart was one of the foremost keyboard virtuosi of the day and because of this and the great series of piano concertos it's sometimes forgotten that he was equally proficient on the violin in his youth. He reported to his father in 1777 after performances in Munich and Augsberg, 'They all stared – I played as though I were the finest fiddler in Europe.' The D Major Concerto is, arguably, the best of the five he composed in the one year, with Mozart's familiar inexhaustible supply of melody and invention. The slow movement is particularly lovely, while the finale is a stately rondo.

MOZART
VIOLIN CONCERTO
NO. 4 IN D
(1775)

C

The last and most brilliant of the set composed in 1775 is known as the *Turkish* because, in the last of its three movements, Mozart treats us to a splurge of Hungarian gypsy music before digressing into a thumping march imitating the then popular vogue for Turkish music (it was a theme he borrowed from an earlier ballet of his called *The Jealous Woman of the Harem*) – all this in the middle of a witty and graceful minuet!

MOZART
VIOLIN CONCERTO
NO. 5 IN A
'TURKISH'
(1775)

C

MODEST
MUSSORGSKY
1839-81
RUSSIAN
A NIGHT ON THE
BARE MOUNTAIN
(1867, rev. Rimsky-
Korsakov 1886)

O

'On the eve of St. John's Night, June 23 1867, I finished, with God's help, St. John's Night on the Bald Mountain [near Kiev], a tone picture consisting of the following episodes,' wrote Mussorgsky to Rimsky-Korsakov. '1. Assembly of the Witches, Hubbub and Chatter 2. Satan's Pageant 3. Ceremonies in Honour of Satan 4. Witches' Dance.' Originally, Mussorgsky intended the work to be part of an opera (begun in 1863) but changed his mind. The version we usually hear is by Rimsky-Korsakov who re-orchestrated the entire thing after Mussorgsky's death. The opening is familiar from a long-running TV commercial for a brand of tape cassette - the one with a guy sitting in an armchair as a gale courses through his sitting room.

MUSSORGSKY
PICTURES AT AN
EXHIBITION
(1874)

I/O

In 1873 the Russian painter and architect Vladimir Hartmann died and Mussorgsky, who had known Hartmann intimately, visited a retrospective exhibition of his work in St. Petersburg shortly afterwards. Deeply affected, he was inspired to write a suite of piano pieces illustrating Hartmann's pictures. The result was this much-loved promenade round the exhibition, ten episodes with, as Mussorgsky explained, 'the composer... walking idly through the gallery, pausing occasionally to observe a picture and think sadly of his friend.' The suite is one of the most important pieces of Russian piano music but is more familiar today in the orchestral version by Ravel. There are also others by Lucien Cailliet - better than Ravel's but not as widely known - Henry Wood and Leopold Stokowski.

STANLEY MYERS
1933-93
ENGLISH
CAVATINA
(1970/71)

I

Myers cut his teeth as an arranger and composer in television (he worked on *Z Cars* in the 1960s) before breaking into films. His big hit was *Cavatina*, which he originally wrote for the 1971 film *The Walking Stick*, and then re-used in the Robert de Niro vehicle *The Deer Hunter (1978)*, with its serene and haunting theme of regret. Guitarist John Williams played it on both soundtracks and had a hit single with it in the late 1970's, while it was given a further lease of life by having lyrics added (by Cleo Laine) and called 'He was beautiful'. Not surprisingly, it's very popular at funerals.

N

Nicolai spent most of his brief career in Vienna as a composer and conductor (he helped found the Vienna Philharmonic Orchestra). His masterwork is this comic opera based on Shakespeare's play and its overture is a classic of its kind - tuneful, sprightly and vigorous in the manner of Suppé and Offenbach. Poor Nicolai conducted only four performances of the opera before being felled by an apoplectic stroke at the age of 39.

OTTO NICOLAI
1810–49
GERMAN
Overture to
THE MERRY WIVES
OF WINDSOR
Opera
(1849)

O

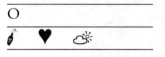

Neglected by all but the Scandinavian countries during his lifetime, Nielsen only became internationally known in the 1950s when he was finally recognised for what he was: Denmark's most important composer. Using Dvořák and Brahms as his models, Nielsen composed six symphonies and in each one tried out something new. The Second was inspired by a group of paintings he had come across in a village pub in Zealand depicting the Four Temperaments (he portrays them as 'Fury, Phlegmatic, Melancholy and Sanguine'). The third movement is particularly poignant and moving; by contrast, the finale has a rollicking swagger that is quite irresistible.

CARL NIELSEN
1865–1931
DANISH
SYMPHONY NO. 2
'THE FOUR
TEMPERAMENTS'
(1902)

O

Nielsen's Fifth, composed between 1920 and 1922, is one of the most original of twentieth century symphonies. It's in two big movements, the first of which can be characterised as presenting a conflict, the second is about the problems arising from it and its optimistic, affirmative outcome. If that description seems obtuse then the music will reveal all. It's a magnificent, approachable work most famous for the passage in the opening movement when a solo side-drum belligerently wipes out the orchestra!

NIELSEN
SYMPHONY NO. 5
(1922)

O

MICHAEL NYMAN
B. 1948
THE PIANO
CONCERTO
(1993)

C

♪   ♥   ☁

Jane Campion's hugely successful 1992 film *The Piano* featured a noteworthy score by Nyman. The solo piano music (played by Holly Hunter as Ada, the pianist in the film) and other material written for the film furnished the subject matter for this single-movement concerto. It is in four sections (*The Beach, The Woods, The Hut* and *The Release*), three of them using popular Scottish folk tunes of the Eighteenth and Nineteenth Centuries - *Flowers of the Forest, Bonny winter's noo awa* and *Bonnie Jean*. It was first performed in September 1993 with Kathryn Stott as soloist.

O

JACQUES OFFENBACH
1819-80
GERMAN-FRENCH
LA BELLE HÉLÈNE
(1864)

OP

♪

Following the resounding success of his *Orpheus in the Underworld* in 1858, Offenbach decided to come up with another operetta based on mythological characters. This is an often hilarious send-up of the legend of Helen of Troy (the 'Fair Helen' of the title) while providing a vehicle for Offenbach's favourite occupation - satirising the government of the day, the social order of the Second Empire, the army, his fellow composers, you name it. The Parisian audiences of 1864 lapped it up and it's still one of the most popular of operettas, a succession of catchy tunes and arias.

OFFENBACH
BARCAROLLE
from The Tales of Hoffmann
(1881)

OP

☁

Offenbach wrote this captivating work right at the end of his life (in fact, he died during rehearsals for the first production). It's quite different in tone from the rest of his output, a grand opera based on three tales by the extraordinary German writer, music critic, caricaturist and composer E.T.A. Hoffmann (the French title of the opera is *Les Contes d'Hoffmann*). The plot is complex but the music is not, and its best-known section is the lovely duet 'Belle nuit, ô nuit d'amour' ('Lovely night, oh night of love') from Act 3, known as the Barcarolle. A barcarolle is a boatman's song, especially associated with the Venetian gondoliers and this one, the most famous of all barcarolles, is a marvellous evocation of the moonlit canals of Venice.

A further reason for the scandal surrounding the operetta *Orpheus in the Underworld* [see below] was the introduction of the 'immoral' cancan after a stately minuet. 'A profanation of holy and glorious antiquity,' wrote one critic, 'in a spirit of irreverence that borders on blasphemy.' The cancan is the boisterous dance where all the girls lift their dresses and petticoats to reveal saucy glimpses of stocking tops and more. Also known as the *chahut*, it had been introduced in about 1840 and so, though not a new dance, became incredibly popular as a result of Offenbach's operetta.

OFFENBACH
CANCAN
from Orpheus in the Underworld
Operetta
(1858)

O

In Act 1, Spalanzani, an inventor, has made a wonderful mechanical doll named Olympia which he hopes will enable him to make back some of the money he has lost in a banking failure. Hoffmann, who appears in his own story, falls in love with Olympia. At a party to introduce her to the public, she sings a tremendously demanding coloratura aria 'Les Oiseaux dans la charmille' ('Songbirds in the Bower') during which, as a clockwork doll, she has to be wound up, of course. Listen to Joan Sutherland to hear how it should be done!

OFFENBACH
'DOLL SONG'
from The Tales of Hoffmann
(1881)

OP

You could say that *Orphée aux Enfers* (the original French title) was the first operetta (i.e. an opera that didn't/couldn't take itself or its subject too seriously). At its opening in Paris in 1858 it was not an immediate success – it poked fun at the great composer Gluck (see his opera *Orpheus and Eurydice*), the current government, Greek legends, and anything else that took Offenbach's fancy. It was a particularly devastating review that provoked the Parisians to turn up in droves to see the show for themselves, which quickly became a *succès de scandale*. Soon it was playing all over Europe and America, a smash hit. More importantly, it established a new form of musical entertainment. The Overture (like many of those to Offenbach's operettas) was not written by Offenbach. This was brilliantly put together by one Carl Binder for the 1860 Vienna production. One vocal highlight is the 'Fly Duet' in Act 3 in which two characters buzz their feelings for one another, as endearingly silly as anything you'll ever hear.

OFFENBACH
ORPHEUS IN THE UNDERWORLD
(1858)

OP

219

OFFENBACH
(arr. Rosenthal)
GAITÉ PARISIENNE
Ballet
(1938)

O

This brilliant one-act ballet came about through the impresario Sol Hurok (1888-1974) and the choreographer and dancer Léonide Massine (1895-1979) who wanted a rollicking musical score for the Monte Carlo Ballet in 1938. They selected a number of choice morsels from Offenbach's works (including *Orpheus in the Underworld*, *La Périchole* and *La Vie parisienne*) and handed them to the French composer and conductor Manuel Rosenthal (b. 1904) to orchestrate. The slim story line (it's set in a fashionable Paris restaurant and revolves around various amours) is put in the shade by the infectious score that Rosenthal produced.

CARL ORFF
1895-1982
GERMAN
CARMINA BURANA
(1937)

CHO

The words for what the composer described as a 'scenic cantata' are taken from an anthology of thirteenth century student poems found in the monastery of Benediktbeuren in Bavaria. They're in Latin and German - bawdy celebrations of drinking, sex and other delights - and the music Orff gave them matches their spirit: raw, rhythmic, energetic, a fusion of traditional, jazz and contemporary techniques. *O fortuna*, the powerful opening chorus, is now forever linked to a well-known brand of after-shave due to a long-running TV commercial in the 1980s.

P

JOHANN PACHELBEL
1653-1706
GERMAN
CANON IN D
(date unknown)

O

Nothing to do with firearms or the clergy. A musical canon is a composition in which a theme played by one voice (or instrument) is repeated by other voices (or instruments) before the previous voice has finished, so that it overlaps ('Frère Jacques' and 'Three Blind Mice' are canons). German-born Pachelbel was more famous in his lifetime as an organist and composer of church music (and he wrote piles of it), but he's remembered now solely for this mightily-popular canon, originally written for three violins and continuo. It's used in many TV commercials and appears on just about every compilation CD of serene and restful music, though you rarely hear the Gigue, its companion piece, which follows it.

For the last decade of the Nineteenth Century until well into the next, Paderewski's name was synonymous with the piano. He was a great Polish patriot who went on to become the Prime Minister of his country's newly-established republic for a short period in 1919. At one time, his Minuet in G for piano was played by everyone (it was always billed as *Paderewski's Celebrated Minuet*) and even today its old-world courtliness is hard to resist. It is actually No. 1 of a collection of six piano pieces entitled *Humoresques de concert*, Op. 14. There are some other works by Paderewski that are well worth getting to know, such as his Piano Concerto in A minor and the *Polish Fantasy* (for piano and orchestra), as well as his Chopin-like Nocturne in B flat.

IGNACE JAN PADEREWSKI
1860-1941
POLISH
MINUET IN G
(1887)

I

♥

The impact of Paganini's career and music on his contemporaries and succeeding generations was truly astonishing. The archetypal Romantic figure, Paganini was the greatest violinist the world had ever seen and his technical wizardry introduced not only virtuosity as an important element in music-making but rocketed the potential of the violin to another level. In part, this was due to the *24 Caprices* for solo violin that were published in 1820. These form a virtual compendium of anything that is possible on the instrument. Liszt and Schumann made piano versions of some of them, several composers wrote piano accompaniments for them, and several more were inspired to write variations on the most famous of them all, Caprice in A minor, Op. 1 No. 24 (see Brahms, Lutoslawski and Rachmaninov).

NICCOLÒ PAGANINI
1782-1840
ITALIAN
24 CAPRICES
for violin
(1801-07)

I

Perpetual Motion is how the title translates and that's exactly what this piece is - a continuous whirl of even notes lasting about three minutes without a let-up - a test of endurance and accuracy for any violinist. How people like James Galway (on the flute) and Wynton Marsalis (on the trumpet) do it without apparently breathing is, well, breathtaking. There's a similar but lesser known *moto perpetuo* called *Perpetuela* written ten years after the famous one. Paganini is said to have played its 2,242 notes in 3 minutes, 3 seconds. He also used the piece in the finale of his Quartet No. 14.

PAGANINI
MOTO PERPETUO
(c. 1822)

I

PAGANINI
I PALPITI
(1819)

I

$\oint$

The most popular opera aria of the early 1800s was 'Di tanti palpiti' ('From such heart-ache') from Rossini's 1813 opera *Tancredi*, one of those hit tunes that everyone went around whistling. It's known as the 'Rice Aria' because Rossini was alleged to have written it in four minutes while his rice was cooking. Paganini and Rossini knew each other well and the demon fiddler wrote this set of tremendously difficult variations based on Rossini's tune and designed them to stun his audience into disbelief.

PAGANINI
LE STREGHE
(1813)

I

$\oint$

Paganini's most celebrated set of 'variations on a theme' is this, *The Witches' Dance*. He had seen a production of a ballet by Süssmayr called *Il Noce di Benevento* at La Scala, Milan and the tune he uses for this fiendishly-taxing piece comes from that. Paganini's other thrilling variations for the violin include *Fantasy on the G String* (based on themes from Rossini's opera *Moses in Egypt* and played on just the G string of the violin), *Variations on 'Nel cor più non me sento'* (from Paisiello's *La Molinara*) and *Variations on 'God save the Queen'*. They're all quite easy to find on disc.

PAGANINI
VIOLIN CONCERTO
NO. 1 IN D
(c. 1817)

C

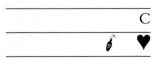

Like most of Paganini's music, none of the six violin concertos he wrote was published during his lifetime. Paganini was a canny operator who didn't want anyone else to play his music (not that many could!) and jealously guarded the scores to prevent anyone copying his secrets. Until the 1950s, only Concertos Nos. 1 and 2 were played but now all six have been recorded and we can marvel not just at Paganini's melodic invention and the dazzling effects he produced but at his great skill as an orchestrator. No. 1 alternates between the bravura and lyrical, ending with a vivacious rondo that is electrifying in the hands of a great player like Michael Rabin or Salvatore Accardo.

First performed by Paganini in 1827, nearly a decade after the première of No. 1, the Second Concerto is famous for its last movement, a rondo known by its nickname of *La Clochette* or *La Campanella* (*The Little Bell*) because it features the sound of a bell which the soloist matches on the upper reaches of the violin. It's equally celebrated through Liszt's version of the tune for solo piano. Paganini's other four concertos make compelling listening, all of them substantial works lasting well over half an hour, the best of which is, arguably, No. 4 in D minor, composed in 1831.

PAGANINI
VIOLIN CONCERTO
NO. 2 IN B MINOR
(1826)
and others

C

♥

Though a big name in his day, Paisiello has been almost totally forgotten despite notching up over 100 operas. Among these are *La Molinara* (see entry on Paganini's *Le Streghe*) and *The Barber of Seville* (1782) which was still hugely popular when Rossini wrote his own version of the same story in 1816. Though many contemporary composers have written for the mandolin (Stravinsky, Prokofiev and Webern among them) the most effective use was in the concertos and sonatas written between the time of Vivaldi (1678-1741) and Hummel (1778-1837). Paisiello's are charming three-movement examples of the genre.

GIOVANNI PAISIELLO
1740–1816
ITALIAN
MANDOLIN
CONCERTOS
IN C AND E FLAT
(dates unknown)

C

Verdi said of Palestrina, 'He is the real king of sacred music, and the Eternal Father of Italian Music.' In Palestrina, music for the Catholic Church reached a high point; he was one of the great masters of choral music whose work is still held up as a model for students today. He composed over 100 settings of the Mass alone and this one is particularly effective, written for six high voices with several exuberant sections. It's known as an *imitation* mass, that is a work based on an already existing composition such as a motet or a madrigal. In this case, Palestrina used his motet *Dum complerentur* as a kind of stockpile of ideas from which to create a new composition.

GIOVANNI DA
PALESTRINA
c. 1525–94
ITALIAN
MISSA DUM
COMPLERENTUR
(1569)

CHO

PALESTRINA
MISSA PAPAE
MARCELLI
(?1563)

CHO

The *Pope Marcellus Mass* is the one that captured the public imagination like no other work by Palestrina and ensured his place in musical history (he is buried in St. Peter's, Rome, his coffin bearing the epitaph 'Musicae Princeps'). It has always been assumed that the Mass was written in 1555 for Pope Marcellus II (who reigned just 55 days and never heard it). Now scholars think it may have been written for the Council of Trent (1563) or still later in 1565 when a group of cardinals gathered to listen to some unnamed masses to hear whether the texts were audible. Whatever, close your eyes, imagine you're in St. Peter's and listen to this ethereal music filling that awe-inspiring building.

MARIA THERESIA VON PARADIES
1759–1824
AUSTRIAN
SICILIENNE
(date unknown)

I

I rather like the sound of Maria Theresia von Paradies, the daughter of an Imperial Councillor in Vienna and named for her godmother the Empress. Despite being blind from the age of five, she became an excellent pianist, organist, singer and composer, she had 60 concertos in her repertoire and Mozart dedicated his Piano Concerto No. 18 in B flat (K456) to her. Her *Sicilienne* is the slightest of things (usually heard played by violin and piano) but so completely charming that it had to be included here. And if it was good enough for violinists of the calibre of Menuhin, Milstein, Thibaud and Perlman, then it's good enough for me. A footnote, yes, but let's not forget the footnotes.

PIETRO DOMENICO PARADIES
1707–91
ITALIAN
TOCCATA IN A
(1754)

I

Another footnote, no relation to the above, and an even shorter piece. The keyboard sonatas of Paradies were much admired by fellow composers Clementi, Cramer and Mozart. The set of 12 that appeared in 1754, each with two movements, include an extraordinary variety of ideas. This toccata comes from Sonata No. 6 and is one minute and a half of non-stop semi-quavers. It's the only piece by Paradies played today and is quite dazzling - listen to the recording by George Malcolm.

Parry's music has made a bit of a comeback in recent years giving the lie to the old canard that no one was writing decent music in England before Elgar. His choral works are particularly fine and this one is a real spine-tingler. It's the anthem Parry composed for the coronation of Edward VII, an exultant setting of Psalm 122, heard at every coronation service since. For the 1953 crowning of Queen Elizabeth II, the cries of 'Vivat Regina Elizabetha' were added.

HUBERT PARRY
1848–1918
ENGLISH
I WAS GLAD
(1902)

CHO

Parry's most famous work is also one of his shortest. The idea of setting William Blake's poem ('And did those feet in ancient times...') to music was suggested to Parry by the then Poet Laureate Robert Bridges. It quickly caught on after its first performance in 1916 and was adopted as the campaign anthem for the Votes for Women movement (Parry's wife was a suffragette). Later, it was taken up by the National Federation of Women's Institutes. Now it's a second national anthem and an integral part of the BBC's *Last Night of the Proms* ritual. Strange that no one has thought to revive Parry's other rousing patriotic anthem *England*, a setting of John of Gaunt's speech from Shakespeare's *Richard II* - 'This royal throne of kings, this scepter'd isle... '. Not as good as *Jerusalem*, but still pretty powerful.

PARRY
JERUSALEM
(1916)

CHO

The final years of Parry's life were marred by depression and sadness - the war with Germany, his isolation from his wife, a rift with his fellow composer Stanford, all contributed to a state of mind which is eloquently caught in these six motets. Parry took the words of Psalm 39 ('Lord, let me know mine end') and poems by Vaughan, Campion and Donne among others for these deeply moving and personal testaments. No. 3 is *Never weather-beaten sail*, but the most familiar is the first of the set, the elegiac *My soul, there is a country*.

PARRY
SIX SONGS OF
FAREWELL
(1916-18)

CHO

Arvo Pärt
B. 1935
ESTONIAN
THE BEATITUDES
(1990, rev. 1991)

CHO

The setting of *The Beatitudes* (Matthew v, 3-12, which begins 'Blessed are the poor in spirit, for theirs is the kingdom of heaven') was Pärt's first use of an English text. It's a work in which he uses the technique he describes as *tintinnabulation* [for an explanation see *Summa* below] where the music seems to be standing still for much of the time but which, in this case, builds to a climactic 'Amen' underpinned by the organ.

Pärt
DE PROFUNDIS
(1980)

CHO

Coming where he does in this book, the Estonian-born composer is well placed, for many of his choral works have elements with which both Palestrina and Parry would have been familiar. *De Profundis* is scored for male choir, organ and percussion (including tam-tam and tubular bell), and is notable for the relentless thumping of the bass drum which has been likened to 'a primeval heartbeat'. The words are a setting of Psalm 130 ('Out of the depths have I called you, Lord') and it was written shortly after Pärt moved from his native country to live in Berlin.

Pärt
SUMMA
(1977)

CHO

Summa is a setting of the *Latin Creed* ('I believe in one God, the Father Almighty, Maker of heaven and earth…'). This is one of Pärt's creations in which he uses *tintinnabulation* - hard to define but throughout a *tintinnabuli* piece there's the constant unchanging sound of the same chord rather, as one writer aptly put it, 'like the way in which a bell continues to ring long after the note has been sounded'. The effect is strangely restful and hypnotic. *Summa* also exists in (wordless) versions for string quartet and string orchestra.

Johann Adam Hiller, a now-forgotten eighteenth century German composer, one of many who have made 'reworkings' of this choral masterpiece, wrote 'I know of no music that, from beginning to end, has had the same emotional impact on me as Pergolesi's, and the man who could remain cold and unmoved when hearing it does not deserve to be called a human being.' Pergolesi, who died from consumption at the age of 26, is said to have completed the work only days before his death. The setting of the Latin text 'Stabat mater dolorosa' ('A grieving mother stood in tears beside the Cross...') is in 12 brief sections sung by a soprano and contralto with string orchestra.

GIOVANNI PERGOLESI
1710–36
ITALIAN
STABAT MATER
(1736)

V

Not to be confused with Léon Jessel's *Parade of the Tin Soldiers* (1905), Pierné's miniature march is nevertheless another quintessential example of the European light music tradition. It's one of those simple, catchy little tunes you can't get out of your head for days but can never remember what it's called. This one began life as a piano piece in 1887 and comes from a collection called *Album for My Little Friends*. Pierné himself was a pupil of Massenet and Franck, and was a fine organist and conductor who left a vast amount of rarely-performed music in virtually every form.

GABRIEL PIERNÉ
1863-1937
FRENCH
MARCH OF THE
LITTLE LEAD
SOLDIERS
(date unknown)

O

The suite that the American composer Piston fashioned from the music of his ballet *The Incredible Flutist* turned out to be his most popular work (Arthur Fiedler and the Boston Pops gave the first performance). Easy to see why - it's colourful, tuneful and witty. The suite (in 12 very short sections) follows the story of the ballet which involves a circus arriving in a village one hot afternoon, led by the remarkable, charismatic Flutist. He seems to cast an amorous spell on the inhabitants, but before anything gets out of hand, the band strikes up, the spell is broken and the circus leaves.

WALTER PISTON
1894-1976
AMERICAN
THE INCREDIBLE
FLUTIST
Ballet
(1938)

O

AMILCARE PONCHIELLI 1834–86
ITALIAN
LA GIOCONDA
(1876)

OP

♥

La Gioconda (*The Joyful Girl*) was Ponchielli's only international success; in the last decade left to him, he could never repeat the high artistic level of this operatic masterpiece. There's a celebrated tenor aria (Enzo's idyll to the beauty of the night, 'Cielo e mar' from Act 2) and the heroine's dramatic 'Suicidio' in Act 4 when she plans to kill herself. But the most familiar part of the opera isn't a vocal item. The *Dance of the Hours* is heard in Act 3 at a sumptuous ball where dancers, in groups of six, come out impersonating the hours of dawn, day, evening and night. It was one of the 'classical pops' featured in Walt Disney's *Fantasia* and which some of us know thanks to American comedian Alan Sherman's send-up: 'Hello muddah, hello faddah/Here I am at Camp Granada'.

FRANCIS POULENC 1899–1963
FRENCH
ADAGIETTO
and RONDEAU
from Les Biches Ballet
(1924)

O

🎵

Les Biches is a one-act ballet featuring three handsome, muscle-bound boys who flex their pecs before their sexually-ambiguous hostess. The title translates as *The Hinds*, but more colloquially as *The Little Darlings*. Get the picture? Poulenc's scores in any musical genre are full of rhythmic energy which made him a natural ballet composer (this was premièred by Diaghilev's Ballets Russes at Monte Carlo in 1924), and this one also features popular French folk-songs. The orchestral Adagietto and Rondeau (respectively Nos. 4 and 2 from the score) are hummable 'oh-so-that's-where-they-come-from' numbers.

POULENC
BABAR THE ELEPHANT
(1940-45)

I (with narrator)

🎵

The book L'Histoire de Babar le petit éléphant was written by the painter Jean de Brunhoff for his two sons. It first appeared in 1931 (the first English edition in 1933 had a preface by A.A. Milne). Poulenc was holidaying at Brive-la-Gaillarde in the summer of 1940 with 11 of his nephews and nieces and, so the story goes, one of the children interrupted Uncle Francis playing his own music with, 'How horrid that music is - come on, play me this.' The child thrust a copy of *Babar the Elephant* on to the piano and the amused composer began improvising round the story and pictures. Five years later he worked on the ideas from that occasion and published the work, dedicating it to the 11 boys and girls who had made up that first audience. It's now a staple item of children's concerts.

Few composers have ever been as good as Poulenc at switching from boisterous high spirits to heart-breaking lyricism in a matter of moments. Try this minor masterpiece and you'll see what I mean (though the fiery last movement exudes dazzling good humour from start to finish). Poulenc wrote a sonata for two clarinets and another for clarinet and bassoon early in his career but this one (and an oboe sonata) were his last works and not premièred until after his death. It was dedicated to the jazz clarinettist Benny Goodman and is now an integral part of the clarinet repertoire.

POULENC
CLARINET SONATA
(1962)

CH

Arguably the most successful of all Poulenc's works, the Organ Concerto is unlike any other you've heard. With its thunderous opening chords and general air of gloom you think you're in for a hard time - and then suddenly you're in the variety theatre listening to music that couldn't be more carefree and exuberant. The changes from the sacred to the secular and back again reflect Poulenc's own inner nature. The Concerto is in one continuous movement and is dedicated to the lady who commissioned it, the Princess Edmond de Polignac.

POULENC
CONCERTO IN G
MINOR FOR
ORGAN, STRINGS
AND PERCUSSION
(1938)

C

D minor is generally considered a sombre, tragic key (listen to Brahms's D Minor Piano Concerto). Poulenc offers us an urbane, easy-going concerto whose freshness and charm have made this one of his most played works (the composer himself and pianist Jacques Février gave the première in Venice in the summer of 1932). The second movement (larghetto) will remind you of a Mozart slow movement but with a uniquely Poulenc tang. As one commentator wrote, 'Poulenc understands [the difference] between light music and trivial music; a rather critical distinction in a concerto of this kind, for in the last analysis the difference is one between entertainment and boredom.'

POULENC
CONCERTO IN D
MINOR FOR TWO
PIANOS
(1932)

C

POULENC
GLORIA
(1959)

CHO

Here Poulenc keeps a straight face for this deeply-felt and uplifting choral work, scored for soprano soloist, chorus and orchestra and written towards the end of his life. That's not to say it's a solemn experience throughout (as the opening *Gloria* will tell you), but its moving lyricism and purity matched by a complete lack of pomposity are most affecting. The work has six sections, all sung in Latin.

POULENC
PIANO CONCERTO
(1949)

C

Poulenc described his Piano Concerto as 'lightweight, a sort of *souvenir de Paris* for pianist-composer'. He played it first at a concert in Boston in January 1950. The first movement strikes a serious mood in the middle and the slow movement has a touch of melancholy about it (very much part of Poulenc's make up), but the finale is as witty and spirited as anything he wrote, quoting the French song 'À la claire fontaine' (or is it 'Way down upon the Swanee River'? See what *you* think!). Such 'musical slang' shocked its first audiences who couldn't understand how a serious composer could have a sense of humour.

ZBIGNIEW PREISNER
B. 1955
POLISH
REQUIEM FOR MY
FRIEND
(1996)

CHO

Up till now, the self-taught Polish composer Preisner has devoted himself to film music, most notably for Louis Malle's *Damage*, Agnieska Holland's *The Secret Garden* and his collaborations with director Krzysztof Kieslowski (*The Double Life of Veronique, Three Colours Blue/White/Red*). Kieslowski's death in 1996 prompted this, Preisner's first full-scale work. Part One, as bleak and sparse as a Siberian railway siding, is an atmospheric, ghostly setting of words from the Catholic Mass for the Dead with echoes of Górecki's Third Symphony and plainsong that haunt the memory - especially the vivid *Lacrimosa* with its high soprano part. Part Two, subtitled *Life*, is a (mainly) subdued tribute to Krzysztof using Biblical, Latin and Polish texts with its acclamatory *Ascende huc* and *Veni et vidi* sections particularly striking.

After the Revolution, Prokofiev spent most of the next decade abroad, only returning to Russia in 1927 and not settling there again permanently until 1932. The first music he wrote after his return was for a 1933 movie made by the Russian film corporation, Belgoskino, called *Lieutenant Kijé*. The following year Prokofiev turned the score into a symphonic suite for the concert hall. Kijé was a mythical character, created after Tsar Nicholas I misread the name of a Russian officer – the non-existent Lieutenant of the title – on a report. Afraid to point out to the Tsar his mistake, the courtiers decided to invent an officer, hence all the comical comings and goings illustrated in the score. The best-known bit (and it's included in every Christmas compilation) is *Troika* (*Sleigh Ride*) with its jingling sleigh bells, a setting of an old Russian drinking song.

**SERGEI PROKOFIEV
1891–1953**
RUSSIAN
LIEUTENANT KIJÉ
Suite
(1934)

O

The oranges in this opera are three princesses imprisoned in three oranges by a wicked sorceress. A crown prince falls in love with them, though only one survives her juicy entombment, the last of the trio revived by having a bucket of water thrown over her. It's a fantastical, nonsensical story which Prokofiev used to send up the conventions of grand opera. Along the way is some of his most brilliant writing for the orchestra with his usual spiky, angular tunes spiced with many quotations from Russian and French operas. The short, heavily-accented March is often heard separately, frequently in Prokofiev's own transcription for piano solo.

PROKOFIEV
MARCH
from The Love for Three Oranges
Opera
(1919)

O/I

The first production of this ballet based on Shakespeare's *Romeo and Juliet* was not a success. The Soviet critics found the music 'hard, cold and incongruous' when presented at the Bolshoi Theatre, Moscow in 1935 – and they disapproved of the happy ending Prokofiev had provided (he later restored the tragic one). It was not until he transformed the ballet score into three suites for the concert hall that the music caught on. The second of these opens with the strutting dance of the two rival families, the Montagues (Romeo's lot) and the Capulets (Juliet's).

PROKOFIEV
MONTAGUES AND CAPULETS
from Romeo and Juliet
Ballet
(1935)

O

231

PROKOFIEV
PETER AND THE
WOLF
(1936)

O (with narrator)

'Symphonic fairy tale for narrator and orchestra' is how this evergreen children's entertainment is officially described. Prokofiev wrote it to teach children the sounds of the different instruments of the orchestra (the bird is a flute, the duck an oboe, the cat a clarinet, etc.) and a narrator speaks the text, pausing to allow the music to give a tonal interpretation of what is being described. The story was Prokofiev's own, though his music is far more imaginative than his prose, which has been recorded by everyone from Sir Ralph Richardson and Dame Edna Everage to Sean Connery, Sting, David Bowie - and me!

PROKOFIEV
PIANO CONCERTO
NO. 1 IN D FLAT
(1911-12)

C

Poking fun and defying conventions were two of Prokofiev's pre-occupations as a young composer. He certainly achieved them with the first of his five piano concertos. It marks a significant break from the lush Romanticism of Rachmaninov's concertos, introducing harsh, percussive effects, unexpected melodic twists and angular rhythms that startled its first audiences. He composed it as a vehicle for his debut as a soloist with an orchestra (Prokofiev was an exceptionally fine pianist), and later for his graduation concert from the St. Petersburg Conservatory. Hearing it, you can imagine what a scandal it caused when his fellow students played Liszt and Saint-Saëns.

PROKOFIEV
PIANO CONCERTO
NO. 3 IN C
(1917-21)

C

One of the most frequently played of all twentieth century piano concertos, No. 3 is a masterpiece. The solo part is particularly brilliant with Prokofiev's characteristically percussive writing but is not without some genuinely lyrical passages (you only have to listen to the beautiful opening Russian theme played by the clarinet). Though the Concerto was completed in 1921, most of the themes had been written over the previous decade: you wouldn't know it - the writing seems so spontaneous with white-hot inspiration. Prokofiev gave the first performance in Chicago the same year (just two weeks before the première of *The Love for Three Oranges* in the same city) and later made a revealing recording of the work (though in rather dim sound).

'It seemed to me,' wrote Prokofiev, 'that had Haydn lived to our day he would have kept his own style while adding something of the new at the same time. That was the kind of symphony I wanted to write. When I saw that the idea was working I called it the Classical Symphony.' So, laced with Prokofiev's own sardonic sense of humour and imagination, here's a twentieth century Haydn, full of unexpected twists of harmony and mood in the traditional four movements of the Classical period: Allegro, Larghetto, Gavotte and (lively) Finale. Strange to think that such a witty, spirited work could have been composed in 1917 during the days of the Russian Revolution.

PROKOFIEV
SYMPHONY
NO. 1 IN D
'CLASSICAL'
(1916-17)

O

One of the Twentieth Century's greatest violin concertos has a slow movement that ranks as one of Prokofiev's loveliest creations. Its string of memorable themes (and, of course, Prokofiev's typically incisive, exciting rhythms) are unmistakably Russian, written in a warmer, more approachable vein than even the Third Piano Concerto. Both of them, though, have final movements which can be described as 'tumultuous'. The Second Violin Concerto was written for a French violinist, Robert Soetens, who gave the first performance in Madrid in 1935.

PROKOFIEV
VIOLIN CONCERTO
NO. 2 IN G MINOR
(1935)

C

If you're looking for an introduction to the whole world of opera, *La Bohème* couldn't be a better choice. A touching tale of love, laughter and tears, it has some of the best-known arias ever written, among them this much loved tenor solo from Act 1, 'Your tiny hand is frozen' (known to bawdier members of the singing profession as 'You're tiny – and it's frozen'). It's sung by the hero, Rodolfo, a poet who lives a Bohemian life in a cheerless garret in Paris' Latin Quarter. Into his life comes the beautiful but consumptive seamstress Mimi, who knocks at his door asking for a match. Listen to the recording by Jussi Björling.

GIACOMO PUCCINI
1858-1924
ITALIAN
'CHE GELIDA
MANINA'
from La Bohème
(1896)

OP

♥

PUCCINI
'SI, MI CHIAMANO
MIMI'
from La Bohème
(1896)

OP

♥

'They call me Mimi,' sings the seamstress after her introduction to Rodolfo (who has just fallen head over heels for her). She tells him she embroiders artificial flowers for a living. Lonely and longing for the sunshine, she yearns for the real flowers of the countryside. *La Bohème* was Puccini's fourth opera but, although it contained a string of imperishable numbers like Mimi's aria and was the work that established his international reputation, it was not an immediate success. It's now perhaps the most popular of all operas, still guaranteed to fill a house anywhere in the world.

PUCCINI
'O SOAVE
FANCIULLA'
from La Bohème
(1896)

OP

♥

'O lovely maid in the moonlight' is the duet between Rodolfo and Mimi that comes at the end of Act 1. She hears Rodolfo's friends call him from the street below and goes to the window. In the moonlight she appears even lovelier to him. The yearning theme of this impassioned song of love (always heard in association with Mimi) is quoted earlier in the act and several times afterwards, most tellingly in the last act.

PUCCINI
'MUSETTA'S WALTZ
SONG'
from La Bohème
(1896)

OP

♥

In Act 2 Rodolfo and Mimi have joined their friends in the local café and enter into the Christmas spirit. Among them is Musetta, an old flame of Rodolfo's flatmate Marcello, who has arrived with a wealthy, elderly admirer. 'Quando me'n vo' soletta per la via,' she sings ('As through the streets I wander onward merrily') known as 'Musetta's Waltz Song'. It's one of the highlights of the opera as she makes it obvious she is still in love with Marcello without arousing the suspicions of her aged companion.

In Act 3, Mimi and Rodolfo have quarrelled and decide, regretfully, to part. Then Marcello appears. He's caught Musetta flirting with a stranger. So the two pairs of lovers each sing their farewells, a beautiful and ingenious vocal quartet in which Puccini manages to combine the gentle and melancholy parting of Mimi and Rodolfo ('Addio, dolce svegliare' - 'Farewell, sweet love') with the aggressive and vindictive 'Viper!', 'Toad!' that Marcello and Musetta shout at each other.

PUCCINI
'MIMI'S FAREWELL'
from La Bohème
(1896)

OP

♥

Gianni Schicchi is the third of three one-act operas known collectively as *Il Trittico* (*The Triptych*), the other two being *Il Tabarro* (*The Cloak*) and *Suor Angelica* (*Sister Angelica*). Gianni Schicci is the name of a wily Tuscan peasant who manages to revise a wealthy man's will so that his daughter (Lauretta) will have a dowry and so can marry her boyfriend Rinuccio. 'O mio babbino caro' is high in the opera aria popularity ratings and it's easy to hear why - a typically ravishing Puccini melody full of passion and tears. It's sung by Lauretta as she begs her father to help her so that she can marry her beloved. If he doesn't help her, she says, she'll drown herself!

PUCCINI
'O MY BELOVED FATHER'
from Gianni Schicchi
(1918)

OP

♥

Puccini began writing *Madame Butterfly* in the autumn of 1901. A car accident interrupted work for several months but the work was finally completed in December 1903 (although he revised the score soon after its unsuccessful first outing). Puccini felt this was 'the most felt and most expressive opera that I have conceived' and it was his own personal favourite of all he wrote. This exquisite love duet is a real three-hanky number and comes at the end of Act 1, sung by Pinkerton (a lieutenant in the U.S. navy) and his new wife, Cio-Cio-San (to give Madame Butterfly her real name), a 15-year-old geisha.

PUCCINI
'DOLCE NOTTE'
('Love Duet') from
Madame Butterfly
(1904)

OP

♥ ♦

PUCCINI
'ONE FINE DAY'
(*'Un bel dì'*)
from Madame Butterfly
(*1904*)

OP

♥ ◗

Three years have passed and the Lieutenant, recalled to America, has not returned to his wife in Nagasaki. He has never seen his little boy, 'Trouble', but Cio-Cio-San is convinced he will return. 'Some day he'll come' (or 'One Fine Day' as it's universally known) comes from Act 2; it's one of the most celebrated of soprano arias, a wonderful bit of writing for, despite the searing optimism of the music, you can hear nevertheless that Cio-Cio-San's situation is hopeless.

PUCCINI
'HUMMING
CHORUS'
from Madame Butterfly
(*1904*)

OP

♥ ☁

Pinkerton's ship, the *Abraham Lincoln*, has arrived and Butterfly is convinced that, despite what she has heard to the contrary, her American husband will return to her and stay. As night falls she waits, rigid and motionless, while she listens to the hum of voices drifting up to her from the distant harbour. This is the moving and delicate 'Humming Chorus', an intermezzo suggesting the passage of time between the end of Act 2 and the beginning of Act 3.

PUCCINI
'ADDIO, FIORITO
ASIL'
from Madame Butterfly
(*1904*)

OP

♥

Pinkerton, Sharpless (the U.S. Consul) and Pinkerton's new American wife, Kate, all arrive at Butterfly's home. When Pinkerton sees for himself the proof of Butterfly's total loyalty to him, the flower-decked room to welcome his return and the memories it evokes, he realises how heartlessly he has behaved. After this tearful farewell to the house he knew so well, he rushes away in self-disgust.

PUCCINI
INTERMEZZO
from Manon Lescaut
(*1893*)

O/OP

♥

Puccini's *Manon Lescaut* arrived on the scene nine years after Massenet's version of the same story (page 190) and follows the original Abbé Provost novel more closely. The four acts take place in eighteenth century Amiens, Paris, Le Havre and Louisiana. Listen out in particular for Manon's lovely aria 'In quelle trine morbide' ('In this gilded cage'), one of Puccini's finest. The most famous passage, though, is the orchestral Intermezzo. Stealing a trick from Mascagni in his *Cavalleria Rusticana*, Puccini represents the journey from Paris to Le Havre between Acts 2 and 3.

The Swallow has never been among Puccini's most popular works. It is set in the 1850s in Paris and the Riviera and tells the tale of Magda, the mistress of a wealthy businessman, Rambaldo. She elopes with young Ruggero but finally leaves him to return to Rambaldo. 'Ch'il bel sogno di Doretta' ('Who could guess what Doretta's lovely dream was'), known as 'Doretta's Dream Aria', is sung by Magda in Act 1. Few wrote for the soprano voice better than Puccini and the phrase 'Folle amore! Folle ebrezza!' ('Crazed love! Crazed intoxication!') is one of those glorious, spine-tingling moments that few but he could produce.

PUCCINI
'DORETTA'S DREAM'
from La Rondine (1917)

OP

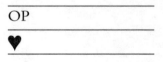

Where *La Bohème* is tender and romantic, *Tosca*, from four years later, is sombre and tragic. It's based on an 1887 play by Victorien Sardou set in Rome in June 1800 when Napoleon's army was greeted by Italian patriots as their liberator from oppressive Austrian rule. The painter Cavaradossi is in love with the celebrated singer Floria Tosca. He decides to hide Angelotti, an escaped political prisoner. In this famous Act 1 aria, Cavaradossi takes out the miniature of his adored Tosca and sings of the beautiful way in which her features blend into a harmonious whole, hence its English translation 'Strange Harmony'.

PUCCINI
'RECONDITA ARMONIA'
from Tosca (1900)

OP

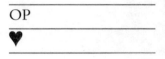

In Act 2 Cavaradossi has been arrested by the feared Chief of Police, Baron Scarpia and, having refused to reveal the hiding-place of Angelotti, is condemned to be shot. Scarpia tells Tosca her lover will be spared if she sleeps with him. In 'I have lived for art', one of opera's most moving and beloved arias, Tosca wonders, having devoted her life to art and love, gone regularly to church and given freely to charity, what she has done to deserve this cruel fate. Then, as Scarpia attempts to take his prize, she stabs him. The legendary recording of this scene between Tito Gobbi and Maria Callas still makes the hairs on the back of your neck stand on end.

PUCCINI
'VISSI D'ARTE'
from Tosca (1900)

OP

PUCCINI
'E LUCEVAN LE STELLE'
from Tosca
(1900)

OP

♥

No wonder tenors have queued up to play the role of Cavaradossi since *Tosca*'s first performance in January 1900 when they are presented with gifts like this: 'When the stars were brightly shining'. Here, having been told he has an hour to live before his execution, Cavaradossi sings a touching farewell, recalling his meetings with Tosca on starlit nights in quiet gardens.

PUCCINI
'IN QUESTA REGGIA'
from Turandot
(1926)

OP

♥

Those expecting the Puccini of *La Bohème* and *Tosca*, or a string of pretty arias like its most famous number (see below), are in for a surprise. Here Puccini, writing in the last year of his life (1924) but always shrewd enough to keep an eye on what was going on around him musically speaking, adopts many features of contemporary music. The plot concerns the ice-princess Turandot, bewitching daughter of the Chinese Emperor, who promises to marry any man of royal blood who can answer three riddles. Those failing to answer correctly will be put to death. Charming! In 'In this same palace' (Act 2), Turandot describes how one of her forebears was cruelly abducted.

PUCCINI
'NESSUN DORMA'
from Turandot
(1926)

OP

♥

Calaf (shall we call this the Pavarotti part?) has answered Turandot's riddle correctly. She balks at the idea of having to marry the son of a foreign slave. Her father insists she keeps her word. Calaf offers to withdraw if she can discover his real name by morning. Turandot decrees that 'none shall sleep' until Calaf's true identity is discovered. He, meanwhile, hangs around the palace garden at night relishing the moment when he will reveal that he is in fact the son of Timur, the exiled King of Tartary. 'None shall sleep,' he sings, a ludicrously inappropriate context for a football theme song. Be that as it may, Luciano Pavarotti's rendition of this one aria, repeated airplays and best-selling status has opened up the world of opera and classical music to millions of people.

The chaconne (or chacony) is a French word describing what was originally a slow Spanish dance in 3/4 time. In practice, it's the same as a passacaglia. Generally it uses a repeated pattern of bass notes (this is called a 'ground bass') which gives rise to a set of variations played on top. Purcell's is among the most famous examples (but see also 'Dido's Lament', below, a vocal chaconne). Though no one is certain of its origins, Purcell's Chaconne in G minor was probably composed for some stage production. It's a work of tranquil beauty in which 18 variations unfold continuously with constantly changing rhythmic patterns.

**HENRY PURCELL
1659–95**
ENGLISH
CHACONNE IN G MINOR FOR STRINGS
(date unknown)

O

While Purcell wrote a considerable amount of music for stage plays, he wrote only one opera, that is a stage work where the entire text is set to music. It remains one of the most significant operas written by an Englishman, yet was commissioned for a girls' boarding school in Chelsea! The libretto was by Nahum Tate who based it on the story in the fourth book of Virgil's *The Aeneid* about the tragic love between Aeneas, the Trojan hero, who is shipwrecked and falls in love with Dido, the Queen of Carthage. The Overture features a short and solemn introduction before bubbling into life much like a French overture by someone like Lully.

PURCELL
DIDO AND AENEAS
(1689)

OP

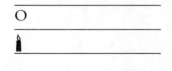

Described variously as 'one of the most touching episodes encountered in opera before Gluck' and 'one of the noblest pages in early opera', 'Dido's Lament' is a powerful illustration of the 'less is more' theory. Two witches and a sorceress have conspired to rob Dido of her love. The Queen is so grief stricken at the announcement of Aeneas' departure that she falls dead from a broken heart, having sung her immortal 'When I am laid in earth'. There have been many fine recordings of this but when Kirsten Flagstad reaches the phrase 'Remember me', none has quite matched her poignancy.

PURCELL
'WHEN I AM LAID IN EARTH'
from Dido and Aeneas (1689)

OP

PURCELL
'FAIREST ISLE'
from King Arthur
(1691)

OP

The amount of incidental music that Purcell wrote for Dryden's play *King Arthur or The British Worthy* in 1691 has led it to be dubbed an opera. Strictly speaking it's a 'play with music' (or 'semi-opera') but, whatever, it has some of Purcell's finest music - the famous *Frost Scene* in Act 3 depicting the frozen wastes from which the Cold Genius arises, the two sirens in Act 4 singing 'Two daughters of this aged stream we are' and, in the final act, this stately and moving song.

PURCELL
'NYMPHS AND
SHEPHERDS'
from The Libertine
(c. 1692)

V

This is the opening vocal number for the music Purcell composed for a play by Thomas Shadwell (c. 1642-92), the dramatist and Dryden's successor as Poet Laureate. Apart from bowdlerising Shakespeare, Shadwell was famous for his comic treatment of contemporary habits and for his crude humour. *The Libertine* is a typical and justly-forgotten example, yet I doubt if there was a primary school child in the inter- and post-war years that didn't sing 'Nymphs and Shepherds' at some time ('This is Flora's holiday, this is Flora's holiday') without having a clue what it was all about. Its popularity was partly due to a best-selling (and stylistically anachronistic) record of it made in 1929 by the Manchester Schoolchildren's Choir with the Hallé Orchestra under Sir Hamilton Harty.

PURCELL
Rondeau from
ABDELAZAR
(1695)

O

Another play for which Purcell contributed incidental music (though not nearly so much as for *King Arthur*) was the 1695 London production of *Abdelazar or The Moor's Revenge*, written by the extraordinary Aphra Behn (1640-89), professional spy and dubbed the first professional woman author in England. The second section of the music is the Rondeau made famous (indeed, resurrected from obscurity) by Benjamin Britten, a great champion of Purcell's genius. He used this noble theme as the basis for his 1946 orchestral *Variations and Fugue on a Theme of Henry Purcell*, better known as *The Young Person's Guide to the Orchestra*.

Like many 'trumpet tunes' of the period, this noble air was originally written for the harpsichord in imitation of the trumpet. And, like the famous Trumpet Voluntary once ascribed to Purcell but now to Jeremiah Clarke, it's never been conclusively proved that this popular piece was by Henry Purcell. The same tune appears in *The Island Princess*, a work by Clarke and Purcell's younger brother Daniel. Whoever composed it, it's a terrific piece to go down the aisle to. Have a listen also to Purcell's Trumpet Sonata No. 1 in D, only discovered in 1950 in York Minster, which is *definitely* by our man!

PURCELL
TRUMPET TUNE
AND AIR IN D
(1696)

I

Q

Eton-educated Quilter is remembered today mainly for his sensitive and atmospheric song settings of Shakespeare and the music he wrote in 1911 for *Where the Rainbow Ends*, a fairy play that was once a regular feature of London's Christmas entertainments. Quilter wrote in a light-handed style somewhere between Delius and Elgar and this adroitly-constructed overture is a delight, a medley of familiar nursery and folk tunes. If you like this then try his *Three English Dances*.

ROGER QUILTER
1877–1953
ENGLISH
CHILDREN'S
OVERTURE
(1919)

O

R

Rachmaninov wrote his First Piano Concerto when he was only 18 and still a student at the Moscow Conservatoire. This is his Op. 1, his earliest work - on the face of it. But what we actually hear today is the almost complete re-write he made 26 years later in 1917, well after the Second and Third Concertos were internationally famous. He used some of the same beautiful themes of his youthful version but in reality it's not an early work. The music is unmistakably Russian - yearning, soulful melodies with passages of high passion and drama - and the piano writing, as you'd expect from a brilliant pianist, is scintillating.

SERGEI
RACHMANINOV
1873–1943
RUSSIAN
PIANO CONCERTO
NO. 1 IN F SHARP
MINOR
(1891, rev. 1917)

C

RACHMANINOV PIANO CONCERTO NO. 2 IN C MINOR *(1901)*

C

♥

The most beloved of all piano concertos was composed under unusual circumstances. Rachmaninov had worked for two years on his First Symphony. Its première, conducted by Glazunov (rumoured to have been drunk), was a disaster and derided by the critics. It cast the composer into the profoundest depression. He entirely lost his creative urge and considered giving up being a composer altogether. Rachmaninov consulted a certain Dr. Nikolai Dahl, famous for his 'magic cures', achieved by auto-suggestion. After daily visits from January to April 1900 for his course of 'positive suggestion therapy' (hypnosis), Rachmaninov found that, miraculously, he could write again. By the summer he had written the second and third movements (Andante and Finale) while the first movement, with its famous opening eight chords on the piano, followed in the spring of 1901. The Second Piano Concerto was dedicated in gratitude 'To Monsieur N. Dahl'. The wonderful, soul-searching themes have endeared the work to millions and, of course, it was used to tissue-drenching effect in David Lean's masterly 1945 film *Brief Encounter*.

RACHMANINOV PIANO CONCERTO NO. 3 IN D MINOR *(1909)*

C

♥

Despite the popularity of No. 2, 'Rach 3' (as it's known in the trade) is the more cleverly constructed as a piece of music - almost all the themes are inter-related with different versions of them cropping up in all three movements. It is also arguably the most technically demanding of any piano concerto in the standard repertoire. With Rachmaninov's Russian melancholy, luxuriant orchestration and brilliant piano writing well to the fore in all three movements, it is the epitome of the grand, late-Romantic concerto. It was dedicated to Rachmaninov's friend, the great pianist Josef Hofmann who, nevertheless, never played it. The 1996 film *Shine*, which told of the mental breakdown of pianist David Helfgott, turned 'Rach 3' into a classical hit.

Look in any reference book or music catalogue and you'll find this deliciously-knowing piano solo described as 'based on a theme improvised by Rachmaninov's father Vassili [or Wasili]' (hence the initials in the title). Wrong. It's actually an elaborate transcription of a piece by the obscure Franz Behr (1837-98) - his *Scherzpolka* or *Turtle Dove Polka*, Op. 303. Rachmaninov must have either assumed it was by his father (who played it frequently to his young son) or forgot to mention it when it was published in 1911. Either way, it provides a witty encore for a piano recital.

RACHMANINOV
POLKA DE W.R.
(1911)

I

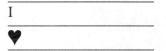

In 1892, Rachmaninov wrote five short pieces for piano, his Op. 3. The second of them became one of the most popular and over-played of all works for the instrument. Rachmaninov nicknamed this C Sharp Minor Prelude 'it', because at every recital he was forced to play 'it' and grew to loathe 'it' (in much the same way that Elgar couldn't abide the singing of his *Pomp and Circumstance March No. 1*). The Prelude is said to depict a dead man rising from his coffin. Maybe, but in a few pages it encapsulates much of Rachmaninov's mature style of music - the Slavic melancholy, Moscow church bells, plainsong chanting and a well-judged emotional climax. Incidentally, the other four pieces of Op. 3 are lovely, especially No. 1, *Elégie*.

RACHMANINOV
PRELUDE IN
C SHARP MINOR
(1892)

I

♥

Rachmaninov wrote a further 23 preludes (plus a couple of juvenile efforts) for piano: one set of ten (Op. 23) between 1901 and 1903 and a second set (Op. 32) in 1910. Like Chopin's Preludes, they cover every major and minor key though are much more taxing to play and have more complex textures. Many display the same nostalgic yearning and Russian day-dreaming as the concertos (try Op. 32 No. 5 in G or Op. 32 No. 10 in B minor, the composer's own favourite). The most popular is the Prelude in G minor, Op. 23 No. 5 with its rugged march rhythm and romantic central section.

RACHMANINOV
PRELUDES
(1901-10)

I

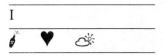

RACHMANINOV
RHAPSODY ON A
THEME OF
PAGANINI
(1934)

C

An alternative title for this work could be *Theme and 24 Variations on a Theme of Paganini for Piano and Orchestra*. The theme Rachmaninov takes is the famous A Minor Caprice for solo violin by Paganini, the last of a set of 24 which revolutionised the instrument when they appeared in 1820. Brahms wrote an exhaustive two-volume collection of variations on the same theme (for solo piano, page 83) in 1863; Rachmaninov's were written in 1934 while he was holidaying at his home on Lake Lucerne. The variations proceed without a break - along the way we hear the tune of the *Dies Irae* alongside the Paganini theme (Variation 7) and a Chopin-like nocturne (Variation 18), the best-known section of the whole work, often heard on its own and used in the mediocre 1953 MGM film *The Story of Three Loves*. As with the four concertos, listen to the recording made by Rachmaninov himself.

RACHMANINOV
SYMPHONY
NO. 2 IN E MINOR
(1908)

O

One of Rachmaninov's most imposing and richly-rewarding works, the Second Symphony has had a far happier history than the disastrous First. It was completed a year before the Third Piano Concerto and its four movements follow the pattern (and to some extent the language) of a Tchaikovsky symphony. You can hear that many of the themes Rachmaninov uses are shared between different movements (for instance, there's a snatch of the first movement at the end of the third, and the vivacious finale quotes a whole range of earlier ideas), a device which binds the whole work together. As in the *Paganini Rhapsody*, Rachmaninov introduces the tune of the *Dies Irae* (in the second movement). It's the Adagio (third movement) which enraptures the ear, though, with one of those searing, yearning melodies that are particularly associated with Rachmaninov.

Few of Rachmaninov's 71 songs are generally well known. Among them are inspired numbers like 'Spring Waters', 'Lilacs', 'To the Children' and 'Daisies'. By far the most famous is the ravishing, wordless 'Vocalise', composed in 1915. There's a recording of Rachmaninov himself conducting his orchestral version but even lovelier than that is the one arranged by Arcady Dubensky and conducted by Leopold Stokowski, with the soprano Anna Moffo. One critic described it as the most perfect vocal recording ever made. Stokowski described the short piece as 'like a self-portrait in tone of the composer - his intense love of Russia as he knew it as a child... his melancholic realisation that it is a dream-world he would never again experience'.

RACHMANINOV
'VOCALISE'
(1915)

V/O

♥

Not every music book mentions poor old Raff, but if he was good enough for his day (when he was extremely highly regarded) then he's good enough for me. You'll see what I mean if you track down his Piano Concerto which, if you like those heart-on-sleeve Romantic piano concertos like the Grieg and Tchaikovsky, you are sure to enjoy. It appeared just a year before Tchaikovsky's Piano Concerto No. 1, and its wealth of memorable melodies, exuberant spirit and lush orchestration will make you wonder why we don't ever hear it in the concert hall. Raff also left some attractive solo piano works and symphonies. Start with Symphony No. 3 (*Im Walde*) with its touches of Brahms and Mendelssohn.

JOACHIM RAFF
1822-82
SWISS-GERMAN
PIANO CONCERTO
IN C MINOR
(1873)

C

♥

Radio announcers have to be extra careful when introducing this, the curtain raiser to what is considered to be Rameau's masterpiece. The story concerns the fraternal devotion of the Heavenly Twins, Castor and Pollux, who both love Thélaîre. It was the most successful of Rameau's operas during his lifetime (it was mounted 250 times at the Opéra before 1785) featuring a prominent ballet role and the kind of pageantry of which Parisian opera-goers of the day were so fond. The Overture, written in the style of Lully, has a solemn introduction before darting into life and, unusually, blending into the choral prologue.

JEAN-PHILIPPE
RAMEAU
1683-1764
FRENCH
Overture to
CASTOR & POLLUX
Opera
(1737, rev. 1754)

O

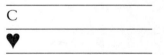

RAMEAU
Overture to
LES INDES GALANTE
Opera-ballet
(1735-61)

O

♪

The Indigo Suitors is how the title of this opera–cum–ballet translates. Once again, the Overture opens with a stately air before a lively introduction to proceedings. These are particularly exotic considering it's a work that dates from 1735, for *Les Indes galantes* tells four different tales of love, each taking place in a different location: Act 1 in Turkey, Act 2 in Peru, Act 3 in Persia and Act 4 in a North American forest. The piece also features an earthquake, a storm at sea and a volcanic eruption.

RAMEAU
LA POULE,
TAMBOURIN
and others
(1706-41)

I

♪

Couperin and Rameau were the two composers who laid the foundations of French keyboard music, Rameau the more theatrical and emotional of the two. His most celebrated contributions are the three sets of pieces for harpsichord that were published between 1706 and 1741 and among them are some little gems: there's *Le Rappel des oiseaux* (*The Summoning of the Birds*) which imitates just that, *Tambourin* (a kind of drum) - Rameau's most famous piece - *Les Tourbillons* (*Whirlwinds*) and *La Poule* (*The Hen*). There are many other charming and descriptive pieces in these *Pièces de clavécin* (the French word for harpsichord).

MAURICE RAVEL
1875-1937
FRENCH
ALBORADA DEL
GRACIOSO
(1905)

I/O

♪

In 1905, Ravel composed a set of five piano pieces which, in terms of his artistic development, were a new departure. They are five 'tone pictures' which reflect, rather than duplicate, their subjects. The most famous number of the suite is this one (No. 4) whose title translates as *Morning Serenade of the Jester*. It is a fearsomely difficult and highly coloured piano solo, both elements of which Ravel manages to capture in his dazzling orchestral version of 1918.

One of the Twentieth Century's landmark scores and considered to be among the finest ballets in the French repertoire. It was commissioned by Diaghilev for his Ballets Russes in 1909 with a story based on the mythical legend of Daphnis and Chloé. It took Ravel two years to complete this extraordinary work which is more like a vast symphony than a ballet. Strange to say, Diaghilev did not like the result and the première, danced by Nijnsky, was not a success. Nowadays you're more likely to hear this atmospheric, impressionistic music in the form of the two suites Ravel prepared from the full score. The second of these is the more popular and contains one of the great musical depictions of a sunrise with *Daybreak*.

RAVEL
DAPHNIS ET CHLOÉ
Ballet
(1912)

O

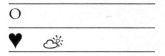

Inspired by a poem by Aloysius Bertrand, Ravel sought expressly to write a piano work of 'transcendental virtuosity', as he described it, one which would equal Balakirev's oriental fantasy *Islamey* in technical difficulty. The result was this, Ravel's masterpiece for the piano, one of the most notable twentieth century works for the instrument. It's in three arresting movements: *Ondine* (portraying a water-spirit), *Le Gibet* (a musical portrait of the gallows) and *Scarbo* (a dwarfish nocturnal imp). There's an exceptional account on disc by Ivo Pogorelich.

RAVEL
GASPARD DE LA NUIT
(1908)

I

Debussy once said of Ravel that he possessed 'the finest ear that ever existed'. Quite a compliment from such a fastidious critic, but listening to a work like this you can see why he said it. The Introduction and Allegro was written for the Parisian harpist Micheline Kahn and is scored for flute, clarinet, harp and string quartet. To hear what is possible with this small and unusual combination is a revelation - and all in the space of barely 11 minutes. After the slow Introduction (one of the most atmospheric passages in chamber music) comes the Allegro and an extended harp solo, utilising the newly-invented chromatic harp, introduced in 1897.

RAVEL
INTRODUCTION AND ALLEGRO
(1905)

CH

RAVEL
JEUX D'EAU
(1901)

I

It was another poem that inspired this, one of music's most impressive impressions of water (the title translates as *Fountains*). The line by de Regnier that caught Ravel's fancy is '… a river god laughing at the waters as they caress him'. Ravel's musical picture has something in common with Liszt's earlier 'water music' for piano - *Au bord d'une source*, for example, and another piece also entitled *Jeux d'eau* - but Ravel created sounds in his piece that had never been heard before. The use of the high notes on the piano was revolutionary and many of his contemporaries, including Debussy, benefited from the new techniques involved in the 'scintillating cascades of notes that make the water laugh and play', as one writer put it.

RAVEL
PAVANE POUR UNE
INFANTE DÉFUNTE
(1899)

I/O

This stately, wistful dance from an earlier age was originally written for the piano in 1899 but is now equally well known in the orchestral version Ravel made in 1905. He chose the title for the alluring sound of the words - not for any particular dead Spanish princess (*Infanta*), and certainly not for a 'dead infant' as the title is sometimes carelessly translated.

RAVEL
PIANO CONCERTO
IN G
(1931)

C

Who can resist this vivacious, jazz-influenced display concerto written, as Ravel explained, 'in the spirit of Mozart and Saint-Saëns'? It took him two years to write (1929-31) and he himself conducted the first performance in January 1932 with Marguerite Long as soloist (they made a recording of it the following year). The first movement flashes by with many brilliant passages from both the soloist and orchestra; the heavenly slow movement is like one of those implacable Bach adagios while the finale bowls along, a miracle of lightness and grace with the spirits of Mendelssohn and Gershwin looking on.

Ravel was much influenced by the French composers of the late Seventeenth and early Eigthteenth Centuries; he was also in the habit of writing for the piano and afterwards making an orchestral arrangement. This suite of six pieces is an example of both. After seeing service on the Front as an ambulance driver, Ravel decided to write a work in homage to the war dead and this one, which he had commenced in 1913 as a tribute to the great French composer Couperin, fitted the bill, serenely reflecting the spirit of an age long gone. The movements, all seventeenth century forms or dances, are: Prélude, Fugue, Forlane, Rigaudon, Menuet and (the best known) Toccata.

RAVEL
LE TOMBEAU DE COUPERIN
(1913-17)

I/O

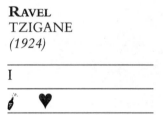

Ravel wrote this piece for the Hungarian-born Jelly d'Arányi (1895-1966), one of two violin-playing sisters who settled in London. *Tzigane* (a Hungarian gypsy) follows the pattern of a traditional Hungarian rhapsody: a long, slow introduction – a very difficult solo cadenza for the violin, played on the G string (shades of Paganini!) – leading to a fiery gypsy melody which, with other tunes and dances, culminates in a whirlwind finale. Ravel originally scored the work for violin and *lutheal*, a short-lived musical invention which was an organ-like attachment to the piano, but subsequently orchestrated the accompaniment.

RAVEL
TZIGANE
(1924)

I

Ravel composed what he called his 'choreographic poem' as the result of a commission by Diaghilev. The score itself includes a written description of the progress of the music: 'Whirling clouds give glimpses, through tiny chinks, of couples dancing. The clouds scatter, little by little. One sees an immense hall peopled with a twirling crowd. The scene is gradually illuminated. The light of the chandeliers bursts forth, fortissimo. An Imperial court, in or about, 1855'. Or you could see it as an elegant Viennese waltz by Johann Strauss which gradually turns into a nightmare as the couples dance themselves to destruction: a portrait of the change between light-hearted pre-war Vienna and its post-war despair and futility. Ravel made three versions of the score (which, incidentally, Diaghilev disliked so heartily that he refused to produce it), one for orchestra, another for two pianos and a third for piano solo, all written in the same period.

RAVEL
LA VALSE
(1919)

O/I

OTTORINO RESPIGHI
1879–1936
ITALIAN
ANCIENT AIRS AND
DANCES FOR THE
LUTE
(1917-33)

O

Respighi learnt how to create colourful orchestral effects from Rimsky-Korsakov. Here he applies his skill to three suites of orchestral transcriptions of short pieces originally written for the lute. Each movement lasts no more than four minutes on average, twentieth century treatments of tunes composed by obscure Italian composers of the Sixteenth and Seventeenth Centuries like Molinaro, Galilei and Besardo.

RESPIGHI
THE BIRDS
(1927)

O

This is a thoroughly charming suite composed 'for small orchestra' in which Respighi once more draws on music from the past. In this case, he uses keyboard and other music by the early eighteenth century composers Pasquini, Gallot, Rameau and the prolific 'Anon.'. Its five short movements portray *The Dove*, *The Hen*, *The Nightingale* and *The Cuckoo*, with an introductory prelude that many of us will remember as the signature tune for BBC TV's *Going For a Song*.

RESPIGHI
THE FOUNTAINS
OF ROME
(1914-16)

O

Respighi's major works are three evocative musical portraits of the Eternal City, a trio of symphonic poems each comprising four movements. *Fontane di Roma* (*The Fountains of Rome*) is generally considered to be the best with each Roman fountain 'contemplated at the hour in which their character is most in harmony with the surrounding landscape' (Respighi). They are: *The Giulia Valley Fountain at Dawn*; *The Triton Fountain in the Morning*; *The Trevi Fountain at Mid-day*; *The Villa Medici Fountain at Sunset*.

RESPIGHI
THE PINES OF ROME
(1924)

O

The second in this series of symphonic poems celebrates 'the century-old trees which dominate so characteristically the Roman landscape, …testimony for the principal events in Roman life'. The four sections, played without a pause are: *The Pines of the Villa Borghese*, *The Pines Near a Catacomb*, *The Pines of the Janiculum* (in this one, Respighi inserts into the score a gramophone recording of the song of the nightingale), and *The Pines of the Appian Way*. The latter ends in a blaze of sound as visions of ghostly legions tramp down the ancient highway.

The four movements of *Feste Romane* depict four very different kinds of festivals, all painted in Respighi's lush and imaginative orchestration. Proceedings open at the Circus Maximus as the mob enjoy the spectacle of Christians being thrown to the lions. Part 2 is *The Jubilee* – a band of pilgrims joyfully catch their first view of Rome from Monte Mario. Next comes *The October Festival* (what we call Harvest Festival) and finally *The Epiphany*, which Italians obviously celebrate more enthusiastically than we do – if the music is anything to go by.

RESPIGHI
ROMAN FESTIVALS
(1928)

O

This is the title of one of the monuments of nineteenth century organ music, a commentary on the *Psalm of Vengeance* ('O Lord, Thou God to whom vengeance belongeth, shine forth'). True, it's never likely to be Top of the Pops and its gloomy opening theme may put you off, but stick with it, for the roughly 23 minutes of four linked sections contain some of the most imposing organ music ever written. It will certainly give your speakers a work-out. Reubke, a pupil of Liszt, died when he was only 24, already a mature composer, and this is his only organ work.

JULIUS REUBKE
1834-58
GERMAN
SONATA ON THE
94TH PSALM
(1857)

I

Rezniček, the son of a princess and an Austrian field-marshal, composed several operas and symphonies. The only piece of his you'll ever hear today is this Overture to his comic opera *Donna Diana*, introduced in Prague in December 1894 (though, with its two principal characters named Carlos and Princess Diana, you'd have thought someone would have revived the whole work by now). The witty and exuberant curtain raiser has always been popular – one of those 'well-I-never-knew-it-was-called-that' bits of music.

EMIL VON REZNIČEK
1860-1945
AUSTRIAN
Overture to
DONNA DIANA
Opera
(1894)

O

JOSEF RHEINBERGER
1839-1901
GERMAN
ORGAN
CONCERTOS
(1884 and 1894)

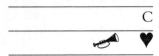

C

A forgotten name (unless you're an organist or organ buff), Rheinberger was as famous during his lifetime as he is little known today. His two organ concertos are among the very few examples by a Romantic composer (Liszt, Saint-Saëns, Brahms and Franck, the most notable composers who wrote for the organ, all failed to get round to writing an organ concerto). No. 1 in F major and No. 2 in G minor are full-blooded, majestic works, chock full of memorable themes matched by superb orchestration. Listen to the second theme in the first movement of the G Minor - a first cousin of *Nimrod* from Elgar's *Enigma Variations* which was written five years later! Rousing, triumphal works that should be better known.

NIKOLAI RIMSKY-
KORSAKOV
1844-1908
RUSSIAN
CAPRICCIO
ESPAGNOL
(1887)

O

It's a strange fact that before Ravel and some of his Spanish contemporaries, the musical spirit of Spain was more effectively captured by Slavic composers than Hispanic. Rimsky-Korsakov was justly proud of this orchestral masterpiece written 'at that period of my creative life at the end of which my orchestration had reached a considerable degree of virtuosity'. It has five short-ish linked sections played without pause using Spanish themes of different dance characters: *Alborada, Variations, Alborada* (a different treatment), *Scene and Gypsy Dance*, and the final *Fandango of the Asturias*.

RIMSKY-KORSAKOV
FLIGHT OF THE
BUMBLE-BEE
from The Legend of
Tsar Saltan
Opera
(1900)

O/I

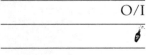

One of classical music's most familiar pieces is actually an orchestral interlude from Act 3 of Rimsky's opera *Tsar Saltan*. It's a realistic attempt to portray in music the buzzing of a bumble-bee. In its original rarely-heard context it sounds very different from the dozens of arrangements that have been made of the piece, played on everything from the accordion to the xylophone. Prominent among these is Rachmaninov's elegant transcription for piano and an amazing elaboration of it (also for piano) played in octaves (!) by the Franco-Hungarian pianist Georges Cziffra.

Like Rachmaninov after him, Rimsky held a lifelong fascination with Russian Church music. The main themes for this orchestral showpiece come from a collection of canticles known as the *Obikhod* from the Russian Orthodox Church. Two of these can be heard in the solemn introduction before the solo violin leads to the main part of the Overture, a lively treatment of these same two themes. According to Rimsky, the music expresses 'the transition from the solemnities of Passiontide to the vociferous communal rejoicings of Easter'.

RIMSKY-KORSAKOV
RUSSIAN EASTER
FESTIVAL
OVERTURE
(1888)

O

Rimsky-Korsakov's most celebrated large-scale composition is based on episodes from *Tales of the Arabian Nights*. The Sultan, convinced of the unfaithfulness of women, is determined to kill each of his wives after the first night he spends with them. One of them, the Sultana Scheherazade, saves her life by diverting him with stories she relates over a period of 1,001 nights. It was a subject that could have been dreamt up specially for Rimsky's musical palette - the exotic setting, the beguiling rhythms of the Orient and the fabulous stories are captured brilliantly in his multi-coloured orchestration. The four separate movements of his symphonic suite depict the tales of: *The Sea and the Vessel of Sinbad*; *The Tale of the Prince Kalender*; *The Young Prince and the Young Princess*; and *The Festival at Baghdad - The Sea - The Vessel is Wrecked*. Finally, the Sultan speaks in a gentle, amorous tone - so everyone lives happily ever after.

RIMSKY-KORSAKOV
SCHEHERAZADE
(1888)

O

Few in the West are familiar with Rimsky's operas though the composer himself thought them his finest achievements. But there are many little snippets from them that have achieved popularity over the years like this sinuous song from his sixth opera, *Sadko*. Sadko, a wandering minstrel, invites three merchants to tell him about their homelands. One of them is a Hindu and he proceeds to tell Sadko about the mystery and magic of India in an Oriental type of song that's also known as 'Chanson hindu'.

RIMSKY-KORSAKOV
'SONG OF INDIA'
from Sadko
(1898)

OP

RICHARD RODGERS
1902-79
AMERICAN
SLAUGHTER ON
TENTH AVENUE
Ballet
(1937)

O

♪ ♥

The composer of *Oklahoma!* and *Carousel* collaborated with Lorenz Hart for the musical *On Your Toes* (1937), one of the many hit shows they wrote in the 1920s and 1930s. From it comes the song 'There's a small hotel' and this mini-ballet, the climax of the evening. A dancer loves a stripper, both are menaced by a gangster and, while trying to kill the dancer, the gangster shoots the stripper. The dancer then shoots the gangster. Rodgers' luscious score mixes jazz and symphonic ideas to great effect, a concert piece that has become an American classic.

JOAQUÍN RODRIGO
1901-99
SPANISH
CONCIERTO DE
ARANJUEZ
(1939)

C

♥ ☁

High in the Classic FM Hall of Fame is Rodrigo's Guitar Concerto, named for the princely town of Aranjuez with its magnificent palace, just outside Madrid. Rodrigo and his wife moved there in the same year that he completed this, the finest guitar concerto of the Twentieth Century, though he had written much of it the previous year when still living in Paris. Composed by a man who was blind from the age of three, has there ever been a more vivid musical picture of Spain? All three of its movements have different, contrasted characters, but it is the inspired central slow movement (Adagio) that has most caught the imagination of music-lovers, ever since the Concerto's première in Madrid in December 1940.

RODRIGO
FANTASIA PARA UN
GENTILHOMME
(1954)

O

♥ ☁

Fantasia for a Gentleman is another guitar-and-orchestra work but based on music by the seventeenth century guitarist and composer Gaspar Sanz. There are four movements: *Villano* (a simple rustic dance) *and Ricercare* (a more complex musical form); *Fanfare of the Cavalry of Naples*; *Dance of the Candles*; *Canario (From the Canary Islands)*. The work is dedicated to the great Spanish guitarist Andrés Segovia (1893-1987) who premièred the work in March 1958.

It has been described as 'the best comic opera ever written' and Beethoven said, 'It will be played as long as opera exists.' He was right. Since its second performance in February 1816 (the first night was a fiasco) *The Barber* has kept its place in the popularity stakes. It's based on one of three hit plays by Beaumarchais concerning the loveable rogue Figaro, the barber of the title (see also Mozart's *The Marriage of Figaro*). The miracle is that Rossini wrote the entire score (600 pages of it) in just 13 days, though the famous Overture has, musically, nothing to do with the opera that follows it! If Rossini ever bothered to write one (doubtful), it is now certainly lost and what has always been played is this reworking of material from some of his earlier failures (*Aureliano in Palmira* and *Elisabetta, Regina d'Inghilterra*).

GIOACHINO ROSSINI
1792-1868
ITALIAN
Overture to
THE BARBER OF SEVILLE
Opera
(1816)

O

Count Almaviva has had to disguise himself as a poor student to further his love for Rosina, the beautiful ward of Doctor Bartolo, whom Bartolo wants for himself. Figaro makes his entrance with this, one of opera's most famous patter songs – 'Make way for the factotum' – explaining that he is called hither and thither by everyone, Mister Fixit, a jack-of-all-trades. It's a favourite bravura solo for high baritones in concerts and singing competitions. Figaro then suggests to Almaviva that he disguise himself as a soldier, pretend to be drunk and seek shelter in Rosina's house. After that the fun begins!

ROSSINI
'LARGO AL FACTOTUM'
from The Barber of Seville
(1816)

OP

Hardly has Rossini given us the show-stopping 'Largo al factotum' (see above) than he gives us another, probably the best-known coloratura aria in opera (Saint-Saëns quotes it amusingly in *Fossils* from *Carnival of the Animals*). The title translates variously as 'A little voice I heard just now' or 'A voice in the distance' and 'A little voice within my heart'. Rosina has heard the Count serenading her from below her window and in Scene 2 sings this pert, flirtatious response.

ROSSINI
'UNA VOCE POCO FA'
from The Barber of Seville
(1816)

OP

ROSSINI
Overture to
LA CENERENTOLA
Opera
(1817)

O

Pronounced 'Chay-nay-ren'tow-lah', the title translates simply as *Cinderella*, the same Cinderella we meet more usually in pantomime. Here are the Ugly Sisters (Clorinda and Tisbe) and their father Don Magnifico, Baron of Mountflagon, mistreating poor Angelina, known as Cinderella. True, in Rossini's version the fairy godmother is Alidoro, the tutor of the Prince, and the glass slipper becomes a silver bracelet – but everyone lives happily ever after in this delightful, quick-fire comic invention. The Overture matches it to perfection, though in fact it was previously used for another opera called *La Gazetta*.

ROSSINI
'NON PIÙ MESTA'
from La Cenerentola
(1817)

OP

At the very end of the opera, Cinders forgives her stepsisters and her stepfather, singing 'No longer sad beside the fire'. It's known as the 'Rondo Aria', a brilliant and very difficult coloratura test, a spine-tingling vocal display guaranteed to bring down the curtain to loud cheers. In recent years, Cecilia Bartoli has made the title role her own and her recording of this aria alone is quite remarkable.

ROSSINI
Overture to
THE ITALIAN GIRL
IN ALGIERS
Opera
(1813)

O

L'Italiana in Algeri was Rossini's first major success in the field in which he was to become so successful and influential. He was 20 at the time and the Venetian audiences loved the combination of high farce, tender love interest and the Oriental setting. The complex plot revolves round the Bey of Algiers tiring of his wife and falling in love with Isabella, shipwrecked off the coast of Algiers. The Overture is a gem, opening with a haunting theme on the oboe followed by a 'Rossini crescendo'. This was a device for which Rossini became famous and which is in almost all his opera overtures, where a short, fast passage is repeated over and over again each time with fuller orchestration, creating a sense of mounting excitement.

This is the last of the 30-odd operas that Rossini wrote in Italy. *Semiramide* (pronounced 'Sem-ear-ram-ee-day') is one of his serious operas and tells the story of Semiramis, Queen of Babylon, who murders her husband with the help of her lover but who subsequently falls in love with a warrior without knowing that he is her son. Serious stuff indeed, but the Overture gives little hint of this. It's a masterpiece and one of the few in which Rossini uses material from the opera itself.

ROSSINI
Overture to
SEMIRAMIDE
Opera
(1823)

O

Semiramide is very rarely revived these days, and it is only by the Overture, the striking Act 2 duet 'Giorno d'Orrore' ('Day of Horror') and this brilliant number that the opera is generally known. A famous soprano aria (with chorus), it comes in Act 1 when Semiramis rejoices that a ray of love will shine into her heart now that her handsome warrior (Arsace) has returned ('A beautiful enchanting gleam of hope and content at last shone for me').

ROSSINI
'BEL RAGGIO LUSINGHIER'
from Semiramide
(1823)

OP

Two early, unsuccessful one-act operas that are rarely seen on stage have overtures that are among Rossini's most popular, sparkling with wit and invention. *La scala di seta* (the 'silken ladder') is used nightly by Dorvil to reach his wife Giulia whom he has secretly married and who is living in the house of her jealous guardian. In the second opera, Sofia is being forced to marry the son of Signor Bruschino whom she has never met. Her lover passes himself off as the son. This latter overture is the one in which there's a passage where the violins are requested to play with the wood of their bows (*col legno*) instead of the hair.

ROSSINI
Overtures to
THE SILKEN LADDER
and
IL SIGNOR BRUSCHINO
Operas
(1812 and 1813)

O

**ROSSINI
SONATAS
FOR STRINGS 1-6**
(1804, rev. 1823)

O

If you weren't told beforehand, you might think these charming little works were apprentice pieces by Mozart or Haydn. You would find it hard to believe that they were written by a 12-year-old who had had no formal musical training and whose only experience of music was listening to the municipal orchestra in which his father played. An old copy of the scores discovered in 1954 bears this inscription by Rossini: 'Six terrible sonatas composed by me... when I was still a child and had not had any lesson in accompaniment; composed and copied in three days, and performed by Triossi, double-bass, his cousin Morri, first violin, and the latter's brother, cello; they all played like dogs and I, second violin, was not the least of the dogs in the group'.

**ROSSINI
STABAT MATER**
(1832)

CHO

Rossini's non-operatic masterpiece is this setting of the Latin hymn *Stabat Mater*. Subdivided into ten sections, the work is written for four soloists, chorus and orchestra. When finally performed in the version by which we know it today, some thought it superior even to Haydn's *The Creation* and, when Donizetti conducted an early performance, the audience surrounded Rossini's apartment demanding his appearance to acknowledge the ovation. The exalted melodies and the immense skill with which the voices are handled make for an inspiring work. The second section is *Cujus animam*, a lofty tenor solo.

**ROSSINI
'DI TANTI PALPITI'**
from Tancredi
(1813)

OP

Tancredi was among the operas that contributed to Rossini's reputation as one of Italy's leading composers. It was his earliest 'serious' success with the usual mix of love, betrayal, infidelity, threats of death and (in this case) a happy ending. It's seldom performed, unlike this aria from Act 1 which was once the most famous operatic aria of all, a huge hit all over Europe. 'From this heart-ache' is how it translates but it is also called the 'Rice Aria' because Rossini is said to have composed it in four minutes while waiting for his rice to cook (both feats, of course, quite impossible). (See also Paganini).

This is the Rossini overture that opens with an arresting roll on two snare drums before a grand, vigorous march. The plot of this rarely-encountered two-act comic opera concerns a servant girl falsely accused of stealing a silver spoon who, just before she goes to the scaffold, is exonerated by the discovery of said spoon in the nest of *la gazza ladra* (the 'thieving magpie').

ROSSINI
Overture to
THE THIEVING
MAGPIE
Opera
(1817)

The most famous opera overture of all? Probably. Indelibly associated by people of a certain age with *The Lone Ranger*, the last section was used as the theme tune for the long-running radio and television series in the 1940s and 1950s. It is actually a miniature symphonic poem, the nearest Rossini ever came formally to producing one independent of an opera. Berlioz described it as 'a work of immense talent which resembles genius so closely as to be mistaken for it'. Prefacing the well-known story of the fourteenth century Swiss hero and his fight to overthrow the despotic Austrian rule and the tyrant Gessler, the Overture is in four sections: a picture of sunrise over the Swiss mountains leading to a storm and a lovely pastoral section. Trumpet calls herald the arrival of the Swiss army and the celebrated gallop which ends this masterpiece.

ROSSINI
Overture to
WILLIAM TELL
Opera
(1829)

In 1936 Benjamin Britten was commissioned by the GPO Film Unit to contribute '14 small sections of about 8-20 seconds each', based on Rossini piano pieces, to accompany a short animated film (it was called *The Tocher*, a Scots word for a dowry) advertising the Post Office Savings Bank. Later, Britten re-scored three movements and added a further two, calling the suite *Soirées musicales* (a further suite was added, *Matinées musicales*, in 1941). The music comes from *William Tell* and Rossini's collection of 180 little piano pieces called *Sins of Old Age*. The jaunty first suite contains: March, Canzonetta, Tirolese, Bolero and Tarantella.

ROSSINI
(arr. Britten)
SOIRÉES MUSICALES
(1936)

ROSSINI
(arr. Respighi)
LA BOUTIQUE
FANTASQUE
Ballet
(1919)

O

After the failure of his grand opera *William Tell* in 1829, Rossini composed little else of importance, though he did trot out dozens of short pieces for his own amusement. They remained forgotten and unpublished until Sergei Diaghilev came across them in a volume disarmingly entitled *Bits of Nothing*. The ballet impresario commissioned Respighi to form a ballet score from them and *The Fantastic Toy Shop* was the result. The mechanical wonders include dancers who do the tarantella and the cancan, plus a squad of Cossacks and a pair of dancing poodles. Great fun.

ANTON RUBINSTEIN
1829-94
RUSSIAN
MELODY IN F
(1852)
and others

I

♥

This Rubinstein (no relation to the celebrated pianist Arthur) was the first great international Russian pianist. He was also a teacher, composer, conductor and visionary - a giant in the musical world of his day. Now he is remembered for just one short work, his *Melody in F* for piano (the first of a set of two pieces of which the second is never played). It's a cousin of Mendelssohn's *Spring Song*, Liszt's *Liebestraume No. 3* and Sinding's *Rustle of Spring*. It was the piece of music that first drew the American composer George Gershwin to the piano when, as a six-year-old, he heard it being played in the street on a pianola. There are many other highly attractive 'salon' and/or virtuoso piano pieces by Rubinstein worth hearing, like his *Romance in E flat*, Op. 44 No. 1, *Kammenoi Ostrow*, Op. 10 No. 22, *Valse-Caprice in E flat* and the *Staccato Étude in C*, Op. 23 No. 2.

RUBINSTEIN
PIANO CONCERTO
NO. 4 IN D MINOR
(1864)

C

 ♥

Of all the piano concertos that were published in the 1860s, only Saint-Saëns' No. 2 in G minor and Brahms' No. 1 in D minor are still in the regular repertoire of pianists. Until 50 years ago, Rubinstein's D Minor was a third. It's a heroic, forceful work, strongly melodic and highly theatrical, the epitome of the grand virtuoso vehicle. If you like the Liszt and Tchaikovsky concertos then you're almost certain to enjoy this.

Few recent choral works have been taken up with such enthusiasm as Rutter's *Requiem*. No wonder - it's written in an accessible (but not condescending) musical language, and few contemporary composers write quite as well for the voice or set texts as sensitively. Rutter wrote it as a response to a personal bereavement, taking the small-scale Fauré and Duruflé requiems as his model. There are seven movements with passages from the Catholic Mass for the Dead, Psalms 130 and 23 (often used at funerals) and some of the Burial Sentences from the 1662 *Book of Common Prayer*. Throughout the 35 minutes of the *Requiem*, the mood is serene, sombre and meditative, with the exception of the brief, animated *Sanctus*.

JOHN RUTTER
B. 1945
REQUIEM
(1985)

CHO

S

This is Saint-Saëns off duty, a *jeu d'esprit* intended for the entertainment of his friends by a man who had a surprising reputation as a whimsical practical joker. He banned publication of the work in his lifetime (apart from its most famous section, *The Swan*) fearing it might damage his reputation as a serious composer (*Carnival* was composed in the same year as his mighty Symphony No. 3). Ironic, then, that this has become his most played work. Scored for two pianos, flute, clarinet, glass harmonica and xylophone, the *Grand Zoological Fantasy* (the work's sub-title) depicts, in 14 short movements, lions, kangaroos, an aquarium and others, liberally parodying Saint-Saëns' fellow composers as well as himself: the Cancan from Offenbach's *Orpheus in the Underworld* in *Tortoises*, Berlioz' *Dance of the Sylphs* and Mendelssohn's *A Midsummer Night's Dream* in *The Elephant*, French folk-songs, Rosina's aria 'Una voce poco fa' from *The Barber of Seville* and his own *Danse macabre* in *Fossils*.

CAMILLE
SAINT-SAËNS
1835-1921
FRENCH
CARNIVAL OF THE ANIMALS
(1886)

CH/O

SAINT-SAËNS
CELLO CONCERTO
NO. 1 IN A MINOR
(1872)

C

♥

The Swan is far and away the best known cello work by Saint-Saëns (it's arguably the best known cello work of all), but Saint-Saëns composed many other attractive works for the instrument including two sonatas, the lovely (but rarely-heard) *Chant saphique* and two cello concertos. The Concerto No. 1 in A minor has always been popular (the legendary Pablo Casals chose it for his London debut in 1905), a single-entity work but subdivided into three 'movements', providing the soloist with a brilliant and highly-effective showpiece.

SAINT-SAËNS
CELLO CONCERTO
NO. 2 IN D MINOR
(1902)

C

♥

By contrast to No. 1, the Second Cello Concerto is relatively unknown - a shame because, though a slighter work than the A Minor Concerto, it has some beautiful passages, not least the andante section which is among the most poignant of all Saint-Saëns' slow movements. The Concerto is in two movements (each one having two linked sections) and was written for the Dutch cellist Joseph Hollmann who gave the first performance in 1905.

SAINT-SAËNS
DANSE MACABRE
(1874)

O

♪

Saint-Saëns' most famous tone poem was in fact originally written as a song for voice and piano in 1873 to a poem by Henri Cazalis. The opening lines are: 'Zig-a-zig-a-zig - hark! Death beats a measure/Drums on a tomb with heels hard and thin' (so the Spice Girls were not the first to sing 'Zig-a-zig-a-zig'). When Saint-Saëns transformed the song the following year into a purely orchestral work, he depicted skeletons rising from their graves at the stroke of midnight for a wild, ghostly dance. This rises to a climax, the strains of the *Dies Irae* are heard, the oboe imitates the cock crowing at dawn and the skeletons disappear into the mist.

Saint-Saëns wrote two sets of études (studies), each containing six pieces designed to address a particular technical problem while mingling purely poetical and musical concerns, exactly like the studies of Chopin and Liszt. The collection of studies designated as Op. 52 conclude with this *Study in Waltz Form*, evocative of the elegant drawing-room pieces of the time, brilliant, showy displays designed to send the audiences into raptures. In this, Saint-Saëns is totally successful but there's just a hint that he's got his tongue firmly in his cheek and is sending up the whole genre.

SAINT-SAËNS
ÉTUDE EN FORME
DE VALSE
(1877)

I

According to the composer's biographer, James Harding, the inspiration for this favourite violin work came from 'a memory of the crackling of a wood fire that somehow took musical shape'. Perhaps not so surprising when you know that Saint-Saëns admitted that he had to compose in order to fulfil a natural function as an apple tree produces apples. Around this 'wood fire' theme, he wove a languorous, insinuating dance rhythm - the *havanaise* (or *habanera* as it's known in Spain).

SAINT-SAËNS
HAVANAISE
(1887)

I

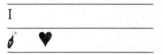

This is the earliest of Saint-Saëns' concert works for violin, composed when he was 28 and dedicated (as his Violin Concertos Nos. 1 and 3 would be) to the Spanish virtuoso Pablo de Sarasate. It is in two sections, as the title suggests: a questioning, plaintive Introduction followed by the Rondo, among the composer's most instantly recognisable tunes. Described as 'one of the golden apples of Saint-Saëns' tonal garden', the work demands the ultimate in classical poise and control - 'grace under fire' is needed to bring it off successfully. Bizet made an arrangement for violin and piano and, early on in his career, Debussy turned it into a work for two pianos.

SAINT-SAËNS
INTRODUCTION
AND RONDO
CAPRICCIOSO
(1863)

I

♥

SAINT-SAËNS
MARCHE MILITAIRE
FRANÇAISE
from Suite algérienne
(1879)

O

Saint-Saëns was an inveterate globe-trotter and a frequent visitor to Morocco and neighbouring countries. The Suite is a three-movement picture postcard of Algeria, preceded by a prelude which portrays the composer's reaction on first glimpsing land from aboard ship. It's the last movement, however, that is heard most often, an exuberant French military march said to have been inspired by Saint-Saëns' joy and security at coming upon a French garrison. James Harding, in his study of the composer, feels that the March is almost a self-portrait of Saint-Saëns at the time he wrote the piece, finding in the music the same 'bird-like gestures, the quick and eager speech that never succeeded in keeping pace with his thoughts, and the urge to have done with a work because the idea for another was already plaguing his restless brain'.

SAINT-SAËNS
PIANO CONCERTO
NO. 2 IN G MINOR
(1868)

C

Saint-Saëns was, among his many other accomplishments, a virtuoso pianist - there are several ancient recordings that testify to this. He wrote five piano concertos in all, this one being the most popular, one in which Bach (in the first movement) meets Offenbach (in the last movement). Saint-Saëns produced it in just 17 days after the great Russian pianist/composer Anton Rubinstein, scheduled to conduct a concert in Paris, invited Saint-Saëns to appear as soloist. The première was not a success for, although he managed to finish the Concerto in time, Saint-Saëns had not mastered the extremely demanding solo part and only the second movement (a scherzo) went off well. It's a work of undemanding, ear-tickling delight from start to finish with its dramatic first movement, rumty-tumpty Mendelssohn-like second and scorching tarantella finale.

The Fourth Concerto is not as immediately attractive as the Second but is a more satisfying work to listen to. The way it is constructed is unusual in that it has two movements, the first one split into two sections and the second into three, rather like the *Organ Symphony* (which, incidentally, also uses chorale-like melodies, begins in C minor and ends in C major). Saint-Saëns also cleverly uses the same themes (or variations of the themes) throughout the work. The finale is particularly impressive, a folk-song kind of tune with a sparkling part for the soloist.

SAINT-SAËNS
PIANO CONCERTO
NO. 4 IN C MINOR
(1875)

C

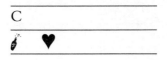

If his earlier four concertos are a continuation of the styles of Chopin, Mendelssohn and Liszt, in his Fifth Concerto Saint-Saëns boldly goes where no one had gone before, incorporating elements of Arabic music into this essentially European form. The central section is based on a Nubian marriage song and there are unmistakable sounds of the gamelan elsewhere (gamelan orchestras had caused a stir at the Paris Exhibition of 1889). The final movement, though, is meant to depict the sound of the ship's engines as it starts on the voyage home - an exhilarating toccata which Saint-Saëns also used in the last of his studies for solo piano, Op. 111. *The Egyptian* was launched on 3 June 1896 to celebrate the 50th anniversary of Saint-Saëns' debut as an 11-year-old virtuoso.

SAINT-SAËNS
PIANO CONCERTO
NO. 5 IN F
'EGYPTIAN'
(1896)

C

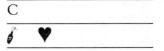

This is an exquisite vocalise (that is, a song without words - other good examples are by Rachmaninov and Villa-Lobos). It was written as part of the music Saint-Saëns contributed to a production of a spectacular play by Dieulafoy put on at the Béziers Festival in 1902 and based on the life of the bloodthirsty queen of Persia. 'Le Rossignol et la rose' (its French title) takes the soprano soloist up into the stratosphere with long-breathed phrases in imitation of the nightingale.

SAINT-SAËNS
'THE NIGHTINGALE
AND THE ROSE'
from Parysatis
(1902)

V

SAINT-SAËNS
'SOFTLY AWAKES
MY HEART'
from Samson and Delilah
(1877)

OP

♥ 🎇

Of the 12 operas that Saint-Saëns composed, only this has retained a place in the regular repertoire. The others have disappeared from view (Bernard Shaw wrote of one entitled *Ascanio*: 'I can recall no alleviation to my prodigious boredom'). *Samson and Delilah*, based on the story in the *Book of Judges*, is an undeniably powerful and beautiful work, if short on psychology and characterisation. 'Mon coeur s'ouvre à ta voix' is the most famous number in the score, sung in Act 2 by the treacherous Delilah (a mezzo-soprano role) as she seduces Samson. It's often heard separately and was among the first things that Saint-Saëns composed for the opera.

SAINT-SAËNS
BACCHANALE
from Samson and Delilah
(1877)

OP

♪

Samson has had his hair cut off, thus rendered harmless. He is carted off to prison and blinded (Act 3, Scene 1). Act 3, Scene 2 takes place in the great hall of the temple of Dagon, its vaulted roof supported by two pillars. It is dawn and after the High Priest and other dignitaries enter, Delilah and a group of dancing girls come in carrying goblets of wine. After a victory chorus, there is this wild *bacchanale*, a favourite orchestral showpiece which, after its 'Fry's Turkish Delight' introduction, gets faster and faster, building to a frenzy of excitement.

SAINT-SAËNS
SEPTET IN E FLAT
(1881)

CH

♪

This is unquestionably one of Saint-Saëns' finest chamber works, and it's a rather endearing one too. It's scored for the unusual combination of string quartet, bass, piano and trumpet - with the emphasis on the trumpet, for Saint-Saëns wrote it for a music society known as La Trompette. The Septet is in the form of a five-movement suite, mainly light-hearted, even jocular in mood, with a military air about it (in fact, Saint-Saëns quotes a French army regimental call at one point).

This glorious work - Saint-Saëns' *Organ Symphony* as it's generally called - was popularised by its use in the 1995 film *Babe*. Before that, the same theme from the final movement was turned into a pop hit in 1978 called 'If I had words'. The famous bit - where the full organ comes thundering in - is actually the same tune (played in a major key) as the tune at the very opening of the Symphony (played in a minor key). And that opening theme is itself derived from the Latin plainchant *Dies Irae*. It crops up throughout the Symphony in various guises, even in the reposeful slow movement when the organ makes its first appearance. Clever chaps, these composers. Saint-Saëns dedicated this, the last of his three mature symphonies, to the memory of his friend Franz Liszt.

SAINT-SAËNS
SYMPHONY
NO. 3 IN C MINOR
'ORGAN'
(1886)

O

In the same year as his *Danse macabre* appeared came Saint-Saëns' first work for two pianos, a medium he instinctively understood and to which he brought a refreshingly novel approach. The theme he used is from the middle bit (the Trio) of the minuet movement from Beethoven's Piano Sonata in E flat, Op. 31 No. 3 and consists of an Introduction, Theme, seven Variations, Fugue and Finale. It's a fun piece with a breathless ending that keeps both pianists on their toes - if you see what I mean!

SAINT-SAËNS
VARIATIONS ON A
THEME OF
BEETHOVEN
for two pianos
(1874)

I

Saint-Saëns enjoyed one of the longest creative careers in musical history. He began composing when he was six and went on writing until he was 86. Amongst this prodigious output are eight works for violin and orchestra (some are included here) three of which are violin concertos. The last of these, dedicated to the Spanish virtuoso Sarasate, is the finest but, though much recorded, has never become as familiar as the Tchaikovsky and Brahms fiddle concertos composed two years earlier in similar romantic vein. The final movement has one of Saint-Saëns' most passionate and soaring themes.

SAINT-SAËNS
VIOLIN CONCERTO
NO. 3 IN B MINOR
(1880)

C

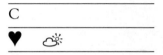

SAINT-SAËNS
VIOLIN SONATA
NO. 1 IN D MINOR
(1885)

CH

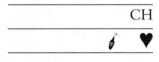

If the idea of a 'violin sonata' sounds somewhat forbidding and serious, then have a go at this. It has four short movements full of memorable tunes and ideas - the third, for instance, is a sweet little waltz while the finale is a hectic cross-country gallop that puts both fiddler and pianist through their paces in passages of great brilliance. Saint-Saëns wrote the Sonata for a famous Belgian (yes, another one!) violinist called Martin Marsick. Fans of Marcel Proust's *Remembrance of Things Past* will know that it was a phrase from the first movement of this D Minor Sonata that inspired his description of the *Vinteuil Sonata* in the book.

PABLO DE SARASATE
1844–1908
SPANISH
CONCERT FANTASY
ON CARMEN
(c. 1883)

I

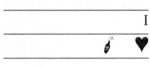

Pablo Martín Melitón Sarasate y Navascuez, to give him his full name, first performed in public at the age of eight. As a composer he was a miniaturist - he wrote no sonatas or concertos, though Saint-Saëns, Dvořák, Bruch, Lalo, Sir Alexander Mackenzie and Henryk Wieniawski all dedicated violin concertos to him. The *Carmen Fantasy* is a great test for any player. It is in five seamless sections (fast-slow-fast-slow-fast) with an ingenious treatment of the famous 'Habañera' from Act 1 of Bizet's opera. There are two other sets of Carmen variations for violin, one by Jenö Hubay, the other by Franz Waxman written for the 1946 film *Humoresque* starring John Garfield as a struggling violinist.

SARASATE
ZIGEUNERWEISEN
('Gypsy Airs')
(1878)

I

Those who heard Sarasate play came away uniformly awed. George Bernard Shaw heard him and was amazed by 'a speed, a delicacy of touch, and an exquisite precision of intonation that would have astonished Tartini's devil'. We can hear proof of this in Sarasate's own performance of this, his most popular composition - one of the most popular of all violin pieces, come to that - on one of the nine discs he recorded way back in 1904. The soulful central theme was used to distraction in the silent movie era to denote sad, pathetic, tearful events and sung to: 'Take me home, oh mother, take me home'.

Satie wrote only about 100 pieces and most of them last only a few minutes (some only a few seconds). But, as Jean Cocteau pointed out, 'Satie's work is small the way a keyhole is small - everything changes the minute you look or listen through it.' This is a suite of four short movements for piano duet with Satie's characteristically catchy tunes and ideas, and bearing such typical Satie titles as *Franco-lunar March* and *Waltz of the Mysterious Kiss in the Eye*. It was written for a 'music-hall' ballet featuring the eccentric dancer Caryathi, hence the title, and was orchestrated by Satie in 1920.

ERIK SATIE
1866–1925
FRENCH
LA BELLE
EXCENTRIQUE
(1908-12)

I/O

These three short hypnotic lullabies are de rigeur for any aspiring beginner on the piano. Nos. 1 and 3 are equally popular in their orchestral versions by Debussy. Satie, half-Scottish half-French, was renowned for his surreal sense of humour and quirky ideas. It's thought that he got his inspiration for these pieces from a Greek vase decorated with naked youths performing a stately dance before the statues of their gods at the Gymnopedia - a yearly festival held in honour of those who fell at Troy.

SATIE
TROIS
GYMNOPÉDIES
(1888)

I

The world première recording of Sauer's romantic E Minor Concerto won both the Concerto and Gramophone Disc of the Year awards in 1996, proof that you don't have to be called Beethoven to win prizes or sell records. Here was a work that had not been heard since the early 1900s by a composer whom not one in 1,000 would have known - and the public has lapped it up. No wonder: it's beautifully written with gorgeous themes and a glittering solo part (the serene Cavatina movement is particularly popular).

EMIL VON SAUER
1862–1942
GERMAN
PIANO CONCERTO
NO. 1 IN E MINOR
(1884)

C

♥

**DOMENICO
SCARLATTI
1685-1757**
ITALIAN
KEYBOARD
SONATAS
(c. 1719-57)

I

Scarlatti composed nearly 600 sonatas for the harpsichord, though only about 30 were published during his lifetime. They are nothing like as long as Mozart's (let alone Beethoven's) but are an amazing body of work. The music ranges from imitations of Spanish guitars and folk music, to whirlwind keyboard acrobatics, witty musical jokes, rapidly-repeated notes, frequent crossings of hands and long-breathed elegiac melodies. Whether they are played on the harpsichord or piano, the best thing to do is buy a disc with a selection of them and just dip in. It's a real treasure house. Identifying each one is a problem: many are written in identical keys, of course, and there are two different systems of numbering them - L numbers and Kk numbers (after Alessandro Longo and Ralph Kirkpatrick, the two musicians who catalogued them).

SCARLATTI
(arr. Tommasini)
THE GOOD-
HUMOURED LADIES
*Ballet
(1917)*

O

A ballet fashioned from various movements of Scarlatti sonatas - that's what this is, formally entitled 'a one-act choreographic comedy'. The idea was concocted by the dancer and choreographer Léonide Massine who based the ballet on a story by Goldoni about an ageing countess who falls for a waiter disguised as a prince. Commissioned by Diaghilev for the Ballets Russes, the Italian composer Vincenzo Tommasini (1878-1950) engagingly captures the lightness, colour and character of the Scarlatti pieces (usually heard in the form of a five-movement suite), a considerable achievement for a man whose enormous wealth allowed him to lead the life of a scholarly recluse on his Italian estates, cultivating his interests in music and translating the more arcane Greek philosophers.

Here is one of the great Romantic virtuoso concertos of the Nineteenth Century, now rarely heard in public and best known through an astonishing world première recording by the American pianist Earl Wild made in 1969. It was composed two years after Tchaikovsky's First Piano Concerto and was dedicated to Liszt who admired and played it (as - incidentally did Mahler - the only recorded instance of this composer as the soloist in a concerto). The three movements require a scintillating bravura technique to get round the notes - guaranteed to tickle the senses, featuring a sparkling central scherzo and a heroic, sweeping finale that builds to a shattering climax.

XAVER SCHARWENKA 1850–1924
POLISH–GERMAN
PIANO CONCERTO NO. 1 IN B FLAT
(1876)

C

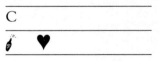

Of Scharwenka's four piano concertos this is arguably the finest and was the one work for which Scharwenka himself wished to be remembered. However, until its world première, award-winning recording by Stephen Hough in 1994 it had not been heard for the best part of a century for reasons which must remain a mystery: it's a tremendous work. The first performance took place in New York in 1910 with the composer as soloist, and Mahler conducting. One critic wrote after the event: 'It is writing of an exalted kind... [and] the piece closes with truly Dionysian and bewildering brilliancy.'

SCHARWENKA
PIANO CONCERTO NO. 4 IN E MINOR
(1908)

C

A century ago this little piano piece was as ubiquitous as Rubinstein's Melody in *F*, Rachmaninov's C Sharp Minor Prelude or Paderewski's Minuet in G. 'My foolish dance' was how Scharwenka later referred to it. He wrote it when still in his teens and sold it outright for five dollars to the publishers Breitkopf and Hartel who made nearly a million dollars out of it. The *Polish Dance* opened the doors of the musical world to its composer but, though he produced several other sets of *Polish Dances* over the years, he never had a hit like this again.

SCHARWENKA
POLISH DANCE
Op. 3 NO. 1
(1869)

I

PAUL SCHOENFIELD
B. 1947
AMERICAN
FOUR PARABLES
(1983)

C

♪

When there has been so much unapproachable music written in the last half of the Twentieth Century, it's good to come across a work that says, 'Come on in, the water's fine!' *Four Parables* is a suite for piano and orchestra reflecting four different experiences in the composer's life. Schoenfield's music takes in a whole range of musical styles - jazz, folk, pop, the classical tradition - and the results are exhilarating: Gershwin-meets-Stravinsky-meets-Broadway. The titles of the movements may make you even more intrigued: *Rambling Till the Butcher Cuts Us Down*, *Senility's Ride*, *Elegy* and *Dog Heaven*. The same composer's *Vaudeville* (a concerto for piccolo trumpet) is equally irresistible.

FRANZ SCHUBERT
1797-1828
AUSTRIAN
FANTASIA IN F
MINOR
(1828)

I

♥ ☁

If you play the piano and can enlist a piano-playing friend to join you for this four-hand work, have a crack at the first few pages at least. It opens with one of Schubert's most sublime melodies - one that will haunt you for days after - which returns throughout the Fantasy. Though played without interruption, there are four clearly defined contrasting movements. If you feel really ambitious, try Schubert's other great piano duet, the *Grand Duo in C*.

SCHUBERT
IMPROMPTUS,
Op. 90, D899 *and*
Op. 142, D946
(1828)

I

☁

An impromptu is a short composition (usually for piano) which sounds exactly as you'd expect - spontaneous, improvised and, well, impromptu - though it was probably Schubert's publisher who thought of the title, not Schubert. He composed two sets of four impromptus, the one in G flat (Op. 90 No. 3) being a particular favourite. The other famous one is Op. 142 No. 3 in B flat which uses the same tune that Schubert used in the incidental music to *Rosamunde* and in the slow movement of his A Major String Quartet. (Note: All Schubert's compositions are identified by Opus numbers and/or D or Deutsch numbers, Deutsch being the musicologist who first published a catalogue of all Schubert's music in 1951.)

A popular one for the piano duet team, one of about 20 marches Schubert wrote for four hands to play. This one, an evergreen 'classical pop', is from a group of three he called *Military Marches*, though it's not exactly full of martial fervour - far too good-humoured and jolly for that. It's often played in orchestral versions and sometimes in an elaborate, virtuoso arrangement for solo piano made by a pupil of Liszt called Carl Tausig.

SCHUBERT
MARCHE MILITAIRE
NO. 1 IN D
(1818)

I

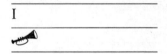

The idea of the *moment musical* (a 'musical moment') was Schubert's and is not dissimilar in style to an impromptu. This form so suited the composer for, with the profusion of ideas that came to him, he liked to encapsulate a mood in a moment - and then move on to the next one. (Several large musical projects were left unfinished for this reason.) These six *Musical Moments* are delightful miniatures and not too difficult for amateurs to play, which helps explain their enduring appeal. Jaunty No. 3 in F minor (sometimes known under the publisher's title of *Air Russe*) is the best known.

SCHUBERT
MOMENTS
MUSICAUX
(1823-28)

I

When Count Ferdinand de Troyer requested a work in a similar style to Beethoven's Septet, Schubert responded with alacrity completing the five movements between 24 February and 1 March 1824. It is his only significant piece of chamber music for more than five instruments, scored for clarinet, bassoon, French horn, two violins, viola, cello and double bass (the same as Beethoven's model except for an extra violin). The music, which is light-hearted in mood except for the darker finale, had to wait until 1853 to be published.

SCHUBERT
OCTET IN F
(1824)

CH

SCHUBERT
Overture and incidental music to
ROSAMUNDE
(1823)

O

♥ ☁

What a sad early history this wonderful music had: Schubert was asked to write the music for an 1823 production of a play called *Rosamunde* by one Wilhelmine von Chézy (she also wrote the libretto for Weber's opera *Euryanthe*). It was a disaster and lasted two nights after which the manuscript gathered dust. Along with five of Schubert's symphonies and 60 songs, it was unearthed by chance 45 years later in Vienna by George Grove (founder and first editor, 1879-89, of the monumental *Grove Dictionary of Music and Musicians*) and Arthur Sullivan (of Gilbert and Sullivan fame). Most frequently heard today are the Overture (actually an overture that Schubert had written three years earlier for an operetta), the Ballet Music in G major and the Entr'acte No. 3 in B flat. The last is one of Schubert's most heavenly tunes, one he used again in the A Minor String Quartet and the B Flat Impromptu.

SCHUBERT
PIANO QUINTET
IN A
'TROUT'
(1819)

CH

🎻 ♥ ☁

Schubert dreamt up this loveable work in the beautiful countryside of Steyr – 'a secret collaborator in this quintet', observed one commentator, for happy melodies and a carefree spirit permeate every bar of this masterpiece of chamber music. It's scored for piano, violin, viola, cello and double bass (the latter replacing the customary second violin), an unusual line-up which Schubert modelled on Hummel's then-popular Piano Quintet composed seven years earlier. There are five movements: the third and fifth are based on Austrian and Hungarian folk melodies while the fourth, the main cause of the Quintet's popularity, is a set of five variations on Schubert's own song 'Die Forelle' ('The Trout').

SCHUBERT
PIANO SONATA
NO. 21 IN B FLAT
(1828)

I

🎻 ♥ ☁

Schubert completed 21 sonatas for the piano. The last three of these, considered to be the best of the bunch, are known as the 'posthumous sonatas' because they were not published until ten years after Schubert's death. The finest of these is the B Flat Sonata, required playing for all pianists, required listening for all lovers of the piano. The first movement alone (observing repeats) lasts over 20 minutes; the slow movement has been described as among the greatest slow movements ever composed. It is profoundly personal music, written when Schubert was in the last year of his short life.

'One glance at Schubert's Trio (Op. 99) – and the troubles of our human existence disappear and all the world is fresh and bright again.' This was Schumann's view of this sunny, radiant piece with all of Schubert's usual melodic and rhythmic invention. It has four movements and was composed in the summer of 1827 but, although it was given a private performance, was not heard in public or published in Schubert's lifetime. The buoyant spirit of the Trio has still never been captured more effectively than on the celebrated historic recording made in 1927 by the cellist Pablo Casals, violinist Jacques Thibaud and the pianist Alfred Cortot.

SCHUBERT
PIANO TRIO
NO. 1 IN B FLAT
(1827)

CH

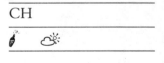

The second of Schubert's two piano trios is far less well known today yet it was Schubert's favourite and, despite being written after the Trio No. 1 in B flat, was performed and well received by the public in his own lifetime. Some find it over-long and with less inspiring melodies. In that case they haven't listened to the second movement (Andante) whose main theme is based on a Swedish folk song and was featured on the soundtrack of Stanley Kubrick's 1975 film *Barry Lyndon*.

SCHUBERT
PIANO TRIO
NO. 2 IN E FLAT
(1827)

CH

Schubert's songs (or *lieder*) are among the most beautiful ever composed – and he wrote exactly 603 of them, the first of them ('Hagars Klage') when he was just 14. 72 of them alone are settings of poems by Goethe, 47 by Mayrhofer and 46 by Schiller, adorned with Schubert's inexhaustible treasure chest of melody. 'An die musik' is a good starting point – 'To Music' – a radiant song in praise of music with words by the composer's friend Franz von Schober, composed in 1815 (a good year for Schubert, for he wrote 144 songs in that period and, on 13 October, wrote eight in a single day!). 'An Sylvia' ('Who is Sylvia') from 1826 is

SCHUBERT
SONGS
(1811-28)

V

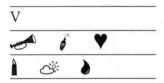

one of the best known, using a German translation of verses from Shakespeare's *Two Gentlemen of Verona*. The most popular, however, is 'Ave Maria'. It may come as a surprise to learn that the words have no relation to the Roman Catholic prayer (as are most of the myriad songs called 'Ave Maria') but are taken from Sir Walter Scott's *The Lady of the Lake*. 'Die Forelle' ('The Trout') has a tune that Schubert later used for his Piano Quintet in A (see above). 'Erlkönig' ('The Erl-King') was Schubert's first published song (1821), his Op. 1, and is a dramatic setting of Goethe's tale of the father and his dying son riding through night and wind. Among many others to look out for are: 'Hark, hark the lark', 'Heidenröslein', 'Litanei', 'Auf dem wasser zu singen', 'Wiegenlied' and 'Gretchen am Spinnrade'.

SCHUBERT
SONG CYCLES
(1824-28)

V

Apart from the individual songs (above), Schubert wrote several song cycles, that is a group of songs united by a single theme. Among them are many incomparable masterpieces. *Die schöne Müllerin* (*The Lovely Miller Maid*, 1824) is a collection of 20 songs using poems by Wilhelm Müller (1794-1827), in which an apprentice and the miller's daughter of the title pass through the stages of joy, disillusionment and thoughts of suicide. From this come 'Das Wandern', 'Wohin?' and 'Ungeduld'. *Die Winterreise* (*The Winter Journey*, 1827) has 24 songs, again with lyrics by Müller, though the mood here tends to be more melancholic (Schubert was at a low ebb at the time). Here you can find 'Gute nacht', 'Der Lindenbaum', 'Die Krähe' and 'Frühlingstraum'. *Schwanesgesang* (*Swan Song*) is a cycle put together after Schubert's death by his publisher. 14 songs by various poets are mainly filled with optimism. Of these, the most famous are 'Liebesbotschaft', 'Am Meer' and 'Ständchen'.

Schubert's one string quintet is his last chamber work. It is also, by general consent, his finest, composed during August and September 1828 and thus, together with the Piano Sonatas in C minor, A and B flat, among the handful of masterpieces he completed during the last months of his life. Amazingly, though a rehearsal of the Quintet took place in October, there is no record of a public performance prior to 1850 and it wasn't published until three years after that. Scored for two violins, one viola and two cellos, it has four movements. Words cannot do justice to the sublime beauty of the second (Adagio), certainly the most exquisite movement in the whole of Schubert's instrumental music and one of the most ethereal in classical music.

SCHUBERT
STRING QUINTET
IN C
(1828)

CH

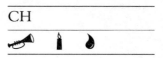

Schubert composed his First Symphony aged just 16; his Fourth and Fifth were completed by the time he was 19. Both the latter had amateur premières but were not otherwise heard in public until the Fourth was performed in Leipzig in 1849, 21 years after Schubert's death. The 'Tragic' (a subtitle that Schubert added to the title page of the manuscript some time after completing the work), is the first of his nine symphonies in which he found his true powers of expression – the originality of the material, the beauty of its lyrical themes and the ability to build a large-scale structure are a great advance on his earlier attempts. The four movements are not 'tragic' in a sombre, melancholy way, but more tempestuous and ardent.

SCHUBERT
SYMPHONY
NO. 4 IN C MINOR
'TRAGIC'
(1816)

O

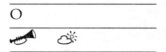

If No. 4 is called the 'Tragic', then No. 5 might well be nicknamed the 'Joyful', its four movements a striking contrast to those of its predecessor. Schubert composed it in a little over three weeks with its first performance given by the amateur orchestra that had grown out of the string quartet in which Schubert himself played the viola. Otherwise, it seems likely that the Fifth Symphony wasn't heard again until a concert at the Crystal Palace in February 1873. It is now the most popular of Schubert's early symphonies.

SCHUBERT
SYMPHONY
NO. 5 IN B FLAT
(1816)

O

**SCHUBERT
SYMPHONY
NO. 8 IN B MINOR
'UNFINISHED'
(1822)**

O

♥   ☁☀

No one is quite certain why Schubert left his Eighth Symphony unfinished. All we know is that he began its composition in Vienna on 30 October 1822 intending it as a gift to the city of Graz who had elected him an honorary member of the Music Society. What they ended up getting was one movement in B minor, a second in E major and just nine bars of a scherzo. Whatever the reason (and thousands of words have been written in speculation on the subject), this, one of the most beloved of all symphonies, was not heard until 30 years after Schubert's death after its discovery in a pile of other Schubert manuscripts by George Grove and Arthur Sullivan (see entry on *Rosamunde* music, above). After the sombre opening bars of the first movement, listen to the famous tune that follows. If you want to remember how it goes, it fits these words: 'This is/ the symph-on-y/That Schubert wrote but never fin-ished'.

**SCHUBERT
SYMPHONY
NO. 9 IN C
'GREAT'
(1825-28)**

O

🎺   ♥   ☁☀

By far the most vast of Schubert's symphonies, the *Great* (so called to distinguish it from his slighter Symphony No. 6 in C major) encompasses a range of profound emotions and is far more complex and individual than anything Schubert had attempted previously. Schumann, who discovered it in 1838, described it as a work 'of heavenly length'; Mendelssohn thought it 'bright, fascinating and original throughout' (it was he who gave it its first performance). The distinguished critic Ralph Hill felt that the music 'is simply enjoying itself and its logic is that of a cross-country run... a musical tonic [that] is loved for its invigorating winds and its freedom from care'.

In four movements played without interruption, this mighty work for piano solo is so called because its opening theme is that of Schubert's own song 'Der Wanderer' (composed in 1816 to a poem by Georg Lübeck: 'Ich komme vom Gebirge her' – 'From the mountains I have come'). It's a work that is frequently heard in the piano and orchestra arrangement made by Liszt in 1851 at a time when Schubert's works, a quarter of a century after his death, were still little known. Liszt's countless piano transcriptions of Schubert's songs, together with this mini piano concerto, contributed a great deal to making Schubert's name known and appreciated.

SCHUBERT
WANDERER
FANTASY
(1822)

I

Clara Wieck, as she was before her marriage to Robert Schumann, was just 13 when she wrote in her diary on 13 January 1833, 'I have begun to compose a concerto'. A child prodigy, she was already well-known in musical circles throughout Europe and, when she completed her one-movement work for piano and orchestra ten months later, her musical marriage to Schumann already established, it was he who orchestrated it. Later, she added and orchestrated two shorter movements herself and the première of her A Minor Concerto was conducted by Mendelssohn in November 1835. Music written by a woman at this time was one thing but a confident, large-scale concerto - and by one so young - was something else. It's an undemanding, pleasant listen in the style of Chopin, Mendelssohn and Robert Schumann himself, the last movement of the three (the first to be written) in a lively polonaise rhythm.

CLARA SCHUMANN
1819-96
GERMAN
PIANO CONCERTO
IN A MINOR
(1835)

C

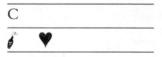

ROBERT SCHUMANN
1810–56
GERMAN
ADAGIO AND
ALLEGRO
(1849)

CH

In 1849 the Schumanns were living in Dresden, the home of the foremost horn player of the day, Joseph Rudolph Lewy (it was he who played first horn in the premières of Wagner's *The Flying Dutchman* and *Lohengrin*). Inspired by his playing and the recent invention of the valve horn, Schumann wrote the Adagio and Allegro in the space of four days in February 1849, the first work of major importance for the new instrument (the Allegro is wonderfully fresh and passionate). Shortly after, he began a sketch of the brilliant *Konzertstücke* for four horns and orchestra, a centrepiece of the horn repertoire.

SCHUMANN
CARNAVAL
(1835)

I

During a brief departure from his obsession with Clara Wieck, Schumann wrote this much-loved piano masterpiece for Ernestine von Frick. Ernestine lived in the Bohemian town of Asch. In German musical notation, 'ASCH' can become musical notes: A, Es [S] (what we call E flat), C and H (what we call B natural). These four notes (which also happen to correspond to the only musical letters in SCHumAnn's name) provide the theme for *Carnaval*, a succession of character sketches he subtitled *Little Scenes for the Piano on Four Notes*. Among those clearly depicted are: *Eusebius* and *Florestan* (two of Schumann's pen-names which represent the contrasting sides of his personality), *Chiarina* (Clara Wieck), *Estrella* (Ernestine von Frick), *Chopin* and *Paganini*.

SCHUMANN
CELLO CONCERTO
IN A MINOR
(1850)

C

Written in a burst of inspiration shortly after Schumann's arrival in Düsseldorf as Director of Music, the Cello Concerto is among the most personal and introspective of all the great concertos for the instrument. Its three movements do not provide the conventional display vehicle for the soloist but are of a more intimate, lyrical nature. In the first movement we can hear the two sides of Schumann's creative personality (Eusebius and Florestan), the idyllic second is dominated by Eusebius, while Florestan takes over for the finale.

Schumann's youthful ambition to be a great piano virtuoso was curtailed in 1832 after he tried to rectify an ailment in the fingers of his right hand by the use of a patent mechanical device. It left him with a permanently crippled right hand. This did not prevent him from making some of the most important contributions to the literature of the piano, not least this masterpiece which he dedicated to Liszt. Writing to his beloved Clara, Schumann confided, 'I do not think I ever wrote anything more impassioned than the first movement. It is a profound lament about you.' After this comes a heroic march and then a final movement that has been described as 'a pure stream of beatific melody'.

SCHUMANN
FANTASIE IN C
(1838)

I

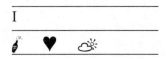

Schumann used the same pseudonyms Eusebius and Florestan (see *Carnaval* and Cello Concerto, above) for his contributions as music critic of the *Zeitschrift für Musik*. These eight short contrasted piano pieces reveal the opposing sides of their natures, the two sides of Schumann's personality - one forceful and dominant, the other a gentle dreamer. The first four blend the two together, and it is interesting to note that Schumann thought up the titles *after* he had written the music. The three best known of these, among Schumann's most popular works for piano, are *Traumes Wirren (Dream Confusion)*, *Des Abends (At Evening)*, *Warum? (Why?)* and *In der Nacht (By Night)*.

SCHUMANN
FANTASIESTÜCKE
Op. 12
(1837)

I

Here is another set of short descriptive pieces bound together under one title (a favourite device of Schumann), this one translated as *Scenes from Childhood*. These charming sketches are Schumann's fond observations of children and their world. So among the 13 numbers in the album are musical pictures of games, story-telling, make-believe and a wide range of moods, while in every number 'a gentle hand strokes a fair face', as one writer put it. Every student pianist knows No. 7, *Träumerei (Daydreams)*, one of the best known of all short piano pieces.

SCHUMANN
KINDERSZENEN
(1838)

I

**SCHUMANN
PAPILLONS
('Butterflies')
(1829-31)**

I

A forerunner of *Carnaval, Butterflies* is a collection of 12 short pieces whose unifying theme is festivity and celebration. It was inspired by different characters and episodes in a work called *Flegeljahre* by the German novelist and humorist Jean Paul (1763-1825), of whose imaginative and eccentric writings Schumann was a lifelong admirer. Spring is in the air, there's a masked ball in progress (it opens with a tune Schumann later re-used in *Florestan* in *Carnaval*). You can hear the clock chiming six in the finale for the end of festivities. Here Schumann also quotes an old German song frequently sung at weddings ('Grossvaterlied') which recurs in the finale of *Carnaval* where it is used to represent the dense artistic 'Philistines'.

**SCHUMANN
PIANO CONCERTO
IN A MINOR
(1841-45)**

C

More than a decade after the Concerto's first appearance, the musical Philistines of London indulgently passed off Clara Schumann's performance of this concerto as 'praiseworthy efforts… to make her husband's curious rhapsody pass for music'. At that time it was novel to have a concerto that was not an obvious vehicle for virtuoso display, and even Liszt had to give up playing the work in the face of public indifference. Nowadays it is one of the most played and popular in the repertoire. Despite its famous opening dramatic flourish, Schumann's Piano Concerto is introspective and gentle. By the time he completed it in 1845 he was beginning to suffer from the mental instability that would eventually lead to his total insanity.

**SCHUMANN
PIANO QUINTET
IN E FLAT
(1842)**

CH

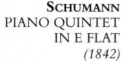

Schumann's most frequently performed chamber work, composed for string quartet and piano, was influential in providing the inspiration for later works of the same ilk by Brahms, Dvořák and Franck. It was written in a white-hot burst of creativity in September 1842, its four contrasted movements being sketched in five days and completed (fully scored) in a fortnight. Schumann dedicated it to Clara who was to have been the pianist at its first performance. At the last moment she fell ill, her place taken by Mendelssohn who played the difficult piano part at sight. Not to be confused with Schumann's Piano Quartet in the same key, an only slightly less distinguished masterpiece.

As a writer himself and a connoisseur of the latest offerings in the literary world, Schumann applied a more sophisticated, intellectual approach to song-writing than Schubert. There is greater unity between words and music in the more than 250 songs he composed, some of their accompaniments aspiring to independent piano pieces, while others seem to be commentaries on the hidden significance of the poem. Schumann's favourite poets were Heinrich Heine (1797-1856) and the other great Romantics of the day. Some of his best known songs, are 'Im Walde' ('In the Wood'), 'Der Nussbaum' ('The Almond Tree'), 'Widmung' ('Devotion'), 'Die beiden Grenadiere' ('The Two Grenadiers') and 'Mondnacht' ('Moonlight') among many others.

SCHUMANN
SONGS
(1840-52)

V

Three monumental song collections, all composed in 1840 when his marriage to Clara was a certainty, contain more miniature vocal masterpieces. These are: *Liederkreis*, Op. 24 (Song Cycle, nine songs), *Frauenliebe und Leben*, Op. 42 (*Woman's Life and Love*, eight songs) and *Dichterliebe*, Op. 48 (*A Poet's Love*, sixteen songs). The first and last are settings of poems by Heine, while *Frauenliebe und Leben* uses rather sentimental lyrics by the German poet and biologist Adalbart Chamisso (1781-1838) - the cycle tells the story of a young woman's love, her happiness, her wedding and then sorrow over her beloved's death. The finest collection is undoubtedly *Dichterliebe* ('unique in its astonishing diversity of inspiration, composition and atmosphere', says one commentator) which includes the lovely 'Ich grolle nicht' ('I will not grieve').

SCHUMANN
SONG CYCLES
(1840)

V

**SCHUMANN
SYMPHONY
NO. 1 IN B FLAT
'SPRING'
*(1841)***

O

Schumann's First Symphony was sketched in the remarkably short time of four days at the end of January 1841; all four movements were completed by 20 February. It was inspired by a poem by the obscure Adolph Böttger but, as Schumann himself admitted, it was 'the season in which the Symphony originated [that] has influenced its form and made it what it is.' From this you can gather that you're in for a genial, energetic and immediately-attractive work bursting with Mendelssohnian high spirits and melodic inspiration. The Symphony was dedicated to Friedrich August, King of Saxony and the first performance was conducted by Mendelssohn.

**SCHUMANN
SYMPHONY
NO. 3 IN E FLAT
'RHENISH'
*(1850)***

O

This was Schumann's last essay in symphonic form but designated No. 3 because it was published before his D Minor Symphony (No. 4). The inspiration for the work came after Schumann and his wife had gone on a pleasure trip to Cologne, on the banks of the Rhine. They were especially impressed by its magnificent Gothic cathedral and the enthronement they witnessed of the Archbishop of Cologne as Cardinal (the fourth of the Symphony's five movements is called the *Cathedral Scene*, an evocation of the event). The Rhine held a particular fascination for Schumann - Symphony No. 3 was originally subtitled *Episode in a Life on the Banks of the Rhine River* - and two of his songs ('Sonntags am Rhein' and 'Im Rhein, im heiligen') celebrate the river. In 1854 Schumann took things a step further and tried to drown himself in it.

**SCHUMANN
TOCCATA IN C
*(1830, rev. 1833)***

I

Schumann's Toccata puts the fear of God into most pianists, being a notorious test of musicality versus stamina, but a marvellous piece of music of great originality. It's a brief, early work which requires enormous endurance to be played effectively. There's a famous live recording of it from 1947 by the astonishing Simon Barere where he rattles it off in four-and-a-half minutes flat. Asked why he played it so fast, Barere replied, 'Because I can!'

Until 1900, Scriabin was a kind of latter-day Russian Chopin composing the sort of piano pieces the Polish composer might have written if he'd still been around. (After 1900, Scriabin changed and increasingly came to believe he was God!) Among the best of these early gems are the *12 Studies*, Op. 8, and the most famous of these is the last of the set, Scriabin's most performed work. 'Whoever plays it,' wrote Louis Biancolli, 'feels momentarily like a god. To have composed that étude is to have married the piano.'

ALEXANDER SCRIABIN 1872-1915
RUSSIAN
ÉTUDE IN D SHARP MINOR,
Op. 8 No. 12
(1894)

I

♥

Not a masterpiece, but with some luscious and highly attractive passages in the course of its three movements. The second (slow) movement is a set of five variations on a song-like theme but the finale, though it opens with a rather dull rondo, goes on to have one of the most searingly-romantic themes of any late-nineteenth century piano concerto. If Scriabin had written nothing else but this tune, he would have merited a mention here.

SCRIABIN
PIANO CONCERTO IN F SHARP MINOR
(1896)

C

♥

Born and died in Paris, Senaillé is remembered today (if at all) through a short transcription for bassoon. In the mid-1920s, bassoonist Archie Camden was recording Mozart's Concerto in B flat (probably the first-ever recording of a complete woodwind concerto) and, needing a fill-up, came up with this perky arrangement he had made of a movement from one of Senaillé's 50 forgotten violin sonatas (No. 4, in fact). It is now an accepted classic for the instrument, cheeky, bubbling - and fun.

JEAN BAPTISTE SENAILLÉ 1687-1730
FRENCH
ALLEGRO SPIRITOSO
(c. 1710)

I

♪

**DMITRI
SHOSTAKOVICH
1906-75**
RUSSIAN
CONCERTO FOR
PIANO, TRUMPET
AND STRINGS
(1933)

C

Described variously as 'fun-poking and mighty refreshing', 'without exaggeration… disagreeable music' and sounding as if 'it might have been written by a schoolboy with his cap set rakishly on the back of his head', Shostakovich's Concerto is both entertaining and exhilarating. The trumpet part is extensive, using both its bravura and lyrical capabilities to the full in music that has echoes of Poulenc, Prokofiev and even Rachmaninov. The Concerto's four short movements end with a coruscating finale, including a piano cadenza inspired by Beethoven's rondo *Rage Over a Lost Penny*. There's a splendid recording of the composer himself as soloist in the work.

**SHOSTAKOVICH
JAZZ SUITES NOS. 1
(1934)
AND 2
*(1938)***

O

Shostakovich's idea of jazz is about as far away from the real thing as synchronised swimming is from being an Olympic sport. In 1934 the Soviet authorities, with their customary with-it outlook, wanted to raise the level of the country's jazz to a more professional standard. In response, Shostakovich wrote his first *Jazz Suite* 'pour encourager les autres'. Scored for a small instrumental ensemble, the Suite consists of three snappy tea-time dances. The more extensive Second Suite has eight short Strauss-like dance movements. Both suites are perkily tuneful, expertly and wittily orchestrated, and immediately attractive - light music (not jazz) at its best.

**SHOSTAKOVICH
PIANO CONCERTO
NO. 2 IN F
*(1957)***

C

Shostakovich wrote his Second Piano Concerto (the Piano and Trumpet Concerto is thought of as No. 1) for his 19-year-old son Maxim when the boy was a student at the Moscow Conservatory. There are many private family and musical jokes, though none gets in the way of the listener's fun. In the first movement there's a constant return to a tune that sounds remarkably similar to 'What shall we do with the drunken sailor?' and the finale is a vigorous rondo (with some references to five-finger piano exercises), but the slow movement is quite different - a long, slow, soulful melody that puts one in mind of Rachmaninov.

The Leningrad Dance Company commissioned Shostakovich to write his first ballet, *The Age of Gold*. It was described as 'an indictment of the non-Soviet man' – the story involves a fight between some fascists and a Soviet football team. The ballet was soon withdrawn though, accused of 'minimising the conflicts of class war and ideological destructiveness'. What fun. Shostakovich, though he afterwards compiled a concert suite from the score, mentions neither the ballet nor the music in his autobiography. One gem survives in the repertoire – the Polka, a genuinely humorous orchestral lollipop that can literally raise a smile. There's also a piano solo version which can do the same in the right hands.

SHOSTAKOVICH
POLKA
from The Age of Gold Ballet
(1929)

O/I

Many twentieth century composers seem either incapable or too embarrassed to write a singable melody. Shostakovich, some of whose music is distinctly dissonant and jarring, was also a superb writer of tunes. Here is a straightforward, romantic film theme, part of the music he wrote for a 1955 Russian movie called *The Gadfly* but which became popularised in the UK as a result of being used as the theme music for the 1983 TV series *Reilly, Ace of Spies*.

SHOSTAKOVICH
ROMANCE
from The Gadfly
(1955)

O/I

♥

In early 1936, Stalin expressed his outrage at Shostakovich's opera *Lady Macbeth of Mtsensk* and the composer suddenly found himself not only out of public favour but in fear of his life. His crime had been to 'lose himself in musical chaos and petty-bourgeois formalism' (whatever that means!). His Fifth Symphony was Shostakovich's tight-rope response, a work that would appease the Soviet authorities while remaining true to his musical ideals. It was premièred in November 1937 to public and critical acclaim and has since become by far the most frequently heard of all Shostakovich's 15 symphonies. Its four movements are written in striking contrast to each other – a dramatic and powerful opening, a waltz-like scherzo, a profoundly-felt slow movement and a march-like finale which ends in a blaze of brass and timpani.

SHOSTAKOVICH
SYMPHONY
NO. 5 IN D MINOR
(1937)

O

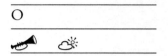

**SHOSTAKOVICH
SYMPHONY
NO. 7 IN C
'LENINGRAD'**
(1941)

Begun in July 1941, a month after the Nazis had invaded the USSR and were laying siege to Leningrad, the Seventh Symphony was planned as an expression of what Shostakovich called, 'the majestic ideas of the patriotic war. Neither savage raids, German planes, nor the grim atmosphere of the beleaguered city could hinder the flow of ideas. I worked with an inhuman intensity I have never before reached.' You can imagine from this what the music sounds like: canons, conflict, requiems, victory, outrage at tyranny - and optimism.

**JEAN SIBELIUS
1865–1957**
FINNISH
**AT THE CASTLE
GATE**
*from Pelléas and
Mélisande
(1905)*

A number of composers have been inspired by Maeterlinck's sombre play. Debussy based his opera of the same name on it and Fauré wrote an attractive suite of incidental music for the theatre. Sibelius' orchestral suite for the play has as its opening section *At the Castle Gate*, made famous by its use as the introductory music for television's long-running *The Sky at Night* (presented by Patrick Moore). It's an apt choice for it seems to conjure up the unfathomable, limitless mysteries of the heavens.

**SIBELIUS
FINLANDIA**
(1899, rev. 1900)

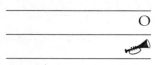

Sibelius' most celebrated work is a tone poem written (in the form we know it today) in 1900. It was originally the fourth movement of a suite entitled *Finland Awakes* composed a year earlier as part of a series of entertainments inaugurated to raise funds to fight Russia's suppression of the press and free speech in Finland. It's said that the one movement we now call *Finlandia* did more to bring about Finnish independence than any speech, pamphlet or other propaganda (no performance was permitted in Finland until 1905). The noble central section has become a second Finnish national anthem; in the UK and the States it has become the hymn 'Be still, my soul'.

Karelia is an area in the eastern part of Finland where the inhabitants are said to have a much jollier disposition than their counterparts in the west. This is reflected in some of the most carefree and exuberant music Sibelius ever wrote. The three short orchestral movements that make up the *Karelia Suite* are: Intermezzo, Ballade and *Alla Marcia*, taken from the incidental music he provided in 1893 for a student theatre production at the University of Viborg.

SIBELIUS
KARELIA SUITE
(1893)

O

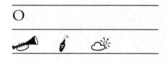

Sibelius explained this exquisite, plaintive work as depicting 'Tuonela [the Finnish equivalent of Hades], the Kingdom of Death… surrounded by a broad river of black water and rapid currents, in which the Swan of Tuonela glides in majestic fashion and sings'. The story comes from the epic Finnish poem *Kalevala* and the music is the second of a suite in four sections inspired by *Kalevala* entitled *Lemminkainen Legends*. The Swan is portrayed by the cor anglais and is one of the most beautiful solos ever written for the instrument.

SIBELIUS
THE SWAN OF
TUONELA
(1893, rev. 1897 and 1900)

O

The two most popular (and accessible) of Sibelius' seven symphonies are No. 2 and No. 5. Not only was he the first great Finnish composer but the first to reflect the character and nature of his country. The Second Symphony, emotional, extravagant, theatrical and colourful, is regarded by the Finns as a sort of national testament: the first movement has a rustic feel (a picture of Finnish pastoral life, perhaps), the second is more yearning and melancholy, the third is a lively scherzo said by some to represent the awakening of Finnish patriotic spirit, while the finale is exultantly optimistic depicting 'the hope entering the breasts of the Finns and comfort in the anticipated coming of a deliverer [from Russian oppression]'.

SIBELIUS
SYMPHONY
NO. 2 IN D MINOR
(1901)

O

SIBELIUS
SYMPHONY
NO. 5 IN E FLAT
(1915, rev. 1919)

O

The mighty Fifth Symphony was written in the second year of the First World War, a period during which Sibelius suffered not only financial but spiritual trials. Profoundly shocked by the conflict, he struggled to express his feelings in the best way he knew how – the symphonic form. Its completion proved, in the words of Karl Ekman, 'an expression of its creator's great optimism, gained through suffering; an elevating testimony, in an evil period, to an unshakeable faith in the ever-renewing power of life'. The first version, premièred in 1915, was withdrawn, heavily re-written and not presented in the form we know today until 1919. The heroic final movement has been described as 'Thor swinging his hammer' and it ends with a famous succession of separated, crunching chords (always hard to know which is the last one!).

SIBELIUS
VALSE TRISTE
(1903)

O

It is not unusual for the least significant work of a composer to be his most popular. At one time, this sentimental little waltz, one of the numbers Sibelius wrote to accompany a production of a play called *Kuolema* (*Death*) by his brother-in-law Arvid Järnefelt, was played by the band of every café in Europe. The music tells the story of a dying woman rising from her bed to dance with strange visionary couples; the music rises to a climax, there's a knock on the door, the spectral figures vanish and there on the threshold is Death.

SIBELIUS
VIOLIN CONCERTO
IN D MINOR
(1903, rev. 1905)

C

The violin was Sibelius' first study instrument and at one time he entertained thoughts of becoming a soloist (as late as 1891 he auditioned for the strings of the Vienna Philharmonic). You can call this the 'Sibelius Concerto' because this is the only concerto he wrote for any instrument. It's one of the cornerstones of the violinist's repertoire and all the great artists have risen to its challenge since its first appearance, Heifetz, Ginette Neveu, Ivry Gitlis and Tasmin Little being four of its most notable exponents on disc. Not an easy work to play, the Concerto has three movements: the first is one of romantic ardour, the second poignant and poetic, the last passionate and impulsive with enormous rhythmic vitality.

Although he wrote symphonies, concertos, tone poems and chamber music numbering 132 separate works, it's by this short piano solo that Sinding's name is remembered universally. A quintessential piece of what is sneeringly referred to by some critics as 'salon music', *Rustle of Spring* was once the aspiration of every young pianist (though in fact it's not at all easy to play well). Now considered hackneyed, it's rarely heard in the concert hall. Our loss, because it's a fine piece of its kind. It's actually the second of his *Six Pieces*, Op. 32 (which are never played at all) but if you want to hear more of Sinding's music (and if you like Grieg you'll like Sinding), try his Suite in A minor for violin and orchestra and his Piano Concerto.

**CHRISTIAN SINDING
1856–1941**
NORWEGIAN
RUSTLE OF SPRING
(1896)

I

Smetana made five versions of this, one of the most loveable of all comic operas, known in the trade as *The Battered Bride*. Starting out as incidental music to accompany a play by Karel Sabina, the score was developed into a fully-fledged opera and heard for the first time in Prague in 1866. The story revolves round the love of Marenka and Janik - everyone else in the tiny Bohemian village in which the action takes place has different ideas for them. The effervescent Overture, often heard on its own, is a merry affair. Gustav Mahler thought it was so much in the spirit of the entire work that he used to place it before the second act so that latecomers might not miss it.

**BEDŘICH SMETANA
1824–1884**
BOHEMIAN (CZECH)
Overture to
THE BARTERED
BRIDE
Opera
(1866)

O

Smetana's gift for writing dance rhythms and folk melodies in the Bohemian idiom is apparent throughout all his music but nowhere more successfully than in this opera, one which laid the foundations for Czech national music. Three purely instrumental sections have long been concert favourites - the *Polka*, a favourite Bohemian dance, gives the first act an exciting finish as the locals celebrate in holiday spirit in the village square; the *Furiant* (a fiery Bohemian dance) comes in the second act when the villagers perform a dance at a local inn; the *Dance of the Comedians* accompanies a circus troupe who come to entertain the villagers in the third act.

SMETANA
POLKA, FURIANT
and DANCE OF THE
COMEDIANS
from The Bartered Bride
(1866)

O

SMETANA
MÁ VLÁST
(1872-76)

O

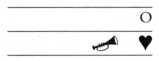

Written when Smetana was at the height of his powers, before the onset of deafness, syphilis and insanity, *Má Vlást (My Homeland)* is a series of six remarkable tone poems depicting his beloved country. The second of these is Smetana's most famous work. It's called *Vltava* (or *The Moldau*), a picture in music of the great River Moldau as it passes on its way from the forests of Bohemia to the sea, one of the most vivid pieces of descriptive music ever written. Its wonderful melodies (ironically, its main theme is derived from Swedish, not Czech, folk music) and colourful orchestration have helped to make this a perennially popular work.

JOHN PHILIP SOUSA
1854-1932
AMERICAN
KING COTTON
March
(1895)

O

Sousa was the 'March King of America': he wrote 136 marches in all (and a great deal of other music besides, including a number of comic operas). The most famous ones follow a similar pattern - an arresting introduction, a skittish first melody (repeated) followed by a broader tune (repeated), progressing to the Trio (the main march melody) and onwards, after a series of repeats, to a big climax with the main theme treated in different orchestral colours. *King Cotton* was written to mark the occasion of the engagement of the Sousa Band at the Cotton States Exposition in Atlanta, Georgia.

SOUSA
THE LIBERTY BELL
March
(1893)

O

The title comes from the occasion when the Sousa Band took part in a parade in Philadelphia to honour the return of the Liberty Bell. The first of Sousa's marches to achieve widespread popularity was *The Gladiators* (1886) - it sold over a million copies - but *The Liberty Bell* was one of the first marches to bring Sousa substantial financial rewards.

SOUSA
SEMPER FIDELIS
March
(1888)

O

The motto of the US Marine Corp is 'Semper Fidelis' and Sousa wrote this immensely popular march when he was leader of the US Marine Band. Whenever there's a parade of any description, *Semper Fidelis* will be played, yet Sousa never capitalised on it - he sold the copyright outright for $35. Sousa made one of the earliest gramophone recordings in 1890 of this and two other marches (*The Thunderer* and *The Washington Post*). *Semper Fidelis* is now credited as the first hit of the US record industry.

Arguably the best-known march in the world was composed on board the *SS Teutonic* while Sousa was travelling back from Italy via England to the United States in the autumn of 1896 (one source says the whole march was composed on Christmas Day of that year). Sousa described how he 'paced the deck with a mental brass band playing the march fully a hundred times during the week I was on the steamer'. It's a stirring, patriotic piece. Piano fans will also know it in a sensational transcription for piano solo by Vladimir Horowitz - two hands or ten?!

SOUSA
THE STARS AND
STRIPES FOREVER!
March
(1896)

O

Another all-time Sousa favourite and one of the few of his marches that he himself bothered to record (once in 1890 and again in 1926). The Sousa Band left many recordings but he himself was suspicious of 'mechanical music' - it was he who coined the term 'canned music' - and conducted only a handful of his band's discs. He certainly knew what he was about when he did take up the baton, however, proving that he lived up to his famous dictum that 'a march should make a man with a wooden leg step out'.

SOUSA
THE THUNDERER
March
(1889)

O

This was commissioned, not surprisingly, by that great American newspaper for the ceremonies attending the presentation of prizes in a student essay contest. It was taken up as a *two-step*, a dance that was then all the rage, and brought international fame to the capital's paper. (There's an ancient recording of this by the Sousa Band conducted by the band's virtuoso trombone soloist, Arthur Pryor, remembered today as the composer of the novelty number *The Whistler and his Dog*.)

SOUSA
THE WASHINGTON
POST
March
(1889)

O

JOHN STAINER
1840–1901
ENGLISH
THE CRUCIFIXION
(1887)

CHO

Stainer's *The Crucifixion* was a staple feature of English choral societies for well over half a century. Its piety and emotional simplicity have meant that it has now rather fallen out of fashion. A pity – there is some magnificent and moving music in this score for tenor and bass soloists, choir, congregation and organ. The title page tells us this is 'A meditation on the sacred passion of the holy Redeemer, the words selected and written by the Rev. J. Sparrow-Simpson' (how charmingly Victorian!). Among its passing delights are the rousing chorus 'Fling wide the gates' and the heroic tenor solo 'King ever glorious'.

CHARLES STANFORD
1852–1924
IRISH
THE BLUEBIRD
(1910)

CHO

Stanford's music, long unfashionable and underrated, has been making a comeback in recent years. Some pieces – especially his vocal writing – have always been cherished and this short unaccompanied song for choir is one of them. It is a setting of a poem by Mary Coleridge of enormous delicacy and sensitivity – 'The lake lay blue below the sky...'. A famous old recording by the Glasgow Orpheus Choir contributed greatly to its popularity, the final high single note from a solo soprano fading magically into the ether.

STANFORD
CLARINET
CONCERTO
IN A MINOR
(1904)

C

To my mind, this is one of the loveliest of all woodwind concertos. The influence of Brahms is clear but not at the expense of Stanford's own idiomatic style. Stanford met the clarinettist Richard Mühlfeld for whom Brahms had written his Clarinet Quintet and sonatas and, having completed his Concerto, dedicated it to Mühlfeld. Alas, the most celebrated player of the day refused to accept the work, deeply offending the composer. Who could fail to respond to the dreamy, romantic theme of the second section (the Concerto, though in a single-movement, has three distinct parts) or be captivated by the virtuoso final allegro?

In 1911, a few months before he began work on this, the most ardently romantic piano concerto by a British composer, Stanford had conducted the British première of Rachmaninov's Second Piano Concerto with the composer as soloist. The opening of Stanford's Second Concerto (he wrote three altogether) is clearly reminiscent of Rachmaninov's but the heart-rending second theme could only have been written by an Irishman, likewise the hints of folk-song in the slow movement and the vigorous dance of the finale. A glorious work that deserves to be better known.

STANFORD
PIANO CONCERTO
NO. 2 IN C MINOR
(1915)

C

The Staffordshire-born poet and lawyer Sir Henry Newbolt (1862-1938) wrote many poems revealing his deep love of the sea and seafarers (when he wasn't writing about *esprit de corp* and encouraging us all to 'Play up! play up! and play the game!'). Stanford set a number of Newbolt's poems for baritone soloist, chorus and orchestra: *Songs of the Fleet* (1910) contains 'The Little Admiral' while the five *Songs of the Sea* has the stirring 'The "Old Superb"' and, most famously, 'Drake's Drum' - 'Drake he's in his hammock till the great Armadas come. (Capten, art tha sleepin' there below?)'. Splendid stuff.

STANFORD
SONGS OF THE SEA
(1904)

CHO

♥

Stanford's Third Symphony was the first significant and certainly the most successful symphony by a British composer before Elgar's First. It won Stanford an international reputation, was chosen to open the new Concertgebouw in Amsterdam, and was given many times in Europe and North America - Mahler thought highly enough of it to conduct two performances with the New York Philharmonic. Listen to the lively second movement and you'll see why the symphony is subtitled 'Irish', while the third and fourth movements actually quote Irish traditional tunes: the lament of the *Sons of Usnacht* (very similar to the theme of the slow movement in Brahms's Fourth Symphony), *Molly McAlpin* and *Let Erin remember the days of old*.

STANFORD
SYMPHONY
NO. 3 IN F MINOR
'IRISH'
(1887)

O

STANFORD
TE DEUM
from Services in B Flat
(1879)

CHO

Stanford in B Flat, as choirmasters up and down the land refer to this setting of the Services, was published when Stanford was 27, his first major contribution to the liturgy. The *Te Deum* ('We praise thee, O God: we acknowledge Thee to be the Lord') is one of the Church's great hymns of praise. Stanford opens his Services with it in a rousing setting that was performed at the coronation of King Edward VII in 1902.

JOHN STANLEY
1712–86
ENGLISH
TRUMPET
VOLUNTARY IN D,
Op. 6 No. 5
(1752)

I

The term *voluntary* has been around since the mid-Sixteenth Century to describe an improvised piece of keyboard music. Today it almost always means the organ solo at the beginning and end of an Anglican church service. Stanley, blinded by accident at the age of two, was one of the greatest organists of his day, enjoyed the friendship and esteem of Handel and became Master of the King's Band of Music. He wrote 30 voluntaries (three sets of ten, published in the 1740s and 1750s) for the organ. This one, exploiting the instrument's trumpet stop, is the best known, a great favourite at weddings. No. 6 from this set, also in D, is a fine less well-known alternative.

JOHANN STRAUSS I
1804–49
AUSTRIAN
RADETZKY MARCH
(1848)

O

The most celebrated composition by Johann Strauss Senior, the 'Father of the Waltz', is actually a march. It was written at the end of his life to celebrate the victory over the Italians by the Austrian general Count Joseph Radetzky von Radetz (1766-1858). Almost at once it became the musical symbol of Hapsburg Vienna and Austrian military power. Not to be confused with the Rakóczy March (see Berlioz), this one is always the final number of the New Year's Day concert in Vienna, accompanied by the audience clapping (roughly) in time.

Johann Strauss II made his debut as a conductor and composer in Hietzing, near Vienna, on 15 October 1844, just five years before the early death of his famous father. The first of the more than 400 waltzes he was to compose aroused immense enthusiasm, prompting the editor of the local paper to report: 'Goodnight, Lanner [Strauss I's rival]. Good evening, Father Strauss. Good morning, Son Strauss.' Among the most loved of those he would produce over the next half century is *Künstlerleben*, Viennese to its core, quintessential Strauss with its light-hearted expression of an artist's life. A fairy-tale, of course, like the rose-coloured picture of Vienna that Strauss offered to the world and which ended with the First World War.

JOHANN STRAUSS II
1825–1899
AUSTRIAN
AN ARTIST'S LIFE
(1867)

O

♥

Unquestionably the most famous waltz ever written, *An der schönen, blauen Donau* (to give it its original title) has a claim to being the most widely-known piece of classical music. It was originally a choral work composed for the Vienna Men's Singing Society, a setting of a poem by Karl Beck in praise of Vienna and the River Danube - not that anyone has ever seen the blue Danube (it's generally a shade of dirty grey). It caused a sensation when it was first performed, indeed everywhere it was presented, and when Strauss made his American debut in Boston he conducted the waltz played by an orchestra of 1,000 instruments and a chorus of 1,000 voices! Today, it's a second Austrian national anthem and always heard in its purely orchestral garb, though there is also a scintillating piano transcription by the obscure Artur Schulz-Evler (1854–1905) which many great virtuoso pianists once had in their repertoire. (See also Brahms: Waltzes, page 84)

JOHANN STRAUSS II
THE BLUE DANUBE
(1867)

O

♥

JOHANN STRAUSS II
EMPEROR WALTZ
'KAISER WALTZ'
(1889)

O

♥

There are two conflicting explanations for the title. One is that it was written in 1888 to celebrate the 40th anniversary of the reign of the Austrian emperor Franz Joseph I; the other story has it that in the autumn of 1889, Strauss was in Berlin to conduct some of his works and brought with him an extended waltz called *Hand in Hand*, intended to complement the links between Berlin and Vienna. It was Strauss's publisher who changed the title to *Kaiser-Walzer*, reflecting a recent meeting between Franz Joseph and Emperor Wilhelm II, who had just ascended the German throne. Whatever its history, the *Emperor Waltz* is one of Strauss's most distinguished waltzes. The second of its four main themes was turned into the song 'I'm in love with Vienna' for the 1939 Hollywood film *The Great Waltz*.

JOHANN STRAUSS II
Overture to
DIE FLEDERMAUS
Operetta
(1874)

O

♥

The Bat was Strauss's third operetta and the only one by the 'Waltz King of Vienna' to be set in that city. The libretto was written by Meilhac and Halévy, the same guys who wrote *Carmen*, and Strauss was so inspired by the comic plot that he completed the entire score in 43 days. With its elegant sets and gowns, its dramatic intrigue, infectious gaiety and lively, mocking spirit, it's no wonder that it has remained such a firm favourite in the opera houses of the world for well over a century. The Overture is often heard independently and uses several of the operetta's principal melodies including the waltz that comes at the climax of the second act.

JOHANN STRUASS II
'LAUGHING SONG'
from Die Fledermaus
(1874)

OP

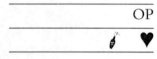 ♥

From Act 2 comes 'Mein Herr Marquis' ('My Dear Marquis') known as the 'Laughing Song'. It's sung by Adele at Prince Orlovsky's masked ball. She is the maid of Eisenstein's wife Rosalinde and Eisenstein, who has been introduced as Marquis Renard, thinks he recognises the girl. Orlovsky and the rest of the guests laugh at him for such a curious mistake and Adele, too, makes fun of her employer in this famous soprano showpiece. For a different kind of laugh, though, you should dig out the recording made by the legendary Florence Foster Jenkins - a hoot in more than one sense.

Another thrilling vocal display number, also from Act 2, is sung by Rosalinde. Disguised as a Hungarian Countess, she has been watching her husband flirting outrageously with the masked Adele. Soon Eisenstein moves on to the mysterious Countess but when Adele suggests that she is not really Hungarian at all, Rosalinde launches into 'Klänge der Heimat' ('Strains of my Homeland'), a czardas in which 'no genuine Hungarian could sing more movingly of the pain of separation from the beloved homeland, or of the fire in the Hungarian breast that drives them to the dance', in the words of critic Ernest Newman.

JOHANN STRAUSS II
Czardas from
DIE FLEDERMAUS
(1874)

OP

Not far behind the popularity of *Die Fledermaus* comes *Die Zigeunerbaron*, premièred in Vienna in 1885. The operetta tells the story of Sandór Brinkay who returns to his ancestral home having left it as a child. The house is occupied by gypsies and he falls in love with one of them, Saffi. The Overture is made up of themes from the operetta, most notably the celebrated music from Act 2, the rapturous *Schatz* (*Treasure*) *Waltz* when Saffi and her foster-mother Czipra uncover some buried treasure.

JOHNANN STRAUSS II
Overture to
THE GYPSY BARON
Operetta
(1885)

O

♥

The *Morgenblätter* waltz was written for a ball for a Viennese press club, the Concordia. Offenbach had previously written a set of waltzes entitled *Evening Papers* which was played the same evening as the Strauss première. The journalists expressed their preference for Offenbach's, a verdict that posterity has decidedly reversed.

JOHANN STRAUSS II
MORNING PAPERS
(1864)

O

♥

**JOHANN STRAUSS II
PERPETUUM
MOBILE
*(1862)***

O

One of Strauss's best known works is neither a waltz, a march nor a polka. He himself described it as 'a musical jest', a short, high velocity orchestral work-out in perpetual motion. In theory, once begun it has no ending, for when they reach the end of the printed music the players are instructed to start again from the top without a break *ad infinitum*. In performance it's usually concluded by a couple of big chords, or by the orchestra gradually playing softer and softer until the conductor turns to the audience with the words, 'And so on!'

**JOHANN STRAUSS II
POLKAS
*(1846-88)***

O

Apart from waltzes and operettas, Strauss was a prolific composer of polkas. The best of these are the *Pizzicato Polka* (1870), an exercise in plucked strings and written in collaboration with his brother Josef; *Thunder and Lightning Polka* (1868) - plenty of opportunities for the percussion department; *Tritsch-Tratsch Polka* (1858), as infectiously jolly a piece as was ever written and the subject of an ear-boggling piano transcription by the virtuoso Georges Cziffra. Others include *Annen-Polka, Champagne Polka, Electrophorus Polka, Explosions Polka…* the list seems as endless as Strauss's high-spirited melodic invention.

**JOHANN STRAUSS II
ROSES FROM THE
SOUTH
*(1880)***

O

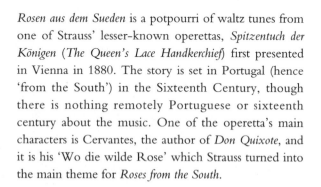

Rosen aus dem Sueden is a potpourri of waltz tunes from one of Strauss' lesser-known operettas, *Spitzentuch der Königen* (*The Queen's Lace Handkerchief*) first presented in Vienna in 1880. The story is set in Portugal (hence 'from the South') in the Sixteenth Century, though there is nothing remotely Portuguese or sixteenth century about the music. One of the operetta's main characters is Cervantes, the author of *Don Quixote*, and it is his 'Wo die wilde Rose' which Strauss turned into the main theme for *Roses from the South*.

Written for an Austrian nobleman and performed for the first time by Strauss's orchestra in 1868, this is an orchestral tone poem depicting the beauties of Nature in the forests skirting Vienna. After its stately opening and a serene melody on the cello, the woods are represented by a waltz played on the zither.

JOHANN STRAUSS II
TALES FROM THE
VIENNA WOODS
(1868)

O

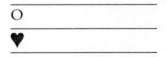

Vienna Blood, or *Vienna Life*, is another of Strauss's hymns in praise of his native city and its inhabitants, though this one is distinctly more dreamy and sentimental in character than his usual light and carefree waltzes. Some other Strauss tributes to Vienna include *Die jungen Wiener* (*Young Viennese*), *Wien, mein Sinn!* (*Vienna, My Soul!*), *Wiener Punsch-Lieder* (*Viennese Punch Songs*), *Wiener Frauen* (*Viennese Women*) and, of course, *Tales from the Vienna Woods*.

JOHANN STRAUSS II
VIENNA BLOOD
(Wiener Blut)
(1873)

O

♥

'Frühlingsstimmen', Strauss's Op. 410, is a vocal waltz (words by one Richard Genée), an exuberant celebration of spring. Nowadays it's more generally heard in its orchestral version. The waltz was dedicated to the great Viennese pianist Alfred Grünfeld (1852-1924) who recorded his own version of it on an ancient disc back in 1913, a rare link to one of the giants of musical history.

JOHANN STRAUSS II
VOICES OF SPRING
(1883)

O

♥

(Not *Wine, Women and Song* as its German title *Wein, Weib und Gesang* is often mistranslated.) The waltz has one of Strauss's most spacious introductions, almost an independent composition, before the four waltz melodies which follow. Legend has it that when Wagner first heard this music, he was so moved that he grabbed the baton from the hand of the conductor, Anton Seidl, and conducted the rest of the piece himself. For an alternative to the original orchestral version, try the elaborate piano transcription by Leopold Godowsky (he also wrote paraphrases of *Die Fledermaus*, *An Artist's Life* and *The Gypsy Baron*).

JOHANN STRAUSS II
WINE, WOMAN AND
SONG
(1869)

O

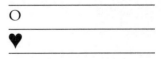

JOHANN STRAUSS II
(arr. Benatzky)
'NUN'S CHORUS'
from Casanova
(1928)

OP

There have been numerous stage and film productions of works using the music of the Strauss family. One of these was by the Czech-born composer, author and producer Ralph Benatzky (1884-1957), best known for his operetta *White Horse Inn* (1930). In 1928, he adapted a number of Strauss works for an operetta loosely based on the life of the eighteenth century adventurer Casanova. From it comes this inspirational soprano solo, famous in an evergreen recording by the show's original Berlin star Annie Frind.

RICHARD STRAUSS
1864-1949
GERMAN
AN ALPINE
SYMPHONY
(1911-15)

O

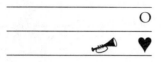

Richard Strauss made his mark on the musical world with a series of five audacious orchestral tone poems (see below), all composed in the decade after 1888. *An Alpine Symphony*, begun and completed in February 1915, is really an extended tone poem, consisting of 22 sections portraying the ascent to the summit of a great Alpine peak by a group of climbers. They pass through a forest, by a brook, a waterfall, cross meadows, traverse a glacier, until they reach their goal - followed, perhaps predictably, by a thunderstorm. It's a tremendous (50-minute) work scored for double woodwind, 20 horns and organ, with thunder and wind machines, in addition to the full orchestra. And it all begins with one of music's most glorious sunrises.

RICHARD STRAUSS
ALSO SPRACH
ZARATHUSTRA
(1896)

O

A tone poem as long as a three-movement symphony, *Thus Spake Zarathustra* takes its title from the philosophic work by the German writer and scholar Friedrich Nietzsche (1844-1900) and was intended, according to the composer, 'to convey an idea of the development of the human race from its origin, through the various phases of evolution, religious as well as scientific, up to Nietzsche's ideas of the Superman'. The opening of the work was an obvious candidate for the opening of Stanley Kubrick's overrated cult film *2001: A Space Odyssey* (described by one critic as 'somewhere between hypnotic and immensely boring'). Now, Strauss' *Also Sprach Zarathustra* is, for better or worse, inescapably linked to space exploration - at least the thunderous opening minutes are, with its speaker-crunching pages of full orchestra and organ. Have you heard the rest of the work?

This is the first of Strauss's famous tone poems (the first that made an impression, that is, for he had written an earlier one called *Macbeth*). Its musical story is based on a poem by the Hungarian Nikolaus Lenau about the celebrated, insatiable lover and his search for the perfect woman. Strauss threw aside all the influences that had shaped his music thus far (he was only 24 at the time) writing in a daring and bombastic way which many found offensive - the ardent, passionate nature of the music created a storm of controversy when it was first performed. It made Strauss' name and today it's a classic of the orchestral repertoire.

RICHARD STRAUSS
DON JUAN
(1888)

O

After Strauss completed his last opera, *Capriccio*, in 1941, he declared, 'From now on it will all be for harps.' In fact, far from hanging up his pen after a creative period of six decades, he turned out a series of autumnal masterpieces topped by these *Vier letzte Lieder* begun early in 1947 and completed less than a fortnight after his 84th birthday. All were conceived for the orchestra as much as the voice: the first three end with a solo passage for the French horn, an instrument as close to Strauss' heart as the soprano voice for which they were written; all are written in a mood of accepting, calm serenity. Their first performance took place in May 1950 nearly nine months after Strauss' death. The first to be composed was the last song in the published set: 'Im Abendrot' ('At Sunset') with words by Eichendorff; the other three have words by Hermann Hesse – 'Frühling' ('Spring'), 'September', and 'Beim Schlafengehen' ('Going to Sleep') many people's favourite of the four .

RICHARD STRAUSS
FOUR LAST SONGS
(1948)

V

RICHARD STRAUSS
HORN CONCERTO
NO. 1 IN E FLAT
(1882)

C

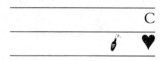

Strauss' father was the cantankerous first horn-player of the Munich Court Orchestra and Richard's affection for his father's instrument lasted all his life - *Till Eulenspiegel* has one of the most difficult passages ever written for the instrument, there are important parts for the French horn in the *Four Last Songs* and the Horn Concerto No. 2 was among the last works Strauss wrote. The First Horn Concerto was written as a gift for his father who celebrated his 60th birthday in 1882. It was completed the following year and first performed two years later, a short work in three linked movements ending with a demanding and lively Rondo.

RICHARD STRAUSS
DER
ROSENKAVALIER
(1911)

OP

To many people *The Cavalier of the Rose* (which is how the title translates) is the last great Romantic opera. It is certainly the most popular German opera of the Twentieth Century. 'A comedy for music' is how the composer described the work which combines the elements of intrigue, farce, passionate emotions and truly touching pathos. Strauss' two earlier operas, *Salome* and *Elektra*, were written in a harsh, dissonant musical language, but for this one he reverted to lush romantic writing that pulls at the heart strings. Set in eighteenth century Vienna, it tells the story of the love between the Princess von Werdenberg (known as the Marschallin), her young suitor Octavian (a soprano trouser role) and his beloved Sophie. *Der Rosenkavalier* was once summed up as 'an immense concert waltz' and, indeed, Strauss took many of the waltzes from the opera to form independent orchestral suites. The vocal climax, one of the most ravishing passages in all opera, is the Trio from Act 3 sung by the three protagonists.

RICHARD STRAUSS
SONGS
(1885-1948)

V

Because of the fame of his operas and tone poems, Strauss the songwriter is often overlooked. He composed more than 135 of them, the greatest written before his 30th birthday, though he was still in his teens when he produced his first group of songs for voice and piano. These *Eight Songs* (Op. 10) from 1885 include 'Zueignung' ('Dedication'), 'Die Nacht' ('The Night') and 'Allerseelen' ('All Soul's Day'), all miniature masterpieces. From his *Six Songs* (Op. 17) of 1885 comes the lovely 'Ständchen' ('Serenade') and the

Four Songs (Op. 27) of 1894 has 'Cäcilie' and 'Morgen' ('Tomorrow') - but dip in anywhere and you'll come up with treasures.

'Till Owlglass' is how you would translate the name of this character in German legend, a cheat and a rogue, found in the folklore of every country (for example, in Russia he is Ivan the Fool, in Italy he is Lochinello). In this tone poem, Strauss tells Till's story from his early pranks and practical jokes, Till causing mischief and mayhem, Till in love, Till rejected, to Till caught, tried and hanged. In the legend, he escapes the gallows but Strauss lets him swing. It's all there in the music painted with Strauss's ingenious and colourful orchestration.

RICHARD STRAUSS
TILL EULENSPIEGEL'S MERRY PRANKS
(1895)

O

The great impresario Sergei Diaghilev and the dancer and choreographer Mikhail Fokine approached the Russian composer Anatol Liadov to write a ballet score based on the old legend of the firebird. Liadov, remembered now for his unpretentious piano piece *A Musical Snuff-box*, can be said to have unwittingly changed the course of music because inspiration was not forthcoming and the job went instead to the 27-year-old Stravinsky. *The Firebird* made his name, for the music is of stunning originality, with brilliant orchestration, a distinctive melodic invention and rhythmic drive. The ballet was a triumph when it was premièred in Paris in 1910. Its story is a compilation of several firebird fairy tales. Here, the hero Ivan spares the life of the enchanted bird who in return prevents him from falling under the power of the evil magician Kastchei. 12 princesses appear to warn him of the danger and, when Ivan succeeds in destroying Kastchei, he is rewarded with the loveliest of the princesses with whom he has fallen in love. Especially popular from the three concert suites Stravinsky fashioned from the score are the *Dance of the Princesses* and Finale.

IGOR STRAVINSKY
1882-1971
RUSSIAN
THE FIREBIRD
Ballet
(1910)

O

STRAVINSKY
PULCINELLA
Ballet
(1920)

O

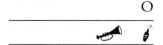

Another Diaghilev ballet commission, *Pulcinella* is a one-act ballet with songs based on the eighteenth century music of Pergolesi. But Stravinsky goes further than merely adapting bits and pieces of Pergolesi and provides a musical portrait of Pergolesi and his times. Pulcinella is the traditional hero from the Neopolitan *commedia dell'arte* theatre and the plot is one of those 'A thinks B is C' disguise comedies which, with some magic, some slapstick and a lot of confusion, all ends happily ever after. The work's 18 original sections were arranged by Stravinsky in 1922 as a concert suite of 11 sections with vocal parts being replaced by instruments.

STRAVINSKY
THE RITE OF
SPRING
Ballet
(1913)

O

If the sophisticated pre-First World War audience of Paris thought they had heard modern Russian music in Stravinsky's *The Firebird* and *Petrushka*, nothing could have prepared them for *Le Sacre du printemps* (*The Rite of Spring*), subtitled *Scenes of Pagan Russia*. Its première on the night of 29 May 1913 caused a riot. Saint-Saëns walked out, Ravel and Debussy were on their feet yelling their support. The cause of such high emotion was the extraordinary music that Stravinsky had dreamt up. To some people it was the work of a madman, a violent wrench from every musical tradition that had gone before. Stravinsky introduced weird and discordant effects, rapid and frequent changes of tempo and unusual combinations of instruments. No one had heard such primordial, elemental music before as Nijinsky and the Ballets Russes portrayed the scenes of a sacrificial pagan fertility rite in which a young girl dances herself to death. Less then 30 years later, though, Stravinsky's music had become so much part of the standard repertoire that it was included in Walt Disney's 1940 film *Fantasia*.

By the time that this, the 12th Gilbert and Sullivan collaboration, appeared, the librettist and composer had quarrelled frequently. Paradoxically, when they did eventually bury the hatchet, they produced the longest and sunniest of their works. Its convoluted plot revolves round two gondoliers, Giuseppe and Marco, the brides they have chosen (blindfolded) and an unlikely tale of cradle snatching which determines the heir to the throne of Barataria. The most popular numbers from a hit-stacked show are: 'We're called Gondolieri', 'The Duke of Plaza-Toro', 'When a merry maiden marries', 'Rising early in the morning' and Marco's serenade 'Take a pair of sparkling eyes'.

**ARTHUR SULLIVAN
1842–1900**
ENGLISH
THE GONDOLIERS
(1889)

OP

This was the fourth operetta from Gilbert and Sullivan's partnership if we include the lost score of *Thespis* (1871). It followed *Trial by Jury* (1875) and *The Sorcerer* (1877). *Pinafore*, written the following year, was a colossal success on both sides of the Atlantic, notching up 700 consecutive performances in London. It was the only one of the G & S operettas to be officially premièred in New York and, in its first season, 90 different companies presented the work in the United States. In New York alone there were five simultaneous productions. Not even Andrew Lloyd Webber can match that. Pinafore is one of the strongest of Sullivan's scores. It's a witty satire on the Admiralty (in particular the First Sea Lord of the time, William H. Smith) and on social class. The story revolves round Captain Corcoran's daughter Josephine who refuses to marry Sir Joseph Porter, First Lord of the Admiralty, because she is in love with humble Ralph Rackstraw. The hits from the show are its Overture, 'I'm called little Buttercup', 'I am the Captain of the Pinafore', 'When I was a lad' and 'He is an Englishman'.

SULLIVAN
HMS PINAFORE
(1878)

OP

SULLIVAN
IOLANTHE
(1882)

OP

Gilbert transferred his satirical targets into a fairy kingdom in this comic opera, taking some swipes at the Lord Chancellor and the House of Lords in the process. It's a complicated plot (which of Gilbert's inventive story lines isn't?) involving the Lord Chancellor's opposition to the marriage of his ward Phyllis to Strephon, who is half fairy (I know, I know), half mortal son of Iolanthe, the heroine (who is a full fairy). The Overture is Sullivan's best and the string of well known songs include 'Loudly let the trumpet bray', 'When I went to the Bar', 'When all night long a chap remains', 'When Britain really ruled the waves' and, most celebrated of all, 'When you're lying awake with a dismal headache', the epitome of all patter-songs known as the 'Nightmare Song'.

SULLIVAN
THE LOST CHORD
(1877)

V

By far the most successful song of the late Victorian era had lyrics by Adelaide Proctor set to music by Sullivan. 'Seated one day at the organ/I was weary and ill at ease...,' it begins. In fact, Sullivan was seated at his brother's deathbed when the music for the song came into his head. Frederick Sullivan, who had created the role of the judge in Gilbert and Sullivan's *Trial by Jury*, died at the age of only 39 (Adelaide Proctor also died young in 1864). Shortly after the tune was written, the soprano Antoinette Sterling called on Sullivan with a copy of the same poem asking if he would set it to music for her. He was able to hand her the finished manuscript there and then.

SULLIVAN
THE MIKADO
(1885)

OP

With this masterly comic operetta, Gilbert and Sullivan were at their creative peak and for many people *The Mikado* is their favourite. In its first 15 years it totalled over 1,000 performances in London and over 5,000 in America; it's been filmed and adapted in different versions more than any other opera or operetta. Much of its appeal was due to the (then novel) exotic Japanese setting: the story concerns Nanki-Poo, son of the Mikado, who flees in disguise having been promised in marriage to the unattractive Katisha; he falls in love with Yum-Yum who, in turn, is being sought by her guardian Ko-Ko, the Lord High Executioner. There is scarcely an unfamiliar number in the entire score but particular highlights are: the Overture, 'A wandering minstrel I', 'Three little maids from school', 'The sun, whose rays are all ablaze', 'A more humane Mikado', 'The flowers that bloom in the spring' and 'Willow, titwillow'.

SULLIVAN
THE YEOMAN OF THE GUARD
(1880)

OP

This is by far the most serious of Gilbert and Sullivan's work; indeed it was hailed as 'a genuine English opera' after its triumphant opening. That said, its individual numbers like 'When maiden loves' and 'I have a song to sing-o', have never been as universally popular as others. The Overture, though, is one of Sullivan's masterpieces. Set in Elizabethan England, the story is about Colonel Fairfax, under sentence of death in the Tower, and his search for a sorceress bride who will save him from execution. Jack Point and Elsie Maynard, two strolling players, save the day.

SULLIVAN
(arr. Mackerras)
PINEAPPLE POLL
Ballet
(1951)

O

In 1951, the conductor Sir Charles Mackerras was able to realise a long-held ambition to create a ballet from the scores of Gilbert and Sullivan operas (with the vocal parts being played by instruments). While playing in the orchestra at Sadler's Wells, he suggested the idea to the choreographer John Cranko, and deciding on Gilbert's 'The Bumboat Woman's Story' (one of his *Bab Ballads*) as a storyline, scored his patchwork quilt of tunes from the G & S canon. Even experts find it hard to spot where some of the tunes of this exuberant and colourful score come from for, apart from those mentioned above, there is reworked material from *The Sorcerer, Patience, Ruddigore, The Pirates of Penzance, Princess Ida*, Sullivan's *Overture di Ballo* and even *Cox and Box* (which had music by Sullivan but lyrics by F.C. Burnand). *Pineapple Poll* was first performed at Sadler's Wells in 1951.

FRANZ VON SUPPÉ
1819–95
AUSTRIAN
Overture to
THE BEAUTIFUL
GALATHEA
Operetta
(1865)

O

𝅗𝅥

Suppé had to wait until 1865 for his first real success as a composer of light opera. In *Die schöne Galathee* he took Offenbach's lead in parodying a tale from Greek mythology (Offenbach's *La belle Hélène* had been a hit in Vienna only a few months earlier). In Suppé's piece, the sculptor Pygmalion falls in love with the statue he has made of the beautiful Galathea, who promptly asks for a meal of schnitzel and pickled gherkin and turns out to be an outrageous flirt. The Overture features themes from the operetta, notably the opening *Drinking Trio* and the music that accompanies Galathea's transformation into life.

SUPPÉ
Overture to
THE JOLLY
ROBBERS
Operetta
(1867)

O

𝅗𝅥

Though only his operatic overtures are known today, Suppé wrote prolifically - over 300 stage works plus a variety of instrumental, orchestral and sacred music. In 1867 the Carl-Theater in Vienna mounted a benefit performance for the now fashionable composer and it was on this occasion that the first performance of his one-act operetta *Banditenstreiche* (*The Jolly Robbers*) was given. The Overture gives full rein to Suppé's love of Italian music.

SUPPÉ
Overture to
LIGHT CAVALRY
Operetta
(1866)

O

𝅗𝅥

None of Suppé's operas has survived in the repertoire but their overtures still enliven many a concert programme with their high spirits and melodic charm (not for nothing was Suppé known as the 'German Offenbach'). *Leichte Kavallerie* was the first real operetta on army life and its military subject matter is reflected in the Overture. After its introductory fanfare comes the well-known equestrian gallop.

Ein morgen, ein Mittag, ein Abend in Wien was a popular local, now long-forgotten play produced in Vienna in 1844 for which Suppé wrote the music. It's an affectionate tribute of a grateful son to the adopted city that had opened its heart to him (of Belgian descent, he had been born in Austria but raised in Italy). After a forceful opening, the Overture slips into one of Suppé's most inspired themes, a song for the cello against plucked strings. Though an early work, it follows the same pattern as most of his later overtures – a more lively section leading to an exciting, ever-faster conclusion.

SUPPÉ
Overture to
MORNING, NOON AND NIGHT IN VIENNA
(1844)

O

Dichter und Bauer was a 'comedy with songs' that appeared in 1846 and provided the impetus for what is, arguably, Suppé's most popular work, a classic of music in the lighter vein. In fact, the music of his *Poet and Peasant Overture* had been used for at least three other plays before he introduced it to the Theatre an der Wien where he had begun work the same year (1846). Here it was a hit and so it acquired its fourth, permanent title. Heard all over the world and much beloved of brass bands, the Overture has been adapted for over 60 different combinations of instruments.

SUPPÉ
Overture to
POET AND PEASANT
(1846)

O

During the late 1860s, Svendsen found himself in Paris playing the violin in various theatre orchestras and composing incidental music for plays. This colourful orchestral showpiece (it lasts about 12 minutes) was written several years later to evoke the festive processions he remembered from his time in what he called 'the most glorious city on earth'. *Carnival in Paris* wasn't composed in Paris: he began work on the piece in New York, continued it in Leipzig and finished it in Bayreuth.

JOHAN SVENDSEN
1840–1911
NORWEGIAN
CARNIVAL IN PARIS
(1872)

O

SVENDSEN
ROMANCE IN G
(1881)

I

♥ ☁️

Here is one of those delicious bon-bons which sound immediately familiar but you can never put a name to. Svendsen began his career as a violinist until paralysis of the hand confined his activities to conducting and composing. His publisher commissioned this violin piece after an earlier success but Svendsen did not deliver. On Svendsen's next visit, so the story goes, his publisher locked him in a room until he had finished the music he'd been paid to write! The Romance was subsequently reprinted 64 times during Svendsen's lifetime but, as the publisher had bought it outright, he never saw another krone from it.

T

THOMAS TALLIS
C. 1505-85
ENGLISH
SPEM IN ALIUM
(c. 1571)

CHO

🕯️

Tallis (or 'Tallys' as he himself wrote his name) was the first important English composer and *Spem in alium* (literally *Sing and Glorify*) is his masterpiece. Tallis asks for eight (unaccompanied) choirs, each of five voices, to enter one after the other, their independent vocal lines gradually building in volume and complexity in one sustained, magisterial hymn of praise. What makes this remarkable even today is that for some considerable part of the work, the 40 different voices join together to sing 40 completely different vocal lines simultaneously!

FRANCISCO TÁRREGA
1852-1909
SPANISH
RECUERDOS DE LA
ALHAMBRA
(date unknown)

I

☁️

The Spanish guitar virtuoso and composer was a formative influence on the great Andrés Segovia (1893-1987) who, more than anyone else, was responsible for the twentieth century renaissance of the guitar. Tárrega was a shy man who disliked performing in public and who used only his bare finger tips to achieve the delicate shadings he called for in his music. *Memories of the Alhambra*, one of the most frequently played of all classical guitar solos, is an exercise in tremolo - rapid repeated notes - with a wistful melody typical of the salon music of the day. Segovia, incidentally, is quoted as saying of Tárrega, 'He was very dedicated, but playing without fingernails is absolutely stupid.'

Tartini's famous Sonata was written, he related, after he dreamt he had sold his soul to the Devil and heard his servant playing 'a sonata so miraculous and beautiful... that it exceeded all flights of imagination'. On wakening, Tartini attempted to write down what he had heard in his dream. It's a nice story and the fact is that this is a work of extraordinary daring and originality for the 1740s, the date he probably wrote it (no manuscript has survived). The music is highly romantic, unconventional and technically demanding. Today, it is usually heard in the version made by the great violinist Fritz Kreisler (1875-1962) who added five minutes of assorted trills and *tremolandos* for an extra audience thrill.

After a high-profile start to his career (his 1967 theatrical oratorio about Jonah, entitled *The Whale*, was the first classical piece issued on the Beatles' Apple label), Tavener appeared to have lost his way. After he joined the Russian Orthodox Church in 1977 music became for him 'a form of prayer' and the deep spirituality of his later work 'taps a well of unconscious emotion' to which many people, some of whom would otherwise not dream of listening to a contemporary composer, intuitively respond. *The Protecting Veil*, an elegiac, mesmeric cello concerto written for Steven Isserlis in 1987, restored Tavener's standing as an important figure in today's musical world and has since become one of the most successful of all modern classical works.

The funeral of Diana, Princess of Wales on 6 September 1997 made Tavener one of the world's most famous contemporary composers overnight. His *Song for Athene*, the concluding anthem of the service, sung as the pall bearers carried the coffin from Westminster Abbey, had a profoundly moving effect on the millions watching. The work had originally been written in memory of a young family friend. One of Tavener's most recent works, *Eternity's Sunrise*, a setting of Blake's poems, was commissioned just after Diana's death and dedicated to her memory.

GIUSEPPE TARTINI
1692-1770
ITALIAN
VIOLIN SONATA
IN G MINOR
'DEVIL'S TRILL'
(c. 1740)

I

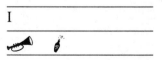

JOHN TAVENER
B. 1944
ENGLISH
THE PROTECTING
VEIL
(1987)

C

TAVENER
SONG FOR ATHENE
(1993)

CHO

PETER TCHAIKOVSKY
1840–93
RUSSIAN
Andante Cantabile from
STRING QUARTET
NO. 1 IN D
(1871)

CH

Tchaikovsky wrote three string quartets between 1871 and 1876 while he was a professor at the Moscow Conservatory, but chamber music was not a medium to which he was greatly attracted. The Quartets Nos. 2 in F and 3 in E flat minor are played infrequently, certainly compared with No. 1, and even that is not particularly well known - except, that is, for its magical slow movement, one of the most affecting in all chamber music. The theme is based on the folk-song 'Sidel Vanya' ('Uncle Vanya sat on a divan') which, while visiting his sister at Kamenka in the summer of 1869, Tchaikovsky heard a baker sing.

TCHAIKOVSKY
CAPRICCIO ITALIEN
(1880)

O

In February 1880, Tchaikovsky wrote from Rome to his friend and patron Nadezhda von Meck that he was working on a sketch for an 'Italian Fantasy' based on folk-songs. 'Thanks to the charming themes, some of which I have taken from collections and some of which I have heard in the streets, this work will be effective.' The brilliant orchestral showpiece, which was premièred the same year, opens with a tune for the trumpet that Tchaikovsky is said to have heard from a military barracks in Rome, and ends with an exciting tarantella. It's noisy, colourful and brash, effective rather than profound, a piece in which, as one writer put it, 'Tchaikovsky says nothing of great importance but says it very well indeed'.

TCHAIKOVSKY
1812 OVERTURE
(1880)

O

'The world's worst and noisiest overture,' it's been called. Well, it's certainly noisy but its melodramatic music and extraordinary power have never lost their grip on audiences since its first performance. It was written to dramatise and commemorate the withdrawal of French troops under Napoleon in 1812 (a strategic retreat but one which the Russians have always regarded as a victory) and was premièred during the consecration of the Temple of Christ the Redeemer in Moscow, built as a memorial to the 'victory'. The introductory theme is the Russian hymn 'God, preserve Thy people' followed by an all-too-real depiction of the Battle of Borodino in which the 'Marseillaise' and 'God Save the Czar' fight it out for musical supremacy (though in actual fact neither tune was in official use at the time of the battle). The Russian anthem triumphs accompanied by canons and the bells of Moscow.

The fifth of Tchaikovsky's ten operas, *Eugene Onegin* (pronounced Yoo'-jeen On-yay'-ghin) is an undisputed masterpiece (though others, *The Maid of Orleans* and *The Queen of Spades* deserve to be far better known). Based on Pushkin's poem of the same name, Tchaikovsky's opera is set in St. Petersburg in about 1815 and tells the story of the love the young, gauche Tatiana feels for the elegant Onegin. He rejects her, then, six years later, he encounters a very different Tatiana, now the radiant and sophisticated wife of a retired general, and falls head over heels for her. Tatiana struggles with her emotions but finally rejects Onegin. Composed at the same time as the Fourth Symphony [see below], the opera is an intimate stage work more concerned with poetry and psychological insights than theatrical effects. The outstanding passage in the work, one of the most moving in all opera (and the first section that Tchaikovsky composed), is the *Letter Scene* from Act 1 in which Tatiana releases her pent-up feelings of love and writes a letter to Onegin. In Act 2 there's the celebrated Waltz to which the guests dance at a party given in Tatiana's honour, followed by 'Lensky's Aria' in which Lensky, engaged to Olga, Tatiana's sister, challenges his friend Onegin to a duel, a moving, lyrical outpouring of farewell before he is mortally wounded. Then there's the magnificent Polonaise in Act 3, played at the St. Petersburg ball where Onegin re-meets Tatiana. Piano buffs will want to hear Liszt's version of the Polonaise and Paul Pabst's elaborate paraphrase on themes from the opera.

TCHAIKOVSKY
EUGENE ONEGIN
Opera
(1879)

OP

TCHAIKOVSKY
MARCHE SLAVE
(1876)

O

Among the best of Tchaikovsky's shorter compositions for orchestra, *Marche slave* was written for a benefit concert held in honour of the wounded Slavic soldiers of the Turko-Serbian war. It is in three parts: a funeral hymn, leading to a section made up of two Russian folk dances and concluding with a jubilant treatment of the Russian National Anthem, a tune also used in Tchaikovsky's better-known *1812 Overture*. This, though, is the more interesting of the two works, despite its flashy, if impressive, climax.

TCHAIKOVSKY
THE NUTCRACKER
Ballet
(1892)

O

A little girl dreams on Christmas Eve that the gift of a household nutcracker doll comes to life. She defends it in battle against the Mouse King and his cohorts and, when it changes into a handsome prince, she visits the enchanting world of the Sugar Plum Fairy. The ballet is based on E.T.A. Hoffman's fairy tale *The Nutcracker and the Mouse King* and inspired Tchaikovsky to write some of his most captivating music, without a hint of his characteristic melancholy. The concert suite from the full score is universally popular containing the *Miniature Overture, March, Dance of the Sugar Plum Fairy, Russian Dance, Arab Dance, Chinese Dance, Dance of the Flutes* and *Waltz of the Flowers*. It featured in Walt Disney's cartoon *Fantasia* and there's also a spectacular version for solo piano by the Russian virtuoso Mikhail Pletnev.

TCHAIKOVSKY
PIANO CONCERTO
NO. 1 IN B FLAT
MINOR
*(1875, rev. 1879
and 1889)*

C

The world's most played and recorded piano concerto opens with a majestic theme from the orchestra accompanied by dynamic chords from the piano. After a cadenza and a brief exchange of ideas, the opening is repeated. It's among the most arresting passages from any concerto but, despite its effectiveness, is never heard again. For the main body of the first movement Tchaikovsky uses a folk-like tune which, it's said, he heard sung by a blind beggar in the Ukraine, and a tender melody for French horns and woodwind. The slow movement's elegiac theme is interrupted by a glittering scherzo-waltz, while the finale features a

Russian dance and a lyrical song which becomes the overwhelming climax of the Concerto. When Tchaikovsky first played it through (on Christmas Eve 1874) to his friend Nicholas Rubinstein, the latter pronounced it 'utterly worthless, absolutely unplayable... bad, trivial, vulgar'. After its phenomenal success at its première in Boston in 1875 and subsequently across Europe, Rubinstein relented and admitted his error by performing it brilliantly at the Paris Exhibition of 1878. The 1958 recording by Van Cliburn became the first classical album to go gold (it spawned two other million sellers, the saccharine song hits 'Concerto for Two' and 'Tonight we love') but, whatever other version of the Concerto you buy, the live recording made in 1943 by pianist Vladimir Horowitz and conductor Arturo Toscanini has never been equalled for sheer incandescent excitement.

It's a puzzle why Tchaikovsky's Second Piano Concerto is not better known: it's full of glorious melodies, of course (what Tchaikovsky work isn't?), exhilarating writing for the soloist and a feast of delightful ideas. It was a triumph when it was premièred in Moscow in 1882 but then, for some reason, fell into neglect. It's a long work (as long as a symphony) in three movements. After the dramatic first movement, the second is a lyrical romance for piano, solo violin and solo cello (in the past, this was usually played with massive cuts made by the pianist and teacher Alexander Siloti). The finale is a brilliant rondo. If you like No. 1, you're sure to enjoy No. 2 – then why not investigate Piano Concerto No. 3 and Tchaikovsky's other under-appreciated works for piano and orchestra, the *Concert Fantasy* and the *Andante and Finale*?

TCHAIKOVSKY
PIANO CONCERTO
NO. 2 IN G
(1880)

C

♥

TCHAIKOVSKY
ROMEO AND JULIET
Fantasy-overture
(1869, rev. 1870
and 1880)

O

♥

The idea of writing a tone poem based on Shakespeare's play came from Balakirev. Tchaikovsky, in 1869, was still a relatively inexperienced composer and he was advised and encouraged in its composition by Balakirev (having completed the work, he subsequently revised it twice, the third version being the one we know today). *Romeo and Juliet* is not an overture in the usual sense - it is not a curtain raiser for an opera, for example, but a descriptive concert piece, the 'fantasy' element of the title referring to the music's freedom of form. It doesn't follow the play but incidents in the drama are easy to spot: the religious chant for clarinets and bassoons which opens the work represents Friar Lawrence; the turbulent passage which follows paints the feud between the Montagues and Capulets. Then there's the rapturous, poignant lover's theme for Romeo and Juliet, clearly written from the heart - Tchaikovsky composed it after he had been jilted by the beautiful singer Désirée Artôt.

TCHAIKOVSKY
SERENADE FOR
STRINGS IN C
(1880)

O

♥   ☼

Written on impulse, this charming four-movement work for string orchestra was written at the same time as the *1812 Overture*. It could not be more different, its second and third movements particularly popular - an elegant Parisian waltz and an eloquent elegy. Tchaikovsky confided that while writing it he 'felt it deeply from start to finish'. It is also a textbook example of how to write economically and poignantly for strings, from its sonorous hymn-like opening to the Russian dance finale.

TCHAIKOVSKY
THE SLEEPING
BEAUTY
Ballet
(1890)

O

 ♥   ☼

The première of *Swan Lake* [see below] was a disaster - it was only after Tchaikovsky's death that it was revived successfully - and it took the composer a decade to come up with another ballet score, this time for the St. Petersburg Imperial Theatre. And this time, his creation was greeted with acclaim, establishing Tchaikovsky as an important ballet composer. Basing it on the familiar fairy tale, Tchaikovsky casts the ballet into five sections: the christening when the wicked fairy (Carabosse) utters her curse; the scene in which Princess Aurora pricks her finger; the hunting scene where Prince Charming is shown a vision of the Sleeping Princess; the awakening; and finally a divertissement featuring characters from other fairy tales, including *Puss-in-Boots* and *Little Red Riding Hood*. The luscious *Rose Adagio* from Act 1 is danced (much of it on point) by Princess Aurora with her four suitors, each of whom presents her with two roses.

The earliest of Tchaikovsky's three ballet scores, *Swan Lake* owed its origins to a little dance piece performed in 1871 for children at the country estate of Tchaikovsky's sister. In 1875, when the Imperial Opera commissioned Tchaikovsky to compose a ballet, it was these dance sequences that he developed into a full ballet. *Swan Lake* tells the story of the beautiful Odette who has been transformed into a swan by the magician, Rothbart. Every midnight, Odette and her companions revert to human form and on one such occasion she meets and falls in love with Prince Siegfried. Of course, it wouldn't be a proper ballet if the spell wasn't eventually broken and everyone didn't live happily ever after. From the 33 numbers in the score, the Waltz from Act 1, Scene from Act 2 and the *Dance of the Cygnets* are perennial concert favourites.

TCHAIKOVSKY
SWAN LAKE
Ballet
(1877)

O

Like most of Tchaikovsky's major works, the Fourth Symphony was the outcome of an emotional crisis, in this case the failure of his disastrous marriage to a mentally-unstable 28-year-old music student, Antonina Milyukova. After attempting suicide, Tchaikovsky left his teaching post at the Conservatory and took the well-practised neurotic's cure - a trip through Western Europe. Eventually, his creative juices started flowing again and within a few months he had completed the Fourth Symphony and his opera *Eugene Onegin*. The Symphony is modelled on Beethoven's Fifth, and its underlying theme is the same - Man and his Destiny. The opening brass fanfare, Tchaikovsky revealed, symbolised his 'vain terrors' and 'fear of the unknown' (in this first movement, by the way, when the introductory theme is repeated, there is a striking similarity with a passage in the Prelude to Bizet's *Carmen*). The slow movement is of rustic simplicity, followed by a scherzo featuring pizzicato strings. The

TCHAIKOVSKY
SYMPHONY
NO. 4 IN F MINOR
(1877)

O

finale is boisterous and exuberant, and uses the Russian folksong 'Over in the meadow stands a birch tree'. The work was given its première on 17 February 1878 in Moscow and is dedicated to Tchaikovsky's patron, Madame von Meck.

**TCHAIKOVSKY
SYMPHONY
NO. 5 IN E MINOR**
(1888)

O

Tchaikovsky thought the symphony 'the most lyrical of all musical forms'. 'Should it not express,' he asked, 'all the things for which words cannot be found, which nevertheless arise in the heart and demand expression?' Above the opening sketches for the Fifth, he scribbled 'Complete resignation before Fate'. Yet, rather than weigh down the listener with gloomy pessimism, the music offers instead a healing balm. The four movements are awash with a miraculous supply of melody with which Tchaikovsky expresses his heart-on-sleeve emotions. Who can resist the second movement (*andante cantabile*) with its melting theme introduced by the solo French horn? Or the third movement waltz based in part on a street song Tchaikovsky heard in Florence. Or the finale which opens with an optimistic (major key) version of the very first tune of the Symphony and ends in a blaze of bravura orchestral writing?

**TCHAIKOVSKY
SYMPHONY NO. 6 IN
B MINOR
'PATHÉTIQUE'**
(1893)

O

The most famous and popular of Tchaikovsky's symphonies is a magnificent conception from beginning to end. It is the composer's swan song. Returning from a tour of Europe in February 1893, he wrote to his nephew Vladimir Davidov that he had the idea for a symphony based on a programme but 'a programme that shall remain an enigma for everyone - let them try to puzzle it out if they like'. By the end of August the Symphony was complete and Tchaikovsky was delighted with his brother's suggestion that it be subtitled *Pathétique*. However, two days after the first performance (28 October 1893), he cancelled the name and added a dedication to his nephew. A week later Tchaikovsky was dead. To some extent, the Symphony is autobiographical (is this its enigma?). 'The programme is subjective through and through,' wrote Tchaikovsky, 'and during my journey I often wept bitterly while composing it in my head.' Among the many points of interest along the way is the quote from the Russian requiem service ('And rest him with the Saints'), the unusual five-four beat of the second movement (the 'waltz which isn't a waltz') and the over-confident third-movement march (to which my naughty orchestral friends sing the words: 'I'm going camping to Scotland/But I'm not going to take my wife'). Most remarkable of all is the last movement, generally acknowledged as one of the finest symphonic finales in music, 'incomparably noble, dignified and unspeakably tender' - a lament for terrible woes.

One of the four big violin concertos that every soloist has in their repertoire (the others are by Beethoven, Mendelssohn and Brahms), the Tchaikovsky fiddle concerto is more lyrical and in a lighter vein than the piano concertos. It was dedicated to the legendary violin teacher Leopold Auer who pronounced it unplayable. (One of Auer's most eminent pupils, Jascha Heifetz, made a classic recording of the work in 1957 conducted by Fritz Reiner.) It took four years before it was heard in public (Vienna, 1881) where, though hard to believe now, it was savaged by the critics. Throughout the work, Tchaikovsky uses Russian-sounding themes, especially in the finale. 'My melodies and harmonies of folk-song character,' he wrote to Madame von Meck, 'come from the fact that I grew up in the country, and in my earliest childhood was impressed by the indescribable beauty of the characteristic features of Russian folk music.'

TCHAIKOVSKY
VIOLIN CONCERTO
IN D
(1878)

C

TCHAIKOVSKY
VARIATIONS ON A
ROCOCO THEME
(1876)

O

♪ ♥

It's strange that Tchaikovsky wrote so little for the cello, the instrument closest in timbre to the human voice and perfect in its ability to express his rich, melancholic Romanticism. Only the *Pezzo Capriccioso* (1887) and these Variations were originally conceived for the cello, but this consummate work is the closest Tchaikovsky came to writing a cello concerto. Inspired by his love of Mozart (he himself admitted that the very mention of Mozart's name could bring tears to his eyes), Tchaikovsky dreamt up an elegant eighteenth century rococo theme (*rococo* in musical terms has come to mean the light, decorative style of the late-Baroque/early-Classical era) and wrote seven variations which alternate the brilliantly virtuosic with forlorn lyricism. It was written for and premièred (in 1877) by the German-born cellist Wilhelm Fitzenhagen.

GEORG PHILIPP
TELEMANN
1681–1767
GERMAN
LA BOUFFONNE
(date unknown)

O

♪

Music, thought Telemann, 'ought not to be an effort' and disarmingly asserted that 'a good composer should be able to set public notices to music'. Handel observed of him: 'Telemann could write a motet for eight voices as easily as one could write a letter'. His music combined the operatic elements of Italy, the German contrapuntal style, and the French school of dance-based suites. This delightful six movement suite is a good example - the opening Overture, the most substantial part of the work, is written in the French manner (slow introduction, followed by a lively section), succeeded by five short dances in contrasting tempos.

TELEMANN
CONCERTO FOR
VIOLA AND
STRINGS IN G
(date unknown)

C

♪ ☁

Telemann has a claim to being the most prolific composer in history, producing almost as much as J.S. Bach and Handel put together (he was far more highly regarded during his lifetime than either of them). Inevitably, not all of it is of equal quality and even dipping into the 600 overtures or suites, the 200 concertos, 40 operas and over 1,000 pieces of church music, one piece can begin to sound like another ('diddle-diddle' music, as some cynics describe it). But his finest music is extraordinary - forward-looking, individual and compelling. I can recommend the amiable Viola Concerto in four short movements as an introduction to Telemann's style. The opening Largo is unexpectedly touching.

Among Telemann's most recorded works is this little (ten-minute) concerto typical of his infectious spirit and melodic grace. Then there's the Concerto in A for flute, violin & cello, the Concerto in D for three horns, violin and orchestra, the Double Horn Concerto in E flat... the list is almost endless. There is, not surprisingly, a lot of Telemann's music that you, me and everyone else has never had the chance or time to hear. One friend of mine has guided me towards the following: a choral work called *Singet Gott, lobsinget seinem Namen*, the oratorios *Die Auferstehung und Himmelfahrt Jesu* and *Der Tag des Gerichts*, the 1723 *Music for the Admiralty* and the 1761 opera *Don Quichotte der Löwenritter* - these are pleasures I have yet to discover.

TELEMANN
CONCERTO FOR
TRUMPET AND
STRINGS IN D
(date unknown)

C

One of Telemann's best known works is this seven-movement suite written when he was in his early twenties. It's a genuine little masterpiece. Its musical inspiration comes from the four corners of Europe - there's the French-style Overture, for instance, *Air à l'Italien* (a song-like movement from the land of Scarlatti), there are two versions of the passepied (a gently rhythmic dance from Brittany) and, finally, a polonaise, a souvenir from his time at Pless (an ancient Polish province, then part of the Hapsburg Empire).

TELEMANN
SUITE IN A MINOR
for recorder and strings
(date unknown)

O

The only one of Thomas's 20 operas to survive - and only on the fringes of the repertoire - is *Mignon*, a blemished masterwork that had a huge vogue when it appeared and made Thomas one of the most successful opera composers of his time. Indeed, Thomas became the first opera composer in history to live long enough to attend the 1,000th performance of a work he had written (a gala performance of *Mignon* in Paris, May 1894). His music is, as one writer described it, 'for hearts susceptible to honest emotions and for a public of average assimilative powers which enjoys melodies easy to remember'. The Overture consists of the opera's two best-known numbers, Mignon's air 'Connais-tu, le pays?' and...

AMBROISE THOMAS
1811-96
FRENCH
Overture to
MIGNON
Opera
(1866)

O

THOMAS
'IO SON TITANIA'
from Mignon
(1866)

OP

The plot of *Mignon* is as unlikely as they get in opera (which is saying a lot) but at least has a happy ending. It's a tale of a deranged minstrel (Lothario) in search of his long-lost daughter (Mignon) who has been adopted by gypsies. Meister buys her freedom and hires her as his servant. To cut a very complicated story short, Mignon becomes jealous of Meister's *amour* Philine, an actress. After a performance of A *Midsummer Night's Dream*, Philine is surrounded by her admirers and sings this celebrated coloratura polonaise 'I am Titania', still a popular soprano display piece. The castle at which the actors have been performing then bursts into flames. In the last act (in Italy), Lothario regains his marbles and realises he's a nobleman and that Mignon is his daughter, and Meister falls in love with Mignon.

MICHAEL TIPPETT
1905-98
ENGLISH
FANTASIA
CONCERTANTE ON
A THEME OF
CORELLI
(1953)

O

A gracious, pastoral string work, the *Corelli Fantasia* is based on a theme from Corelli's Concerto Grosso Op. 6 No. 2 in F. As in the original concerto, Tippett divides his forces, in this case two violins and cello playing against a section of the string orchestra. It was commissioned by the Edinburgh Festival in 1953 to celebrate the tercentenary of the birth of Corelli and has proved to be one of Tippett's most enduring works (musical detectives will look out for the Puccini-pastiche in the middle and, in the fugue section, a quote from Bach's organ *Fugue on a Theme by Corelli*, BWV 579). The Fantasia was used most effectively in Sir Peter Hall's 1974 film of Suffolk rural life, *Akenfield*.

Vaughan Williams' love of English folk-song began in the early 1900s through the recently-formed English Folk Music Society. V.W. and fellow composer Gustav Holst made a serious study of their country's indigenous music, much of which had never been written down or catalogued before (Vaughan Williams, it was said, dressed 'as though stalking the folk song to its lair'). His *Folk Song Suite* was inspired by another enthusiasm - British military bands - and its first performance was given at Kneller Hall, the home of British military music, near Twickenham, London. Its three sections feature 'Seventeen Come Sunday', 'My Bonny Boy' and, in the final march, *Folk Songs from Somerset*. Today, it's more generally heard in the orchestral version by the composer and one-time pupil of Vaughan Williams, Gordon Jacob.

RALPH VAUGHAN WILLIAMS
1872-1958
ENGLISH
ENGLISH FOLK SONG SUITE
(1923)

O

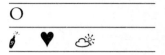

A beloved, quintessential piece of English music, the *Tallis Fantasy* was introduced at the Three Choirs Festival in Gloucester in 1910. The theme is the third of eight tunes that Tallis composed in 1567 for the *Metrical Psalter* of Matthew Parker, Archbishop of Canterbury. Vaughan Williams had inserted the theme into the *English Hymnal* (No. 92, 'Thou wast, O God, and thou wast blest') which he edited in 1906. In this treatment he used a string orchestra divided into two, and a string quartet (played by the leaders of each group) to achieve an antiphonal effect, a popular device in sixteenth century music where two distinct groups played in response to each other, a kind of Tudor stereo system. More importantly, this was the work that finally emancipated English music from continental influence.

VAUGHAN WILLIAMS
FANTASIA ON A THEME OF THOMAS TALLIS
(1910)

O

VAUGHAN WILLIAMS
FANTASIA ON
'GREENSLEEVES'
(1934)

O

♥ 🌤

This short instrumental piece, scored for harp, flute and strings, is made up of two folk-songs: 'Greensleeves' (an Elizabethan melody of unknown authorship) and 'Lovely Joan', a tune which V.W. himself came across in Norfolk in 1908. The 'Ballad of My Lady Greensleeves' was registered in 1575 and is mentioned more than once by Shakespeare, making it a suitable candidate for inclusion in the incidental music Vaughan Williams composed for (a 1912 production of) *The Merry Wives of Windsor* in which Falstaff commands, 'Let the sky rain potatoes, let it thunder to the tune of "Greensleeves".' Later still, V.W. used it in his 1929 opera *Sir John in Love* (sung by Mistress Ford when she visits Sir John Falstaff). The Fantasy, perhaps surprisingly, was written as recently as 1934.

VAUGHAN WILLIAMS
THE LARK
ASCENDING
(1914, rev. 1920)

O

♥ 🌤

There are few who have not fallen under the spell of this ethereal fantasy for solo violin and orchestra. It is a musical translation of the poem of the same name by George Meredith (1828-1909) which begins: 'He rises and begins to round/He drops the silver chain of sound/Of many links without a break/In chirrup, whistle, slur and shake...'. The violin soars above the discreet orchestral accompaniment, there is a folk-like central section after which the violin/lark again takes flight. Vaughan Williams wrote the work for the English violinist Marie Hall (1884-1956) and she played the first performance in the old Queen's Hall, London on 14 June 1921, with the British Symphony Orchestra under Adrian Boult.

VAUGHAN WILLIAMS
Overture to
THE WASPS
(1909)

O

🎵

In 1909, Vaughan Williams wrote the incidental music for a Cambridge University production of Aristophanes' comedy, *The Wasps*. From this, the composer made an independent suite but its Overture is the only section to survive in the popular repertoire. It opens with the buzzing of the wasps which is followed by themes that are not in the least bit ancient Greek but very Vaughan Williams.

Among the earliest champions of Vaughan Williams' music was the redoubtable Sir Henry Wood, co-founder of the Promenade Concerts and one of the leading figures in British musical life for more than half a century. For Sir Henry's Golden Jubilee Concert at the Royal Albert Hall on 5 October 1938, Vaughan Williams composed this setting of Lorenzo's speech in Act 5, Scene 1 of Shakespeare's *The Merchant of Venice*: 'How sweet the moonlight sleeps upon this bank!/Here will we sit, and let the sounds of music/Creep in our ears:...'. The Serenade is dedicated to Wood 'in grateful memory of his services to music' and is surely one of the finest of any Shakespeare settings, the magical orchestral introduction setting the nocturnal mood, followed by the solo voices (in the first performance) of 16 British singers with whom Sir Henry had been associated. Quite a present.

VAUGHAN WILLIAMS
SERENADE TO MUSIC
(1938)

CHO

♥   ☁☀

Arguably one of the finest symphonies of the Century, Vaughan Williams' Sixth was composed when he was 75 years old. It is certainly one of Vaughan Williams' greatest works. The war and post-war period reverberate throughout the Symphony, its four movements played without a break, reflecting the anguish and tragedy, turmoil and terror of the previous years. The Symphony ends with some of the most serene music you'll ever hear (the longest section), 'a whisper from beginning to end', ebbing away into uncertain optimism and 'a stillness made audible'.

VAUGHAN WILLIAMS
SYMPHONY NO. 6
IN E MINOR
(1947, rev. 1950)

O

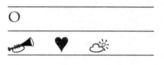

Aida (pronounced Eye-ee'-dah') is what grand opera is all about - spectacle, a reasonably credible story, a string of memorable arias and choruses, high emotion, convincing characterisation - and since its first outing in 1871 it has never lost its appeal. Early on in the Opera comes this most celebrated of tenor arias, the radiant 'Heavenly Aida' in which Radames, a captain in the Egyptian Guard, sings the praises of his divine Aida, an Ethiopian slave held captive by Amneris, daughter of the King of Egypt. (Oh dear. He doesn't know that Aida is an Ethiopian princess or that Amneris is in love with him.)

GIUSEPPE VERDI
1813-1901
ITALIAN
'CELESTE AIDA'
from Aida
(1871)

OP

♥

VERDI
GRAND MARCH
from Aida
(1871)

OP

Verdi closes the second act of Aida with perhaps the most magnificent conception of his career - the 'Hymn of Victory' ('Gloria all' Egitto') followed by a glittering procession led by Radames at the head of the Egyptian army (among the captured is Amonasro, the King of Ethiopia, Aida's father). The *Grand March*, with or without elephants, never fails to impress - somewhat bizarrely, given its origins, it's a popular choice for English church weddings.

VERDI
'O PATRIA MIA'
from Aida
(1871)

OP

♥

By the time Act 3 arrives, Amneris is going to marry Radames and goes to the temple to invoke divine blessings on the union. Aida emerges from the shadows and sings nostalgically of her homeland ('Oh native land, I shall not see thee more'). Radames has asked to meet her, perhaps for a last farewell - if so, she will drown herself in the Nile. It's one of the finest of all arias in the Italian repertory for a dramatic soprano. Incidentally, though commissioned by the Khedive of Egypt to celebrate his native land, and though *Aida* was premièred at the Cairo Opera House, the opera did not enter the regular repertoire there until 1987 when it was lavishly staged in ancient Luxor: Egyptian scholars regarded *Aida* as a European and very un-Egyptian entertainment.

VERDI
Overture to
LA FORZA DEL
DESTINO
Opera
(1862, rev. 1869)

O

Following the successes of *Rigoletto*, *La Traviata* and *Il Trovatore*, *The Force of Destiny* is musically more advanced, with greater emphasis on dramatic atmosphere but with no loss of melody. The story of the opera is a gloomy one of love, accidental murder, disguise and vengeance, a quite nonsensical plot which Verdi's colourful and vivid score triumphantly conceals. The Overture is often heard independently in concerts, though not in its original version. Verdi revised the opera in 1869 for a production at La Scala, Milan and added the more substantial introduction we know today.

Verdi's only masterpiece not intended for the stage has nevertheless been described as 'Verdi's best opera' and 'Verdi's latest opera, in church vestments'. There's more than a grain of truth in these verdicts. The death of his friend, the poet and novelist Alessandro Manzoni, in 1873 inspired Verdi to write this heartfelt and stirring setting of the Requiem Mass (sometimes called the *Manzoni Requiem*). It was first performed in May 1874 on the anniversary of Manzoni's death. Its success all over Europe was instant (Verdi took it on tour and played to full houses), the work combining the elegiac and spiritual (the tenor soloist's *Ingemisco*, for instance, often sung as a concert item) with the powerful and dramatic (try the *Dies irae* and *Tuba mirum* sections).

VERDI
REQUIEM
(1874)

CHO

The best known numbers from this operatic masterpiece are often heard separately, giving the mistaken impression that they are 'set pieces' and not part of the action. Not so. Every one of the 'hit arias' is a marvel of truthful characterisation and germane to the progress of the plot - it's just that Verdi's melodic gift was so powerful that it's easy for it to appear otherwise. In Act 1, the Duke (one of the most rewarding tenor parts in any Verdi opera) sings 'One woman or another, for me all are the same' to carefree, airy music that immediately tells you about the character of the Duke and his amorous way of life.

VERDI
'QUESTA O QUELLA'
from Rigoletto
(1851)

OP

Ever since its first performance, *Rigoletto* has held its place in the opera houses of the world. 'Caro nome' ('Beloved name, the first to move the pulse of love within my heart') is still one of the most celebrated and exacting of soprano arias. It's sung in Act 1 by Gilda, the beautiful daughter of the hunchback Rigoletto, whom the Duke has wooed while pretending to be a struggling student named Walter Maldè (there's one for the opera buffs!). She, poor darling, falls for it hook, line and stinker.

VERDI
'CARO NOME'
from Rigoletto
(1851)

OP
♥

VERDI
'LA DONNA È
MOBILE'
from Rigoletto
(1851)

OP

'Woman is fickle as a feather in the wind', sings the libidinous Duke of Mantua in Act 3 of Verdi's opera. Talk about the pot calling the kettle black! The fickle Duke sings this famous tenor aria while disguised as a soldier at the seedy inn of the assassin Sparafucile. It is such a hackneyed recital number out of context that it's easy to forget just how adroit a piece of writing it is. It reflects the Duke's character with its light-headed, buoyant rhythm and final flashy cadenza yet is sung in particularly unsavoury surroundings.

VERDI
QUARTET
('Bella figlia dell' amore')
from Rigoletto
(1851)

OP

This is *the* great vocal quartet in all opera, sung in Sparafucile's inn by the Duke, who is wooing Maddalena ('Fairest daughter of love, I am a slave to your charms'), Sparafucile's buxom sister who pretends to repulse him ('Ah! That is really laughable - how cheap such talk is!'), Gilda who is nearby, heartbroken ('O wretched heart betrayed') and Rigoletto, who vows to take revenge on the Duke ('It will be quick, it will be deadly'). All these different expressions are welded effortlessly into one sublime unit of great ingenuity. It all ends in tears of course. Liszt wrote a famous paraphrase for the piano based on the Quartet's music.

VERDI
Preludes to Acts 1 and 3 of
LA TRAVIATA
Opera
(1853)

O

The last of the three great operas from Verdi's middle period, following *Rigoletto* and *Il Trovatore*, *La Traviata* (literally *The Fallen Woman*) was the first serious opera that had nothing to do with kings and queens, intrigues, murder, mythology or the like. It's set in the elegant Paris drawing rooms of the time and is concerned with the bourgeois world struggling with all-too-recognisable human problems. The story is based on the novel by Alexandre Dumas *fils, La Dame aux camélias*, itself based on the life of the legendary courtesan Marie Duplessis who died from tuberculosis in 1847. In the novel she becomes Marguerite Gautier; in the play and film (starring Greta Garbo), she is Camille; in Verdi's opera she is called Violetta Valéry. The Prelude to Act 1 is an extraordinarily effective psychological portrait of our heroine with glimpses of the music associated with Violetta's death and her impassioned 'Amami Alfredo' aria from Act 2. The

Prelude to Act 3 sets an atmospheric introduction for the final scene, a sad and tender piece of great beauty opening with delicate, fragile sounds on the violins – Violetta is dying.

Act 1, and there's a party at Violetta's. Gaston has brought his friend Alfredo and tells his hostess that Alfredo is seriously in love with her. Alfredo is introduced and toasts her in the spirited 'Let us drink from the wine-cup o'erflowing' in which the chorus joins lustily. Violetta then takes it up. This is known as the 'Brindisi' ('Drinking Song'), the most familiar of several other operatic brindisis.

VERDI
'LIBIAMO, LIBIAMO'
from La Traviata
(1853)

OP

Left alone after the revels, Violetta realises that her heart has been touched for the first time by Alfredo and quietly wonders if he is 'the one of whom I dreamed'. In a moment she has banished such thoughts and launches into this brilliant coloratura aria 'Ever free I shall still hasten madly on from pleasure to pleasure'.

VERDI
'SEMPRE LIBERA'
from La Traviata
(1853)

OP

The middle opera of Verdi's trilogy of the early 1850s (*Rigoletto* and *La Traviata* are the others), *The Troubadour* has a notoriously imponderable plot. This did nothing to prevent it becoming the most popular opera of the Nineteenth Century, entirely due to the ravishing score Verdi was inspired to write. From Act 2 comes one of the most famous of opera choruses known as the 'Anvil Chorus' in which a band of gypsies work at their forges, swinging their hammers down in clanking rhythm with the music.

VERDI
'ANVIL CHORUS'
from Il Trovatore
(1853)

OP

VERDI
'DI QUELLA PIRA'
from Il Trovatore
(1853)

OP

A thrilling tenor aria sung by Manrico, the troubadour of the title, as he draws his sword and gathers his soldiers together in an attempt to rescue his supposed mother, the gypsy Azucena. 'From that dread pyre' is a tour de force which ends with a long, held top C - Pavarotti used to hit this spectacularly well - though it's not in the score. It's undoubtedly effective, but the high C that Verdi *did* write comes earlier in the aria on the line 'O teco almeno corro a morir' ('Or, all else failing, to die with thee').

VERDI
MISERERE
from Il Trovatore
(1853)

OP

♥

At one time, not so long ago, this was the most popular tune from any opera. In Act 4, Leonora, the heroine, has hatched a plan to rescue from prison her lover Manrico who is under sentence of death. The *Miserere* ('Have mercy on a spirit approaching the departure which has no return') is chanted by a chorus of monks from within the prison with Leonora's heart-broken cries sung over it, while Manrico is heard singing from his cell in the prison tower. Old hat it may be, but it works every time.

VERDI
'AI NOSTRI MONTI'
from Il Trovatore
(1853)

OP

♥

In the final scene of the opera, Azucena and Manrico are in a prison cell and each tries to console the other. The duet 'Ai nostri monti' ('Home to our mountains') is another of opera's 'top hits' in which mother and son hope that some day they will return to their home in the mountains where they were once happy. A few minutes later, Manrico is led away to be executed while Azucena is forced to watch.

Nabucco, originally entitled *Nabucodonosor* (*Nebuchadnezzar*), was a turning point in Verdi's career. The opera's instant success brought him fame throughout Italy and one reason for it was this chorus, a poignant hymn. Nabucco, the King of Babylon, has defeated the Hebrews and in Act 3 the Hebrew slaves 'in their chains, at forced labour' sing of their homeland with the words 'Fly, thought, on wings of gold; go settle upon the slopes and the hills, where, soft and mild, the sweet airs of our native land smell fragrant'. Verdi's audience drew a parallel between the Hebrews and their own situation under oppressive Austrian rule and 'Va, pensiero' became a national anthem for Italian independence. Verdi himself became a symbol of the Italian resistance.

VERDI
'VA, PENSIERO'
(Chorus of the Hebrew Slaves)
from Nabucco
(1842)

OP

It was 16 years after the success of *Aida* before Verdi completed his next opera, a powerful and moving work thought by many to be the most perfect of its kind ever written, quite an achievement for a man of 74. Based on Shakespeare's play, it was first seen in 1887 and the singer who created the title role, Francesco Tamagno, lived to record two of Otello's arias, a remarkable link with Verdi who had been born back in 1813. In Act 4 comes the 'Willow Song' - 'O Salce! salce! salce!' ('Oh willow, willow, willow!') in which Desdemona movingly recalls a tale of a girl deserted by her lover - it's a mesmerising aria of great beauty capped by a truly heart-wrenching cry of farewell to her lady-in-waiting, Emilia. Left alone, Desdemona kneels before the image of the Madonna to sing an exquisite setting of the *Ave Maria* - 'Hail Mary... in the hour of death. Hail!... Amen!'. The whole sequence is one of pure genius, heightened by the fact that you know the fate that is about to befall Desdemona.

VERDI
'WILLOW SONG'
and
AVE MARIA
from Otello
(1887)

OP

♥ 🕯

TOMÁS LUIS DE VICTORIA
c. 1548-1611
SPANISH
REQUIEM
(1603)

CHO

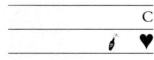

In 1583, Victoria (or Vittoria as he is known in Italy, where he worked for 20 years) entered the service of the Dowager Empress Maria of Austria. She was a Renaissance lady of high attainments and frightfully well connected - daughter of the Emperor Charles V, sister of King Philip II of Spain, and the wife of Emperor Maximilian II. When she died in 1603 it was Victoria's responsibility to write the music for the funeral rites and his magnificent, stately *Missa Pro Defunctis* (*Requiem Mass*) is his lasting legacy. If you like the choral masterpieces of Allegri or Palestrina, you're sure to enjoy this, for Victoria, though influenced by his friend Palestrina, wrote in a more dramatic, richly-textured style, as you'll hear. The *Requiem* is scored for a cathedral choir of male voices: basses, baritones, tenors and high falsettists. The moving *Kyrie* ('Lord have mercy, Christ have mercy, Lord have mercy') comes second in the service.

LOUIS VIERNE
1870-1937
FRENCH
CARILLON DE WESTMINSTER
(1927)

I

Vierne was a celebrated (blind) organist and composer, a pupil of Franck and Widor, who developed the 'organ symphony' pioneered by his teachers - the Finale from Symphony No. 1 is a terrific piece for weddings (if the organ is big enough and the organist is up to it). Vierne died with his boots on, mid-service at the organ of Notre-Dame, Paris. *Carillon de Westminster* is an exciting organ toccata played against the familiar chimes of Big Ben, which you can hear passing softly from hand to hand and then to the pedals, increasing in volume amidst a whirl of notes until the scintillating final pages.

HENRI VIEUXTEMPS
1820-81
BELGIAN
VIOLIN CONCERTO NO. 4 IN D MINOR
(1850)

C

It's a shame this adorable work is not taken up by more violinists. Tchaikovsky was much taken with it ('beautiful, poetical, very effective and excellently orchestrated') and in the hands of a player like Heifetz or Menuhin, both of whom recorded the Concerto, it can seem like a masterpiece. Vieuxtemps himself, one of those rare 'famous Belgians', was a prodigy violinist who toured from the age of seven. His Fourth Concerto is rather different from the standard three-movement affairs of its day. It's more like four musical pictures with a prologue, reflecting the life and struggles of a mythical hero. It begins with an impassioned slow movement, followed by a lyrical *andante religioso*. After that comes one of the most difficult movements in the literature, a lightning-quick 'hunting' scherzo. The Concerto ends with a heroic march.

The Fifth Concerto of Vieuxtemps is a three-movements-in-one work and shares with No. 4 the same technical skill, original voice and fund of distinguished thematic material. The first section especially has some impassioned, romantic writing to which all lovers of the violin concertos by Paganini, Mendelssohn and Bruch will readily respond. The other five violin concertos Vieuxtemps composed have now been unearthed after years of neglect. True, none is as uniformly good as Nos. 4 and 5, but all are well worth a listen. So is his Viola Sonata in B flat, his once popular *Elégie* and *Fantasia-Appassionata* (both for violin) and Cello Concerto No. 1 (try the dazzling last movement).

VIEUXTEMPS
VIOLIN CONCERTO
NO. 5 IN A MINOR
(1861)

C

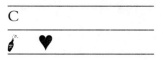

The prolific Villa-Lobos produced nine suites under the same apt title – music that fused characteristic Brazilian rhythms and melodies with the style of J.S. Bach. By far the best known item from these suites is the serene, wordless soprano aria (the *Cantilena*) from the Fifth Suite, a vocalise sung to the syllable 'Ah' that floats over the pizzicato accompaniment of eight cellos. It's a remote relation – but nevertheless a relation – of the famous Air from Bach's Suite No. 3 in D. The second part (*Danza*) of *Bachianas Brasileiras No. 5* is less well known and was added later in 1945. Villa-Lobos himself conducted a classic recording of the Aria with soprano Victoria de los Angeles in 1956.

**HEITOR VILLA-LOBOS
1887–1959**
BRAZILIAN
Aria from
BACHIANAS
BRASILEIRAS NO. 5
(1938)

V

The least Bach-like of the *Bachianas Brasileiras* suites is No. 2, made up of orchestrations of unconnected works originally intended for piano and cello. The last of its four short movements is an inspired musical depiction of a little train puffing its way through the Brazilian countryside until, with a realistic scraping and squealing, it finally grinds and wheezes to a halt.

VILLA-LOBOS
THE LITTLE TRAIN
OF THE CAIPIRA
*from Bachianas Brasileiras
No. 2
(1930)*

O

VILLA-LOBOS
CHÔROS
NO. 1 IN E MINOR
and other pieces for guitar
(1920)

I

♥   ☁

Villa-Lobos wrote so much music in such a profuse array of styles, he's difficult to pin down. Not all of it is of equal interest, but one instrument that Villa-Lobos played himself was the guitar and, as a virtually self-taught musician, he brought an original and fresh approach to it both technically and musically. At one time he played the guitar in popular street bands or *chôroes* - hence the title of this catchy solo, written in the style of the music in which the street band played. Others to look out for are his *Five Preludes* for guitar (1940), especially the expressive Prelude No. 1 in E minor and the jaunty little Prelude No. 2 in E.

TOMASO VITALI
1663-1745
ITALIAN
CHACONNE IN G
MINOR
(date unknown)

I

🎺 🕯

Tomaso Vitali gets the credit for this work, a cornerstone of the violin repertoire ever since its discovery and publication in 1867. No one is quite sure who wrote it, though it almost certainly pre-dates J.S. Bach. When the 17-year-old Jascha Heifetz stunned the musical world with his American debut in 1917, it was with this piece that he began his recital - not, as was customary, with a piano accompaniment but with an organ, in an arrangement by Ottorino Respighi. Many years later, Heifetz recorded it - a disc that makes the hairs on the back of your neck stand on end.

ANTONIO VIVALDI
1678-1741
ITALIAN
CONCERTO FOR
TWO TRUMPETS IN C
(date unknown)

C

🕯

One of the splendours of the Baroque era of music is this brilliant concerto, probably the most successful of all those written within the limitations of the natural trumpet (the modern valve trumpet, which enables a player to get around the notes with far greater ease, didn't appear until after Beethoven's time; its first appearance in a score was not until 1835 for an opera called *La Juive*). The first and third movements are full of brilliant runs and fanfares while the shortest of slow movements avoids the soloists having to play anything slow and lyrical by not using them at all.

The fifth concerto of *Il cimento dell'armonia e dell' inventione* (see *The Four Seasons*) is entitled *La tempesta di mare* (in E flat), another descriptive violin concerto. *La tempesta di mare* is also the title of a concerto in F major, the first of a collection of six flute concertos that appeared in print in 1728 but which had probably been written about 20 years earlier. This one opens with a glittering, ebullient 'storm at sea', followed by a temporary stilling of the waters in the calm second movement. The second concerto is called *La notte* (*The Night*) – there's a Vivaldi bassoon concerto with the same title. This one, unusually, begins with a slow movement, then proceeds to an episode called *Fantasmi* (*Visions*) - agitated dreams, from the sound of it - while the last slow section is called *Il sonno* (*Sleep*). The third of the *Six Flute Concertos* is the best known: *Il cardellino* (*The Goldfinch*), an extraordinarily fresh and carefree virtuosic concerto of bird song.

VIVALDI
FLUTE CONCERTOS
(1728)

C

Of the nearly 400 instrumental concertos that Vivaldi composed, 230 alone are for his own instrument, the violin. He was the prototype of the modern virtuoso, bewitching his audiences with his technical prowess and, as a composer, creating some of the most original and innovative music of the age. The four concertos that make up *The Four Seasons* are just part of a collection of 12 published in 1725 under the collective title of *Il cimento dell'armonia e dell'inventione* (*The Contest between Harmony and Invention*). Each of the *Seasons* has three movements (fast-slow-fast) according to the convention of the day but what is remarkable about them are the endearing musical characterisations Vivaldi includes: No. 1, *Spring*, has the goatherd's trusty dog barking (the viola); No. 2, *Summer*, has bird-song, a shepherd pestered by insects and a frightening summer storm; No. 3, *Autumn*, has a drunken harvest celebration and a stag hunt; No. 4, *Winter*, presents the chattering cold and, in the lovely slow movement, rain dripping on the trees while the fortunate ones are sat next to a warm fire.

VIVALDI
THE FOUR SEASONS
(1725)

C
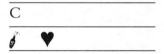

VIVALDI
GLORIA
from Gloria in D
(date unknown)

CHO

From 1713 onwards, Vivaldi began to compose an increasing amount of choral and sacred music, the vast majority of which remained totally unknown until the 1920s. Among those of his works which have survived the centuries is the *Gloria in D*, RV 589 (there's another Vivaldi *Gloria in D*, catalogued as RV 588, which is rarely heard). It's in 12 short sections, scored for two soprano soloists, contralto, choir and orchestra and its lively opening, which is simply a setting of the words 'Gloria in excelsis Deo', has become deservedly popular. (For explanation of RV numbering see Glossary.)

VIVALDI
MANDOLIN
CONCERTOS
(dates unknown)

C

Among the composers who have written for the mandolin are Handel, Mozart, Hummel, Paisiello, Donizetti, Verdi, Mahler, Respighi, Casella, Schoenberg, Stravinsky, Prokofiev and Webern. There are few concertos for the instrument that have caught on, though, and three are by Vivaldi. The most popular is the Concerto in D for mandolin, RV93 (which was originally written for the lute) followed by the Concerto in C for mandolin, RV425 and the Concerto in G for two mandolins, RV532 - all of them excellent: you couldn't wish for a livelier, jollier start to the day. (For explanation of RV numbering see Glossary.)

VIVALDI
NULLA IN MUNDO
PAX SINCERA
from Motet in E, RV630
(date unknown)

V

Though ordained as a priest in 1703 (the year in which he also began his long association with the Ospedale della Pietà in Venice, a charitable foundation for girl orphans), Vivaldi wrote little sacred music until 1713. His 12 surviving motets are all for soprano or contralto soloist with orchestra, a choice influenced by his duties at 'La Pietà'. All have non-liturgical texts written in a rather free Italianised Latin. This one, the first part of which has become immensely popular with Classic FM listeners, is in four sections: aria-recitative-aria-allelujah (allegro). The title warns against the world's hidden evils: 'There is no peace in this world without poison'.

The legend of the mariner condemned to sail the seas in his spectral ship until the end of time greatly appealed to Wagner. The curse could only be redeemed by the love of a faithful woman, and the power of the redemption of love was a theme that seems always to have obsessed Wagner. The Overture to this early opera contains every vital element of the story which follows: the theme associated with the unfortunate Dutchman opens the piece followed by one of the mightiest musical storms ever written – the wind whistles through the rigging, huge waves crash over the side of the boat. The calm after the storm features an air known as 'Senta's Ballad' which the heroine will sing in Act 2 of the opera. There's a jolly sailor's dance and another reference to 'Senta's Ballad' before the Overture closes peacefully.

**RICHARD WAGNER
1813–83**
GERMAN
Overture to
THE FLYING
DUTCHMAN
*Opera
(1843)*

O

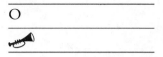

The ghostly Flying Dutchman has put into port in a Norwegian fishing village, the visit to dry land he is permitted to make once every seven years. He meets up with Captain Daland. Daland introduces him to his romantically-inclined daughter, Senta. She knows the legend of the Flying Dutchman and, when she sees him, knows that it is her destiny to save the man from eternal perdition. In Act 2, Senta and a group of girls are busy spinning, and sing the famous 'Spinning Chorus' (almost as famous in Liszt's transcription for solo piano). Senta then sings her own song, 'Traft ihr das Schiff im Meere an' ('Senta's Ballad'), in which she tells her friends all about the Flying Dutchman.

WAGNER
SPINNING CHORUS
*from The Flying Dutchman
(1843)*

OP

♥

WAGNER
Prelude to Act 1 of
LOHENGRIN
Opera
(1850)

O

Lohengrin tells the story of Elsa who, accused of murdering her brother, has a mystic dream of a knight who will defend her from the charge. Lo and behold, her knight in shining armour arrives in a boat drawn by a swan. He turns out to be Lohengrin, the son of Parsifal, guardian of the Holy Grail. Wagner chose to write a prelude to his opera, (rather than an overture consisting of the work's themes) in order to highlight the story's inner significance. The music suggests a vision of the Holy Grail (the cup that, according to medieval legend, Christ used at the Last Supper). It descends from heaven shedding, in Wagner's description, 'glorious light on the holder like a benediction' before ascending again to the 'ethereal height of tender joy'.

WAGNER
Prelude to Act 3 of
LOHENGRIN
(1850)

O

Elsa does not know the identity of her knight for he has told her that he can stay only on condition that she never asks his name or whence he came. She agrees, he defeats her accuser in combat and the two of them marry. By contrast to the Act 1 Prelude, the Prelude to Act 3 is a brilliant impression of wedding festivities, strings, woodwind and brass to the fore with the trombones blaring out an exuberantly joyful theme. Played before the curtain rises, it leads directly to...

WAGNER
BRIDAL CHORUS
from Lohengrin
(1850)

OP

Elsa, Lohengrin and half the court enter the bridal chamber to one of the best-known tunes in the world - though few of the countless brides who have walked down the aisle to its strains have a chorus singing 'Treulich bewacht bleibet zurück' ('Faithful and true we lead you forth') which is what you hear in the opera. Most of us learnt very different words: 'Here comes the bride/Full, fat and wide/Twice round the gas-works/And once inside'. *Lohengrin* was premièred in 1850 in Weimar. This and Mendelssohn's *Wedding March* were first linked together at the wedding of Princess Victoria and Prince Frederick William of Prussia in 1858, establishing a tradition that is still with us.

For his 1845 opera *Tannhäuser*, Wagner took the subject of the aristocratic medieval Minnesingers (groups of nobles who sang of love). In *Die Meistersinger von Nürnberg* (*The Mastersingers of Nuremberg*), he took the later middle-class trade guilds who modelled themselves on the Minnesingers. The most famous Mastersinger was the shoemaker, poet and dramatist Hans Sachs (1494-1576), who lived in Nuremberg. The Overture is a work of real genius and often heard independently. It's a compression of all the principal themes that crop up in the course of the drama - the solid, burly Mastersingers' motif, followed by the love motif of Walther and Eva, the march motif of the tradesman-musicians, a tune representing 'love confessed' (which will turn into 'Walther's Prize Song') and another agitated theme portraying 'love's ardour' - until, at the climax, all five are combined simultaneously with tremendous skill - and to overwhelming effect.

WAGNER
Overture to
DIE
MEISTERSINGER
Opera
(1868)

O

Walther and Eva have fallen in love but her father, Veit Pogner, has decreed that Walther must qualify to become a Mastersinger before he can marry his daughter. The pedantic critic Beckmesser (based on the eminent critic and Wagner-hater Eduard Hanslick) has his own designs on Eva. In the end, Beckmesser wins precisely 'nul points' in the great Nuremberg Song Contest while Walther surpasses himself with this hit song, an impassioned tenor solo, which is enough to win the Contest, become a Mastersinger and, of course, get the girl.

WAGNER
'PRIZE SONG'
from Die Meistersinger
(1868)

OP

♥

In ancient Scandinavian mythology, the Valkyries were the fierce warlike daughters of Odin (Wotan in *The Ring*) whose duty was to snatch up the fallen in battle and bear them to Valhalla. These warrior maidens rode through the skies on great steeds, accompanied by thunderclouds and lightning. In Act 3 of *The Valkyrie* (the second opera in the *Ring* cycle), Wagner produces this extraordinary orchestral musical depiction of the neighing and galloping of horses, the cries of the warrior women and the sound of the coming storm as the Valkyries ride through the heavens.

WAGNER
RIDE OF THE
VALKYRIES
from Die Walküre
Opera
(1850)

OP

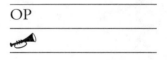

WAGNER
SIEGFRIED IDYLL
(1870)

O

♥   🕯   ☁

Wagner's wife, Cosima, was born on Christmas Day 1837, the daughter of Franz Liszt and the Countess d'Agoult. For her 33rd birthday she received a birthday present which the whole world has been able to share with gratitude, the *Siegfried Idyll*. This eloquent lullaby for chamber orchestra was conceived in secrecy by Wagner for his new bride and young son Siegfried. On Christmas morning 1870, at half past seven, 15 musicians assembled quietly on the stairs leading to Cosima's bedroom and played this 'beautiful and intolerably poignant serenade'. The themes are drawn from *Siegfried*, the third opera in the *Ring* cycle (particularly the love music from Act 3), but the work also quotes the old German cradle song 'Schlaf, mein Kind'.

WAGNER
SIEGFRIED'S
FUNERAL MARCH
from Götterdämmerung
(1876)

OP

🎺

Götterdämmerung (*Twilight of the Gods*) was the first of the four mammoth operas Wagner wrote that make up *Der Ring des Nibelungen* (*The Ring of the Nibelung*), always referred to as *The Ring*. In performance, though, *Götterdämmerung* is the last opera of the cycle, preceded by *Das Rheingold* (*The Rhine Gold*), *Die Walküre* (*The Valkyrie*) and *Siegfried*. Siegfried, one of *The Ring*'s principal figures, has been killed by the treacherous Hagen and his body is borne on a shield into the Hall of the Gibichungs. His *Funeral March* comes right at the end of *The Ring* – you'll have sat through 15 hours of music by then – and, in ten minutes or so, reviews in a masterly way all the themes associated with various scenes and characters in the four music dramas.

WAGNER
Overture to
TANNHÄUSER
Opera
(1845)

O

🎺

The opera's full title is *Tannhäuser and the Singing Contest on the Wartburg*. Its subject is taken from legend and history – Tannhäuser actually existed, as did the singing contests. He was a Minnesinger born around 1205, one of a group of poets and musicians, mainly of noble birth, who sang of love and beauty, frequently holding contests for the purpose (see also *Die Meistersinger*). The opera tells the story of the doomed love affair between Tannhäuser and Elisabeth, niece of the Landgrave of Thuringia. The Overture is one of the finest and most famous of all opera curtain-raisers, presenting many of the musical themes Wagner presents in the course of the work, one of which is...

Tannhäuser has escaped from the world to revel in the sensual delights of Venus and her court beneath a mountain (the Venusberg). Eventually he tires of physical pleasures and yearns to return to the real world. At the mention of the Virgin Mary's name, Venus disappears and Tannhäuser finds himself in a valley where a band of pilgrims is chanting a hymn as they make their way towards Rome. In the last act of the opera the same 'Pilgrims' Chorus' is heard again to magnificent effect as Elisabeth scans in vain the faces of pilgrims returning from the Eternal City to see if her beloved Tannhäuser is amongst them.

WAGNER
'PILGRIMS' CHORUS'
from Tannhäuser
(1845)

OP

In Act 2, Elisabeth is rapturous at the news of the return of her beloved Tannhäuser (though he's a little coy about telling her exactly where he's been). Knights, nobles and pages enter the Hall of the Minstrels in the Castle of the Wartburg to witness the song contest, the winner of which will receive Elisabeth's hand in marriage. Wagner sets the scene with the brilliant *Festival March* as the guests take their place with grave dignity before lifting their voices in a chorus of praise to the Hall.

WAGNER
PROCESSION OF
THE GUESTS
from Tannhaüser
(1845)

OP

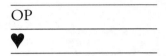

For singing the praise of carnal pleasures in the song contest, Tannhäuser has been banished and sent to Rome for absolution from the Pope. When Elisabeth sees that her love is not among the pilgrims returning from Rome, she prays to be taken from this earth. Tannhäuser's friend Wolfram overhears her and, when she leaves, entreats the evening star to guide and protect her in this poignant baritone solo, 'O du mein holder Abendstern' (sometimes called the 'Song to the Evening Star').

WAGNER
'O STAR OF EVE'
from Tannhaüser
(1845)

OP

♥

WAGNER
Prelude to
TRISTAN AND
ISOLDE
(1865)

O

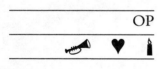

Based on Arthurian legend, *Tristan* is another story of doomed love - the clandestine passion between the knight Tristan and Isolde, betrothed to the Cornish King Mark. It is more a psychological music drama than an opera dominated by plot and action. In Wagner's own words, Tristan is a story of 'endless yearning, longing, the bliss and wretchedness of love... [with] one sole redemption - death, surcease, a sleep without awakening'. The Prelude begins with a four-note fragment played on the cellos - the grief motif. Overlapping it is an answering phrase from the oboes - the desire motif. The point when these two motifs meet produces the famous 'Tristan chord', one heard throughout the opera. Various other significant themes from the opera are heard before the Prelude reaches a climax - an outpouring of hopeless love - before quickly subsiding.

WAGNER
'LIEBESTOD'
from Tristan and Isolde
(1865)

OP

In the opera, the 'Liebestod' ('Love Death') aria comes in the final section. Tristan has been wounded by a treacherous friend and Isolde arrives just in time for him to die in her arms. In a trance-like ecstasy she sings her impassioned song of farewell, surely one of the most sensual and moving declarations of love ever written, before falling lifeless herself on Tristan's body. Wagner himself combined the beginning of his great music drama with its ending to produce an independent concert piece. And if all this emotion isn't enough, there's a wonderful *Tristan and Isolde Fantasy* which Franz Waxman contributed to the 1947 Hollywood film, *Humoresque*, when the 'Liebestod' is turned into a mini violin-and-piano concerto.

Besides his myriad original compositions (250 waltzes alone), Waldteufel made arrangements of other composers' music, resulting in two of his biggest successes. One is *Estudiantina* (*Band of Students*), a then-popular vocal duet by one Paul Lacome, to which Waldteufel added some Spanish songs to create a four-part waltz. It's one of those 'oh-so-that's-what-it's-called' numbers. You'll recognise his waltz *España* because it's a waltz-time version of Chabrier's famous orchestral rhapsody which also incorporates a duet from Chabrier's one-act operetta *Une Éducation manqué* and some additions of Waldteufel's own invention.

Andrew Lamb, Waldteufel's biographer, admits that while his music doesn't scale great architectural heights like Johann Strauss II, Waldteufel 'seeks to enchant by the grace and charm of his melodies and their gentle harmonies'. Strauss's music is Austrian, more masculine; Waldteufel's is French and more feminine. Waldteufel conducted all over Europe. He was particularly popular in London (his dances were regularly featured at Queen Victoria's state balls at Buckingham Palace) and on one such trip, in 1885, he struck up a friendship with Dan Godfrey, conductor of the band of the Grenadier Guards (later, Godfrey would become a dominating force in British music and championed Elgar's Cello Concerto after its initial failure). Waldteufel's joyous *The Grenadiers* (*Valse militaire*) is dedicated to Godfrey.

EMILE WALDTEUFEL 1837–1915
FRENCH
ESTUDIANTINA *(1883) and*
ESPAÑA *(1886)*

WALDTEUFEL
THE GRENADIERS *(1886)*

WALDTEUFEL
THE SKATERS'
WALTZ
(1882)

O

♪ ♥

Born in Strasbourg in December 1837 just seven weeks after Johann Strauss the elder had given his very first concert on French soil in that same city, Waldteufel, like Strauss, came from a family of dance musicians (despite his German name, the family were French, hailing from Alsace). Waldteufel spent most of his life in Paris and by the 1870s he had won world-wide fame for his dance music. *Les Patineurs (The Skaters)* is his best-known work today though it was not until the 1920s that it became an international success. Toscanini, no less, thought so highly of it that he recorded it in a re-orchestrated version of his own. A wintry scene, skaters gliding around on the ice gradually becoming more confident, the arrival of a sleigh with sleigh-bells - it's all here, no doubt inspired by the fact that in the late 1870s and early 1880s the Seine regularly froze over completely.

WILLIAM WALTON
1902–83
ENGLISH
BELSHAZZAR'S
FEAST
(1931)

CHO

🎺 🕯

Although officially labelled 'cantata', this is the most significant English oratorio since Elgar's *The Dream of Gerontius*. Originally commissioned in 1929 by the BBC who asked for a small-scale choral work, by 1930 the work had grown so large that the BBC released Walton from his contract. It requires a solo baritone, chorus and orchestra plus an expanded brass section, the latter supposedly in response to Sir Thomas Beecham's remark before the first performance in Leeds: 'As you'll never hear the thing again, why not throw in a couple of brass bands?' *Belshazzar's Feast* is a thrilling and powerful experience, 'a paean of praise for the god of gold', and Walton's choral writing, in the best Anglican tradition, is masterly.

The BBC commissioned this march in November 1936 for the crowning of Edward VIII. In the event, of course, it became a coronation march for his brother, George VI, and accompanied the entry of the Queen Mother (Queen Mary) to Westminster Abbey on 12 May 1937. In fact the work had already been recorded a month earlier and had even been broadcast (on 9 May). Similarities to Elgar's *Pomp and Circumstance Marches* are obvious. It uses the same successful formula of brisk march - quieter, stately second section (the Trio) - return of brisk march - triumphant, full orchestra repeat of Trio in different key - exhilarating ending.

WALTON
CROWN IMPERIAL
(1937)

O

It was in 1923 that Walton made a name for himself. He was 21 years old when his 'melodrama for reciting voice and seven instruments', *Façade*, was first given in London to the considerable discomfort of an audience who hadn't a clue what it was all about. It consisted of a series of abstract poems by Edith Sitwell declaimed through a megaphone behind a curtain to the accompaniment of Walton's irreverent, jazzy, brilliantly-orchestrated music. Today, it's a favourite concert item, especially at music festivals when a celebrity is usually on hand to get his or her tongue round the tricky delivery of the text. There are two suites for full orchestra (without the verses): Suite No. 1 (the best known, from 1926) features *Polka* (quoting the old music-hall song 'See me dance the polka'); *Valse* (which reminds us that Walton earned money in the 1920s from arranging dance band music); *Swiss Yodelling Song* (cow bells and quotes from *William Tell*); *Tango-Pasodoblé* (snatches of Ravel and 'I do like to be beside the seaside'); *Tarantella* (with a touch of Stravinsky). The Second Suite includes *Popular Song*, signature tune of BBC TV's *Face the Music* panel game.

WALTON
FAÇADE
(1922)

CH

WALTON
HENRY V SUITE
(1944)

O

The first Shakespeare film for which Walton wrote the score was *As You Like It* (1936). During its making he met Laurence Olivier who, seven years later, asked him to compose the music for his film of *Henry V* (Walton would go on to provide the music for Olivier's films of *Hamlet* and *Richard III*). Much of the music was written before Walton had even seen the rough cut, taking his inspiration purely from Shakespeare's text. The result ranks as one of the finest of all film scores (Olivier said that 'the music actually made the film'). The short five movement suite arranged from the score is by Muir Mathieson who conducted the music for the soundtrack.

WALTON
ORB AND SCEPTRE
(1953)

O

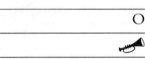

Walton's second coronation march was written for the crowning of Elizabeth II on 2 June 1953, and was heard as part of the orchestral music before the service. Like *Crown Imperial*, it had its first performance at a recording session (in March of that year) and follows the same jubilant *Pomp and Circumstance* pattern. There's a third Walton coronation march - the one he wrote for the crowning of Edward IV in Olivier's film of *Richard III*. Clearly he'd had enough of coronation marches by then for he added the facetious direction for the score to be played 'Con prosciutto, agnello e confitura di fragole' ('With ham, lamb and strawberry jam')!

WALTON
PARTITA
(1957)

O

The baroque title (*partita* simply means 'suite') belies the nature of this delightful, little-known orchestral *jeu d'esprit* consisting of a sparkling Toccata, a gentle and exquisite *Pastorale Siciliana*, and a high-spirited *Giga burlesca* to conclude. Walton wrote it as part of the 40th anniversary celebrations for the Cleveland Orchestra and its dictatorial conductor George Szell. He evidently enjoyed its composition: 'It poses no problems, has no ulterior motives or meaning behind it, and makes no attempt to ponder imponderables. I have written it in the hope that it may be enjoyed straight off'.

This is Walton's earliest orchestral piece and dedicated to Siegfried Sassoon. It gets its title and inspiration from a print by Thomas Rowlandson (1756-1827) depicting the animated life of the Portsmouth quayside - a money lender, a tavern of drunken, sprawling, singing customers, the masts of ships. A short, punchy work, the Overture is in Walton's best irreverent manner, brilliantly scored, full of energy and good humour that doesn't let up for a second. Other Walton overtures in the same breezy style are: *Scapino, Johannesburg Festival Overture* and *Capriccio Burlesco*.

WALTON
PORTSMOUTH
POINT
Overture
(1925)

O

The Prelude finds Walton in 'English ceremonial mode' once more - a really grand and, ultimately, rather moving march. It was composed for the film *The First of the Few* which told the story of the Spitfire and its designer, R.J. Mitchell (played by Leslie Howard). The Prelude plays over the opening credits while the lively Fugue accompanies the production-line assembly of the aircraft parts. The solo violin passage portrays the exhausted and dying Mitchell - but you don't need to see the film to enjoy the music, a great concert favourite.

WALTON
SPITFIRE PRELUDE
AND FUGUE
(1942)

O

Peter Warlock was the pen-name used by the English composer Philip Heseltine who committed suicide in his London flat by gassing himself. Profoundly influenced by Delius and by his great love for Elizabethan music, most of Warlock's output is for voice. Paradoxically, his best known work is his delightful *Capriol Suite* for string orchestra, six softly-spoken French dances based on tunes found in a collection published in 1588 called *Arbeau's Orchésographie*. The Pavane from this is the same tune used by Delibes in his incidental music for Victor Hugo's play *Le Roi s'amuse*.

PETER WARLOCK
1894-1930
ENGLISH
CAPRIOL SUITE
(1926)

O

♥

CARL MARIA VON
WEBER
1786–1826
GERMAN
BASSOON
CONCERTO IN F
(1811, rev. 1822)

C

Good works for bassoon and orchestra are few and far between and Weber wrote two of the best. His Bassoon Concerto was for the Munich-based player Georg Friederich Brandt. Though it's cast in the conventional three-movement format (fast-slow-fast), there are many unconventional passages - at times the soloist sounds as though he is singing in one of Weber's operas. The central *Romanza* is a wonderful inspiration of great tenderness showing off the bassoon's wistful quality, contrasted in the finale by its witty, playful side. Weber's other masterpiece for the instrument is the *Andante and Hungarian Rondo* in C minor, originally composed for viola and orchestra in 1809 but reworked for Brandt in 1813. You'd have to be hard of heart not to warm to the perky *Rondo* theme, one of those carefree, reassuring movements that make the sun shine when it's raining.

WEBER
CLARINET
CONCERTO NO. 1 IN
F MINOR
(1811)

C

Just as Mozart's friendship with the clarinettist Anton Stadler led to the great Clarinet Concerto and Clarinet Quintet, and Brahms' admiration for the virtuoso Richard Mühlfeld inspired numerous masterpieces for the instrument, so Weber's close relationship with Heinrich Bärmann (1784-1847) produced a string of major works for the clarinet. Both of Weber's clarinet concertos are brilliant and highly-virtuosic, and display every aspect of the instrument without descending into the empty note-spinning of which many contemporary works were guilty - here the spectacular passages unfold as part of the music. Their jolly final rondos are guaranteed to send you on your way rejoicing. What distinguishes the F Minor Concerto is its slow movement, a long drawn-out wistful song over strings, interrupted magically by a trio of horns which the soloist joins just as if they were sharing a secret apart from the orchestra - a stroke of genius.

Weber's first piece for Bärmann, the principal clarinettist of the Bavarian Court Orchestra in Munich, was the little Concertino in C minor (also worth a listen) that triumphantly concluded Bärmann's solo debut in Munich in April 1811. The two Clarinet Concertos were commissioned as a result, polished off within a few weeks of each other in the spring of 1811 (though not published until a decade later). Both are dedicated to Bärmann who was able to advise Weber on the instrument's possibilities and limitations. He must have been quite a player, for there are many demanding passages in both works that test even modern virtuosi. The Second Concerto, like the First, abounds in celebratory high spirits and memorable themes (listen to the exuberant final Rondo!). Try also the Clarinet Quintet in B flat (another work dedicated to Bärmann) and the virtuoso *Grand Duo Concertant* of 1816 (the only Weber clarinet work that's not).

WEBER
CLARINET
CONCERTO
NO. 2 IN E FLAT
(1811)

C

Weber was Mozart's first cousin by marriage (Constanze Mozart was Weber's niece). Just 20 years after Mozart wrote the last of his horn concertos, Weber wrote his one concerted work for the instrument. Although he called it a concertino ('short concerto'), it's as long as most of Mozart's and, like the *Konzertstück* (page 353), is a four-movements-in-one work. Having originally written it in 1809, he revised it for a Munich horn player called Rausch, giving him in the last section (a scintillating polonaise) some of the most difficult music ever composed for the instrument. One earlier passage asks the performer to create chords on the instrument by simultaneously playing one note and humming another.

WEBER
CONCERTINO
FOR HORN
IN E MINOR
(1809, rev. 1815)

C

WEBER
Overture to
DER FREISCHÜTZ
Opera
(1821)

O

The opera's title is usually translated as *The Freeshooter* - a marksman who uses magic bullets. It is one of the most important operas ever written for, with this one work, Weber established German (as distinct from Italian) opera as a distinctive theatrical form. Discarding the usual plots of intrigue and mistaken identity, he based the story on the legends of his own country, involving magic, the supernatural and religious themes. It was a short step from here to Wagner's monumental *Ring* cycle which is based on entirely the same ideas. The story of *Der Freischütz* has echoes of the Faust legend: in exchange for a man's soul, the evil spirit of the forests can provide magic bullets to hit any target. The Overture, often heard independently, is a brilliant curtain-raiser, the first to include complete melodies from the music that was to follow and which in themselves form a commentary on the mood and content of the whole drama.

WEBER
'AGATHE'S PRAYER'
from Der Freischütz
(1821)

OP

Prince Ottokar's head ranger Cuno has two assistants, Max and Kaspar. Max is in love with Agathe who has promised to be his bride if he can prove to be the best marksman in the Prince's shooting contest. Kaspar outshoots Max who falls under the power of the evil wild huntsman Samiel, the provider of magical bullets. In this exquisitely beautiful aria from Act 2, 'Leise, leise, fromme Weise' ('Gently, gently, lift my song') known as 'Agathe's Prayer', Agathe looks out of her window in the moonlight and sings of her love for Max. (Max, by the way, shoots his girl by mistake with the last magic bullet, a mysterious hermit revives her, Max is forgiven and lo! – a happy ending.)

WEBER
INVITATION TO THE
DANCE
(1819)

I/O

Of Weber's many piano works, by far the most familiar is this, *Aufforderung zum Tanz*, a waltz-rondo in D flat that is now generally heard in the orchestral arrangement by Berlioz. It was composed as early as 1819, way ahead of its time for it provided the Waltz Kings of Vienna (Lanner and the Strauss family) with a prototype for their dance music. Like the *Konzertstück*, *Invitation to the Dance* tells a story - an obvious one of a man asking a lady for the next dance to which she assents (slow introduction); they swirl round the dance floor to entrancing music (the main central section);

Weber then daringly brings the dance to a definite close (cue premature hand-clapping from audience) before tagging on a quiet, poetic ending as the gentleman returns the lady to her seat. Two other occasional piano works by Weber are worth getting to know: his *Polacca brillante in E* 'L'Hilarité' and the *Rondo brillante in E flat* 'La Gaité'.

Unconnected to any opera, the *Jubel-Ouvertüre* (or *Jubilee Overture*) for orchestra was written on the occasion of the 50th anniversary of the reign of Weber's patron, the King of Saxony. A slow introduction leads to the vigorous main theme of the Overture succeeded by a contrasting light-hearted one. After both ideas have been repeated, the music builds to a climax for a thunderous version of the national song 'Heil dir im Siegerkranz'. 'Hang on,' you say, when it appears, 'Isn't that "God save the Queen"?' The very same. The Saxons nicked it from us, of all the cheek. There's an impressive organ arrangement of the *Jubilee Overture* by W.T. Best, a favourite item in Victorian organ recitals.

WEBER
JUBILEE OVERTURE
(Jubel-ouvertüre)
(1818)

O

In many respects, this one-movement mini piano concerto is the touchstone of all romantic concertos. Weber composed the *Concert Piece* in 1821, the first such work to have a programme (or story) dictating its musical content, a device that many later Romantic composers emulated (Mendelssohn, Liszt, Berlioz and Wagner were just four giants hugely influenced by Weber). There are four distinct sections, played without a break, that tell a story set in the period of the Crusades: a lady sits in her tower gazing sadly into the distance wondering if she'll ever see her knight again (slow first section); she has a vision of him being slain on the battlefield (passionate second section); hark! what is that distant sound? an army of knights returning! (third section – march); it is he! happiness without end! joy unbounded! love triumphant! she is in his arms again (fast and furious finale). There are many beautiful and effective passages throughout (the opening woodwind theme for instance) while the piano writing glitters and bewitches to produce a masterpiece of the lyrical romantic literature.

WEBER
KONZERTSTÜCK
IN F MINOR
(1821)

C

WEBER
Overture to
ABU HASSAN
Opera
(1811)

O

Abu Hassan, a one-act opera based on a tale in *The 1,001 Nights*, gave Weber his first real success in the theatre, though it's rarely staged now. It's all about Abu Hassan and his wife Fatime trying to pay off their debts by raising funeral money for each other's faked deaths. The Overture is a breathless little gem which lasts just three and a half minutes.

WEBER
Overture to
EURYANTHE
Opera
(1823)

O

The contest between darkness and light in *Der Freischütz* is renewed in this opera of two years later. It's concerned with an evil couple (Lysiart and Eglantine) struggling to destroy the good guys (Adolar and the heroine Euryanthe). The impetuous opening of the Overture suggests the world of knightly romance and chivalry until a change of pace and a moment's silence lead to a strange, mystical passage. In the Opera, this represents a ghost whose troubled soul must find rest, a spiritual air '[of the kind] that must have given Wagner the vision of a new world, for it is not difficult to find a kinship between this music and the Prelude to *Lohengrin*', as one writer aptly put it. The chivalric theme returns to press the Overture to a galloping conclusion.

WEBER
Overture to
OBERON
Opera
(1826)

O

Fairyland was obviously in the air in 1826, for Mendelssohn wrote his overture to *A Midsummer Night's Dream* at the same time that Weber completed his three-act opera *Oberon*. The King of the Fairies and Titania feature in this, Weber's last opera (written for London), but any connection with Shakespeare's drama quickly disappears in a complex tale of magic horns, shipwrecks off Greece, slavery in Tunis, murder and infidelity. What is notable about the Overture is the masterly way in which the four different themes which Weber introduces are eventually drawn together before he ends with a rousing presentation of the opera's hit soprano aria 'Ocean, thou mighty monster'.

Weber's four piano sonatas written between 1812 and 1822 are extremely difficult to play. This is because he had abnormally large hands and some of the passages put the music beyond the physical possibilities of most players. That is one reason why they are so rarely heard (only the lyrical Sonata No. 2 in A flat occasionally receives an airing). However, the Rondo (final movement) of the First Sonata has always been around, an astounding non-stop whirl of semiquaver notes played *presto* (very fast), a tour de force in perpetual motion which lasts, in the hands of an athletic pianist, three and a half minutes - a real high-wire act, the pianistic equivalent of Paganini's *Perpetuum Mobile* for the violin.

WEBER
PERPETUUM
MOBILE
*from Piano Sonata
No. 1 in C
(1812)*

Second only to Smetana's *The Bartered Bride*, Weinberger's opera *Schwanda the Bagpiper* was the most popular Czech opera of its day, though now it has completely faded from the repertoire. As in Smetana's work, it is the folk dances from the score that greatly contributed to its popularity and the Polka, which Schwanda plays on his bagpipes when he enters in the second scene of Act 1, is a lusty peasant dance that was once a mainstay of 'light music' programmes. The Fugue, whose main theme is suggested by the Polka, is heard in the opera's closing scene with the Polka set against the Fugue, played by full orchestra and organ. From 1939 Weinberger lived in the USA, the same year in which he composed his *Variations and Fugue on 'Underneath the Spreading Chestnut Tree',* inspired by seeing a newsreel film of King George VI taking part in the song at a boys' holiday camp.

**JAROMÍR
WEINBERGER
1896-1967**
CZECH–AMERICAN
POLKA AND FUGUE
*from Schwanda the
Bagpiper
Opera
(1927)*

SAMUEL WESLEY
1766–1837
ENGLISH
AIR AND GAVOTTE
(1816)

I

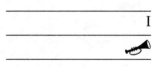

The second son of Charles Wesley who, with his brother John, founded the Methodist movement, Samuel grew to become the foremost organist of his day and a fine composer. His choral work *In exitu Israel* (1810) is unusual for its time, opening with a plainsong chant (from the Catholic church), taking in continental style, Bach, echoes of his teacher Boyce, all with a firm grasp of the English cathedral tradition. His brief Air and Gavotte have been perennial favourites with organists since they were published in 1816, the pretty, rather pensive Air making a perfect partner for the jaunty Gavotte. Both are popular wedding pieces. Poor Wesley: aged 21 he 'fell into a street excavation and was for seven years incapacitated, and ever afterwards subject at intervals to mental aberration'.

SAMUEL SEBASTIAN
WESLEY
1810–76
ENGLISH
CHORAL SONG AND
FUGUE
(date unknown)

I

The natural son of Samuel Wesley 'who gave him his name and a share of his genius', S.S., like his father, became the finest organist in the country. He was (and remains) the only organist to serve five different cathedrals in succession – Hereford, Exeter, Leeds Parish Church (which has the musical status of a cathedral), Winchester and Gloucester. His finest organ work is the Introduction and Fugue in C sharp minor; his most popular piece at one time was *Holsworthy Bells*, written after hearing the bells of Holsworthy in Devon; today, his best-known is the magnificent Choral Song and Fugue – the first part a magisterial and joyous anthem for the organ, followed by one of the jolliest fugues you'll ever hear.

SAMUEL SEBASTIAN
WESLEY
BLESSED BE THE
GOD AND FATHER
(1835)

CHO

Wesley's contribution to church music in the Nineteenth Century was enormous. So highly was he thought of that, three years before Wesley's death, Mr Gladstone recommended to Queen Victoria that he be paid a civil list pension of £100 a year. It was that or a knighthood. Wesley took the money. Many of his hymns, anthems and services are still sung regularly today, his most enduring anthem being this setting of words from the *First Epistle of Peter*. It ends, after a lengthy subdued passage, with a thunderous organ chord introducing the final dramatic line: 'But the word of the Lord endureth for evermore'. A wonderful moment. Wesley, though musically much influenced by Mendelssohn, was careful to note the precise stops on the organ that he required for the organ accompaniments of his anthems, something previously unheard of in cathedral music.

Widor, apart from being distantly related to the Montgolfiers, the legendary balloon pioneers, was the greatest French organist of the age. When he was 26 he took over the organ of Saint-Sulpice in Paris where he reigned for 64 years. In 1872, two years after taking up the post, he began to compose a series of ten organ symphonies - not works for organ and orchestra but works in which the organ plays the part of a symphony orchestra. They were modelled indirectly on Alkan's Symphony and Concerto for solo piano which aimed at the same thing in pianistic terms. The First Symphony has no less than seven movements, the fifth of which is the most spectacular, 'a priests' march of provocative colourfulness' with calmer episodes to contrast the thunderous main theme, an ideal accompaniment to weddings and ceremonial occasions, one that more than lives up to its title.

CHARLES-MARIE WIDOR
1844-1937
FRENCH
MARCHE PONTIFICALE
from Organ Symphony No. 1
(1872, rev. 1901)

Perhaps the most familiar organ piece today is the last of the five movements which make up the fifth of Widor's ten organ symphonies - Widor's Toccata, as it's popularly known. The delirious, relentless whirlwind of notes coupled with the organ pedals booming out its stately theme produce a wonderful feeling of elation. It has been a firm favourite for weddings ever since the Duke and Duchess of Kent went down the aisle to it in 1961. But couples wanting it played at their marriages are sometimes disappointed: not only does it need a large instrument in good mechanical order to achieve its effect (it doesn't work on a harmonium!) but you have to have an organist of a certain standard to play it. For many organists, a request for Widor's Toccata costs them hours of practice and sleepless nights.

WIDOR
TOCCATA IN F
from Organ Symphony No. 5
(1878)

HENRYK WIENIAWSKI
1835–80
POLISH
LÉGENDE
(c. 1860)

I

♥

Wieniawski was arguably the greatest violinist to emerge after Paganini. A child prodigy, he was born in Lubin, Poland and entered the Paris Conservatory aged eight. In 1859 he came to London to participate in a series of quartet concerts. Here he met and fell in love with Isabella Hampton, niece of the composer George Osborne. Wieniawski married her and it is to Isabella that the *Légende* is dedicated (the couple's youngest daughter Irene, later Lady Dean Paul, composed under the pseudonym Poldowski). With either its piano or alternative orchestral accompaniment, it's a short (eight minute) poetic, tender piece in the German-Romantic style of the day, rising to a climax in the middle section where, notably, Wieniawski makes a chord using all four open strings.

WIENIAWSKI
VIOLIN
CONCERTOS NOS. 1
(1853)
AND 2 *(1862)*

C

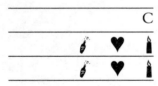

Wieniawski wrote only 24 works in all. With those mentioned above and below, one other composition, the Violin Concerto No. 2 in D minor, has ensured that his music remains an indispensable part of the violinist's arsenal, a masterpiece and one of the great virtuoso Romantic concertos, but one in which bravura passages take second place to the most expressive, lyrical – at times almost soulful – music (try the second movement Romance). It ends with a lively gypsy tune and a blaze of fireworks guaranteed to bring the house down. His Violin Concerto No. 1 in F sharp minor, unlike the Second Concerto, is seldom played, but then many violinists have a propensity to ignore well-written, effective works. It was composed when Wieniawski was still an adolescent and, in the words of Itzhak Perlman, who made his Carnegie Hall debut with it in 1963, it is 'very innocent musically and extremely difficult technically'. Wieniawski himself died at the age of 45, burnt out and virtually destitute.

All Wieniawski's works are for the violin. As a virtuoso violinist-composer, he showed precocious talent: his first work, the *Grand Caprice Fantastique*, was published when he was only 12. Among the pieces that are in the repertoire of every fiddle-player today are the *Polonaise Brillante No. 1 in D,* the popular *Souvenir de Moscow* (a set of variations on two Russian folk tunes) and the dazzling *Scherzo-tarantelle*, which uses the rhythms and melodies of Neapolitan folk dance in a lively perpetual motion. Two short works inspired by the folk music of his native land are the languid *Kuyawiak* and the more extrovert mazurka *Obertas*.

Wolf-Ferrari's *I Giojelli della Madonna*, with its echoes of Mascagni, is a passionate tragedy about the fate of Maliella whose affections the blacksmith Gennaro attempts to win from the swashbuckling Rafaele by stealing jewels from a statue of the Madonna. The orchestral suite is a real charmer: it opens with a boisterous *Festa popolare*, followed by the delicate Intermezzo (this being a Neapolitan melodrama, it's hard not to draw parallels with this and the theme from *The Godfather*); the third movement Serenade, once staple fare for 'light music' orchestras, will have you thinking 'now I know where it comes from!'. The finale is a frenzied *Danza napolitana* marked by Wolf-Ferrari to be 'a regular orgy… of reckless, cruel sensuality'.

Adding his Italian mother's name to that of his German father, Wolf-Ferrari unwittingly mapped out his own destiny. He was born in Venice and died there but spent most of his life in Germany; he studied art in Venice but then changed to study music in Munich; he composed 13 operas with Italian texts but had most success with them in Germany. The one-act *Il segreto di Susanna* was one of these. It's a comedy about a young wife who's a secret smoker, a vice which leads her husband to suspect she has a lover. The short and snappy Overture sparkles like a diamond.

WIENIAWSKI
VIOLIN PIECES
(1847-70)

I

**ERMANNO WOLF-FERRARI
1876-1948**
ITALIAN
INTERMEZZO
from The Jewels of the Madonna
Opera
(1911)

O

WOLF-FERRARI
Overture to
SUSANNA'S SECRET
Opera
(1909)

O

ARTHUR WOOD
1875–1953
ENGLISH
BARWICK GREEN
from My Native Heath
(1925)

O

You've never heard this? Then you are one of the few people who have never listened to *The Archers*! Barwick Green is the title of its signature tune and it comes from a suite written by the Yorkshire-born conductor and composer Arthur Wood. The other three movements are called *Knaresboro' Status*, *Ilkley Tarn* and *Bolton Abbey*. Our piece portrays a maypole dance on the village green of Barwick-in-the-Elmet, east of Leeds – a long way from Ambridge.

HAYDN WOOD
1882–1959
ENGLISH
THE HORSE
GUARDS,
WHITEHALL
from London Landmarks
(1946)

O

No relation to Arthur (above) but a fellow Yorkshireman whose best known orchestral work also became famous through its use as a radio signature tune. *The Horse Guards, Whitehall* introduced the long-running *Down Your Way*, compered by Brian Johnson (and before him Franklyn Engleman). Wood's other fine London suite, *London Cameos*, is another example of the adroitly-crafted, tuneful school of English light music that has undergone such a revival in recent years. Apart from *The Horse Guards*, Wood was the composer of two famous songs: 'Brown Bird Singing' and 'Roses of Picardy'.

Z

DOMENICO ZIPOLI
1688–1726
ITALIAN
ELEVAZIONE
(1716)

O

One of the very first pieces of music I ever heard on Classic FM was by a composer I'd never previously encountered. Zipoli was born in Rome, became an organist and went off to Seville to join the Jesuit order. From there he emigrated in 1717 to Córdoba in Argentina where he spent the rest of his short life. His *Elevazione* (an instrumental composition written to be performed during the Elevation of the Host in the Roman Catholic Church) was composed in 1716 for oboe, organ and strings and has the same serene intensity as Albinoni's Adagio. How's that for an A to Z of music in one sentence!

1812 Overture (Tchaikovsky) 31, **314–15**, 316, 318
2001: A Space Odyssey (film) 302

A Montevideo (Gottschalk) **140**
Abdelazar (Purcell) 18, 86, **240**
Abenslied (Humperdinck) 21, 26, **162**
Abu Hassan (Weber) **354**
Academic festival overture (Brahms) 78, 82
Accardo, Salvatore (violinist) 87, 222
Accursed huntsman (Franck) **126**
Adagietto (Poulenc) **228**
Adagio (Khachaturian) 30, **170**
Adagio and allegro (Schumann) **280**
Adagio for cello and orchestra (Bargiel) **53**
Adagio for organ and strings in G minor (Albinoni) 23, **38**, 360
Adagio for strings (Barber) 19, 33, **52**, 188
Addio, fiorito asil (Puccini) **236**
Adiemus (Jenkins) **166**
Adiemus II (Jenkins) **166**
Adieu, notre petit table (Massenet) **190**
Adieux sonata, Les (Beethoven) **59**
Adventures of Robin Hood (Korngold) **171**
advertisements 48, 90, 106, 166, 190, 216, 220, 266
Africaine, L' (Meyerbeer) **199**
Agathe's prayer (Weber) **352**
Age of anxiety (Bernstein) **71**
Age of gold (Shostakovich) **287**
'Ah! Vous dirai-je, Maman' (Adam) 36, 108
Ai nostri monti (Verdi) **332**
Aida (Verdi) 18, 31, 186, 199, **327–8**, 333
Air and gavotte (Samuel Wesley) **356**
Air on the G string (JS Bach) 26, **48**
Akenfield (film) 324
Alborada del gracioso (Ravel) **246**
Alla Marcia (Sibelius) 22, **289**
Allegro spiritoso (Senaille) **285**
Alpine symphony, An (R Strauss) **302**
Also sprach Zarathustra (R Strauss) **302**
Alt Wien (Godowsky) **138**
Alto rhapsody (Brahms) **78**
Amadeus (play and film) 211, 212
American in Paris, An (Gershwin) **130**
Amor brujo, El (Falla) **120**
Ancient airs and dances for the lute (Respighi) **250**
Andante cantabile (Tchaikovsky) 29, **314**
Andante and rondo capriccioso (Mendelssohn) **192**
Andantino in D flat (Lemare) **177**
Andre, Maurice (trumpeter) 156
Angeles, Victoria de los (singer) 335
Another Dawn (film) 174
Anthony Adverse (film) 174
Anvil chorus (Verdi) 22, **331**
Appalachian spring (Copland) **101**
Appassionata sonata (Beethoven) **59**
Apres un reve (Faure) **121**
Aranyi, Jelly d' (violinist) 249
Archers, The (radio) 99, 360
Aria (film) 172
Aria (Villa-Lobos) 23, **335**
Arlesienne suite No.1 (Bizet) **73**
Arlesienne suite No.2 (Bizet) **73**
Arrival of the Queen of Sheba (Handel) 17, 32, **148**
Artist's life, An (J Strauss II) **297**, 301
As You Like It (film) 348
Ascension, L' (Messiaen) **198**

Ashton, Sir Frederick (choreographer) 51, 128, 157
At the castle gate (Sibelius) **288**
Au fond du temple saint (Bizet) **73**
Auer, Leopold (violinist) 134, 321
Aurora (W Lloyd Webber) **186**
Autumn (Chaminade) **91**
Ave Maria (Caccini) **23**, **90**
Ave Maria (Gounod) 50, **140**
Ave Maria (Verdi) **333**
Ave verum corpus (Byrd) **89**
Ave verum corpus (Mozart) 20, **202**

Babar the elephant (Poulenc) **228**
Baba-Yaga (Liadov) **179**
Babe (film) 267
Bacchanale (Saint-Saens) **266**
Bachianas Brasileiras No.2 (Villa-Lobos) **335**
Bachianas Brasileiras No.5 (Villa-Lobos) 23, **335**
Baez, Joan (singer) 189
Bagatelle No.25 in A minor (Beethoven) 21, **55**
Bailero (Canteloube) 23, 90
Baillie, Isobel (singer) **194**
Baker, Janet (singer) 90
Ballade in F sharp (Faure) **121**
Ballades (Chopin) **93**
Ballet Egyptien (Luigini) **186**
Banks of the green willow (Butterworth) **89**
Barber of Seville (Rossini) 28, 30, 207, 223, **255**, 261
Barbirolli, Sir John (conductor) 114
Barcarolle (Offenbach) 33, **218**
Barere, Simon (pianist) 183, 284
Barmann, Heinrich (clarinettist) 350, 351
Barry Lyndon (film) 275
Bartered bride, The (Smetana) **291**, 355
Bartlett, Ethel (pianist) 49
Bartoli, Cecilia (singer) 90, 133, 256
Barwick Green (A Wood) **360**
Bassoon concerto in B flat (Mozart) 160, **203**, 285
Bassoon concerto in F (Hummel) **160**
Bassoon concerto in F (Weber) 160, **350**
Beast with Five Fingers (film) 46
Beatitudes, The (Part) **226**
Beatrice and Benedict (Berlioz) **67**
Beautiful Galathea, The (Suppe) **310**
Beecham, Sir Thomas (conductor) 68, 143, 148, 152, 346
Bel raggio lusinghier (Rossini) **257**
Bell song (Delibes) **105**
Bella figlia dell'amore (Verdi) **330**
Belle excentrique, La (Satie) **269**
Belle Helene, La (Offenbach) **218**, 310
Belshazzar's feast (Walton) **346**
Benvenuto Cellini (Berlioz) **67**, 69
Berezovsky, Boris (pianist) 51
Berganza, Teresa (singer) 137
Berglund, Tim (singer) 137
Biches, Les (Poulenc) **228**
Birds, The (Respighi) 24, **250**
Bjorling, Jussi (singer) 73, 233
Blessed be the God and Father (SS Wesley) **356–7**
Blue Danube (J Strauss II) 21, 84, 163, 176, **297**
Blue tango (Anderson) **41**
Bluebird, The (Stanford) **294**
Body and Soul (book) 208
Boeuf sur le toit, Le (Milhaud) **199**
Boheme, La (Puccini) **233–5**, 237, 238
Bohemian girl (Balfe) **52**
Bohemian symphony (Dvorak) **113**

Bonney, Barbara (singer) 194
Bouffonne, La (Telemann) **322**
Boult, Sir Adrian (conductor) 326
Boutique fantasque, La (Rossini) **260**
Brain, Dennis (horn player) 206
Brandenburg concertos (JS Bach) 24, **45**
Brandt, Georg Friederich (bassoonist) 350
Bridal chorus (Wagner) 18, **340**
Bridge on the River Kwai (film) 39
Bridgetower, George Augustus Polgreen (violinist) 65
Brief Encounter (film) 242
Bronsart, Hans von (pianist) 182
Browning, John (pianist) 52
Bulow, Hans von (pianist) 81, 180
Butt, Dame Clara (singer) 117
Butterflies (Schumann) **282**
Butterfly lovers violin concerto (Chen Kang and Ho Zhan Hao) **92–3**
By the sleepy lagoon (Coates) **99**

Cailliet, Lucien (conductor) 216
Calinda, La (Delius) **106**
Callas, Maria (singer) 65, 237
Camden, Archie (bassoonist) 285
Campanella, La (Liszt) **179**
Cancan (Offenbach) 22, 163, **219**, 261
Candide (Bernstein) 31, **71**
Canon in D (Pachelbel) 18, 33, **220**
Cantata mundi (Jenkins) **166**
Cantata No.140 (JS Bach) **49**
Cantata No.147 (JS Bach) **47**
Cantata No.208 (JS Bach) **49**
Cantilena (Villa-Lobos) **335**
Cantique de Jean Racine (Faure) 33, **121**
Cantique de Noel (Adam) **35**
Capriccio Espagnol (Rimsky-Korsakov) **252**
Capriccio Italien (Tchaikovsky) **314**
Caprice Espagnol (Moszkowski) **201**
Caprice No.24 in A minor (Paganini) 27, 83, 187, 221, 244
Caprices (Paganini) 180, **221**
Capriol suite (Warlock) **349**
Caractacus (Elgar) **118**
Carillon de Westminster (Vierne) **334**
Carmen (Bizet) 30, **73–4**, 319
Carmina Burana (Orff) 28, 30, **220**
Carnaval (Schumann) **280**, 281, 282
Carnival (Dvorak) **110**
Carnival of the animals (Saint-Saens) 21, 34, 103, 255, **261**
Carnival in Paris (Svendsen) **311**
Caro mio ben (Giordani) **133**
Caro nome (Verdi) **329**
Caruso, Enrico (singer) 109, 125, 178, 199
Casals, Pablo (cellist) 45, 75, 154, 262, 275
Casanova (J Strauss II) **302**
Casta Diva (Bellini) **65**
Castor and Pollux (Rameau) **245**
Caucasian sketches (Ippolitov-Ivanov) **164**
Cavalleria rusticana (Mascagni) 29, 141, 178, **190**, 236
Cavatina (Myers) 20, **216**
Celeste Aida (Verdi) **327**
Cello concerto in A minor (Schumann) **280**, 281
Cello concerto in B flat (Boccherini) **75**
Cello concerto in B minor (Dvorak) **111**
Cello concerto in E minor (Elgar) **114**, 116, 345
Cello concerto No.1 in A minor (Saint-Saens) **262**
Cello concerto No.1 in C (Haydn) **153**
Cello concerto No.2 in D (Haydn) **153**

Cello concerto No.2 in D minor (Saint-Saens) 262
Cello suites (JS Bach) 24, 45, 46
Cenerentola, La (Rossini) 256
Ceremony of carols (Britten) 27, 84
Chaconne (JS Bach) 46
Chaconne in G minor (Vitali) 336
Chaconne in G minor for strings (Purcell) 239
Chanson de matin (Elgar) 114
Chanson de nuit (Elgar) 26, 114
Chasseur maudit, Le (Franck) 126
Che gelida manina (Puccini) 233
Checkmate (Bliss) 74
Childhood of Christ (Berlioz) 27, 67
Children's corner suite (Debussy) 34, 103
Children's Favourites (radio) 39
Children's games (Bizet) 74
Children's march (Grainger) 142
Children's overture (Quilter) 241
Choral fantasy in C (Beethoven) 54, 63
Choral preludes (Brahms) 79
Choral song and fugue (SS Wesley) 356
Choral symphony No.9 (Beethoven) 54, 63, 81
Choros No.1 in E minor (Villa-Lobos) 336
Chorus of the Hebrew slaves (Verdi) 333
Christmas concerto (Corelli) 27, 102
Citizen Kane (film) 158
Clair de lune (Debussy) 33, 104
Clarinet concerto in A (Mozart) 29, 102, 203, 350
Clarinet concerto in A minor (Stanford) 294
Clarinet concerto in C minor (Finzi) 124
Clarinet concerto No.1 in F minor (Weber) 350, 351
Clarinet concerto No.2 in E flat (Weber) 351
Clarinet concerto No.2 in F minor (Crusell) 102
Clarinet quintet in A (Mozart) 21, 203, 350
Clarinet sonata (Brahms) 81, 294
Clarinet sonata (Poulenc) 229
Classical symphony (Prokofiev) 233
Clement (violinist) 64
Cleveland Orchestra 52
Cliburn, Van (pianist) 317
Clockwork Orange (film) 63
Cockaigne overture (Elgar) 114
Colas Breugnon (Kabalevsky) 168
Colonel Bogey (Alford) 39
Colonial song (Grainger) 143
Comedians, The (Kabalevsky) 168
Como, Perry (singer) 90
Concert fantasy on Carmen (Sarasate) 74, 268
Concerti grossi (Corelli) 102, 324
Concerti grossi (Geminiani) 130
Concerti grossi (Handel) 130, 148, 211
Concerto for alto saxophone in E flat (Glazunov) 133
Concerto for coloratura soprano (Gliere) 135
Concerto for flute and harp in C (Mozart) 33, 204
Concerto for flute and strings (Mercadante) 198
Concerto for harp and orchestra (Gliere) 135
Concerto for horn in E minor (Weber) 351
Concerto for organ, strings and percussion in G minor (Poulenc) 167, 229
Concerto for piano, trumpet and strings (Shostakovich) 286
Concerto symphonique No.4 (Litolff) 185
Concerto for three hands (Arnold) 42
Concerto for trumpet and strings in D (Telemann) 323

Concerto for two pianos (Arnold) 42
Concerto for two pianos in D minor (Poulenc) 229
Concerto for two trumpets in C (Vivaldi) 336
Concerto for two violins in D minor (JS Bach) 25, 32, 46
Concerto for viola and strings in G (Telemann) 322
Concierto de Aranjuez (Rodrigo) 29, 254
Consolation No.3 in D flat (Liszt) 180
Coombs, Stephen (pianist) 78, 147
Coppelia (Delibes) 106
Coriolan (Beethoven) 54
Cornish rhapsody (Bath) 53
Coronation march (Meyerbeer) 199
Corsaire, The (Berlioz) 68
Corsaire, Le (Drigo) 110
Cortot, Alfred (pianist) 127, 154, 275
Cosi fan tutte (Mozart) 204
Coucou, Le (Daquin) 103
Country gardens (Grainger) 143
Cranko, John (choreographer) 309
Creation, The (Haydn) 153, 154, 258
Creatures of Prometheus (Beethoven) 56
Crown imperial (Walton) 347, 348
Crucifixion, The (Stainer) 294
Crusell, Bernhard (clarinettist) 102
Cuban overture (Gershwin) 131
Czardas (Delibes) 106
Czardas (J Strauss II) 299
Czerny (pianist) 58
Cziffra, Georges (pianist) 108, 170, 181, 183, 252, 300

Dam busters march (Coates) 99
Damage (film) 230
Damnation of Faust (Berlioz) 68, 69
Damrosch, Walter (conductor) 131
Dance of the blessed spirits (Gluck) 32, 137
Dance of the comedians (Smetana) 291
Dance duet (Humperdinck) 162
Dance of the goblins (Bazzini) 54
Dance of the hours (Ponchielli) 22, 228
Dance of the sylphs (Berlioz) 68, 261
Dance of terror (Falla) 120
Dance of the young maidens (Khachaturian) 170
Dangerous Moonlight (film) 37
Danse Macabre (Saint-Saens) 184, 261, 262, 267
Daphnis et Chloe (Ravel) 247
David, Ferdinand (violinist) 64, 197
Davidov, Carl (cellist) 41
Daydreams (Schumann) 21, 281
De profundis (Part) 226
Death in Venice (film) 189
Deer Hunter, The (film) 216
Depuis le jour (G Charpentier) 23, 91
Desert Island Discs (radio) 99
Devil's trill (Tartini) 313
Di quella pira (Verdi) 332
Diaghilev, Sergei (choreographer) 121, 178, 228, 247, 249, 260, 270, 305, 306
Dido and Aeneas (Purcell) 239
Dido's lament (Purcell) 239
Die tote stadt (Korngold) 172
Diemen, Ursula van (singer) 206
Dies irae (Verdi) 31, 329
Dies natalis (Finzi) 124
Divertissement (Ibert) 163, 196
Djinns, Les (Franck) 126
Dodd, Ken (singer) 58
Dolce notte (Puccini) 235
Doll song (Offenbach) 219

Dolly suite (Faure) 122
Dome epais le jasmin (Delibes) 106
Don Giovanni (Mozart) 30, 183, 204-5, 212, 213
Don Juan (R Strauss) 303
Don Pasquale (Donizetti) 109
Donna Diana (Reznicek) 251
Donna e mobile, La (Verdi) 330
Doretta's dream (Puccini) 237
Double concerto for harpsichord and fortepiano in E flat (CPE Bach) 43
Double Life of Veronique, The (film) 230
Down Your Way (radio) 360
Dream of Gerontius (Elgar) 115, 346
Drum roll symphony (Haydn) 156

E lucevan le stelle (Puccini) 238
Easter hymn (Mascagni) 190
Eclogue for piano and string orchestra (Finzi) 125
Egmont (Beethoven) 56
Egyptian piano concerto (Saint-Saens) 265
Eight English dances (Arnold) 42
Eine kleine nachtmusik (Mozart) 24, 210, 212
Elegie (Massenet) 191
Elegie for cello and orchestra (Faure) 19, 122
Elegy (Alfven) 39
Elevazione (Zipoli) 32, 360
Elijah (Mendelssohn) 100, 192
Elisir d'amore, L' (Donizetti) 109
Elvira Madigan (Mozart) 209
Emperor concerto (Beethoven) 58
Emperor waltz (J Strauss II) 298
Enchanted lake (Liadov) 168
English folk song suite (Vaughan Williams) 325
Enigma variations (Elgar) 19, 114, 119, 252
Entry of the gladiators (Fucik) 129
Erdeli, Ksenia (harpist) 135
Eroica piano variations (Beethoven) 56
Eroica symphony (Beethoven) 19, 56, 61
Es ist ein ros' entsprungen (Brahms) 17, 79
Escales (Ibert) 163
Espana (Albeniz) 37
Espana (Chabrier) 90, 345
Espana (Waldteufel) 90, 345
Estudiantina (Waldteufel) 345
Etude in D sharp minor (Scriabin) 285
Etude en forme de valse (Saint-Saens) 263
Etudes (Chopin) 40, 94, 138
Etudes in all the minor keys (Alkan) 40
Eugene Onegin (Tchaikovsky) 22, 315, 319
Euryanthe (Weber) 274, 354
Evening prayer (Humperdinck) 21, 26, 162
Exultate, jubilate (Mozart) 18, 205

Facade (Walton) 347
Face to Face (television) 65
Face the Music (television) 347
Fairest isle (Purcell) 240
Falstaff (Elgar) 115
Fanfare for the common man (Copland) 31, 101
Fantaisie in F minor (Chopin) 94
Fantaisie-Impromptu (Chopin) 94
Fantasia (film) 50, 110, 228, 306, 316
Fantasia concertante on a theme of Corelli (Tippett) 102, 324
Fantasia in F minor (Schubert) 272
Fantasia and fugue in G minor (The great) (JS Bach) 46
Fantasia on Greensleeves (Vaughan Williams) 30, 32, 326
Fantasia para un gentilhomme (Rodrigo) 254

INDEX

Fantasia on Scottish folk tunes for violin,
orchestra and harp (Bruch) **86**
Fantasia and sonata in C minor (Mozart) **210**
Fantasia on a theme of Thomas Tallis
(Vaughan Williams) 25, **325**
Fantasie in C (Schumann) **281**
Fantasiestucke (Schumann) **281**
Faust (Gounod) **141**, 179
Faust Waltz (Liszt) **180**
Ferrier, Kathleen (singer) 137
Feux follets (Liszt) **180**
Fevrier, Jacques (pianist) 229
Fidelio (Beethoven) 22, **55, 60**
Fiedler, Arthur (flautist) 227
Field, John (pianist) 95
Fille aux cheveux de lin, La (Debusy) 21, 105
Fille mal garde, La (Herold) **157**
Fingal's cave (Mendelssohn) **193**, 196
Finlandia (Sibelius) **288**
Firebird, The (Stravinsky) **305**
First of the Few, The (film) 349
Fischer, Edwin (pianist) 50, 189
Fitzenhagen, Wilhelm (cellist) 322
Flagstad, Kirsten (singer) 239
Flanders and Swann (song writers) 206
Fledermaus, Die (J Strauss II) 66, **298-9**, 301
Flight of the bumble-bee (Rimsky-Korsakov)
252
Flower duet (Delibes) **106**
Flute concertino (Chaminade) **91**
Flute concertos (CPE Bach) **44**
Flute concertos (Vivaldi) **337**
Flying Dutchman (Wagner) 280, **339**
Fokine, Mikhail (choreographer) 305
Football world cup 122, 238
Forget Venice (film) 137
Forsyte Saga (television) 100
Forza del destino, La (Verdi) **328**
Fountains of Rome (Respighi) **250**
Four last songs (R Strauss) **303**, 304
Four parables (Schoenfield) **272**
Four sea interludes (Britten) **85**
Four seasons (Vivaldi) **337**
Four temperaments symphony (Nielsen) **217**
Fournier, Pierre (cellist) 122
Fox, Virgil (organist) 167
Francs-Juges, Les (Berlioz) **68**
Freischutz, Der (Weber) **352**, 354
Frind, Annie (singer) 302
From foreign lands (Moszkowski) **202**
Fugal concerto for flute, oboe and strings
(Holst) **158**
Funeral march of a marionette (Gounod) **140**
Funeral march sonata (Chopin) 19, **97**
Fur Elise (Beethoven) 21, **55**
Furiant (Smetana) **291**
Furtiva lagrima, Una (Donizetti) **109**
Furtwangler (conductor) 173

Gade, Niels (conductor) 197
Gadfly (Shostakovich) **287**
Gaite Parisienne (Offenbach) **220**
Galante, Inessa (singer) 90
Galli-Curci, Amelita (singer) 98, 133
Galop (Kabalevsky) **168**
Galop (Khachaturian) **171**
Galway, James (flautist) 91, 198, 221
Gardiner, Sir John Eliot (conductor) 129
Gaspard de la nuit (Ravel) **247**
Gavotte (Boyce) **78**
Gayaneh (Khachaturian) **170**
Gerhardt, Charles (conductor) 173
German requiem (Brahms) **79**
Gianni Schicchi (Puccini) **235**

Gigli, Beniamino (singer) 90, 109
Gioconda, La (Ponchielli) 22, **228**
Giselle (Adam) **35**
Gitlis, Ivry (violinist) 290
Glagolitic mass (Janacek) **165**
Glasgow Orpheus Choir 294
Gloria (Poulenc) **230**
Gloria (Vivaldi) 44, **338**
Gloria in D (Vivaldi) **338**
Gluck das mir verblieb (Korngold) **172**
Gnomenreigen (Liszt) **184**
Gobbi, Tito (singer) 237
Godfrey, Dan (conductor) 345
Godowsky, Leopold (conductor) 37, 301
Gods go a'begging, The (Handel) **152**
Going for a Song (television) 250
Gold and silver waltz (Lehar) **176**
Goldberg variations (JS Bach) 26, **47**
Gondoliers (Sullivan) **307**
Good-humoured ladies (Scarlatti) **270**
Goodman, Benny (clarinettist) 71, 229
Goodman, Roy (boy soprano) 40
Goreyescas (Granados) **143**
Graham, Martha (choreographer) 101
Grand Canyon suite (Grofe) **146**
Grand choeur in D (Guilmant) 17, **146**
Grand duo concertant (Weber) 32, 351
Grand, grand overture (Arnold) **42**
Grand Hotel (film) 138
Grand march (Verdi) 18, 31, 199, **328**
Grand septet in B flat (Berwald) **72**
Grand sextet in E flat for piano and strings
(Glinka) **136**
Grande messe des morts (Berlioz) 67, **69**
Great fantasia and fugue (JS Bach) **46**
Great mass (Mozart) 56, 206, **207**
Great symphony (Schubert) **278**
Great Waltz (film) 298
Greater love hath no man (Ireland) **164**
Grenadiers (Waldteufel) **345**
Grunfeld, Alfred (pianist) 301
Grutzmacher, Friedrich (cellist) 75
Guitar concerto (Rodrigo) **254**
Guitar quintet in D (Boccherini) 24, **75**
Guitar quintet in E minor (Boccherini) 24, **75**
Gustav Adolf II suite (Alfven) **39**
Gymnopedie No.1 (Satie) 20, 269
Gypsy airs (Sarasate) **268**
Gypsy Baron (J Strauss II) **299**, 301
Gypsy trio (Haydn) **154**

Hall, Marie (violinist) 326
Hallelujah chorus (Handel) 28, **149**
Hamburg symphonies (CPE Bach) **44**
Hamelin, Marc-Andre (pianist) 40, 157
Hamlet (film) 348
Hansel and Gretel (Humperdinck) 21, 26, 34,
162
Harmonious blacksmith (Handel) 22, **148**
Harold in Italy (Berlioz) **68**
Harp concerto in C (Albrechtsberger) **38**
Harpsichord concerto in D minor
(CPE Bach) **44**
Harty, Sir Hamilton (conductor) 240
Harvest hymn (Grainger) **143**
Hary Janos (Kodaly) **171**
Havanaise (Saint-Saens) **263**
Hear my prayer (Mendelssohn) **194**
Hebrides, The (Mendelssohn) **193**
Heifetz, Jascha (violinist) 54, 66, 83, 86, 87,
92, 107, 134, 174, 194, 290, 321, 334,
336

Helfgott, David (pianist) 242
Henry V suite (Walton) **348**
Herbert, Victor (cellist) 111
Herman, Woody (bandleader) 71
Hess, Dame Myra (pianist) 47
Hiawatha's wedding feast (Coleridge-Taylor)
100
HMS Pinafore (Sullivan) **307**
Hoe-Down (Copland) 22, **101**
Hoffnung, Gerard (musical humorist) 42
Hofmann, Jossef (pianist) 201, 242
Holberg suite (Grieg) **144**
Holliday, Michael (singer) 90
Hollmann, Joseph (cellist) 262
Holy city (Adams) **36**
Homage march (Grieg) **144**
Home Alone (film) 35
Hora staccato (Dinicu) **107**
Horn concerto No.1 in E flat (R Strauss) **304**
Horn concerto No.3 in E flat (Mozart) **205**
Horn concerto No.4 in E flat (Mozart) 25,
206
Horowitz, Vladimir (pianist) 74, 201, 293,
317
Horse Guards, Whitehall (H Wood) **360**
Hough, Stephen (pianist) 127, 160, 271
Howard's End (film) 114
Hubermann, Bronislav (violinist) 83, 174
Humming chorus (Puccini) 21, **236**
Humoresque (film) 268, 344
Humoresque in G flat (Dvorak) **111**
Hungarian dances (Brahms) **79**, 113
Hungarian fantasy (Liszt) **180**
Hungarian march (Berlioz) **69**
Hungarian rhapsodies (Liszt) 69, 180, **181**

I am the jolly birdcatcher (Mozart) 28, 207
I dreamt I dwelt in marble halls (Balfe) **52**
I vow to thee, my country (Holst) 159
I was glad (Parry) **225**
Iberia (Albeniz) **37**
Images for orchestra (Debussy) **104**
Images sets 1 and 2 for piano (Debussy) **104**
Imagined oceans (Jenkins) **167**
Imperial march (Elgar) **115**
Impromptu No.4 in C sharp minor (Chopin)
94
Impromptus (Schubert) **272**, 274
In London town (Elgar) **114**
In a nutshell (Grainger) **142**
In questa reggia (Puccini) **238**
In the steppes of Central Asia (Borodin) **76**
In Town Tonight (television) 99
Incoronazione di Poppea, L' (Monteverdi)
200
Incredible flutist (Piston) **227**
Indes galante, Les (Rameau) **246**
Instruments of the Orchestra (film) 86
Intermezzo (Kodaly) **171**
Intermezzo (Mascagni) 29, **190**
Intermezzo (Puccini) 190, **236**
Intermezzo (Wolf-Ferrari) **359**
Introduction and allegro (Elgar) **116**
Introduction and allegro (Ravel) **247**
Introduction and rondo capriccioso
(Saint-Saens) **263**
Inventor and the Comedians, The (play) 168
Invitation to the dance (Weber) **352-3**
Invocation (W Lloyd Webber) **186**
Io son Titania (Thomas) **324**
Iolanthe (Sullivan) **308**
Irish symphony (Stanford) **295**
Islamey (Balakirev) **51**, 247
Isserlis, Steven (cellist) 53, 122, 313

Italian concerto (JS Bach) **47**
Italian girl in Algiers (Rossini) **256**
Italian Straw Hat, The (play) 163
Italian symphony (Mendelssohn) **197**

Jamaican Rumba (Benjamin) **66,** 98
Jazz suites Nos.1 and 2 (Shostakovich) **286**
Jenkins, Florence Foster (singer) 298
Jerusalem (Parry) **225**
Jesus Christ Superstar (musical) 197
Jesu, joy of man's desiring (JS Bach) 17, **47**
Jeunehomme piano concerto (Mozart) **208**
Jeux d'eau (Ravel) **248**
Jeux d'enfants (Bizet) **74**
Jewel song (Gounod) **141**
Jewels of the Madonna (Wolf-Ferrari) **359**
Joachim, Joseph (violinist) 64, 83, 87
John Field suite (Field) **124**
Johnson, Emma (clarinettist) 102
Jolly robbers (Suppe) **310**
Jota Aragonesa (Glinka) **136**
Joy of the blood of the stars (Messiaen) **198**
Juarez (film) 174
Jubilee overture (Weber) **353**
Judas Maccabeus (Handel) **151**
Judex (Gounod) **141**
Jupiter symphony (Mozart) **214**

Kahn, Micheline (harpist) 247
Kaiser waltz (J Strauss II) **298**
Kamarinskaya (Glinka) **136**
Kanawa, Kiri te (singer) 149, 158
Karelia suite (Sibelius) 22, **289**
Katchen, Julius (pianist) 51
Keyboard sonatas (Scarlatti) **270**
Kikimora (Liadov) **179**
Kinderszenen (Schumann) 21, **281**
King Arthur (Purcell) **240**
King Cotton (Sousa) **292**
King's College, Cambridge choir 40
King's row (Korngold) **172**
Kismet (musical) 77
Kol Nidrei (Bruch) **86**
Konzertstuck in F minor (Weber) 351, 352,
   353
Kreisler, Fritz (violinist) 111, 119, **174-5,** 313
Kreutzer, Rudolph (violinist) 65
Kreutzer sonata (Beethoven) 60, **65**
Kuolema (play) 290

Lady Surrenders, The (film) 53
Ladykillers, The (film) 76
Lakme (Delibes) **105, 106**
Land of hope and glory (Elgar) 28, **116**
Land of the mountain and the flood
   (MacCunn) **187**
Land of smiles (Lehar) 135, **177**
Landowska, Wanda (harpsichordist) 47
Largo (Handel) 20, **150**
Largo al factotum (Rossini) 28, **255**
Lark ascending (Vaughan Williams) 33, **326**
Last Night of the Proms (television) 225
Last rose of summer (Flotow) **125**
Laudate Dominum (Mozart) 20, 27, **206**
Laughing song (J Strauss II) **298**
Legend of Tsar Saltan (Rimsky-Korsakov)
   252
Legende (Wieniawski) **358**
Leggierezza, La (Liszt) **181**
Leningrad symphony (Shostakovich) **288**
Leonore overture No.3 (Beethoven) **55**
Let the bright seraphim (Handel) 17, **149**
Leutgeb, Ignaz (horn player) 205, 206
Lewy, Joseph Rudolph (horn player) 280

Libertine (Purcell) **240**
Liberty bell (Sousa) **292**
Libiamo, libiamo (Verdi) **331**
Liebestod (Wagner) **344**
Liebestraume No.3 in A flat (Liszt) 26, **181,**
   260
Lieutenant Kije suite (Prokofiev) 27, **231**
Light cavalry (Suppe) **310**
Lipatti, Dinu (pianist) 210
Listen with Mother (radio) 122
Little, Tasmin (violinist) 290
Little night music (Mozart) **212**
Little sonata for beginners (Mozart) **210**
Little train of the Caipira (Villa-Lobos) **335**
Lloyd Webber, Julian (cellist) 186
Loesser, Arthur (pianist) 49
Lohengrin (Wagner) 18, 280, **340,** 354
London landmarks (H Wood) **360**
London suite (Coates) **99**
London symphony (Haydn) **156**
London symphony (Vaughan Williams) 89
Lone Ranger (radio and television) 259
Long, Marguerite (pianist) 248
Lost chord (Sullivan) **308**
Lough, Ernest (boy soprano) 194
Louise (G Charpentier) 23, **91**
Love duet (Puccini) **235**
Love, the magician (Falla) **120**
Love for three oranges (Prokofiev) **231,** 232
Love Story (film) 53
L-Shaped Room, The (film) 80
Luca, Giuseppe De (singer) 133
Lucia di Lammermoor (Donizetti) **109**
Lullaby (Brahms) **84**
Lympany, Moura (pianist) 170
Lyric pieces (Grieg) **145**

Ma vlast (Smetana) **292**
Madame Butterfly (Puccini) 21, **235-6**
Magic flute (Mozart) 28, 203, 204, **206-7**
Magnificat in D (CPE Bach) **44**
Malcolm, George (pianist) 224
Manchester Schoolchildren's Choir 162, 240
Mandolin concertos (Vivaldi) 24, **338**
Mandolin concertos in C and E flat (Paisiello)
   223
Manilow, Barry (singer/songwriter) 96
Manon (Massenet) **190,** 236
Manon Lescaut (Puccini) 190, **236**
Mantovani (orchestra leader) 39
M'appari (Flotow) **125**
March (Prokofiev) **231**
March of the little lead soldiers (Pierne) **227**
Marche heroique (Brewer) 17, **84**
Marche joyeuse (Chabrier) **915**
Marche militaire Francaise (Saint-Saens) **264**
Marche militaire No.1 in D (Schubert) 22,
   273
Marche pontificale (Widor) **357**
Marche slave (Tchaikovsky) **316**
Marche triomphale (Karg-Elert) 17, **169**
Marches (Coates) **99**
Marriage of Figaro (Mozart) 204, **207,** 209,
   213, 255
Mars (Holst) 31, **159**
Marsalis, Wynton (trumpeter) 156, 221
Marsick, Martin (violinist) 268
Martha (Flotow) **125**
Martin, Sir George (organist) 115
Martin, Philip (pianist) 139
Masquerade (Khachaturian) **171**
Mass in B minor (JS Bach) **48,** 56

Mass No.18 in C minor (The great) (Mozart)
   56, 206, **207**
Massine, Leonide (choreographer) 121, 220,
   270
Mathieson, Muir (conductor) 348
Mattinata (Leoncavallo) **178**
Mazurka (Delibes) **106**
McCormack, John (singer) 189
Meditation (Gounod) **140**
Meditation (Massenet) 26, 134, **191**
Meditation in D (Glazunov) **134**
Meistersinger, Die (Wagner) **341,** 342
Melodie (Gluck) 32, **137**
Melody in F (Rubinstein) **260,** 271
Menuhin, Yehudi (violinist) 119, 224, 334
Mephisto waltz No.1 (Liszt) **182**
Mer, La (Debussy) **104**
Merrill, Robert (singer) 73
Merry Widow, The (Lehar) 66, **176, 177**
Merry wives of Windsor (Nicolai) **217**
Merry Wives of Windsor (play) 326
Messiah (Handel) 28, 100, 146, **149,** 192
Michailowski, Alexander (pianist) 98
Midsummer night's dream (Mendelssohn) 17,
   26, 34, 192, **193, 194,** 261, 354
Midsummer vigil (Alfven) **39**
Mignon (Thomas) **323**
Mikado (Sullivan) **308-9**
Military piano septet (Hummel) **161**
Military symphony (Haydn) **155**
Milnes, Sherrill (singer) 109
Milstein, Nathan (violinist) 134, 138, 224
Mimi's farewell (Puccini) **235**
Minuet (Boccherini) 32, **76**
Minuet in G (Paderewski) **221,** 271
Minuet will-o-the-wisps (Berlioz) **68,** 180
Minute waltz (Chopin) 95, **98**
Miracle symphony (Haydn) **155**
Miserere (Allegri) **40**
Miserere (Verdi) **332**
Missa dum complerentur (Palestrina) **223**
Missa Papae Marcelli (Palestrina) 27, **224**
Missa solemnis in D (Beethoven) **56**
Mitropoulos, Dmitri (conductor) 174
Moffo, Anna (singer) 245
Moiseiwitsch, Benno (pianist) 193
Moments musicaux (Schubert) **273**
Montagues and Capulets (Prokofiev) 22, **231**
Moonlight sonata (Beethoven) 26, 55, **58,** 60
Morning, noon and night in Vienna (Suppe)
   311
Morning prayers (J Strauss II) **299**
Morning serenade of the jester (Ravel) **246**
Mors et vita (Gounod) **141**
Motet in E (Vivaldi) **338**
Moto perpetuo (Paganini) 41, 221, 355
Much ado about nothing (Korngold) **172**
Muhlfeld, Richard (clarinettist) 81, 294, 350
Musetta's waltz song (Puccini) **234**
Music for the royal fireworks (Handel) **149**
Music-box (or Musical snuff-box) (Liadov)
   178, 305
Music While You Work (radio) 99
My native heath (A Wood) **360**
My soul, there is a country (Parry) 20, 225

Nabucco (Verdi) **333**
Navarra (Albeniz) **37**
Nelson mass (Haydn) **153**
Nessun dorma (Puccini) 28, **238**
Neveu, Ginette (violinst) 290
New world symphony (Dvorak) 112, **113**
Night on a bare mountain (Mussorgsky) **216**
Night Mail (film) 85

Night in the tropics (Gottschalk) **139**
Nightingale and the rose, The (Saint-Saens) **265**
Nights in the gardens of Spain (Falla) **120**
Nimrod (Elgar) 19, 103, 116, **119**, 252
Nocturnes (Chopin) 26, **95**, 119, 123
Nocturnes (Field) 95, **123**
Non piu mesta (Rossini) **256**
Norma (Bellini) **65**
Nuits d'ete, Les (Berlioz) **70**
Nulla in mundo pax sincera (Vivaldi) 32, **338**
Nun danket alle Gott (Karg-Ellert) 17, **169**
Nun's chorus (J Strauss II) **302**
Nutcracker (Tchaikovsky) 27, 34, 110, **316**
Nymphs and shepherds (Purcell) **240**

O del mio dolce ardor (Gluck) **137**
O for the wings of a dove (Mendelssohn) **194**
O fortuna (Orff) 28, 220
O my beloved father (Puccini) **235**
O paradis (Meyerbeer) **199**
O patria mia (Verdi) **328**
O silver moon (Dvorak) **111**
O soave fanciulla (Puccini) **234**
O star of eve (Wagner) **343**
Oberon (Weber) **354**
Oboe concerto in C minor (Cimarosa) 30, **98**
Oboe concerto in D minor (Marcello) **189**
Oboe concertos (Albinoni) **38**
Octet in F (Schubert) 25, **273**
Octet for strings in E flat (Mendelssohn) 24, **194**
Ode to Joy (Beethoven) 28, 54, **63**, 81
Ogdon, John (pianist) 93
Oistrakh, David (violinist) 92
Old Vienna (Godowsky) **138**
Ombra mai fu (Handel) **150**
On hearing the first cuckoo in Spring (Delius) 103, **107**
On the town (Bernstein) **72**
On wings of song (Mendelssohn) **195**
One fine day (Puccini) **236**
Onedin Line (television) 170
Orb and sceptre (Walton) **348**
Orchestral Suite No.2 in B minor (JS Bach) **48**
Orchestral Suite No.3 in D (JS Bach) 26, **48**, 335
Organ concertos (Rheinberger) **252**
Organ concertos (Handel) 103, **150**
Organ symphony (Saint-Saens) 147, 261, 265, **267**
Organ symphony No.1 (Vierne) 18, **334**
Organ symphony No.1 (Widor) **357**
Organ symphony No.1 in D minor (Guilmant) **147**
Organ symphony No.5 (Widor) 18, **357**
Ormandy, Eugene (conductor) 53
Orpheus and Euridice (Gluck) 32, **137**, 219
Orpheus in the underworld (Offenbach) 22, 218, **219**, 220, 261
Otello (Verdi) **333**
Overtures (Auber) **43**

Pacific 231 (Honegger) **159**
Pagliacci (Leoncavallo) **178**, 190
Palladio (Jenkins) **167**
Palpiti, I (Paganini) **222**
Panis angelicus (Franck) **126**
Papillons (Schumann) **282**
Parade of the tin soldiers (Jessel) **167**, 227
Paride ed Elena (Gluck) **137**
Partita (Walton) **348**
Parysatis (Saint-Saens) **265**

Pas de deux (Drigo) **110**
Pastoral symphony (Beethoven) **62**
Pathetique sonata (Beethoven) 25, **58**
Pathetique symphony (Tchaikovsky) 25, **320-1**
Pavane (Faure) **122**
Pavane pour une infante defunte (Ravel) **248**
Pavarotti, Luciano (singer) 109, 133, 199, 238, 332
Pearl Fishers (Bizet) **73**
Peer Gynt (Grieg) **145**
Pelleas and Melisande (Faure) **122**, 288
Pelleas and Melisande (Sibelius) 122, **288**
Perlman, Itzhak (violinist) 138, 224, 358
Perpetuum mobile (Paganini) 41, 221, 355
Perpetuum mobile (J Strauss II) **300**
Perpetuum mobile (Weber) **355**
Perry Mason (television) 87
Peter Grimes (Britten) **85**
Peter and the wolf (Prokofiev) 34, **232**
Peterloo overture (Arnold) **42**
Philadelphia Orchestra 53
Piano, The (film) 218
Piano concerto (Barber) **52**
Piano concerto (Nyman) **218**
Piano concerto (Poulenc) **230**
Piano concerto in A minor (Grieg) **146**, 157, 187, 245
Piano concerto in A minor (Hummel) **160**
Piano concerto in A minor (Clara Schumann) **279**
Piano concerto in A minor (Schumann) **282**
Piano concerto in B minor (Hummel) **160**
Piano concerto in C minor (Raff) **245**
Piano concerto in D (Haydn) **154**
Piano concerto in D flat (Khachaturian) **170**
Piano concerto in E (Moszkowski) **201**
Piano concerto in F (Gershwin) **131**
Piano concerto in F (Haydn) **154**
Piano concerto in F minor (Henselt) **157**
Piano concerto in F sharp minor (Scriabin) **285**
Piano concerto in G (Ravel) **248**
Piano concerto No.1 in B flat (Bortkiewicz) **78**
Piano concerto No.1 in B flat (Scharwenka) **271**
Piano concerto No.1 in B flat minor (Tchaikovsky) 157, 245, 260, 271, **316-17**
Piano concerto No.1 in C (Beethoven) **57**
Piano concerto No.1 in D flat (Prokofiev) **232**
Piano concerto No.1 in D minor (Brahms) 79, **80**, 229, 260
Piano concerto No.1 in E (Hahn) **147**
Piano concerto No.1 in E flat (Liszt) **182**, 260
Piano concerto No.1 in E minor (Chopin) **95**, 160
Piano concerto No.1 in E minor (von Sauer) **269**
Piano concerto No.1 in F sharp minor (Rachmaninov) **241**
Piano concerto No.1 in G minor (Mendelssohn) **195**
Piano concerto No.2 in A (Liszt) **182**
Piano concerto No.2 in A flat (Field) **123**
Piano concerto No.2 in B flat (Brahms) **80**
Piano concerto No.2 in C minor (Rachmaninov) 29, 241, **242**, 295
Piano concerto No.2 in C minor (Stanford) **295**
Piano concerto No.2 in D minor (MacDowell) **187**

Piano concerto No.2 in D minor (Mendelssohn) **195**
Piano concerto No.2 in F (Shostakovich) 33, **286**
Piano concerto No.2 in F minor (Chopin) **95**
Piano concerto No.2 in G (Tchaikovsky) **317**
Piano concerto No.2 in G minor (Saint-Saens) 187, 260, **264**, 265
Piano concerto No.3 in C (Prokofiev) **232**, 233
Piano concerto No.3 in C minor (Beethoven) **57**
Piano concerto No.3 in D (Kabalevsky) **169**
Piano concerto No.3 in D minor (Rachmaninov) 31, 201, 241, **242**, 244
Piano concerto No.4 in C minor (Saint-Saens) **265**
Piano concerto No.4 in D minor (Rubinstein) **260**
Piano concerto No.4 in E minor (Scharwenka) **271**
Piano concerto No.4 in G (Beethoven) **57**, 123
Piano concerto No.5 in E flat (Beethoven) **58**
Piano concerto No.5 in F (Saint-Saens) **265**
Piano concerto No.9 in E flat (Mozart) **208**
Piano concerto No.10 in E flat for two pianos (Mozart) **208**, 212
Piano concerto No.20 in D minor (Mozart) **208**, 209
Piano concerto No.21 in C (Mozart) **209**
Piano concerto No.23 in A (Mozart) **209**
Piano concerto No.24 in C minor (Mozart) 57, **209**
Piano concerto No.27 in B flat (Mozart) **210**
Piano quintet (Schumann) 112, **282**
Piano quintet in A (Dvorak) 112, **282**
Piano quintet in A (Schubert) 32, **274**, 276
Piano quintet in E flat (Hummel) **161**, 274
Piano quintet in E flat (Schumann) **282**
Piano quintet in F minor (Franck) **127**, 282
Piano rags (Joplin) **168**
Piano septet in C (Hummel) **161**
Piano septet in D minor (Hummel) **161**
Piano sonata in B minor (Liszt) **183**
Piano sonata No.1 in C (Weber) **355**
Piano sonata No.3 in F minor (Brahms) **80**
Piano sonata No.8 in A minor (Mozart) **210**
Piano sonata No.8 in C minor (Beethoven) 25, **58**
Piano sonata No.10 in C (Mozart) **210**
Piano sonata No.11 in A (Mozart) 25, **211**
Piano sonata No.14 in C sharp minor (Beethoven) 26, **58**
Piano sonata No.21 in B flat (Schubert) **274-5**, 277
Piano sonata No.21 in C (Beethoven) **59**
Piano sonata No.23 in F minor (Beethoven) **59**
Piano sonata No.26 in E flat (Beethoven) **59**, 267
Piano trio in D minor (Arensky) **41**
Piano trio in G (Haydn) **154**
Piano trio No.1 in B flat (Schubert) **275**
Piano trio No.1 in D minor (Mendelssohn) **196**
Piano trio No.2 in E flat (Schubert) **275**
Piano works (Gottschalk) **139**
Pictures at an exhibition (Mussorgsky) 179, **216**
Pie Jesu (Faure) 19, 123
Pie Jesu (A Lloyd Webber) 20, **185**
Piece heroique (Franck) **126**
Pilgrims' chorus (Wagner) **343**

Pineapple Poll (Sullivan) **309**
Pines of Rome (Respighi) **250**
Pizzicato (Delibes) 21, 31, 106
Pizzicato polka (J Strauss II) **300**
Plaisir d'amour (Martini) **189**
Planets (Holst) 31, **159**
Platoon (film) 52
Pletnev, Mikhail (pianist) 316
Plus que lente, La (Debussy) **104**
Poeme (Chausson) 23, **92**
Poet and peasant (Suppe) **311**
Pogorelich, Ivo (pianist) 247
Polish dance (Scharwenka) **271**
Polka (Shostakovich) **287**
Polka (Smetana) **291**
Polka and fugue (Weinberger) **355**
Polka de W R (Rachmaninov) **243**
Polkas (J Strauss II) **300**
Polonaise (Tchaikovsky) 22, 315
Polonaises (Chopin) **96**
Polovtsian dances (Borodin) **77**
Pomp and circumstance march No.1 in D
   (Elgar) 28, 84, **116**, 243, 347, 348
Pomp and circumstance march No.4 in G
   (Elgar) **116**
Pons, Lily (singer) 105
Porgy and Bess (Gershwin) **131**
Portsmouth Point (Walton) **349**
Poule, La (Rameau) 246
Pourquoi me reveiller (Massenet) **191**
Praeludium (Jarnefelt) 166
Prague symphony (Mozart) 213
Pre, Jacqueline du (cellist) 114, 122
Prelude (M-A Charpentier) **92**
Prelude a l'apres-midi d'un faune (Debussy)
   105
Prelude, aria and finale for piano (Franck) **127**
Prelude in C sharp minor (Rachmaninov)
   243, 271
Prelude, chorale and fugue for piano (Franck)
   127
Prelude and fugue in D (JS Bach) **48**
Prelude, fugue and riffs (Bernstein) **71**
Prelude No.4 in E minor (Chopin) 19, 96
Prelude No.7 in A (Chopin) 25, **96**
Preludes (Chopin) 19, 25, **96**, 104, 243
Preludes (Debussy) 21, **105**
Preludes (Rachmaninov) 96, **243**
Preludes (Verdi) 23, **330–1**
Preludes (Wagner) **340**, **344**
Primrose, William (viola player) 66
Prince of Denmark's march (Clarke) 17, **98**
Prince Igor (Borodin) **77**
Prince and the Pauper (film) 174
Prisoners' chorus (Beethoven) 22, 55, **60**
Private lives of Elizabeth and Essex
   (Korngold) **173**
Prize song (Wagner) **341**
Procession of the guests (Wagner) **343**
Prophete, Le (Meyerbeer) **199**
Protecting veil (Tavener) **313**
Pryor, Arthur (trombonist) 293
Pulcinella (Stravinsky) **306**
Pur ti miro (Monteverdi) **200**
Puritani, I (Bellini) **66**

Quartet (Verdi) **330**
Questa o quella (Verdi) **329**
Quintet for clarinet and strings in B minor
   (Brahms) **81**, 294
Quintet for piano and strings in A minor
   (Elgar) **116**

Rabin, Michael (violinist) 222
Radetzky march (J Strauss I) **296**
Rakoczy march (Berlioz) **69**, 296
Rapsodie Espagnole (Liszt) **183**
Rausch (horn player) 351
Rauzzini, Venanzio (castrato) 205
Recondita armonia (Puccini) **237**
Recuerdos de la Alhambra (Tarrega) **312**
Red poppy (Gliere) **135**
Reilly, Ace of Spies (television) 287
Reiner, Fritz (conductor) 83, 321
Remembrance of Things Past (book) 268
Remenyi, Edouard (violinist) 79
Reminiscences de Don Juan (Liszt) **183**
Reminiscences on `A Life for the Tsar'
   (Balakirev) **51**
Requiem (Berlioz) **69**
Requiem (Faure) 19, 121, **123**, 261
Requiem (A Lloyd Webber) 20, **185**
Requiem (Mozart) 206, **211**
Requiem (Rutter) **261**
Requiem (Verdi) 20, 31, 141, **329**
Requiem (Victoria) **334**
Requiem for my friend (Preisner) **230**
Resurrection symphony (Mahler) **188**
Rhapsody for alto voice, men's chorus and
   orchestra (Brahms) **78**
Rhapsody in blue 131, **132**, 146
Rhapsody in C (Dohnanyi) **108**
Rhapsody on a theme of Paganini
   (Rachmaninov) 33, 83, 184, 187, **244**
Rhapsody on Ukranian themes (Liapunov)
   179
Rheingold, Das (Wagner) 342
Rhenish symphony (Schumann) **284**
Rice aria (Rossini) 222, 258
Richard III (film) 348
Richter, Hans (conductor) 114, 116
Richter, Sviatoslav (pianist) 184
Ride of the Valkyries (Wagner) **341**
Rigoletto (Verdi) 109, 184, 328, **329–30**, 331
Rigoletto paraphrase (Liszt) **184**
Ring cycle (Wagner) 52, **341–2**, 352
Rio Grande (Lambert) **175**
Rios, Waldo de los (bandleader) 214
Rite of Spring (Stravinsky) **306**
Ritual fire dance (Falla) **120**
Robertson, Ray (pianist) 49
Rodeo (Copland) 22, **101**
Roi s'Amuse, Le (play) 349
Roman carnival (Berlioz) 67, **69**
Roman festivals (Respighi) **251**
Romance (Shostakovich) **287**
Romance in G (Svendsen) **312**
Romance for violin and orchestra No.1 in G
   (Beethoven) **60**
Romance for violin and orchestra No.2 in F
   (Beethoven) 30, **60**
Romantic symphony (Bruckner) **87**
Romeo and Juliet (Prokofiev) 22, **231**
Romeo and Juliet (Tchaikovsky) **318**
Romeo et Juliette (Gounod) **142**
Rondeau (Poulenc) **228**
Rondeau (Purcell) 18, 86, **240**
Rondine, La (Puccini) **237**
Rondo aria (Rossini) **256**
Rosamunde (Schubert) 272, **274**, 278
Rose has bloomed, A (Brahms) 17, **79**
Rosenkavalier, Der (R Strauss) **304**
Rosenthal, Moriz (pianist) 98
Roses from the south (J Strauss II) **300**
Rostropovitch (cellist) 153
Rothwell, Evelyn (oboist) 8
Rubinstein, Anton (pianist) 64, 97, 260

Rubinstein, Nicolas (pianist) 64, 317
Ruins of Athens (Beethoven) **57**, 64
Rule, Britannia (Arne) 28, **41**
Rumanian rhapsody No.1 in A (Enescu) **120**
Rusalka (Dvorak) **111**
Ruslan and Ludmilla (Glinka) **136**
Russian Easter festival overture
   (Rimsky-Korsakov) **253**
Russian sailor's dance (Gliere) **135**
Rustic wedding symphony (Goldmark) **138**
Rustle of Spring (Sinding) 260, **291**

St Anthony Chorale (Brahms) **83**
St Cecilia mass (Gounod) **142**
St Matthew passion (JS Bach) 19, **49**
St Paul's suite (Holst) **159**
Sabre dance (Khachaturian) 168, **170**
Sadko (Rimsky-Korsakov) **253**
Salammbo (Herrmann) **158**
Salomon, J P (violinist) 155
Salut d'amour (Elgar) 29, **117**
Sammons, Albert (violinist) 119
Samson (Handel) 17, **149**
Samson and Delilah (Saint-Saens) **266**
Sanctuary of the heart (Ketelbey) **169**
Sarasate, Pablo de (violinist) 74, 175, 263,
   267, 268
Sargent, Sir Malcolm (conductor) 86, 108
Scaramouche (Milhaud) **200**
Scheherazade (Rimsky-Korsakov) **253**
Scherzi (Chopin) **96**
Scherzo (Litolff) 182, **185**
Scherzo (Mendelssohn) **193**
Scherzo capriccioso (Dvorak) **112**
Schumann, Clara (pianist) 53, 157, 279, 282
Schwanda the bagpiper (Weinberger) **355**
Scottish fantasy (Bruch) **86**
Scottish symphony (Mendelssohn) **196**
Sea Hawk (Korngold) **173**
Sea pictures (Elgar) **117**
Seasons (Glazunov) **134**
Seasons (Haydn) **154**
Secret Garden (film) 230
See the conqu'ring hero comes (Handel) **151**
Segovia, Andres (guitarist) 254, 312
Sellick, Phyllis (pianist) 42
Semele (Handel) **151**
Semiramide (Rossini) **257**
Semper fidelis (Sousa) **292**
Sempre libera (Verdi) 28, **331**
Septet in E flat (Saint-Saens) 161, **266**
Serenade (Heykens) **158**
Serenade in E minor for strings (Elgar) 29,
   112, **117**
Serenade to music (Vaughan Williams) **327**
Serenade No.6 in D (Mozart) **211**
Serenade No.10 in B flat for thirteen wind
   instruments (Mozart) **212**
Serenade No.13 in G (Mozart) 24, **212**
Serenade for strings in C (Tchaikovsky) 24,
   112, **318**
Serenade for strings in E (Dvorak) **112**
Serenata notturna (Mozart) **211**
Serse (Handel) 19, **150**
Services in B flat (Stanford) **296**
Sextet (Donizetti) **109**
Sgambati, Giovanni (pianist) 137
Sheep may safely graze (JS Bach) **49**, 51
Shepherd Fennel's dance (Gardiner) **129**
Shine (film) 242
Si, mi chiamano Mimi (Puccini) **234**
Short ride in a fast machine (Adams) **36**
Sicilienne (Maria T von Paradies) **224**
Siegfried idyll (Wagner) 23, **342**

Siegfried's funeral march (Wagner) **342**
Signor Bruschino, Il (Rossini) **257**
Sigurd Jorsalfar (Grieg) **144**
Silken ladder (Rossini) **257**
Silver swan (Gibbons) **133**
Simple symphony (Britten) **85**
Sinfonia concertante in E flat for violin and
   viola (Mozart) 208, **212**
Sinfonietta (Janacek) **165**
Singuliere symphony (Berwald) **72**
Six songs of farewell (Parry) 20, **225**
Skaters' waltz (Waldteufel) 27, **346**
Sky at Night, The (television) 288
Slaughter on Tenth Avenue (Rodgers) **254**
Slavonic dances (Dvorak) 42, 112, **113**
Sleepers awake (JS Bach) **49**
Sleeping beauty (Tchaikovsky) 34, 110, **318–
   19**
Sleepwalking girl (Bellini) **66**
Slower than slow (Debussy) **104**
Smith, Cyril (pianist) 42
Soetens, Robert (violinist) 233
Softly awakes my heart (Saint-Saens) **266**
Soirees musicales (Britten) **85**, 259
Soirees musicales (Rossini) **259**
Soldiers' chorus (Gounod) **141**
Solemn melody (Walford Davies) 19, **103**
Solemn vespers (Mozart) **206**
Solomon (Handel) 17, 32, **148**
Solti, George (conductor) 108
Sombrero de tre picos (Falla) **121**
Sonata No.2 in B flat minor (Chopin) 19, **97**
Sonata No.3 in B minor (Chopin) **97**
Sonata on the 94th Psalm (Reubke) **251**
Sonata for violin and piano in A (Franck) **127**
Sonatas for strings (Rossini) **258**
Song for Athene (Tavener) 20, **313**
Song cycles (Schubert) **276**
Song cycles (Schumann) **283**
Song of India (Rimsky-Korsakov) **253**
Song of Norway (operetta) 145
Song of Summer (Delius) **107**
Songs (Hahn) **147**
Songs (Schubert) 140, **275–6**
Songs (Schumann) **283**
Songs (R Strauss) **304–5**
Songs of the Auvergne (Canteloube) 23, **90**,
   163
Songs my mother taught me (Dvorak) **112**
Songs of sanctuary (Jenkins) **166**
Songs of the sea (Stanford) **295**
Songs without words (Mendelssohn) **196**
Sonnambula, La (Bellini) **66**
Sorcerer's apprentice (Dukas) 34, **110**, 179
Sortie in B flat (Lefebure-Wely) **176**
Sospiro, Un (Liszt) **181**
Spalding, Albert (violinist) 53
Spanish dances (Granados) **144**
Spanish dances (Moszkowski) **202**
Spanish overture No.1 (Glinka) **136**
Sparky and his Magic Piano 94
Spartacus (Khachaturian) 30, **170**
Spem in alium (Tallis) **312**
Spinning chorus (Wagner) **339**
Spitfire prelude and fugue (Walton) **349**
Spring sonata (Beethoven) **65**
Spring song (Mendelssohn) 196, 260
Spring symphony (Schumann) **284**
Stabat Mater (Pergolesi) **227**
Stabat Mater (Rossini) **258**
Stadler, Anton (clarinettist) 203, 350
Standing stone (McCartney) **192**
Stars and stripes forever! (Sousa) **293**
Stefano, Di (singer) 109

Stenka Razin (Glazunov) **134**
Stilgoe, Richard (lyricist) 98
Sting, The (film) 168
Stokowski, Leopold (conductor) 50, 216, 245
Story of Three Loves (film) 244
Stott, Kathryn (pianist) 218
Streghe, Le (Paganini) **222**
Streisand, Barbra (singer) 98
String quartet in D (Franck) **128**
String quartet No.1 in D (Tchaikovsky) 29,
   314
String quartet No.2 in D (Borodin) **77**
String quartets (Mozart) **213**
String quintet in C (Schubert) 24, **277**
String quintet in E (Boccherini) 32, **76**
Study in waltz form (Saint-Saens) **263**
Suggia, Guilhermina (cellist) 122
Suite in A minor for recorder and strings
   (Telemann) **323–4**
Suite Algerienne (Saint-Saens) **264**
Suite bergamasque (Debussy) 33, **104**
Suite in F sharp minor (Dohnanyi) **108**
Suite gothique (Boellmann) 17, **76**
Summa (Park) **226**
Summer days suite (Coates) **100**
Summer nights (Berlioz) 33, **70**
Surprise symphony (Haydn) 32, **155**
Susanna's secret (Wolf-Ferrari) **359**
Sutherland, Joan (singer) 109, 219
Swallow, The (Puccini) **237**
Swan, The (Saint-Saens) 261, 262
Swan Lake (Tchaikovsky) 318, **319**
Swan of Tuonela (Sibelius) **289**
Swedish rhapsody No.1 (Alfven) **39**
Sylvia (Delibes) **106**
Symphonic dances (Bernstein) 31, **71**
Symphonic mass (Lloyd) **185**
Symphonic serenade in B flat (Korngold) **173**
Symphonic variations for piano and orchestra
   (Franck) **128**
Symphonie concertante (Jongen) **167**
Symphonie Espagnole (Lalo) **175**
Symphonie fantastique (Berlioz) 68, **70**, 184
Symphony in C (Bizet) **74**
Symphony in D minor (Franck) **128**
Symphony in F sharp (Korngold) **174**
Symphony on a French mountain song
   (d'Indy) **163**
Symphony in G for viola and orchestra
   (Berlioz) **68**
Symphony No.1 (Gottschalk) **139**
Symphony No.1 in A flat (Elgar) **118**, 214,
   295
Symphony No.1 in B flat (Schumann) **284**
Symphony No.1 in C (Beethoven) **60**
Symphony No.1 in C minor (Brahms) 80, **81**,
   82
Symphony No.1 in D (Mahler) **188**
Symphony No.1 in D (Prokofiev) 233
Symphony No.2 (Bernstein) **71**
Symphony No.2 (Gottschalk) **140**
Symphony No.2 (Nielsen) **217**
Symphony No.2 in C minor (Mahler) **188**
Symphony No.2 in D (Brahms) **81**, 82
Symphony No.2 in D minor (Sibelius) **289**
Symphony No.2 in E flat (Elgar) **116**
Symphony No.2 in E minor (Rachmaninov)
   29, **244**
Symphony No.3 (Gorecki) 23, **139**, 230
Symphony No.3 in A minor (Mendelssohn)
   196
Symphony No.3 in C (Berwald) **72**
Symphony No.3 in C minor (Saint-Saens)
   147, 261, 265, **267**

Symphony No.3 in E flat (Beethoven) 19, **61**
Symphony No.3 in E flat (Schumann) **284**
Symphony No.3 in F (Brahms) **82**
Symphony No.3 in F minor (Stanford) **295**
Symphony No.4 in A (Mendelssohn) **197**
Symphony No.4 in C minor (Schubert) **277**
Symphony No.4 in E flat (Bruckner) **87**
Symphony No.4 in E minor (Brahms) **82**, 295
Symphony No.4 in F (Boyce) **78**
Symphony No.4 in F minor (Tchaikovsky)
   315, **319–20**
Symphony No.4 in G (Mahler) **188**
Symphony No.5 (Nielsen) **217**
Symphony No.5 in B flat (Schubert) **277**
Symphony No.5 in C minor (Beethoven) 31,
   61, 319
Symphony No.5 in C sharp minor (Mahler)
   188–9
Symphony No.5 in D minor (Shostakovich)
   287
Symphony No.5 in E flat (Sibelius) 289, **290**
Symphony No.5 in E minor (Tchaikovsky)
   320
Symphony No.6 in B minor (Tchaikovsky)
   25, **320–1**
Symphony No.6 in E minor
   (Vaughan Williams) **327**
Symphony No.6 in F (Beethoven) **62**
Symphony No.7 in A (Beethoven) 19, **62**
Symphony No.7 in C (Shostakovich) **288**
Symphony No.7 in E (Bruckner) **88**
Symphony No.8 in B minor (Schubert) **278**
Symphony No.8 in C minor (Bruckner) **88**
Symphony No.8 in E flat (Mahler) **189**
Symphony No.8 in G (Dvorak) **113**
Symphony No.9 in C (Schubert) **278**
Symphony No.9 in D minor (Beethoven) 28,
   54, **63**, 77, 81
Symphony No.9 in E minor (Dvorak) **113**
Symphony No.38 in D (Mozart) 24, **213**
Symphony No.39 in E flat (Mozart) 24, **214**
Symphony No.40 in G minor (Mozart) 24,
   214
Symphony No.41 in C (Mozart) **214**
Symphony No.94 in G (Haydn) 32, **155**
Symphony No.96 in D (Haydn) **155**
Symphony No.100 in G (Haydn) **155**
Symphony No.103 in E flat (Haydn) **156**
Symphony No.104 in D (Haydn) **156**
Symphony of sorrowful songs (Gorecki) 23,
   139
Symphony of a thousand (Mahler) **189**
Szell, George (conductor) 52, 348

Tagliafero, Magda (pianist) 147
Tales of Hoffmann (Offenbach) 33, 106, **218**,
   219
Tales from the Vienna woods (J Strauss II)
   301
Tam O'Shanter (Arnold) **43**
Tamagno, Francesco (singer) 333
Tambourin (Rameau) **246**
Tancredi (Rossini) 22, **258**
Tango in D (Albeniz) **37**
Tannhauser (Wagner) 341, **342–3**
Tanti palpiti, Di (Rossini) **258**
Taras Bulba (Janacek) **165**
Tauber, Richard (singer) 158, 177
Te Deum (Bruckner) **88**
Te Deum (M-A Charpentier) 17, **92**
Te Deum (Stanford) **296**
Thais (Massenet) 26, 134, 190, **191**
These You Have Loved (radio) 78
Thibaud, Jacques (violinist) 154, 224, 275

Thieving magpie (Rossini) **259**
Things to come (Bliss) **75**
This is the record of John (Gibbons) **133**
Three chorales for organ (Franck) **129**
Three Colours Blue/White/Red (film) 230
Three-cornered hat (Falla) **121**
Three dance episodes (Bernstein) **72**
Three dances from Henry VIII (German) **130**
Three dances from Nell Gwynn (German) **130**
Three Elizabeths suite (Coates) **100**
Three preludes for piano (Gershwin) **132**
Thunder and lightning polka (J Strauss II) 300
Thunderer (Sousa) 292, **293**
Thurston, Frederick (clarinettist) 124
Till Eulenspiegel's merry pranks (R Strauss) 43, 304, **305**
Tintagel (Bax) **53**
Titan symphony (Mahler) **188**
To a wild rose (MacDowell) **187**
Toccata in A (P D Paradies) **224**
Toccata in C (Schumann) **284**
Toccata in F (Widor) 18, 50, **357**
Toccata and fugue in D minor (JS Bach) **50**
Tocher, The (film) 85, 259
Tombeau de Couperin (Ravel) **249**
Toreador (Adam) **35**, 36
Tosca (Puccini) **237–8**
Toscanini, Arturo (conductor) 52, 178, 317, 346
Totentanz (Liszt) **184**
Toy symphony (L Mozart) 34, **202**
Toytown in Children's Hour (radio) 167
Tragic overture (Brahms) **82**
Tragic symphony (Schubert) **277**
Transcendental studies (Liszt) 179, **180**
Transports de joie (Messiaen) **198**
Traviata, La (Verdi) 23, 28, 328, **330–1**
Triple concerto in C (Beethoven) **63**
Tristan and Isolde (Wagner) 53, 103, **344**
Tritsch-tratsch polka (J Strauss II) 300
Triumphal march (Elgar) **118**
Troika (Prokofiev) 27, 231
Trois gymnopedies (Satie) 25, **269**
Trojan march (Berlioz) **70**
Trojans, The (Berlioz) **70**
Trout quintet (Schubert) 32, **274**, 276
Trovatore, Il (Verdi) 22, 328, 330, **331–2**
Trumpet concerto in E flat (Haydn) **156**, 162
Trumpet concerto in E flat (Hummel) **162**
Trumpet tune (M-A Charpentier) 17, **92**
Trumpet tune and air in D (Purcell) 18, **241**
Trumpet voluntary (Clarke) 17, **98**, 241
Trumpet voluntary in D (Stanley) 18, **296**
Tuba tune (Cocker) **100**
Turandot (Busoni) **89**
Turandot (Puccini) 28, 89, 135, **238**
Turangalila symphony (Messiaen) **198**
Turkish march (Beethoven) 57, **64**
Turkish rondo (Mozart) **211**
Turkish violin concerto (Mozart) 211, **215**
Twinkle, twinkle little star **36**, 108
Tzigane (Ravel) **249**

Unfinished symphony (Schubert) **278**
Upshaw, Dawn (singer) 139

Va, pensiero (Verdi) **333**
Valois, Ninette de (choreographer) 74
Valse, La (Ravel) **249**
Valse triste (Sibelius) **290**
Vanity Fair (Collins) **101**
Variations on `America' (Ives) **164**

Variations and fugue on a theme of Henry Purcell (Britten) **86**, 240
Variations on a nursery song (Dohnanyi) **108**
Variations on an original theme (Elgar) **119**
Variations on a Rococo theme (Tchaikovsky) **322**
Variations on a Shaker hymn (Copland) **101**
Variations on a theme of Beethoven for two pianos (Saint-Saens) **267**
Variations on a theme by Haydn (Brahms) **83**
Variations on a theme of Paganini (Brahms) **83**, 187, 244
Variations on a theme of Paganini (Lutoslawski) 83, **187**
Vespers (Monteverdi) 27, **200**
Vesti la giubba (Leoncavallo) **178**
Vienna blood (J Strauss II) **300**
Viennese clock (Kodaly) **171**
Vigno, Salvatore (choreographer) 56
Violin concerto (Barber) 29, **53**
Violin concerto in A (JS Bach) **50**
Violin concerto in A minor (Glazunov) **134**
Violin concerto in A minor (Goldmark) **138**
Violin concerto in B minor (Elgar) **119**
Violin concerto in D (Beethoven) **64**, 321
Violin concerto in D (Brahms) 79, **83**, 87, 138, 267, 321
Violin concerto in D (Korngold) **174**
Violin concerto in D (Tchaikovsky) 30, 138, 267, **321**
Violin concerto in D minor (Sibelius) 134, **290**
Violin concerto in E major (JS Bach) **50**
Violin concerto in E minor (Mendelssohn) **197**, 321
Violin concerto No.1 in D (Paganini) **222**, 223
Violin concerto No.1 in F sharp (Wieniawski) **358**
Violin concerto No.1 in G minor (Bruch) 29, **87**
Violin concerto No.2 in B minor (Paganini) 180, 222, **223**
Violin concerto No.2 in D minor (Bruch) 87
Violin concerto No.2 in D minor (Wieniawski) 358
Violin concerto No.2 in G minor (Prokofiev) **233**
Violin concerto No.3 in B minor (Saint-Saens) **267**
Violin concerto No.3 in D minor (Bruch) 87
Violin concerto No.3 in G (Mozart) **215**
Violin concerto No.4 in D (Mozart) **215**
Violin concerto No.4 in D minor (Vieuxtemps) **334–5**
Violin concerto No.5 in A (Mozart) 211, **215**
Violin concerto No.5 in A minor (Vieuxtemps) **335**
Violin partita No.2 in D minor (JS Bach) 46
Violin pieces (Kreisler) **174**
Violin pieces (Wieniawski) **359**
Violin sonata in G minor (Tartini) **313**
Violin sonata No.1 in D minor (Saint-Saens) **268**
Violin sonata No.5 in F (Beethoven) **65**, 127
Violin sonata No.9 in A (Beethoven) **65**, 127
Vissi d'arte (Puccini) **237**
Vocalise (Rachmaninov) 23, 135, **245**, 265
Voce poco fa, Una (Rossini) **255**, 261
Voices of Spring (J Strauss II) **301**
Volodos, Arcadi (pianist) 211

Waldesrauschen (Liszt) **184**
Walk to the paradise garden (Delius) **107**

Walking Stick, The (film) 216
Walkure, Die (Wagner) **341**, 342
Waltz (Khachaturian) 171
Waltz No.6 in D flat (Chopin) **98**
Waltz song (Gounod) **142**
Waltzes (Brahms) **84**
Waltzes (Chopin) **97**, 98
Wanderer fantasy (Schubert) **279**
Warsaw concerto (Addinsell) **37**
Washington Post (Sousa) 292, **293**
Wasps (Vaughan Williams) **326**
Water music (Handel) 21, 30, 124, **151**
We (play) 39
Wedding march (Mendelssohn) 17, 163, **194**, 340
Weidlinger, Anton (trumpeter) 156, 162
Weingartner, Felix (conductor) 74
Well-tempered clavier (JS Bach) 2, **50**, 140
Werther (Massenet) **191**
West side story (Bernstein) 31, **71**
What is life (Gluck) **137**
What the Papers Say (television) 42
When I am laid in earth (Purcell) 20, **239**
Where e'er you walk (Handel) **151**
Where the Rainbow Ends (play) 241
White Horse Inn (Benatzky) **66**, 302
Whiteman, Paul (bandleader) 132, 146
Wiegenlied (Brahms) 26, **84**
Wiener blut (J Strauss II) **300**
Wild, Earl (pianist) 51, 271
Wilhelmj, August (violinist) 48
Willcocks, Sir David (King's College Choir) 40
William Tell (Rossini) 259, 260, 347
Williams, John (guitarist) 216
Willow song (Verdi) **333**
Wine, woman and song (J Strauss II) **301**
Wise virgins (JS Bach) 51
With the wild geese (Harty) **152**
Wood, Sir Henry (conductor) 50, 98, 119, 216, 327

Xerxes (Handel) 19, **150**

Yeoman of the guard (Sullivan) **309**
You are my heart's delight (Lehar) **177**
Young Musician of the Year (television) 102
Young person's guide to the orchestra (Britten) 34, **86**, 240
Your tiny hand is frozen (Puccini) **233**
Youth piano concerto (Kabalevsky) **169**
Ysaye, Eugene (violinist) 92, 127

Z Cars (television) 216
Zabaleta, Nicanor (harpist) 38
Zadok the Priest (Handel) 28, 44, **152**
Zampa (Herold) **157**
Zigeunerweisen (Sarastae) **268**
Zinman, David (conductor) 139